EVEN UNTO BLOODSHED

Even unto Bloodshed

An LDS Perspective on War

Duane Boyce

Salt Lake City, 2015
Greg Kofford Books

Copyright © 2015 Duane Boyce
Cover design copyright © 2015 Greg Kofford Books, Inc.
Cover design by Loyd Ericson
"Flag raising on Iwo Jima." Joe Rosenthal, Associated Press, February 23, 1945. National Archives and Records Administration (ARC Identifier: 520748).

Portions of this book are a revision of the article, "Were the Ammonites Pacifists?" *Journal of the Book of Mormon and Other Restoration Scripture* 18, no. 1 (2009), published by the Neal A. Maxwell Institute for Religious Scholarship.

Published in the USA.

All rights reserved. No part of this volume may be reproduced in any form without written permission from the publisher, Greg Kofford Books. The views expressed herein are the responsibility of the author and do not necessarily represent the position of Greg Kofford Books.

ISBN 978-1-58958-630-7

Greg Kofford Books
P.O. Box 1362
Draper, UT 84020
www.gregkofford.com

2019   18   17   16   15   5   4   3   2   .

Library of Congress Control Number: 2015939960

For Sariah

Contents

Acknowledgments	ix
Introduction: Thinking about War	1

Part 1
Just-War Theory and Pacifism: Secular Arguments

1.	The Common-Sense Secular View of War	7
2.	Pacifism: The "Anti-Violence" Version	17
3.	Pacifism: The "Anti-War" Version	33

Part 2
Scriptural Arguments for Pacifism

4.	Were the Ammonites Pacifists? Part One	49
5.	Were the Ammonites Pacifists? Part Two	59
6.	On Righteousness, Discussion, and the Non-necessity of War	73
7.	Self-Defense and the Lord's Involvement in War	89
8.	A "Narrative" Reading of the Book of Mormon: Part One	109
9.	A "Narrative" Reading of the Book of Mormon: Part Two	131
10.	Three Arguments for Pacifism	151
11.	Eugene England's Anti-Violence Ethic	175
12.	Self-Defense, Pre-Emptive Action, and Holocaust	191

Part 3
Toward an LDS Theory of War

13.	Getting Past Pacifism	213
14.	The Sermon on the Mount	223
15.	Alma 48 and Doctrine and Covenants 98	241
16.	Two Modern Prophets	257
17.	An LDS Framework Regarding War	271

Appendices

Appendix 1. Considering the Size of the Ammonite Population	281
Appendix 2. The Promises to Nephi and Lehi	287
Appendix 3. A Sketch of Joseph Smith's Divine Manifestations	289
Bibliography	293
Index	307

Acknowledgments

I have acquired debts to all who read this manuscript in whole or in part in various stages of its development: Royal Skousen, Dan Peterson, Cody Carter, Katie Williams, Neil Mayhew, Jim Faulconer, Terry Warner, Brian King, Rita Lewis, Andrew Shelton, and Hannah Mendenhall. Others who have also contributed include Kinsey Lynn, Catherine Hansen, Nina Kramer, and Remington Naves. Although I troubled only three of them to summarize their reactions, I have profited from the comments and suggestions made by all, and the book is significantly improved as a result. My wife, Merralee, is a talented editor and routinely forced me to write with increased clarity. Whether my prose actually satisfies her at this point, or whether she has just given up, I can't say. The same goes for others who have contributed to the creation of this book. Of course, the errors, oversights, and other weaknesses that remain are solely my responsibility and exist despite the efforts of others to assist me. My apologies to them all.

The topic of the book is of great importance and I feel in no way equal to it. Nevertheless, I have thought that I should at least join the conversation. Herewith, my two cents.

Introduction

Thinking about War

Suppose that you live during a time of war, that the village you inhabit lies in a battle zone, and that a military commander one day demands your help in fighting the enemy. You refuse, whereupon the troops take your two small daughters, aged six and eight, and rape them, murder them, and throw their bodies into a well to pollute the drinking water of the village.[1]

This is an account of an actual event, and it helps frame the matter of violence and non-violence in a serious and arresting way. Suppose that the reason you refuse to help the military commander in the first place is because doing so would involve you in acts of cruelty and murder of innocent people. Suppose further that you can prevent the military commander's act of utter barbarism against your children only by shooting him and that shooting him will result in the commander's death. Also, assume that the act will be secret and will have no effect on the wider war or its participants. Is it morally permissible to perform this act of violence?

This case is illuminating for two reasons. First, most people feel that it is morally permissible to kill the commander. Indeed, many who fall in this category will feel that it is not only permissible, but morally *obligatory* to do so. Certainly, the parents of these children would feel this way, as most any parent would. Second, a fair number of people (at least in personal experience) who say that they are opposed to all violence actually waver when faced with a concrete circumstance of this sort. They find themselves opposed to most violence, as it turns out, but not all.

When we enlarge the topic from a single act of violence to the scale of all-out war, people's intuitions are similar. Most feel that war is justified under certain circumstances and, when faced with specific details of aggression and horror, many who describe themselves as opposed to war will find that they can actually support it under such circumstances. Thus, while many were able to condemn the very idea of war in the aftermath of World War I, they found themselves relenting in the face of the monstrous Nazi and Japanese threat of World War II.[2]

---

1. The first-hand account of this incident can be found in Lawrence Freedman, ed., *War*, 53. This volume contains twenty-three first-person accounts of war experience, starting with an account from the Battle of Trafalgar in 1805.

2. See John Howard Yoder's historical treatment in his *Christian Attitudes to War, Peace, and Revolution*, 271–98.

That is why concrete cases are so important. Most everyone is for peace in the abstract, and as long as the discussion remains in the abstract it is easy to be unyielding in favoring peace over war. Who wouldn't be? Even the slightest pretension to a moral point of view will abhor war and embrace peace when the issue is framed this generally. The problem comes when the question is not, "Morally, should we favor peace over war?" but, "Morally, are we permitted to wage war against a regime that is wantonly attacking and killing us or others?" We do not really know what someone means by a positive answer to the first question until we know their answer to the second.

The Plan and General Conclusions of the Book

These and other considerations are important in any attempt to outline a theory of war and peace, an attempt this book will make in at least a general way. The process will be to first sketch the secular, standard, common-sense structure for thinking about war—a framework that reflects and codifies most people's intuitions on this topic. The framework we will look at both justifies war in certain circumstances *and* establishes the principles that must be followed in waging it (Chapter 1). Basic secular arguments for pacifism—the view that rejects the permissibility of war altogether—will then be considered. Since pacifism is not intuitive to most people it must be accorded due attention, and we should give it every chance to overrule our intuitions (Chapters 2 and 3). With this general secular foundation in place, various approaches to pacifism from a gospel point of view will be considered (Part Two: Chapters 4–12). At the completion of this examination it will then be possible to draw some reasoned conclusions and to suggest a general framework for thinking about war from an LDS perspective (Part Three: Chapters 13–17).

Readers who are interested only in scriptural matters and not in the broader intellectual question of pacifism vs. just-war theory, may wish to proceed directly to Part Two. There is some cost in doing this since later chapters periodically refer to material and concepts covered in Part One, but overall it may be the preferred and best approach for some. Part One is important for those who desire an introduction to the broader intellectual inquiry regarding war and peace and is informed by general issues that appear in the secular literature.

The overall conclusions of this book are two: (1) both secular and scriptural arguments for pacifism ultimately fail, and (2) once such pacifist arguments are examined, rebutted, and respectfully set aside, it is possible to construct a sound framework for a scriptural view of war, at least in general terms. Such a framework is not pacifist, but it is anything but aggressive, and it includes the quality of heart—not to mention, the wisdom—expected of all disciples of Christ, whatever their task or circumstance. It was not an anomaly when the Lord instructed the Nephites to defend their families "even unto bloodshed" (Alma 43:47); comprehensively understood this statement expresses a genuine scriptural principle regarding war and peace. This book will try to show why this is so.

It might seem sufficient to develop a scriptural framework regarding war straightaway and to avoid the work of examining arguments for its alternative—pacifism—as part of the project. But this is mistaken. The only way to have confidence that we have reached a sound conclusion on one matter or another is to pay the price of thoughtfully examining its rivals. It is intellectually sordid (isn't it?) to reach conclusions regarding a dispute without attending carefully to both sides. If pacifism is mistaken this must be shown, not simply assumed or even asserted: *Audi alteram partem*. Moreover, if arguments break down it is important to see why and how. That is how we learn to avoid similar mistakes of our own, at least to the degree that we can. Since a number of LDS authors—including famous ones—have advanced either a pacifist point of view or something close to it, any attempt to develop a theory of war from a Latter-day Saint perspective must take these arguments into account. More importantly, disregarding such authors would miss the chance to be convinced by them if, despite what we might expect at the outset, they turn out to be right upon examination.[3]

Of course, this book does not pretend to achieve anything even close to the final word on the subject of war; it is simply a contribution to the conversation. Others will pursue avenues that are slighted here, and still others will correct mistakes that appear. Over time everyone's ideas will be refined and expanded by our combined efforts, resulting in something ever nearer to the truth. This book is just one contribution along the way. Moreover, the book is written at a certain level for a certain audience; someone writing specifically for a philosophical readership will pursue intellectual subtleties, particularly in Chapters 2, 3, and 12, that are ignored here. Even so, in the end there is not much reason to expect that subtle considerations will yield anything more than subtle modifications (welcome though they would be), leaving substantially intact the basic conclusions that are reached here. This expectation could turn out to be mistaken, of course—sometimes intricate refinements generate large intellectual consequences—but it seems reasonable to suppose that the odds at least do not favor such an outcome. I believe that in the end even the most subtle analyses will yield conclusions that do not differ in essential ways from the conclusions reached here.

---

3. Of course, while reaching a conclusion based on careful examination of its rivals does not guarantee the correctness of our conclusion, it does guarantee its honesty—that it was bought at an appropriate intellectual price. A conclusion reached without consideration of counterarguments is reached too cheaply: it is not born of honest toil *and* it runs the risk of being much further from the truth than a more carefully considered conclusion might be. More thoughts about reason, truth, and humility appear both in my "Of Science, Scripture, and Surprise," 163–214 and "The Spirit and the Intellect: Lessons in Humility," 75–107.

Part 1

Just-War Theory and Pacifism: Secular Arguments

Chapter 1

The Common-Sense Secular View of War

Just-War Theory

As mentioned in the Introduction, there exists a general framework for thinking about war that captures most people's intuitions. For example, most who consider the topic feel that war was morally justified in opposing the Nazi aggression of World War II. Thinking about the justification of war in this way has a long history in Western tradition and has yielded what has come to be known as "just-war" theory.[1] Although its origins are found in Augustine and Aquinas, just-war theory's modern form is secular and captures people's general intuitions about war regardless of their religiosity.

Just-war theory consists of two general parts, one specifying the conditions under which waging war is justified in the first place—*jus ad bellum* or the justice *of* war—and one specifying the moral rules that govern the conduct of a war once it is engaged—*jus in bello* or justice *in* war.[2]

Jus ad Bellum: The Justice of War

To begin, consider the matter of *jus ad bellum*—the rightness or justice *of* war. This dimension of just-war theory identifies the conditions under which waging war is justified in the first place. According to this theory a state must satisfy at least six central principles to be justified in entering conflict (with

---

1. See, for example, Augustine, *The City of God*; Thomas Aquinas, *Summa Theologica*; and Hugo Grotius, *On the Law of War and Peace*, by far the most detailed and comprehensive of the three.

2. All of this assumes that concerns about morality are directly applicable to war. Such concerns include whether some wars are right, and some are wrong, and whether some wartime conduct is right, and some is wrong. There are some, however, who resist applying matters of morality (at least in a strong sense) to war—a view generally referred to as "realism." Walzer treats this view thoroughly; indeed, in one sense his entire volume is a tract against the position. See Michael Walzer, *Just and Unjust Wars*. There are so many expressions of realism—the term is variously applied to figures as diverse as Machiavelli and Niebuhr, for example—that Orend seeks to minimize the complexity by reducing the basic positions to *fourteen*; see Brian Orend, "A Just-War Critique of Realism and Pacifism," 435–77. Since I assume that not many Latter-day Saints hold anything like a strong realist view, it is not an important category for present purposes.

suitable qualifications, these principles also apply to a state acting as a protector of another state):[3]

1. The state must act in defense of fundamental human rights (these include the right of liberty and of freedom from serious harm), and the state must have no other reasonable means of defense at its disposal.
2. The state must act from the right intention, such as acting only to defend and vindicate its rights, and not in furtherance of some other cause (national glory, for example).
3. Legitimate political authority must declare the state of war publicly.
4. The war must be waged only when other means (such as diplomacy) cannot prevent the conflict.
5. Waging war must have a reasonable chance of success, meaning the costs of war (violence, suffering, and destruction) are not to be borne in a cause that is futile.[4]
6. The benefits of the war (defense of rights and the thwarting of aggression) must be reasonably proportional to the costs of the war (such as military and civilian casualties as well as the general misery and destruction that will be suffered).

It is worth pausing on this sixth element for a moment. It asserts that the benefits of a war must be proportional to its costs, and both must be considered

---

3. There are many sources that catalogue the elements of just-war theory. I am following Orend, "A Just-War Critique," 437–41.

4. Some might argue that a threshold for futility is either very high or non-existent—that a victim state should defend itself in practically any circumstance: since dying is preferable to living in slavery, *failing* to resist is the decision that requires justification, even in cases of futility. But this is not the just-war view. A position of this sort would seem reasonable if the effects of war were limited to the adults who made the decision and who themselves could assume combatant roles, but what of the effects of war—including injury and death—on children, the elderly, the infirm, the child-bearing, and others who cannot assume roles of this sort and who are not directly involved in the decision-making process in the first place? Morally, can *they* be subjected to the devastation of a war that is futile—particularly if the risk of civilian injury and death is high? Further, is it right even to put soldiers into a situation of fighting a war they cannot win and thus in which many of them will die without purpose? Although different persons can reach different conclusions on the exact threshold for rejecting defense on the basis of futility, just-war theory assumes that there is at least *some* reasonable threshold of this sort and thus that at some point it is wrong to thrust a population into the ravages of war (especially where civilian risk is high) in order to resist aggression that it cannot really resist. Historically, different states have adopted different stances. Poland, for example, resisted Nazi aggression in 1939, resulting in war, while Czechoslovakia in that same year offered no resistance to its invaders.

with great care. It is crucial not to downplay the horrors of suffering that are certain to be experienced, both by combatants and by civilian populations. It is easy to minimize this suffering when we think of war only in the abstract—as something between two or more impersonal entities, i.e., "states." Thinking so generally we may fail to appreciate that states are comprised of individuals, and that in war countless such individuals (including civilians of all ages and circumstances) will undergo trauma, suffering, and death. To count the cost of war, therefore, is to count the cost to *people*. It is to appreciate fully the countless concrete instances of suffering and misery that war will entail.[5]

At the same time we must take care to count the costs of *inaction* in the face of dire and brutalizing circumstances as well. What would it be like to live in a world dominated by an oppressive and brutal totalitarian regime? What would the cumulative effect be over generations? Such matters are not easily calculated, but all leaders face them when they encounter serious instances of aggression against their own states or against states they are friendly with and desire to protect. There is no precise formula that leaders can employ to decide the matter of proportionality, but they must use the best and wisest judgment they can bring to bear on all the evidence available to do so. Proportionality is a critical dimension that leaders must seek earnestly to satisfy if their entrance into war is to qualify as just.

Note that throughout these provisions of *jus ad bellum* there exists a distinction between an aggressor state and a victim, or aggressed, state. By definition an aggressor state cannot wage a just war because, far from defending important human values, it is actually threatening them. An aggressor state forces individuals in other states to risk their lives in order to preserve their rights to political sovereignty and peace. Therefore, to speak of a just war is to speak specifically of the war that the *victim* state is fighting and does not apply to the actions of the aggressor state.

Jus in Bello: Justice in War

The second dimension of just-war theory is *jus in bello*—rightness or justice *in* war. This aspect of the theory specifies the moral rules that govern the conduct of a war once it is engaged. There are three central principles:

1. The state can aim its military efforts only against the legitimate military threats of the enemy. Noncombatants and noncombatant activities of the enemy are not legitimate targets.
2. A state must weigh the costs and benefits of *each* significant military tactic it pursues within the war. As with the proportional weighing of

---

5. For one chilling treatment of such horrors, see Joana Bourke, *An Intimate History of Killing*. See also, "The Experience of War," in Lawrence Freedman, *War*, 9–64.

the war itself (see Principle 6 under *jus ad bellum*), the benefits of a *given* tactic must also be proportional to its costs.
3. A state must not use intrinsically heinous means or weapons; thus, it is not permissible to wage mass rape campaigns or to employ nuclear, biological, or chemical weapons.[6]

The most important principle of *jus in bello* is the first. While it is legitimate to attack one who presents a direct threat to us (i.e., a soldier who is throwing hand grenades at our position), it would not be permissible "to stop him by machine-gunning his wife and children, who are standing nearby, thus distracting him from his aim of blowing you up and enabling you to capture him."[7] In this example the soldier presents a direct threat, but his wife and children—who are obviously noncombatants—do not, and thus it would be murder to attack them as a means to capture him. The same logic applies to others such as farmers (who feed soldiers) and medical personnel (who treat them). Such citizens of enemy states may not be attacked because they meet the needs of these soldiers as human beings and not specifically as soldiers. As a result, they present no direct threat to us and are thus immune from attack.[8]

The doctrine of double effect. While these considerations describe intuitively some of the moral contours that apply to the treatment of noncombatants, it is impossible in practice to conduct any serious military campaign without jeopardizing civilians and perhaps even killing them in serious numbers. Such outcomes are inevitable side-effects of the conflict that combatants wage against one another. As a result, theorists have developed a principle called the "doctrine of double effect" to identify the proper conduct toward noncombatants, even while engaged in a just war against their host state. The doctrine of double effect asserts that it is permissible to perform wartime acts, even when they are likely to kill noncombatants, if three conditions are met:

---

6. Nagel explains this principle by distinguishing between weapons that attack soldiers as soldiers and weapons that attack them as human beings. He identifies starvation, poisoning, and infectious diseases as weapons "designed to maim or disfigure or torture the opponent rather than merely to stop him." See Nagel, *Mortal Questions*, 71. Nagel admits that such distinctions are difficult to draw with precision, but he argues that some principle of this sort underlies our moral intuitions about these matters.

7. Ibid., 69.

8. Ibid., 69–71. Although others have criticized the usefulness of the concept of directness of threat in distinguishing between those who are subject to attack and those who are not, the idea is sufficient for introducing the basic features of just-war theory. Walzer's way of drawing the distinction, for example, is similar to Nagel's.

a. Those acts are legitimate acts of war.
b. Their direct effect is morally acceptable (the destruction of military supplies, for example, or the killing of enemy soldiers).
c. The intentions of the actors are good: (1) the actors intend *only* to achieve the acceptable military objective; (2) they do *not* intend the harm of noncombatants—they do not even harm noncombatants as a means to their legitimate military ends; and (3) the actors accept greater risks to themselves in order to minimize the risk to noncombatants.[9]

To get a feel for this doctrine, consider the case of pilots bombing a military installation that has a civilian population in close proximity. Obeying the doctrine of double effect, those pilots would seek only to destroy the military installation, have no intention to harm the civilian population that exists nearby, and accept greater risks to themselves in order to minimize the chances of striking that civilian population accidentally (i.e., deliberately fly low enough to increase the accuracy of their attacks even though doing so subjects them to greater threat from anti-aircraft fire). In operating this way the pilots will likely intentionally kill enemy combatants who are legitimate targets of attack, while simultaneously risking, and *un*intentionally causing, the deaths of (some) noncombatants as an unavoidable, but overtly and self-sacrificially minimized, side-effect of that legitimate attack. Assuming that this victim state is complying with all other criteria of the just-war framework, even the second tragic result—because unavoidable—is a permissible outcome of the state's defense of its citizens from assault and killing by their aggressors.

Do all noncombatants enjoy equal moral protection? Natural questions arise in considering the privileged status of noncombatants. The most obvious is whether the civilians of an aggressor state enjoy the identical degree of moral protection enjoyed by the civilians of a victim state. We would not be persuaded, for example, if Hitler argued for the need to launch assaults on the ordinary citizens of Great Britain and other Allied states (assaults which he did in fact launch) on the basis

---

9. I am paraphrasing here Michael Walzer's modern formulation of the doctrine of double effect. See Michael Walzer, *Just and Unjust Wars*, 153, 155. Element (c) is Walzer's more stringent rendering of the classical view, which required only that one not intend injury to noncombatants, not that one must also seek to minimize such injury and accept higher risks to oneself in order to do so. For an incisive critique of the classical formulation, see John C. Ford, S.J., "The Morality of Obliteration Bombing," in Richard B. Miller, ed., *War in the Twentieth Century: Sources in Theological Ethics*, 138–77. Walzer includes a fourth element (proportionality) in the doctrine of double effect, but I follow Orend in listing proportionality as a separate category altogether; see Principle 2 of *jus in bello*. A well-known treatment of the doctrine of double effect is Warren S. Quinn, "Actions, Intentions, and Consequences: The Doctrine of Double Effect," 334–51.

that he needed to do so in order to achieve victory against them. This would strike us as morally preposterous. Since Hitler's desire for victory was unjust in the first place, how could the desire to achieve such an immoral end confer legitimacy on any means thought necessary to achieve it, much less on the act of targeting noncombatants? That much seems obvious, but would we be persuaded if a state argued (as Great Britain ultimately did) that it needed to launch assaults on the ordinary citizens of Nazi Germany in order to defend itself against Hitler's aggression? What if survival by a victim state required that? Would the same moral restriction against deliberate harming of civilians apply in that case?

Just-war theory argues that the answer to these questions may be no. In this way of thinking it is possible to override the constraints of the doctrine of double effect when two conditions are present: (1) when defeat for the victim nation would be genuinely catastrophic, and (2) when such defeat is imminent. This combination of circumstances constitutes a "supreme emergency" and justifies the assault on civilians—regrettable as such action is—if doing so makes the difference between survival and defeat for the victim state. It is on this basis that some, but not all, of Great Britain's bombing of German cities in World War II is generally thought defensible. At the same time the United States' bombing of Nagasaki and Hiroshima is often *not* thought defensible since no similar supreme emergency existed in that case.[10] Of course different people can have different views on exactly what conditions constitute a supreme emergency, but it seems intuitive that there exists some point at which the citizens of an aggressor state may fail to enjoy the privileges enjoyed by those of the aggressed state, even if both are morally innocent. One population is part of a state that is unjustly attacking another, while the other is part of a state that is only defending itself against that attack. Extreme circumstances may exist in which this distinction makes a difference, and if so, then noncombatants do not all enjoy the same moral protection in all circumstances and at all times.

Human shields. It is also important to note that one strategy in war exploits the general restriction against harming noncombatants. This strategy deliberately locates civilians in harm's way by placing them as "shields" of military targets so that any attack on legitimate targets necessarily harms the civilians themselves. Such a strategy generally assumes that it will gain advantage in one of two ways: either the human shields will forestall attacks on the military targets altogether, due to the moral sensibilities of the enemy it seeks to thwart, or, failing that, the deaths of the human shields can at least be used

---

10. Walzer, *Just and Unjust Wars*, 251–68. Elizabeth Anscombe wrote a very famous paper on the latter incidents, hotly condemning the United States' action. See G.E.M. Anscombe, "Mr. Truman's Degree."

to manipulate others by pointing to the large number of civilian casualties inflicted by the enemy.

Assuming all other dimensions of *jus ad bellum* and *jus in bello* to be satisfied—in particular, that the victim state's cause is just and that the benefits both of its defense in general, and of the specific attack, are proportional even to these costs—most agree that it is not forbidden to attack legitimate military targets due to the presence of such noncombatants. Summarizing international law on the subject one scholar states: "If civilian casualties result from an illegal attempt to shield a legitimate military objective with a human shield, those casualties are the responsibility of the side using the human shield, not the attacking side."[11]

The same logic obviously applies when the civilians involved are acting as shields voluntarily; indeed, that kind of action would seem to approximate direct hostile conduct and thus to subvert the very noncombatant status such individuals presumably wish to claim for themselves. Voluntary human shields serve the *military* needs of the humans they protect. They are not like farmers, or medical personnel, who meet the specifically human needs of soldiers. As a result, voluntary human shields are widely understood to have no claim against those who harm them when they do so only in pursuit of legitimate military objectives. From the perspective of international law: "Military objectives protected by human shields remain lawful targets despite the presence of such shields."[12]

All of these principles, both under the rubric of *jus ad bellum* and of *jus in bello*, identify the conditions that must be satisfied for a war and its conduct to be considered just. They stipulate the circumstances under which war is necessary and right, and the kind of military conduct that is and is not right once conflict is underway. Although most people abhor war, they do accept its necessity in certain circumstances even while expecting it to be waged in certain ways. The just-war framework attempts to capture these intuitions and codify them, at least in a general way.[13]

---

11. Gary Solis, *The Law of Armed Conflict: International Humanitarian Law in War*, 320. Michael Walzer reaches the same conclusion in his treatment of just-war theory. See Walzer, *Just and Unjust Wars*, 174.

12. Solis, *The Law of Armed Conflict*, 321.

13. Although this general outline of just-war theory is sufficient for my purposes here, it is susceptible to refinement and modification in the details of its formulation and of its application to varied and complex cases. For a rich example of this, see F. M. Kamm, "Failures of Just War Theory: Terror, Harm, and Justice," 650–92. For a recent treatment of killing in war, including various categories of both combatants and noncombatants, see Jeff McMahan, *Killing in War*.

Just War vs. Justified War

The general view of war sketched above asserts that a war is just if it satisfies the conditions of both *jus ad bellum* and *jus in bello*. This view acknowledges that innocent people will be killed in any conflict large enough to be considered war, but argues that this is an acceptable, if thoroughly regrettable and tragic, consequence of a state defending itself in a just cause. According to this view, if these deaths are unintended, if they are explicitly avoided and minimized, and if combatants impose greater risks on themselves in order to avoid and minimize these deaths, then, assuming all other conditions of *jus ad bellum* and *jus in bello* to be satisfied, the war is just.

But another point of view holds that a war is just only if *no* harm comes to any innocent person in the conflict. It is not sufficient that combatants explicitly minimize such harm, but any war that causes such harm *at all* cannot be considered just. Such a war may be justified (it is something that is morally permissible), but, because it includes individual acts that are not just (the harming of those who are not legitimate targets of attack), it cannot satisfy the higher standard of actually being just.

The distinction between these views allows us to identify a difference among just-war theorists and thus to be aware of the nuances of using a word like *just*, but it also helps us identify the minimum statement on which all just-war theorists agree: namely, that at least some wars are *justified*. Whatever other distinctions or disagreements may exist, this is generally accepted.[14]

Conclusion

The just-war framework does not provide a formula that guarantees agreement among all parties evaluating the justifiability of a state's entrance into war, or the manner in which a given state conducts itself in war. Because both the number and the complexity of the variables related to war are so large, and because information regarding these variables is so often imprecise (if

---

14. The just-war literature in moral philosophy draws a number of distinctions in its attempts to identify the contours of right and wrong regarding war. In addition to the distinctions between "just" and "justifiable" and between "intended" and "unintended," distinctions involving the notions of innocence, microthreat, macrothreat, foreseen, unforeseen, liability, narrow proportionality, wide proportionality, infringing, violating, overriding, doing, allowing, and so forth, also figure prominently in efforts to form the proper view. For one entry point into recent literature, see Jeff McMahan, *Killing in War*; Jeff McMahan, "Debate: Justification and Liability in War"; Michael Neu, "Why McMahan's *Just* Wars Are Only *Justified* and Why That Matters," 235–55.

not categorically false), reasonable people can easily disagree.[15] It is precisely because of such complexity that the just-war framework cannot be thought of as a formula that serves to remove all questions. Instead, it is a framework that simply tells us what questions to ask. It identifies the considerations that it seems we must account for, analyze, and weigh if we want to reach a thoughtful decision regarding both the justifiability of any given entrance into war, and the conduct of war once it is engaged. Again, this does not guarantee agreement, but it does provide a common foundation that helps guide the search for a moral point of view regarding particular conflicts.

---

15. Consider a mere sample of the questions that surround any attempt to think about war in a given case: Is it futile for such and such a state to defend itself against a certain aggressor? And what is the standard for futility in the first place? Is the threshold different for some aggressors than for others? Will the benefits outweigh the costs even if such and such a state *is* able to defend itself successfully? And how certain, in reality, is the distinction between the victim and the aggressor in this case? Could they be equally wrong? And regarding the requirement for diplomacy: At what point is such effort no longer genuine diplomacy, but mere opportunity for an aggressor state to continue its aggression with impunity? Further, what are the risks to civilians if a state enters war to defend itself in a particular circumstance? What are the risks to civilians if a state does *not* enter war to defend itself in that circumstance? What are the risks to civilians if a state pursues one military strategy rather than another? And in each case of risk, exactly how is the risk calculated and with what margin of error? And do some circumstances of aggression justify taking greater risks than other circumstances? If so, what factors determine this and how carefully can they be estimated? Moreover, at what point, exactly, is the military situation of a victim state so dire that it qualifies as a supreme emergency—opening the way to assault on noncombatant citizens of the aggressor state? If the standard is "imminent catastrophe," what is the standard for imminence and what is the definition of "catastrophe"? And what margin of error applies in deciding matters of this moral gravity? Further, how should the propensity of an aggressor state to employ human shields figure into the calculation of the costs and benefits of a state deciding whether it should defend itself or not? What must the benefits be in order to enter war in which the aggressor state is guaranteed to elevate the number of civilian deaths? These questions are but the tip of the iceberg.

Chapter 2

Pacifism: The "Anti-Violence" Version

Getting Clear about Pacifism

Just-war theory is not the only possible view of war, and it is not held universally. The competing point of view, pacifism, straightforwardly rejects the primary assertion of just-war theory that at least some wars are justified. In a nutshell, to pacifists war is prohibited in all circumstances as a matter of principle.

Non-Pacifist Peace Stances

It is important to approach the topic of pacifism with a reasonable degree of care because some attitudes are occasionally identified as pacifist even though they do not reject war in principle, but actually fall within the parameters of the just-war framework. For example, if we accept that war is permissible under certain circumstances, but insist that every effort must be made to resolve hostilities through peaceful means before waging such defensive war, we are simply emphasizing the fourth principle of the *jus ad bellum* criteria. We are not, therefore, repudiating just-war theory, but merely emphasizing one of its elements. A 1942 First Presidency statement captures this attitude: "The Church is and must be against war.... The Church ... cannot regard war as a righteous means of settling international disputes; these should and could be settled—the nations agreeing—by peaceful negotiation and adjustment."[1] This statement emphasizes the rightfulness of peace and the wrongfulness of war, but it does not assert that no war, under any circumstances, is ever justified. That would be an additional claim, over and above the view that international hostilities should be settled by peaceful negotiation, "the nations agreeing."

It is also not a repudiation of just-war theory to embrace an expansive and activist ethic toward peace. For instance, desiring to create a peaceful planet where all international conflict is resolved through peaceful means is not uncommon, and early in the last century was called "pacific-ism." It represented

---

1. "First Presidency address," *Conference Report*, April 1942, 94. See also, F. R. Rick Duran, "Pax Sanctorum," in Patrick Q. Mason, J. David Pulsipher, and Richard L. Bushman, eds., *War and Peace in Our Time: Mormon Perspectives,* 59, where he refers to this statement. Duran uses the term "pacifism" to capture this attitude and others like it, but none of the views he so designates actually departs from the just-war framework; see Chapter 10 herein, the section entitled "A 'Pacifist Manifesto,'" regarding this approach.

an overall sentiment toward peace, but accepted the possibility of waging a justified war, however distasteful and regrettable it might be. By the 1930s, however, the term's meaning had narrowed to denote the absolute rejection of all war. The term dropped out of common usage and was replaced by the term "pacifism" and captured the idea of the wholesale rejection of conflict.[2] There seems to be no word that captures what pacific-ism originally meant—a *non-pacifist peace sentiment*—but it matters little since the concept fits within the framework of just-war theory in any case. The distinctiveness of this term lies only in its overall emphasis on the necessity of actively establishing conditions for peace between states and energetically resisting war as the solution when conflict arises. But this is entirely compatible with just-war theory. We can work assiduously for peace and wish for it in all circumstances and still conceive the possibility of a war that is morally permissible. Such a peace sentiment, by itself, is not a competing theory of war.[3]

Nor is it a rejection of the just-war doctrine simply to insist that violence is evil and therefore that war is evil. No one believes that we have a right to go about inflicting pain on others, whether through war or any other act of violence. Just-war theory presupposes this and this presupposition is evident throughout its provisions. Doing no more than insisting that war is evil, therefore, is not additive, but repetitive of what is already recognized. In his frustration at those who incessantly proclaim the evil of war—but who have nothing more to offer on the subject—one famed journalist observed long ago that "the world is not helped much by being told every morning that two and two are four.... Everyone knows that war is a stupid way to deal with issues, but to repeat this is in no way to deal with the issues.... And unless the advocates of peace can [offer concrete solutions], they might as well paint coal black as insist that war is horrible."[4] We can recognize that war is evil and yet claim that in certain circumstances it is a *necessary* evil and therefore that it can be justified. To qualify as pacifism the view considered here would have to make the claim that war is never permitted, in addition to observing that war is evil.

We also do not repudiate just-war theory by objecting to a particular war because we think it is unjust, or by objecting to how a given war is being waged because we think that is unjust. In neither case do we reject war *per se*, but instead reject only a particular war—and for just-war reasons: namely, because we think it violates one or more of the conditions either of *jus ad*

---

2. See Martin Ceadel, *Thinking about Peace and War*.

3. Eugene England exhibits this type of spirit in the course of discussing how he would handle someone attacking his family. See Eugene England, "A Case for Mormon Christian Pacifism," 96–103.

4. Walter Lippmann, "The Futility of Pacifism," 193–94.

bellum or of *jus in bello*. We obviously do not leave the domain of just-war theory when we repudiate a given conflict on just-war grounds.

Additionally, we do not repudiate just-war theory by objecting simply to our personal participation in war for one reason or another, nor do we do so by objecting to the participation of some group of which we are a part. In such cases we do not repudiate war itself or abandon the parameters of just-war theory, but merely identify some reason why we, or others like us, should not participate in a particular just war. This leaves the justifiability of war itself completely unchallenged and generalizes the prohibition against participating in it only to specific persons for specific reasons. In other words, this objection can hardly be characterized as a morally principled rejection of war, since it has already acknowledged that the war is just, and since what it finds objectionable about participation in war is located within us and not within war itself. In this case, the reach of our attitude is so short, its generalization so narrow, that it is not a general principle at all.

Interestingly enough all of these positions (and more) have been called "pacifist" at one time or another, and thus it is possible to construct a list of varieties of "pacifist" positions. But constructing a list of this sort is valuable only insofar as it categorizes the various motives for opposition to war or the various outward and vocal forms that such opposition has taken over the course of time.[5] While that exercise may be useful on a certain level, it is far from fundamental. In the Book of Mormon alone King Benjamin, Captain Moroni, Alma, Gidgiddoni, Mormon, and Moroni were all opposed to war, and yet they all led thousands of men *into* war. These familiar instances underscore the point that, as mentioned earlier, practically speaking *everyone* is opposed to war (except those who start it, in furtherance of power or greed), including prominent Book of Mormon warriors and just-war theorists themselves. Indeed, the just-war tradition is one of generally condemning war, not of finding ways to justify it.[6]

This widespread abhorrence of war explains why these varieties, loosely called pacifist, while interesting from a sociological or even a psychological perspective, actually have no philosophical interest. All of the attitudes mentioned above either presuppose just-war theory or emphasize something that is completely compatible with it. They are the kind of disagreements and differences that can and do occur among proponents of just-war theory and that

---

5. For instance, Jenny Teichman and John Howard Yoder identify a variety of positions that are called "pacifism" in one general sense or another; see Jenny Teichman, *The Philosophy of War and Peace* and *Pacifism and the Just War*; and John Howard Yoder, *Christian Attitudes to War, Peace, and Revolution*. Teichman uses the expression "anti-war-ism" to distinguish these positions from opposition to violence in general.

6. On this point see Michael Neu, "Why McMahan's *Just* Wars are Only *Justified* and Why That Matters," 251.

fit comfortably within its framework. To emphasize one or another of them is to do nothing that contravenes the theory itself, and that is why, from a philosophical and moral standpoint, they are not distinct from just-war theory even if they have been called pacifist at one time or another. That is why Nagel, Anscombe, Narveson, and others restrict the term pacifism to the view—and only to the view—that war itself is wrong in principle, and that it can never be justified. This approach reflects what Ceadel identifies as the core pacifist position, namely, that "participation in and support for war is always impermissible," and Orend's expression that "war, for the pacifist, is always wrong."[7] This is more than an abhorrence of war, and it is more than a diligent effort to abolish war; it is the moral rejection of war as anything that can ever be justified.[8]

So if this is the core of pacifism—that war can never be justified—what are the intellectual arguments for it? The cases fall into two broad categories: one that argues against violence of any sort, whatever its scale, and one that argues against violence specifically on any scale large enough to qualify as war. This chapter will address the first of these cases. The following chapter will address the second.

"Anti-Violence" Pacifism

Those holding the general view that violence itself is always prohibited would say that any act of violence, even in response to violence itself, is still violence and therefore wrong. Those taking this stance would say it is not permissible to shoot and kill the military commander described in the Introduction to this book, despite the violence the commander will perform if he is not stopped. The prohibition against violence is absolute. In the words of Leo Tolstoy:

> The truth is so simple, so clear, so evident, and so incumbent not only on Christians but on all reasonable men, that it is only necessary to speak it out completely in its full significance for it to be irresistible. The truth in its full meaning lies in what was said thousands of years ago . . . in four words: *Thou*

---

7. Ceadel, *Thinking about Peace and War*, 5. See also, Brian Orend, "A Just-War Critique of Realism and Pacifism," 455. For Anscombe and Narveson, see Elizabeth Anscombe, "War and Murder," 41–53; and Jan Narveson, "Pacifism: A Philosophical Analysis," 63–77. Narveson is both correct and emphatic on the point. His argument regarding the definition of pacifism in regard to non-violence in general applies equally to the case of war in particular. Thomas Nagel also equates pacifism with the absolutist position that war is never justified. See Thomas Nagel, "War and Massacre," 56. Lawrence Masek does the same and Jeff McMahan refers to this as the "traditional" understanding of pacifism; see Lawrence Mask, "All's Not Fair in War: How Kant's Just War Theory Refutes War Realism," 143; Jeff McMahan, "Pacifism and Moral Theory," 44.

8. For a wide range of writings related to non-violence—some of which are genuinely pacifist in the way I have identified, and some of which are not—see Howard Zinn, *The Power of Nonviolence: Writings by Advocates of Peace*.

Shalt Not Kill. The truth is that man may not and should not in any circumstances or under any pretext kill his fellow man.[9]

Tolstoy is opposed to killing in any circumstance. It is no surprise, then, that he goes on, three separate times in the same passage, to equate the killing that occurs in war with murder.

Anti-Violence Based on Harm

One way to take an anti-violence stance is to focus on the harm that violence causes. In this view it is not the violence itself that creates the moral problem, but the harm violence inflicts on others.

While a view of this sort seems intuitively correct at first glance it actually precludes the very result it seeks—the blanket prohibition of all violence. After all, if we are opposed to violence because of the harm it causes, aren't we thereby committed to *reducing* harm whenever possible? Since it seems so, imagine a case in which we can prevent an act of violence that would involve $2x$ amount of harm by committing an act of violence against the perpetrator that would involve only x amount of harm (shooting the commander in the case in the Introduction—thus sparing the lives of two children—presents an example along these lines). Doesn't our opposition to violence and the harm it causes compel us to act violently in this case, and thus to *produce* violence? If we want to reduce harm, by what rationale could we refuse to commit an act of violence that would, in the end, reduce it?

Consider the equally real example of a terrorist slowly beheading innocent civilians (or even combatants for that matter) while filming the act no less. This is a vile and reprehensible act and anyone announcing a rejection of violence must be horrified by it, but the obvious question is whether violence is permissible to prevent *these* acts of violence. What if the only way to prevent beheadings were to shoot the beheader, and suppose that we actually had an opportunity to do this? Would it be permissible to do so? Moreover, if we are opposed to harm why wouldn't it be *obligatory* for us to shoot and kill the beheader in order to prevent the harm he will otherwise cause?

This is the kind of problem encountered when objecting to violence on consequential grounds. Opposition to harm seems *eo ipso* to commit us to performing acts of violence when we can reduce harm by doing so, and since minimizing harm can thus require violence, it is a contradiction to appeal to reducing harm as the reason for prohibiting it. The absolute injunction against violence on these grounds is thus self-defeating.[10]

---

9. Leo Tolstoy, "Law of God vs. Law of the State," 123.

10. For a more complete treatment of this and related points, see Jan Narveson, "Pacifism: A Philosophical Analysis," 63–77. Narveson considers the view to be entirely self-contradictory.

Anti-Violence Based on Wrong Action

However, we might object to violence not so much because of the harm it causes, but because of the kind of *act* it is. Violence itself is a wrong kind of conduct, and is therefore prohibited, irrespective of the exact amount and character of the harm it causes. Patrick Mason seems to be framing this type of concern when he asks regarding Cain, Abel, and Adam: "Should Abel have used violent, even lethal, force to stop Cain's assault? Or if Adam had happened upon them, would violence against his aggressor son be justified to protect and preserve his victim son?"[11] Serious wondering about this matter, as opposed to mere rhetorical fancy, presupposes that violence might be wrong in general, whatever the circumstances might be. If so, then it is a serious question whether violence of any sort can ever really be justified, including in self-defense. This point of view is more common and serious than the first, and thus requires more discussion.

Disregard of important moral distinctions. Although the view that violence is never justified seems at first to have some weight on its side, it comes at the cost of disregarding important moral distinctions. There is a difference, after all, between the moral status of Cain and the moral status of Abel. Cain is an aggressor who is seeking the death of Abel, while Abel is an innocent victim who, in fighting, is only defending himself against one who is unjustifiably attempting to kill him. By encountering and employing violence to help him, Adam is simply the agent of Abel, coming to his defense against an unjustified attack by an aggressor. Adam's moral status is nothing like Cain's, and if he were to kill Cain this act would be nothing like Cain's killing of Abel. The killings are morally distinct. As the aggressor, Cain has no right to act as he is acting, and thus forfeits his right not to have others act against him. As the innocent victim, Abel has every right not to be attacked (he has forfeited nothing) and thus has every right to act in his own defense. As Abel's proxy, Adam has every right to defend the innocent Abel.[12]

---

11. Patrick Q. Mason, "Introduction," in Patrick Q. Mason, J. David Pulsipher, and Richard L. Bushman, eds., *War and Peace in Our Time: Mormon Perspectives*, x.

12. The notion of forfeiture figures prominently in my discussion, but it has not been an uncontroversial concept. Judith Thomson, for one, challenges it in an early paper, but later explicitly invokes it. See Judith Jarvis Thomson, "Self-Defense and Rights," 33–50, and her classic "Self-Defense," 283–310. Charles Fried (my first influence) and Frances Kamm both employ the idea, as does Fiona Leverick, even more fully. See Charles Fried, *Right and Wrong*; F. M. Kamm, *Intricate Ethics: Rights, Responsibilities, and Permissible Harm*; and Fiona Leverick, *Killing in Self-Defence*. Grabczynska and Ferzan criticize Leverick's reliance on forfeiture, but are unpersuasive, and Brian Orend explicitly defends the notion against critics. See

To fail to distinguish between Cain and Abel (or Adam) is to fail to appreciate the opposite moral status of aggressors and victims. Imagine, for example, the case of a woman being raped who can defend herself only by fatally shooting her attacker.[13] In determining the rightness of her conduct we would not reduce the matter to a question of determining which is worse between killing and raping. To frame the matter in this way is to mis-frame it. The relevant distinction is not between the act of killing and the act of raping, abstractly conceived, but between the moral status of the two actors themselves—between the moral status of an aggressor and the moral status of a victim. Here the difference is stark because the rapist is an aggressor who has no right to do what he is doing, while the woman is an innocent victim who has every right to defend herself against attack. Right and wrong do not reduce to a simple comparison of outcomes or even to a comparison of intentional actions considered in the abstract. What matters most is the contrast between the moral status of the two actors themselves: one is an aggressor who is violating someone else's rights and one is a victim who is doing no more than defending and preserving her rights.[14] This same distinction is true in the case of Adam and Cain. If we see this simply as two instances of killing in the abstract we see it mistakenly. Just as the victim enjoys a different moral status from her rapist, Adam enjoys a different moral status from Cain. Therefore their acts, from a moral point of view, could not be more different.

All of this explains why it is unpersuasive to reject violence as an act in itself and as unrelated to the person who is committing it. There is a stark moral difference between aggressors and victims, and there is thus a stark moral difference between an act of violence committed by an aggressor and

---

Arlette Grabczynska and Kimberly Kessler Ferzan, "Justifying *Killing in Self-Defence*," 235–53; and Orend, "A Just-War Critique" 435–77.

13. The justifiability of killing in defense against rape has long been widely accepted, although the idea has recently become more controversial. See Leverick, *Killing in Self-Defence*, 143–58. To avoid unnecessary distractions, I imagine the case in which the victim's only defense is to shoot, but where she is obviously shooting only to repulse the attack, not to cause death per se.

14. It is common to see this kind of distinction drawn in the literature. One forceful and well-known example is Elizabeth Anscombe's. See G.E.M Anscombe, "War and Murder," 41–53. Obviously, not all degrees of defense are justified against all degrees of aggression, because not all rights are equally stringent. I have a right that you not snap your fingers in my ear, but I am not justified in cutting off your fingers to prevent you from doing so. Defensive action must be proportional to the right it defends. Although there is no precise and universally accepted formula for determining such proportionality (or even the stringency of a right, for that matter), the general principle of proportionality is no doubt correct. See Frances Kamm's remarks on stringency in Kamm, *Intricate Ethics*, 249–57, 263–68.

an act of violence committed by a victim. To say that all violence is wrong, without regard for the moral status of the person who performs it, is to deny this distinction, and to deny this distinction is to find ourselves helpless before even the simplest cases of self-defense. It is to discover ourselves thinking that the victims in those cases have somehow done something wrong—and that is surely a very large mistake.

The Relational Foundation of Right and Wrong

For readers who want a further exploration of why a difference exists between aggressors and victims, here's the general idea. Note, to begin, that the account above explains the distinction between right and wrong acts of violence on the basis of the difference in moral status between aggressors and victims, and it claims that this results in a different configuration of rights for aggressors and victims. But how does this work—this differential attribution of rights to different persons? How does one obtain rights in the first place, and how can one then forfeit them? What intellectual framework holds all this together? It is possible to provide no more than a rudimentary outline of the explanation, and then only as it applies to these particular cases. A complete theory of rights (or even anything approaching it) would require examination of many different types of cases, extended across a broad range of applications, and expressing far greater degrees of complexity than the cases we have considered thus far in this volume. Even so, it is possible to sketch a general framework that serves (at least intuitively) to make sense of the moral judgments we commonly make regarding *these* cases and that provides at least a rough explanation for them.[15]

Rights and Obligations[16]

The first element of this framework is the inescapability of our intimate connectedness to one another. To *be* is to be in relationship with others.

---

15. The literature on rights is large; a recent detailed and comprehensive discussion is Kamm, *Intricate Ethics*. My purpose, as I said, is dramatically narrower, leaving many questions unexplored and many possible objections unanswered. For example, I know the arguments against the strict correlativity of rights and duties that my prose in this section assumes, and I am aware of the possibility of duties toward third persons. But I leave consideration of these and many other matters aside. I will be content if my brief comments simply resonate with the intuitions and considered judgments of most readers regarding the particular cases I have identified.

16. My starting point is that zone of philosophical interest where Kant, Buber, and Levinas intersect, and my extremely brief treatment draws on all of them. (I obviously have in mind Kant's second formulation of the categorical imperative and Buber's delineation of I-Thou relationships. I am indebted to Terry Warner—whose understanding of Levinas is deep and subtle—for what grasp I have of Levinas, and also for introducing me to Buber.) On Kant see his *Groundwork of the Metaphysics of Morals*,

Indeed, our connectedness to one another is constitutive of our very lives: we exist in relation to others, or not at all.

However, although we are intimately connected to others in this way, we are also separate from them, just as we are separate from objects in our world. The difference is that while we can appropriate objects—use them and make them ours through consumption or intellectual subjugation—we cannot similarly appropriate other people. We cannot make them ours. And to see them as elements of the world that, though intimately connected to us, are also separate from us—and thus that we cannot appropriate in the way we can appropriate objects—is to see them to be selves just as we are. Thus, to see ourselves as separate from them—to constitute ourselves as separate selves at all—is to acknowledge *their* humanity, and to be guided toward meeting the need that they have to be treated as selves in their own right.

To feel this call is thus to embrace the reality that others count just as much as we do: it is to recognize that they possess a right to treatment as our equal. And this means that they have a right not to be used by us—the right not to be exploited for purposes of our own as if they were less than we are (i.e., as if they were mere means to our end). They are not less than we are; they are not mere means to our end. Nor, similarly, are we less than they are—mere means to their end. Our right to treatment as equals—our right not to be exploited—is a right we share. And this means that we also share an obligation—the obligation to honor, rather than to violate, each other's right not to be used (i.e., not to be treated as less than we are).[17]

---

ed. Mary Gregor and Jens Timmerman. On Buber see his *I and Thou*. On Levinas see Emmanuel Levinas, *Totality and Infinity: An Essay on Exteriority*. A popular treatment of Warner's work is C. Terry Warner, *Bonds That Make Us Free*. For the extension I make of this starting point I am completely indebted to Charles Fried, who first wrote on the relational foundation of right and wrong long ago; see Charles Fried, *Right and Wrong*. I am also indebted to Ronald Dworkin for the conception of equality that I employ; see Ronald Dworkin, *Taking Rights Seriously*, 266–78. Obviously, many authors have emphasized Kant's principle of not using others as mere means, all in more detail than I offer here. To pick up on just one of the threads, see Jonathan Quong, "Killing in Self-Defense," 507–37; and Kimberly Kessler Ferzan, "Self-Defense, Permissions, and the Means Principle: A Reply to Quong," 503–13.

17. Kant would say that we are to treat the humanity in each other as an end in itself. Reference specifically to the humanity in each other (i.e., the features that make us distinctively human) is an important element of his thought, but emphasizing this is not necessary for my purposes in this book and readers might find a continual reference to it distracting. For the most part, therefore, I will be less precise in references to this principle and, as is commonly done, refer simply to treating others as ends in themselves, omitting the point that, for Kant, it is specifically the humanity

Wrong Acts

Acts are wrong when they violate this deep right against being used. Consider, for instance, the case of lying. In the normal course of life it is valuable for you to know the truth—to know the way the world is—so that you can order your life freely and rationally with regard to it. It follows from this that you have a right not to be lied to and, because of my relationship with you, it follows that I have the duty *not* to lie to you. I have no right to keep you from the truth to which you are entitled. If I were to lie to you, I would be using you; I would be laying claim to your mind, asserting the right to manipulate it as I wish, according to my purposes.

You also have the right not to suffer violence from me. You have the right to bodily integrity—obviously entailing the right to life—and, honoring this relationship with you, I have the duty not to exercise violence toward you, either by killing you or in any other way assaulting your person. Were I to do so, I would be using you; I would be laying claim to your *body*, asserting the right to use it as I wish, as a means to accomplishing my personal ends. For these reasons, both lying and committing violence are violations of your rights and, because they are violations of your rights, they are wrong.

The general idea, then, is that as a result of (1) our inherent connectedness to one another, and (2) our shared status as separate selves, we all have the deep right to be treated as an equal: we have the right to be treated as an end in ourselves, not merely as a means to someone else's end. And this implies that we all have a corresponding duty—the duty to *honor* this deep right in one another. This deep right and its corresponding duty find expression in the specific circumstances of life through the more concrete rights and duties that follow from them, e.g., the rights not to be lied to and not to suffer violence, and the corresponding duties not to lie and not to harm.

Appreciating all this helps us see (at least one reason) why wrong acts are wrong. For example, when I lie to you (and therefore violate your right not to be lied to) I violate *you*—and this is what makes my action wrong. It is not the contravention of a rule or of an abstract imperative about lying that makes it wrong; it is the violation, the rupture, of a *relationship*—of what I owe you as a result of my inherent connection to you and of your right, as a separate self, to treatment as my equal. That is what I subvert when I lie to you; I constitute our relationship as one in which I am permitted to exploit you, and that makes my act wrong.[18]

---

in others that we are to treat this way. I also leave aside the Kantian point that we are to treat the humanity in ourselves in the same way.

18. I have restricted myself to secular language and concepts in roughing this out, but it is easy to imagine how these ideas are ennobled and enhanced, to say the least, by the common divine/eternal heritage that is the actual basis of our relationship to one another.

Example: the case of lying. Now, to flesh out this view of lying somewhat, consider a case (now quite famous) that the French philosopher Benjamin Constant (1767–1830) asks us to imagine: (1) a would-be murderer comes to our door asking the whereabouts of a person he seeks to kill, and (2) the person he is seeking is actually hiding in our home. Are we justified in lying to the would-be murderer in order to prevent the murder that he intends?

Almost all people answer positively to this question, and Constant himself gives the core of the reason. He first explains that rights give rise to duties, and then adds that "to tell the truth then is a duty, but only towards him who has a right to the truth. But no man has a right to a truth that injures others."[19] This seems exactly right. As stated above, because of our need for the truth in ordering our lives according to the way the world is, and because of both (1) our shared humanity and (2) our separateness, we all have a right to be treated as an equal (i.e., not to be used merely as a means) and thus not to be lied to. And again, as said earlier, this means that we all have a *duty* not to lie to each other: we have no claim to exploit each other's minds, using them however we see fit in order to achieve our purposes.

It is important to be clear about the connection being identified here: namely, that it is *because* people have a right not to be lied to that we have a duty not to lie to them. This is important because—other things equal, at least—it means that if someone does not, in fact, have a right not to be lied to, then we do not, in fact, have a duty not to lie to them. And this is the case with the would-be murderer. He is specifically treating both us and his ultimate victim as mere means to his end. He is asking for the truth as part of an ongoing intention to kill, and this he has no right to do. This means that he has no right to *any part* of his intention, including possessing the truth. The would-be murderer forfeits his right not to be lied to because of the use to which he intends to put the truth if he is *not* lied to (i.e., if he obtains the truth from us). But he has no right to do what he intends, and thus he has no right to the information that would permit him to realize his intention. And because he has no right to this information, we have no duty to share the truth with him.[20]

---

19. Benjamin Constant, cited in Lenval A. Callender, "In Defence of Kant's 'Infamous' Reply to Constant: 'On a Supposed Right to Lie from Benevolent Motives.'"

20. Although people almost universally agree with Constant in his answer, even if not in his (apparent) reasoning, Kant is not one of them. This is not surprising since Constant was specifically challenging Kant's view of lying in proposing this example in the first place. Kant published a reply to Constant, but some of Kant's reasoning in his reply is widely considered ridiculous. David Sussman, however, defends Kant's overall reasoning by placing it, rightly, I believe, in its proper context: not in the arena of personal morality ("virtue," as Kant referred to this domain of philosophy), but specifically in the context of the relations among free and equal members of a political community with a just legal system (the

So even though people begin with a right not to be lied to, they forfeit this right if their intent is to exploit it in a quest to use other people. In seeking such exploitation, they *eo ipso* render themselves ineligible for the rights that would otherwise attach to them. They render themselves without right to the truth, and thereby render others without duty to tell it to them.

Seeing the matter this way helps us appreciate why Abraham and Sarai were right in lying to the Egyptians, as recorded in the Book of Abraham (Abr. 2:21–25; see also Gen. 12:10–19), and why the Lord would instruct them to tell the lie they told. Because of the end to which the Egyptians would have put the truth (they would have killed Abraham in order to obtain Sarai) they forfeited their right to possess the truth, and because they had no right to possess the truth, Abraham and Sarai had no duty to share it with them. The Egyptians, by their own actions and disposition, rendered themselves without claim to the truth, and this rendered Abraham and Sarai without obligation to tell it to them.[21]

To take an example more mundane than that of Abraham or of a would-be murderer, note that when people leave their homes even for a short period they carefully arrange matters to make it appear that they are not away. That is a lie, but it is not wrong. Those who might take advantage of such owners'

---

ethics of "right," as Kant referred to this domain of philosophy). Contra Kant himself, Sussman finds a way (through the notion of "deputizing") to justify the lie even on Kantian terms; see David Sussman, "On the Supposed Duty of Truthfulness: Kant on Lying in Self-Defense," 224–43. Lenval Callender defends Kant's reasoning in both philosophical contexts, and claims that Constant uses the term "right" in a way different from the way Kant uses it in the first place; see Callender, "In Defence of Kant's 'Infamous' Reply to Constant." Christine Korsgaard argues that the lie is permissible from the standpoint of Kant's first formulation of the categorical imperative, but not from the standpoint of the second or third (if these are unfamiliar, see Immanuel Kant, *Groundwork of the Metaphysics of Morals*). This is because the standard of conduct Kant establishes for us is designed for an ideal state of affairs: one in which everyone is living in accord with Kant's maxims. We are to conduct ourselves *as if* we were living in such a world. She argues that this suggests the need for special principles for dealing with evil—principles that do not assume the ideal state of affairs that Kant generally asks us to assume; see Christine Korsgaard, "The Right to Lie: Kant on Dealing with Evil," 325–49. James Mahon defends Kant on lying, incorporating distinctions both regarding the context of lying and regarding three different kinds of lies addressed in Kant's work; see James Edwin Mahon, "The Truth about Kant on Lies." For one translation of Kant's published reply itself, see Immanuel Kant, "Concerning a Pretended Right to Lie from Motives of Humanity."

21. The Lord could have other reasons, of course, for instructing Abraham to lie in this circumstance. I am sketching only one. Furthermore, Abraham is not the only prophet to have lied in circumstances that imperiled life. See the account of Elisha, for example, in 2 Kings 6:8–22.

absence have no right to the truth regarding their whereabouts, and the owners thus have no obligation to evidence it to them. Would-be burglars have violated the conditions presupposed by the rule of truth-telling and thus, by their own disposition, have nullified their claim to the truth. By seeking to exploit others they forsake their fundamental relationship *with* others, and thereby surrender the truth-claims they have that are born of that relationship and cease to exist without it. No one does wrong in lying to them.[22]

Example: the case of defense. The same conceptual framework applies in the cases of violence we have considered. Think again of Cain. He attacks Abel, seeking to kill him, and this he obviously has no right to do. He is not free to use Abel in this way, and his killing of Abel is murder. But what about Abel? Is he free to exercise violence against Cain in self-defense? If every person has the right not to suffer violence, then Cain would also share this right. If so, then it seems that Abel and Adam would be wrong to attack Cain—even if they were to do so defensively.

But the same relationship that exists between rights and duties in the case of lying exists between rights and duties in the case of violence: it is precisely *because* people have a right not to suffer violence that we have a duty not to exercise violence toward them. And this means that if someone does not, in fact, have a right not to suffer violence, then we do not, in fact, have a duty not to exercise violence toward them. And this is the case with Cain. He is treating Abel as a mere means to his end. Indeed, he is seeking to kill

---

22. It is important to note that this account of lying is not permissive, but prohibits every lie proscribed by the commandment against lying ("Thou shalt not lie; he that lieth and will not repent shall be cast out" D&C 42:21). The contribution of this account lies only in suggesting one reason why there is a commandment against lying in the first place, and why, in certain cases, lying is not actually forbidden—why it seems in those cases to conflict with, and to be overridden by, other commandments, and why we feel (along with the Lord, please note) that it *should* be suspended in those circumstances. What this account tries to show is what those circumstances are and why the proscription against lying does not apply in them. The idea is that the commandment presupposes circumstances in which others have a right to the truth (circumstances which are by far the norm) and thus who would be violated by being misled. It is not necessarily applicable in situations in which others do not actually have a right to the truth and thus who would not suffer violation by being misled. It is not important for my purposes to develop an exhaustive list of the ways people can forfeit their right to the truth; doing so would be a large and subtle task of its own. It is sufficient to appreciate only that such forfeiture at least seems possible and that it provides a coherent explanation for why lying is not always forbidden, despite the commandment against it: the commandment is not applicable in situations in which the conditions presupposed by the commandment do not obtain.

Abel, and this he has no right to do. Cain thus forfeits his right not to suffer violence because of what *not* suffering violence will permit him to do. And because he has no right to do this, he has no right not to be attacked if that is required to prevent him from doing it. Adam does no wrong if he kills Cain to prevent Cain from killing Abel.[23]

So even though we begin with a right not to suffer violence, we forfeit this right if our intent is to exploit it in a quest to use others violently ourselves. In doing so, we *eo ipso* render ourselves ineligible for the rights that would otherwise be ours. We render ourselves without right not to suffer violence, and we thereby render others without duty not to exercise violence toward us.

The Difference between Aggressors and Victims

Understanding the rights born of the conjunction of our shared humanity with our status as separate selves helps us locate the critical difference between the aggressor and the victim in each of the cases we have looked at. In each of these examples—the military commander, the inquiring murderer, Cain, and the rapist—the difference between the aggressor and his victim is the way each constitutes his relationship with the other. The aggressors in these cases, by their act or intention of harm, forge a relationship with others that is based on exploitation. All lay claim to use the body, or indeed the life, of another person as a means to some end. In pursuit of some purpose of their own, they violate their victims' right not to suffer violence. They all use another in a way that they would not themselves consent to being used. That is what makes each of them an aggressor. The inquiring murderer uses even the person at the door in this way. Note that the very existence of communication presupposes that communication is truthful: if people could not assume the truth of the communication they enjoyed with others (including, of course, during the very intricate and time-consuming process of learning a language in the first place), the very idea of communication would be impossible. And this makes the expectation of truthfulness the precondition of communication's very possibility. Thus, even apart from any spiritual commitments we might

---

23. All of this leaves aside, of course, the question of whether we have the positive duty of exercising violence in such cases. It is one thing to say that we have no duty not to assault someone in such circumstances, and another to say that we have a duty *to* assault someone in such circumstances—to say that we are not only permitted to defend someone, but that we are morally obligated to do so. This distinction, among many others, is commonplace in the philosophical literature. But the distinction is not important for my purposes in looking at anti-violence pacifism (which is the topic under discussion), because that view makes the claim that violence is not even morally *permitted*. This obviously precludes the possibility that it could ever be a positive duty, and that is why it is not important to take up the distinction here.

have, we, at the door, are accustomed—even committed—to truth-telling. We *assume* it. And this the inquirer exploits. He uses us as a mere means even as he intends to use the person he is seeking as a mere means.

The same is not the case when we consider the actions of the victims (or their defenders) in the same cases. They are not using the attacker merely as a means to some end of their own. There is no sense in which they constitute the relationship in terms of exploitation; they constitute it in terms of preventing exploitation. For example, when Adam exercises violence toward Cain, killing him, it is *not* because he is using Cain as a mere means to some end. If we thought that Adam was doing this—violating some right of Cain's (e.g., not to suffer violence) in order to save Abel's life—then we would be seeing Adam as balancing the wrong of killing against the good of saving a life. We would still likely want Adam to act in such a circumstance, but we would also likely think that he has some repenting to do because of it: he has exploited Cain by violating his rights, even though for a good cause.

But on the account being outlined here, when Adam kills Cain in defending Abel, he does nothing wrong and has nothing to repent of *at all*. After all, Adam does not violate Cain's right not to suffer violence in this case, because Cain has *forfeited* his right not to suffer violence by virtue of the exploitative and violent nature of the relationship he has constituted with Abel. In killing him (if that is the necessary result) Adam has not violated any of Cain's rights and therefore has done no wrong to him. The same analysis applies in each of the other cases we have considered.[24]

As stated earlier, consideration of these matters explains why rejection of violence itself (as an act and as unrelated to the person who commits it) seems so thoroughly mistaken. Between an act of violence committed by an aggressor (*qua* aggressor) and an act of violence committed by a victim (*qua* victim) lies a gaping moral chasm. Behaviorally the two acts may seem similar, but morally they could hardly be more distinct. Applying a blanket moral condemnation of all acts of violence—without regard for the moral status of the persons committing such deeds—seems, therefore, about as large an error as one can make in moral thinking.

---

24. By the same token, Abraham has no need to repent of lying to the Egyptians, we have no need to repent of lying to the would-be murderer at our door, and homeowners have no need to repent of lying about being home when they are not. We will all feel regret that the world presents us with circumstances in which these are correct actions, but they *are* correct actions in these circumstances and therefore call for nothing like repentance. This becomes more apparent when we recall, again, that in the scriptural account it was the Lord who instructed Abraham to lie in the first place.

Chapter 3

Pacifism: The "Anti-War" Version

"Anti-War" Pacifism: Two Arguments

A principled rejection of violence in general is not the only pacifist alternative to just-war theory. Another fundamental option is the principled rejection of violence specifically as expressed in war. This view holds that violence on a small scale—as in the cases we have considered so far, or in the coercion that police and other civil authorities must exercise in the natural course of their duties—can be justified, but that war itself entails violence on a scale so massive that it can never be acceptable. The arguments for this view take two general, but related forms.[1]

Denying the Factual Possibility of a Just War in the Modern Era

To appreciate the first argument for anti-war pacifism recall that principle six of *jus ad bellum* requires that the benefits of a war outweigh its costs. Recall also that the first principle of *jus in bello* requires both that we never intend the deaths of noncombatants, and that we explicitly minimize those deaths (including accepting greater risks to ourselves in order to do so). But one argument against just-war theory is that principle six of *jus ad bellum* can never be satisfied in the era of modern warfare and that this is partly because the first principle of *jus in bello* can never be satisfied. The idea is that while noncombatant deaths may be unintended, and while greater risks are assumed in order to avoid them, the destructive and undiscriminating force of modern weaponry ensures that such deaths will always be higher than acceptable. The horrors of modern warfare are so sweeping, and the pain it causes is so widespread and destructive (even among civilian populations), that the benefits can never outweigh the costs. In the end there is little comfort in the idea that civilian casualties are unintended. Whether killed by direct intention or by accident, they are equally dead, and that's what matters.

For these reasons, those who make this argument acknowledge the propriety of speaking historically and theoretically about what does and does not

---

1. Useful starting points into the literature on the topics that follow include: Uwe Steinhoff, "Debate: Jeff McMahan on the Moral Inequality of Combatants," 220–26; Jeff McMahan, *Killing in War*; Jeff McMahan, "Pacifism and Moral Theory," 44–68; Seth Lazar, "The Responsibility Dilemma for *Killing in War*: A Review Essay," 180–213; and Michael Neu, "Why McMahan's *Just* Wars Are Only *Justified* and Why That Matters," 235–55.

constitute a justifiable war, but they deny that such a war is actually possible in the modern era. Such an argument obviously strikes at the heart of just-war theory since it rejects, at least with respect to the modern era, precisely what just-war theory assumes—that a just war is even possible.[2]

Rejecting the Centrality of the Concept of "Threat" in Just-War Theory

The second argument for anti-war pacifism builds on this problem of noncombatant deaths. We might speak of these as innocent deaths—and they are always deeply regrettable—but we must not overlook the fact that the deaths of the *combatants* on the just side of a conflict are innocent as well. Because their cause is just such soldiers cannot be faulted for their engagement in war, and therefore the deaths they suffer must be included in the total count of innocent deaths the conflict will cause. All of this is clear and assumed in just-war theory. But suppose we extend this argument further and claim that the combatants on the *aggressor* side of a conflict are innocent as well. After all, they did not start the conflict themselves and are not aware (or at least cannot be assumed to be aware) of the unjust character of the war their state is waging. They are simply acting under the orders of their sovereign. If all of this is true then it is hard to see how they could *not* be innocent. But if aggressor combatants are morally innocent, how can it be right to wage war on them, even in self-defense? On the basis of such assumptions it is possible to say that no war can be justified, because virtually all casualties are innocent.

This line of thinking argues for anti-war pacifism by rejecting a key concept in the just-war framework. From the just-war perspective the soldiers of an aggressor state are characterized as representing an unjust threat against the victim state and therefore may be attacked in self-defense. This idea is embedded in the first principle of *jus in bello* which holds that a state may justly aim its military efforts against those who pose a threat but not against those who do not. But the argument we are considering here rejects this conception of the matter and frames the issue, not in terms of threat, but in terms of *innocence*—the absence of moral blame-ability, even in the soldiers on the aggressor side of the conflict. The idea is that an aggressed state may justly aim its military efforts against those who are not innocent but not against those who are. Because, generally speaking, the combatants of an aggressor state are innocent, it follows that it cannot be just for the victim state to attack them even in defense. The bottom line for this pacifist argument is that when we consider the moral innocence of the people who are killed in war, in addition to whatever noncombatant casual-

---

2. Because this view accepts the idea of a justified war in theory, but rejects the possibility that it can ever actually occur (anymore) in practice, it is called in the war literature "contingent pacifism." For the best-known version of contingent pacifism see Robert Holmes, *On War and Morality*.

ties occur, we must also include *all* of the combatants that are killed. And since no conflict can be justified that commits this much moral wrong, no conflict can be justified. It follows that anti-war pacifism, as the rejection of all war, is the only position that is morally defensible.

Four Problems

Although these two central arguments against the justifiability of war are serious, four considerations make them unpersuasive.

Modern Weaponry

First, the assumption that modern weaponry ensures extreme and unacceptable casualties seems to overstate the case. For example, just because a state has horrifically destructive weapons it does not follow that it will use them indiscriminately in conflict. Nuclear bombs are the quintessential example of modern weapons that do not discriminate between combatants and noncombatants and that thus pose the greatest threat to the rules of war. But the range of choices among modern weapons is actually very wide and their precision has greatly increased, not decreased, in recent decades.[3] It is partly for this reason that one scholar concludes, upon careful scrutiny of the U.S. response to the attacks which occurred on September 11, 2001, that this response satisfied the rules of war despite its use of the most modern weapons.[4] This is not to say that there were no noncombatant deaths, as certainly there were; it is only to say that these deaths did not reach the level that anti-war pacifism seems to consider inevitable.[5] In fact, the variety and sophistication

---

3. The Maverick missile, for instance, is guided by television, infrared, and laser technology, and is accurate to within one meter, and the Tomahawk cruise missile is able to circle for hours, to beam a picture of its target to controllers thousands of miles away and to shift its course on command *instantly*.

4. See Carl Ceulemans, "The Military Response of the U.S.-Led Coalition to the September 11 Attacks," 265–91. Michael Walzer expresses a similar judgment in his *Arguing about War*.

5. It would be unreasonable to rule out modern weapons on the basis that, despite their modernity, they still result in civilian casualties. A state defending itself will always cause noncombatant deaths if it must wage a defensive war in close proximity to civilian populations of one size or another, and this is true regardless of the weapons used. According to the just-war framework, a state must take this matter into account (along with all of the other principles of *jus ad bellum*) in making a decision to defend itself; then, if it does defend itself, it must conduct its war operations in harmony with the provisions of *jus in bello*. It cannot eliminate civilian casualties, but it must explicitly seek to minimize them according to the principles sketched in Chapter 2. According to Ceulemans' detailed analysis (see note 4) we have at least one general

of modern weapon systems make it increasingly possible to imagine a modern war that adheres to the parameters of the just-war framework.[6]

Intention

Second, while it is true that noncombatants are just as dead whether they are killed by accident or by direct intention, it is not true that such deaths are morally equivalent. To claim this is to discount too severely the difference that intention makes in the moral status of our conduct. All else being equal, there is a moral difference between an intentional killing and an accidental killing. And this difference is magnified if those doing the killing are doing so only in the course of justified defense, if they are explicitly *avoiding* harm to noncombatants, and if they are accepting greater risks to themselves in order to avoid this harm. A simple calculation of deaths overlooks these factors, but these features of the act of killing are central to its moral status. Harming by accident—accident that is explicitly avoided by accepting greater risk to oneself—entails an entirely different regard for humanity than harming intentionally. The first honors our shared humanity in the best way that the unjust and threatening circumstances allow, while the second betrays that shared humanity and reduces noncombatants to objects to be used and exploited. Despite the similarity in their consequences the two acts are moral opposites.[7]

---

instance of modern weapon use occurring in conformity with this set of conditions, and, if he is right, this obviously vitiates the claim that doing so is impossible.

6. The question about modern weapons raises the matter of risk generally. Some that I have encountered wonder if it is somehow wrong that certain combatants face no risk at all—as in this case of military personnel who launch long-range missiles and engage the enemy only from a distance. Is it fair that they inflict damage on the enemy when they assume no risk to themselves to do so? But the answer to this question seems to follow from the character of the conflict itself. If the victim state is truly a victim, and is engaged in war only in defense of itself against an aggressor, then it is protecting itself from an assault *that it should not be facing in the first place*. What principle would require combatants in such circumstances to accept risks simply to be "fair" toward their attackers? We would not ask a potential rape victim, who happened to be in possession of a handgun, to use it only if her attacker also possessed a gun—all so that her risk in the situation would be no less than his. As discussed in Chapter 2, the difference in moral status between victims and their aggressors seems both obvious and large, and this difference surely renders irrelevant any concerns about "fairness of risk" between them.

7. One large strand of moral theory sees morality as a function solely of outcomes—of *what happens* (although different theorists define in different ways the outcome that matters)—while another large strand of moral theory emphasizes our actions—what we *do* (which means that the morality of our conduct depends on factors that are in addition to what that conduct brings about). The first strand typically identifies what is right simply as that which maximizes the good, while the second (at a minimum)

Pacifism: The "Anti-War" Version 37

Innocence vs. Threat

It also seems mistaken—for two reasons—to say that we do wrong in defending ourselves against those who, despite their moral innocence, are still threats. First, since an innocent threat is categorically both innocent *and* a threat, certainly both categories are relevant in determining what response is justified. It is as important to ask how we should respond to a threat as it is to ask how we should respond to one who is innocent. Furthermore, soldiers of an aggressor state, though individually innocent, are essential agents of a larger project that is *not* innocent. They are either immediate or proximate threats to the lives of others who are also morally innocent, but who are *not* part of a larger unjust threat against *them*. These two factors are particularly important from the standpoint of heads of state because such leaders are explicitly responsible to secure the safety and lives of their citizens. For leaders of victim nations to see aggressor combatants in only one way—as morally innocent—would be to disregard the sense in which they are also unjust threats to the citizens whose lives such sovereigns are obligated to protect. Aggressor soldiers can be defended against because, despite their innocence, they still have no right to pose a threat to those who are not similarly threatening *them* unjustly. Morally speaking, they are innocent and they cannot be blamed, but practically speaking, they are also unjust threats and can be repelled.[8]

---

includes further considerations, beyond just maximizing the good, in determining what is right. Variations of these basic approaches, as well as the debates among them, are many, though I don't believe consideration of them is necessary here. I am content if my brief remarks make intuitive sense to most readers. Classic moral philosophers of the first (teleological) type are Jeremy Bentham and John Stuart Mill (who express different utilitarian versions of teleology), and classic moral philosophers of the second type (historically called "deontologists" in the moral philosophy literature) are Kant and, more recently, W.D. Ross. See Jeremy Bentham, *An Introduction to the Principles of Morals and Legislation* (1879) in J. Bowring, ed., *The Works of Jeremy Bentham*, vol.1; John Stuart Mill, *Utilitarianism, Liberty, and Representative Government*; Immanuel Kant, *Groundwork of the Metaphysics of Morals*; and W.D. Ross, *The Right and the Good*. The work of John Rawls, the most important political philosopher of the last hundred years, and more, is also a species of deontology. See John Rawls, *A Theory of Justice*.

8. Modern discussion of innocent threats goes as far back as Robert Nozick's brief treatment in his *Anarchy, State, and Utopia*. See also Judith Jarvis Thomson, "Self-Defense," 283–310; and Michael Otsuka, "Killing the Innocent in Self-Defense," 74–94. A recent discussion is Jeff McMahan, "The Basis of Moral Liability to Defensive Killing," 386–405, a revised version of which is found in Jeff McMahan, "Self-Defense Against Morally Innocent Threats," in Paul H. Robinson, Stephen P. Garvey, and Kimberly K. Ferzan, *Criminal Law Conversations*. The matter of innocent threats is obviously relevant to the case of innocent *shields* of enemy threats, mentioned in Chapter 1. To consider the matter in its simplest form, imagine an unjust aggressor state

Second, the idea that all combatants are morally innocent and thus not subject to attack fails to sufficiently regard the moral responsibility we bear for events we allow to happen, in addition to the responsibility we bear for actions we actually perform. For example, if heads of state allow an aggressor nation to attack and kill their citizens because they are unwilling to kill their (morally innocent) soldiers, then what responsibility do these heads of state bear for the deaths of their own (morally innocent) citizens that occur as a result of their inaction? While these heads of state may not have actually killed their own citizens, they *have* allowed them to be killed; indeed there is little if any moral difference between the two in this situation.[9] Furthermore, they have allowed their own people to be killed by aggressor combatants who posed an unjust threat while they were *not* an unjust threat in return. Defense would have been just and right in such a circumstance, and failing to provide it as they should and could have is to bear moral responsibility for what happens to their citizens as a result of their inaction.[10]

---

employing involuntary human shields to discourage attacks against its own legitimate military targets. Such human shields are in some respects like morally innocent soldiers: though innocent, they are also unjust threats. This is because their very purpose is to prevent the aggressed state from defending itself against the unjust assaults of the aggressor state and thus to render that victim state more vulnerable to defeat. Moreover, such involuntary shields present this unjust threat to people who (1) are *also* innocent but (2) who are *not* similarly unjust threats to them. Military action in such cases requires careful evaluation of the matter of proportionality; but if that standard is met, then risking the lives of human shields is justified. Indeed, the test of excessive injury to civilians must be relaxed in such cases because such a test must allow for the higher number of noncombatant casualties that is *guaranteed* by the unjust policy of using human shields; see Gary Solis, *The Law of Armed Conflict: International Humanitarian Law in War*, 320. All of this, of course, simply underscores the utter travesty of war in general, and reminds of the need to calculate the costs extremely carefully before determining that military action is the best response in any situation of conflict.

9. Note that the distinction being drawn here is different from the point, made earlier, about intention. There is indeed a large moral difference between deaths we cause intentionally and deaths we cause by accident. But here there is no issue of accident: if we allow an aggressor state to overrun and kill our citizens, we have not done so by accident; we have done so by our deliberate inaction. Our allowing such assault is itself an intentional act. So the distinction here is not between intending and not intending; it is between intentionally doing something and intentionally *allowing* something. It is reasonable to wonder how large a difference exists between actions that differ only in this respect.

10. For an introduction to the distinction between what we do and what we allow to happen, see Warren S. Quinn, "Actions, Intentions, and Consequences: The Doctrine of Doing and Allowing," 287–312; and John Martin Fisher and Mark Ravizza, "Quinn on Doing and Allowing," 343–52. For additional discussion on the topic, see the section "Doing and Allowing" in Chapter 12.

The Cost of Not Waging Defensive War

Fourth, pacifist arguments pay insufficient attention to the horrors and oppression that can be visited upon a nation by an aggressor state. While theorists in recent years have focused on the moral status of individual combatants, the cost of *not* waging a defensive war in one circumstance or another seems to have been somewhat overlooked in the moral calculations. Recall that the sixth principle of *jus ad bellum* requires that the benefits of a war outweigh its costs, and recall that the pacifist arguments we are considering here effectively deny that this principle can ever be satisfied. After all, it is true that European states could have saved several million innocent lives had they simply capitulated to Nazi Germany and avoided war in the European Theatre altogether. Indeed, in the broadest definition of moral innocence—including civilians and the vast majority of combatants—the saving of such lives through capitulation could have been in the many millions.[11] But surely it is important to note that while capitulating in this way could have saved many millions of lives it would have cost a *way* of life to do so. The Nazification of European society would have been a cultural cataclysm resulting in the ruination of hundreds of millions of lives over generations. It would also have put dramatically increased resources at the disposal of the Nazis, rendering them impossible to repel in other parts of the world.

But if anything, the prospect of life under Japanese domination is even more harrowing to consider. The savagery of Japanese wartime conduct, both during the Sino-Japanese War (1937–1945) and the Pacific Theatre of World War II, exceeded even that of the Nazis. As Japan invaded China and began its crusade of massacre and torture, the Japanese claimed their campaign was meant to "punish the people of China for their refusal to acknowledge the superiority and leadership of the Japanese race and to co-operate with them."[12] As war unfolded it was not uncommon for Japanese soldiers to invade hospitals, miles from the front, and to bayonet patients in their beds, including women and infants.[13] One account of Japan's rape of Nanking reports that "tens of thousands of young men were rounded up and herded to the outer areas of the city, where they were mowed down by machine guns, used for bayonet practice, or soaked with gasoline and burned alive."[14] Another speaks of civilian women fleeing for their lives from fires set by Japanese soldiers, and

---

11. For one estimate of the civilian and combatant casualties suffered in World War II, country by country, see War Chronicle, "Estimated War Dead: World War II."

12. Lord Russell of Liverpool, *The Knights of Bushido: A History of Japanese War Crimes During World War II*, 39. This is a respected one-volume summary of mounds of material collected from the Tokyo war-crimes trials.

13. Ibid., 256, for just one example.

14. Iris Chang, *The Rape of Nanking: The Forgotten Holocaust of World War II*, 4.

who were then "caught and raped by the Japanese who then poured petrol over their hair and ignited it. Other women who were carrying infants had them bayoneted in their arms."[15] "Many soldiers," we are told, "went beyond rape to disembowel women, slice off their breasts, nail them alive to walls. Fathers were forced to rape their daughters, and sons their mothers, as other family members watched." The report continues of the Japanese "hanging people by their tongues on iron hooks or burying people to their waists and watching them get torn apart by German shepherds."[16]

Atrocities of this sort were repeated thousands of times, accounts of them seemingly endless. Both savage warriors and brutal occupiers, the Japanese are estimated to have killed between three million and ten million people from 1937 to 1945, including millions of civilians,[17] and their acts of horror included medical experimentation and cannibalism. Reports of civilian deaths in just one city, Nanking, range from 260,000 to more than 350,000 over just a few months.[18]

So what are we to make of the prospect of subjugation by a regime such as this? Is the cost of the loss of a way of life preferable to the cost of fighting in self-defense? Is it best to succumb to an aggressor state because resisting such a regime can never yield a better outcome than succumbing to it would yield?

If we claim this we might argue that civilian-based defense is an effective alternative to war, and that it is therefore preferable to military means of repulsing enemy attack. In essence, states should allow themselves to be overrun and then practice non-violent citizen resistance in the aftermath.[19] We might also list instances where non-violent revolutions have ultimately succeeded against unwelcome regimes and, on this basis, assert the non-necessity of war.[20]

But while we might make such arguments, they seem far from conclusive. It is true that most believe it would be wrong to sacrifice lives—particularly those of children and other noncombatants—in a cause that was known to be

---

15. Lord Russell of Liverpool, *The Knights of Bushido*, 255.

16. Chang, *The Rape of Nanking*, 6.

17. Rummel settles on an estimate of six million. See R. J. Rummel, "Statistics of Japanese Democide: Estimates, Calculations, and Sources." Johnson puts the figure five times higher. See Chalmers Johnson, "The Looting of Asia," *London Review of Books*. Chang reaches an estimate of 19 million deaths, based on Rummel's numbers for the additional deaths due to starvation and disease that were caused by Japanese wartime conduct. See Chang, *The Rape of Nanking: The Forgotten Holocaust of World War II*, 216–17.

18. See Chang, *The Rape of Nanking*, 4.

19. See, for example, the discussion in Coppieters and Fotion, eds., *Moral Constraints on War*.

20. See, for example, Walter Wink, *Jesus and Nonviolence: A Third Way*. Wink's brief work lists examples, but offers no analysis, so it is difficult to know how, and how carefully, he is calculating the costs and benefits in any of the cases he mentions.

futile. In that case the most that could be done *is* to mount citizen resistance in the aftermath of occupation by a foreign power. However, because that circumstance is already anticipated in just-war theory, a claim of this sort is not a departure from the just-war view but is an expression of it (the fifth principle of *jus ad bellum*). That leaves the case where resistance would *not* be futile—where there is a reasonable chance of success in fighting back and preventing a brutal and savage occupation. In *that* case, is succumbing, followed by non-violent citizen resistance, the right course to follow? Is that preferable to resisting the conquest to begin with?

Although the possibility of such non-violent citizen resistance might be appealing, the idea that it can be applied in every case seems chimerical. Against regimes like the Nazis and Imperial Japan the strategy would be fruitless. As George Orwell remarked regarding the generalizability of Gandhi's campaign of non-violent resistance against British colonialism in India, "It is difficult to see how Gandhi's methods could be applied in a country where opponents of the regime disappear in the middle of the night and are never heard from again."[21] In other words, Gandhi's experience in resisting the British can be generalized to cases in which the occupiers are *like* the British, but it cannot be generalized to cases in which they are not. As one Indian native observed, "If Hitler had been ruling India, Gandhi would be a lampshade."[22] Walzer adds:

> Nor would civilian resistance work well against invaders who sent out squads of soldiers to kill civilian leaders, who arrested and tortured suspects, established concentration camps, and exiled large numbers of people from areas where the resistance was strong to distant and desolate parts of the country. Nonviolent defense is no defense at all against tyrants or conquerors ready to adopt such measures. Gandhi demonstrated this truth, I think by the perverse advice he gave to the Jews of Germany: that they should commit suicide rather than fight back against Nazi tyranny. Here nonviolence, under extreme conditions, collapses into violence directed at oneself rather than at one's murderers, though why it should take that direction I cannot understand.[23]

In the end, the pacifist case that war can never be preferable to subjugation by an oppressive foreign power just seems implausible. The argument seems to treat too lightly what can be at stake. World War II is certainly an example where, though the cost was high, resistance was justified to prevent the horrific prospects that a victorious Nazi Germany and Imperial Japan would have meant for the world. Moreover, it would have been justified to use the most current weapons even of today to accomplish this. Indeed, as mentioned above, serious thinkers about war have carefully examined the ini-

---

21. Cited in Michael Walzer, *Just and Unjust Wars*, 332.
22. Dinesh D'Souza, *What's So Great about America*, 70.
23. Walzer, *Just and Unjust Wars*, 332.

tial engagement of the United States in Afghanistan and the first Gulf War—both fought with modern weaponry—and have defended them, including in terms of their costs.[24] All of this is persuasive in denying the categorical claim that the costs of war always exceed its benefits.

Summary

In the end, none of the pacifist considerations we have examined in this chapter—considerations that focus on the innocence of those who die in war, whether noncombatants or combatants—succeeds in supplying a sufficient moral case for prohibiting defensive war. We have seen that it is possible to use modern weapons in a way that acceptably avoids civilian deaths, that there is a moral difference between innocent deaths that are intended and those that are not, and that it is morally permissible for a state to defend itself against unjust threats despite the innocent status of soldiers who are the instruments of that threat. Thus, while it is probably the case that many, if not most of the combatants carrying out an unjust attack are morally innocent, it is also the case that they present a threat that it is justifiable to thwart and, if they could do so, heads of state would be wrong not to thwart it and to allow their citizens to be killed instead. This is especially true when the result of failing to repel an unjust assault would mean the ruination of a way of life that, when compared to most and particularly to what would replace it, represents a noble and civilized social order for its citizens. It is therefore plausible that threatening soldiers should be subject to defensive attack, whatever their individual moral innocence might be. Finally, while it is the case that innocent civilian deaths are always a tragic feature of war, when avoided in the way that just-war theory requires, this tragedy is not sufficient to outweigh that of subjection to the brutal rule of at least some aggressive nations.

Secular Arguments for Pacifism: Conclusion

Looking at the main outlines from a secular standpoint, both anti-violence pacifism and anti-war pacifism seem wanting. Whatever one might say about the justifiability of any particular war, in the end it seems implausible to say that *no* war is ever justified. Nor, as explained, is Tolstoy's spiritual argument persuasive. To the contrary, it seems possible to have an "evil peace" and thus to have a justified war.[25] In the light of these considerations, war must be at a minimum justifiable, thus defeating the intellectual arguments for pacifism.[26]

---

24. See, for example, Walzer, *Arguing about War* and Ceulemans, "The Military Response of the U.S.-Led Coalition," 265–91.

25. Thomas Aquinas, *Summa Theologica*, Part II.

26. One temptation for those with a pacifist impulse is to grant the idea of weak, defenseless states defending themselves, but to find something morally indelicate in

Pacifism in Latter-day Saint Thought

None of this, however, takes into account the arguments for pacifism advanced by Latter-day Saint authors. Is a compelling case for pacifism to be found in the gospel rather than secular intellectual analyses?

The most prominent Latter-day Saint pacifist, at least in terms of ecclesiastical authority, was J. Reuben Clark Jr., a counselor in the First Presidency from 1933 to 1961.[27] Unfortunately, there is virtually nothing in the historical writings dealing with President Clark that demonstrates the *scriptural* basis for his pacifism. However, Hugh Nibley—the most prominent Latter-day Saint scholar of the twentieth century—wrote abundantly on scriptural topics, including the subject of war. Boyd Petersen, Nibley's official biographer, informs us that Nibley's "commitment to pacifism was constant and unwavering"[28] and Petersen devotes a full chapter of his biography to Nibley's views on the topic. He reports that Nibley eventually opposed war of any kind as a result of experiences that left him convinced that war "is an unnecessary evil." Regarding Nibley's views Petersen writes, "Is there a point at which war is justified? A point at which the evil caused by war would be less than

---

the idea of strong nations doing so—an attitude I have encountered only informally, and in completely inchoate form. Perhaps this distribution of sympathies is due to the general tendency to favor underdogs, or perhaps to the expectation that at least conflicts involving weak nations will be smaller wars and thus cause less devastation. However that may be, I do not see how the sympathy, understandable as it is, can be elevated to an intellectual principle. For notice that such a principle would suggest that a defenseless nation is justified in defending itself only so long as it does not *succeed* in defending itself. After all, to the extent that such a state succeeds in defending itself, it is not really defenseless, and if it is not really defenseless, then, according to such a principle, it has no justification for its defense. So the upshot is that a state is permitted to defend itself only so long as it cannot defend itself, and it is not permitted to defend itself the minute it can defend itself. Such seems to be the logical extension of the allocation of sympathies mentioned above, and that is why it cannot be an intellectual principle: it yields an absurdity.

27. See D. Michael Quinn, "Pacifist Counselor in the First Presidency: J. Reuben Clark Jr., 1933–1961," 141–60 and *J. Reuben Clark: The Church Years*, 197–219. I cite Quinn on this matter although I am not altogether comfortable in doing so. The reasons for my disquietude can be found in George L. Mitton and Rhett S. James, "A Response to D. Michael Quinn's Homosexual Distortion of Latter-day Saint History," 141–263; William J. Hamblin, "That Old Black Magic," 225–394; and my "A Betrayal of Trust," 147–63, which cumulatively treat a massive number of errors and distortions in Quinn's works.

28. Boyd J. Petersen, "The Work of Death: Hugh Nibley as Scholar, Soldier, Peace Activist," 166. The context of Petersen's report suggests that he intends a precise meaning of the term "pacifism," rather than merely a vague anti-war sentiment.

the evil war would remedy? The Hugh Nibley of today doesn't seem to think so."[29] Petersen also reports that Nibley's idea of the perfect response in the face of any conflict is to "refuse to take up arms,"[30] and summarizes Nibley's view saying, "Every conflict must sooner or later be settled by discussion, so 'why not have the discussion now' and end the senseless conflict?"[31]

Years earlier Eugene England read Nibley the same way, reporting that Nibley demonstrated that one message of the Book of Mormon is "a highly specific ethic of pacifism."[32] All of this is consistent with Nibley's own observation that "war is contrary to God's laws . . . whoever chooses war must break most of the Ten Commandments . . . [and] one cannot condone part of [war] without condoning everything that it entails."[33] All of this, in addition to other remarks made by Nibley, indicates the existence of a strong pacifist impulse in Nibley's thinking.[34]

Nibley's pacifism is notable, even today, because his influence continues to be felt. His *Collected Works* is a monumental landmark in Latter-day Saint scholarly publishing, and a recent volume on Latter-day Saints' attitudes toward war illustrates Nibley's enduring, central influence more than once.[35] The problem is that Nibley never developed a comprehensive and systematic argument regarding these matters. There is no single article to examine or book to study in which Nibley carefully sets out his scripturally informed views on war and argues for pacifism as the proper stance.[36] At the same time, he does make editorial comments over the course of his voluminous works that would certainly contribute to such an argument were he to make

---

29. Boyd Jay Petersen, *Hugh Nibley: A Consecrated Life*, 221.
30. Ibid.
31. Ibid.
32. Eugene England, "Hugh Nibley as Cassandra," 111.
33. Petersen, *Hugh Nibley: A Consecrated Life*, 220.
34. Although in his recent paper Petersen assures us that Nibley's pacifism was "constant and unwavering," in his biography he hypothesizes that Nibley might justify war to prevent genocide, calling genocide "the one piece of data [Nibley] has not been able to process in his anti-war philosophy" (ibid., 221), but he cannot say so with certainty. This suggests that Nibley's thinking was not entirely complete on the topic.
35. Patrick Q. Mason, J. David Pulsipher, and Richard L. Bushman, eds., *War and Peace in Our Time: Mormon Perspectives*.
36. The closest Nibley comes to this is a short *Ensign* article from 1971 in which, rather than pressing pacifist claims, he defends the suitability of defensive war; see Hugh Nibley, "If There Must Needs Be Offense," 270–77. This, however, seems to be the last piece in which Nibley adopted a position justifying war; subsequent to it, his comments are generally suspicious and disapproving. In no case, however, does Nibley construct a systematic argument about war, motivated by the desire to examine all the evidence and to reach a comprehensive and deep view of the matter.

one. One of these is Nibley's pacifist reading of the Ammonite episode in the Book of Mormon, an interpretation that appears to be common among the Latter-day Saints. But this is far from all. Nibley makes additional significant claims that, if true, would support pacifism on their own, even without consideration of the Ammonites. These claims include:

1. Book of Mormon wars were always between "bad guys and other bad guys," meaning that we cannot take the Nephites' fighting as our example of righteous response to conflict because the Nephites would have faced no wars at all if only they *had* been righteous.
2. It is perverse to proclaim, "who does not take up the sword shall perish by the sword," and thus it is wrong to justify war in the name of defense.
3. God himself fights the battles of the righteous, meaning that the righteous do not need to defend themselves because God will do that for them.
4. War can be avoided by discussion, which means that war obviously can never be justified since talking to each other will always avert conflict.
5. War is "above all unnecessary," meaning, again, that it cannot be justified: if war is unnecessary, then it obviously cannot be right.

These are significant claims. If they are true, and if they are to be understood as Nibley understands them, they provide substantial scriptural support for adopting pacifism as the proper attitude toward war, particularly for those who earnestly seek to do God's will in their lives. For this reason it is important to look carefully at these claims and to determine the degree of support they find in the scriptural record. Do they or do they not support pacifism?

Nibley, however, is only the most prominent among Latter-day Saint pacifists. Others have written more recently and since their arguments differ from Nibley's they too must be examined. Of course, Eugene England's views prominently bestride the general topic of violence in Latter-day Saint intellectual circles. Though not completely unambiguous in his pacifism, he has opined extensively on the matter of war and peace and is widely admired for his writings on anti-violence. All of these must be addressed before we can be prepared to develop a general framework for thinking about war.

Part 2

Scriptural Arguments for Pacifism

Chapter 4

Were the Ammonites Pacifists? Part One

The Received View: The Ammonites as Pacifists

It is commonplace to consider the Ammonites pacifists. Nibley in particular is useful in understanding this view because he is so adamant about the matter. He finds it instructive, for instance, that the Ammonites seemed to equate the killing that occurs in war with murder. He comments that the Ammonites "repeatedly refer to all their former battles as murders,"[1] and again that "no less than eight times do [the Ammonites] refer to their former deeds of arms as acts of murder for which they are contrite."[2] Elsewhere he notes that the murders they had committed were "acts of war,"[3] and again notes that the Ammonites "repeatedly refer to their former deeds of valor on the battlefield as pure murder, and wonder whether God will ever forgive them."[4] Nibley also reminds us that the Ammonites "utterly rejected taking up arms under any circumstances"[5] after their conversion and, based on their example, recommends the same course to us. As Boyd Petersen reports, Nibley considers the Ammonites' well-known actions in Alma 24 (where they chose to die rather than to defend themselves) "the perfect example of what to do when faced with a conflict: refuse to take up arms."[6]

Nibley thus has no hesitation in asserting that the Ammonites "were complete pacifists."[7] He believes that the acts of killing reflected upon by the Ammonites were acts they had performed in conventional war ("deeds of valor," he calls them), that it is these normal wartime acts that the Ammonites came to see as "pure murder," and that that is why they came to reject even a war of self-defense, reasoning that, if killing in war is murder, war must obviously be

---

1. Hugh Nibley, "Last Call: An Apocalyptic Warning from the Book of Mormon," 517.
2. Hugh Nibley, "Freemen and King-men in the Book of Mormon," 356.
3. Hugh Nibley, "Scriptural Perspectives on How to Survive the Calamities of the Last Days," 487.
4. Hugh Nibley, "The Prophetic Book of Mormon," 466.
5. Ibid.
6. Boyd Jay Petersen, *Hugh Nibley: A Consecrated Life*, 221.
7. Nibley, "Freemen and King-men," 356. See also Hugh Nibley, *Since Cumorah*, 295 and 296; and Hugh Nibley, "Leaders to Managers: The Fatal Shift," 499, where Nibley has them in mind in referring to "conscientious objectors."

wrong. It is for this reason, according to Nibley's reading, that the Ammonites chose to be slaughtered rather than to take another's life, even in self-defense.

Such usage of the term "pacifism" is completely standard and satisfies the characterization set forth in Chapter 2: namely, that "participation in and support for war is always impermissible."[8] Nibley demonstrates the established sense in which he uses the term "pacifism" by ascribing to the Ammonites the view that there is no difference between the act of murder and the act of killing in war. It is no mere abhorrence of violence or some general preference for peace over war that he has in mind; rather it is the genuine rejection of all war. Indeed, so high is Nibley's estimation of the Ammonites' total repudiation of war that he equates it with goodness itself, telling us that we can be certain of one thing regarding Book of Mormon wars: "The good people never fight the bad people; they never fight anybody."[9]

Nibley is far from alone in regarding the Ammonites this way. Eugene England admiringly refers to the Ammonites as "rigorously pacifist," and calls the Ammonite episode "the most powerful Book of Mormon teaching of the nonviolent ethic (besides Christ's 'Sermon on the Mount' to the Nephites)."[10] He also refers to the Ammonites as "the great pacifist martyrs."[11] More recently, authors such as Gordon C. Thomasson, J. David Pulsipher, and F.R. Rick Duran, among others, have also either stated or assumed the pacifist character of the Ammonites.[12]

Indeed, with admiration we read of the Ammonites' repentance, of their literal burial of their weapons of destruction in the earth, and of their willingness, on two separate occasions, to suffer death rather than to take up arms in defense of their lives. These are a people whose story stands out because they refuse to take up arms in a book where taking up arms is virtually routine. After all, even during that rarest of times—a period when the Lamanites became one

---

8. Martin Ceadel, *Thinking about Peace and War*, 5. See the section "Getting Clear about Pacifism" in Chapter 2.

9. Nibley, *Since Cumorah*, 348. Nibley does not specify the Ammonites in his statement, but, given his frequent reference to them as pacifists, it is hard to see what other group he could possibly mean. This is the case especially since he refers here to "the good people" and since (as we will see in Chapter 6) he considers the Nephites to be *unrighteous* whenever they fought.

10. Eugene England, "Hugh Nibley as Cassandra," 112.

11. Eugene England, "Healing and Making Peace, in the Church and in the World," 9.

12. See J. David Pulsipher, "The Ammonite Conundrum," 1–12; F. R. Rick Duran, "Pax Sanctorum," 57–79; Gordon Conrad Thomasson, "'Renounce War and Proclaim Peace': Personal Reflections on Mormon Attempts at Peacemaking," 203–18; and Mark Henshaw, Valerie M. Hudson, Eric Jensen, Kerry M. Kartchner, and John Mark Mattox, "War and the Gospel: Perspectives from Latter-day Saint National Security Practitioners," 235–66. In a footnote citing a work of mine ("Were the Ammonites Pacifists?" 33–47), Pulsipher notes that the Ammonites were not strictly pacifists, but in his text he treats them as if they were.

with the Nephites and were numbered among them—this combined people still took up arms against the Gadianton robbers who were spreading "death and carnage throughout the land" (see 3 Ne. 2:11–17). Indeed, the only reference to anything similar to the Ammonites' story is the brief mention (roughly seventy-five years later), of converted Lamanites who also buried their weapons of war and were willing to suffer death rather than defend themselves (Hel. 15:9).[13] But this brief mention (a single verse) gives us nothing like the details we have regarding the Ammonites. The Ammonite story is prominent because it is virtually unique *and* is shared with us in significant detail. It is no wonder that it has become common to cast the Ammonites in a pacifist light.

But it is not sufficient to let the matter rest there. There is actually more to the Ammonites' history, conduct, and attitude than we often think. If we want to understand if their story truly does portray pacifism it is essential, first, to *understand* their story. We need to know who the Ammonites were, what they were like before their conversion, what they repented of, how they repented, and how they behaved after making the covenant that they "never would use weapons again for the shedding of man's blood" (Alma 24:18). This chapter will consider who they were; the next chapter will consider their repentance and their subsequent behavior. Once we have achieved clarity on these matters, it will then be possible to reach a firm conclusion about the Ammonites' attitudes toward war.

Who Were the Ammonites?

The scriptural account is clear in two respects regarding the Ammonites. First, we know that they were Lamanites who were converted by the sons of Mosiah in the period stretching approximately from 91 BC to 77 BC (Alma 17:4, 6). Second, we know that with one exception none of them were Nephite dissenters (Alma 23:8–14). All of the converts are referred to in the record as "Lamanites" and are in fact contrasted with the Nephite dissenters who lived in the Lamanite kingdom at the time and constituted part of the Lamanite force, a fact the record goes out of its way to tell us. Furthermore, when the Ammonites were later attacked and offered no defense of themselves, the record again goes out of its way to tell us that those Lamanites who repented because of the Ammonites' actions included no Nephite dissenters but were "actual descendants of Laman and Lemuel" (Alma 24:29).

All of this seems worth noting because the designations *Lamanite* and *Nephite* are frequently used in the Book of Mormon to indicate loyalty more

---

13. This pattern began with the large-scale Lamanite conversion precipitated by the miraculous events of Helaman 5. We are told that the Lamanites who were converted at this time "did lay down their weapons of war and also their hatred and the tradition of their fathers" (Hel. 5:51).

than genealogy.[14] Nephite dissenters generally fell under the overall category of *Lamanites* once they were thus allied, and no doubt other non-Nephite populations did so as well. The same is true for groups that allied themselves with the Nephites; they took on the designation *Nephites* even though genetically unrelated to any in Lehi's party.[15] This assumption of peoples into one general category or another is not surprising. In the scriptures it is not uncommon for the Lord to designate a particular "seed" with whom someone will be "numbered," regardless of actual ancestral relationships (see 2 Ne. 4:11; 10:19). The most sweeping example of this is membership in the house of Israel itself, which in the end is a function of spiritual choice rather than of literal ancestry.[16] Indeed, the record tells us that the Ammonites themselves, once they inhabited the land of Jershon, were "numbered" among the Nephites (Alma 27:27).[17] For all of these reasons it is interesting that the record is eager *not* to subsume Nephite dissenters under the general descriptor *Lamanite* in this particular case.

Size of the Ammonite Population

In order to fully understand the Ammonites and the reasons for the commitment they made, it is important to know to what extent various descriptions of the overall Lamanite population generalize to the Ammonite sub-population. Fortunately, the Ammonites were almost certainly a significant fraction of the Lamanite populace and they also held significant status.

---

14. For example, see Jacob 1:14; Mosiah 25:12–13; Alma 3:10–11, 17; 45:13–14; 47:35; Hel. 11:24; 3 Ne. 2:14, 16; and 4 Ne. 1:36–38.

15. See, for example, John L. Sorenson, "When Lehi's Party Arrived in the Land, Did They Find Others There?" 1–34.

16. For example, see 1 Ne. 14:2; 2 Ne. 10:18, 30:2; Hel. 15:13; 3 Ne. 16:13, 21:6, 30:2; Rom. 9:6–7; Gal. 2:7–9, 3:29. For a clarifying account of why, from a purely genetic standpoint, no one since Jacob himself has been a "pure Israelite," see Brian D. Stubbs, "Elusive Israel and the Numerical Dynamics of Population Mixing," 263–81. A thorough treatment of the complex nature of classification for various groups in the scriptures is Matthew Roper, "Swimming in the Gene Pool: Israelite Kinship Relations, Genes, and Genealogy," 225–61. A study that focuses specifically on the spiritual character of ethnic identity in the Book of Mormon is Steven L. Olsen, "The Covenant of the Chosen People: The Spiritual Foundations of Ethnic Identity in the Book of Mormon," 14–29.

17. The word "numbered" does not appear in the current edition of the Book of Mormon. There the verse reads simply, "and they were among the people of Nephi" (Alma 27:27), which implies nothing more than a geographical relationship between the Ammonites and the Nephites. The original manuscript of the text, however, reads "and they were *numbered* among the people of Nephi"—which implies the spiritual family connection discussed in the text. For the wording of the original manuscript, see Royal Skousen, ed., *The Book of Mormon: The Earliest Text*, 378. My thanks to Skousen for bringing this point to my attention.

(See Appendix 1 for the considerations that lead to this conclusion.) It is not unreasonable, therefore, to generalize descriptions of the Lamanites as a whole to this subset who later became converted.

Following their conversion the group desired to distinguish themselves from their former Lamanite society and adopted the name Anti-Nephi-Lehies in order to do so (Alma 23:17). Later, when they were given the Nephite land of Jershon for their protection, they were called by the Nephites "the people of Ammon" and "were distinguished by that name ever after" (Alma 27:26, 43:11), originating the common term *Ammonites* to refer to these people.

What Were the Ammonites Like Before Their Conversion?

In understanding the Ammonites' conversion and repentance it is important to examine what they were like before their change of heart. The record tells us some things about the Ammonites as a group as well as about the Lamanites in general. Since the Ammonites were at least a significant portion of the Lamanite population in size and status, it is plausible to suppose that what the account reveals about the Lamanites in general applies, at least roughly, to the Ammonites themselves. Certainly there is nothing in the record to indicate otherwise. So what does the Book of Mormon tell us?

Lamanite Wars

First, we know that from the beginning the Lamanites were prone to attack and to wage war against the Nephites. Jacob tells us that Nephi himself had to fight to defend his people from Lamanite assault (Jacob 1:10; also 2 Ne. 5:14), and aggressive wars are also reported by Jacob (Jacob 7:24), Enos (Enos 1:20), Jarom (Jarom 1:6), Abinadom (Omni 1:10), Amaleki (Omni 1:24), Zeniff (Mosiah 9, 10, 19–21), and Mormon (W of M 1:13–14)—a record of Lamanite aggression spanning the first four hundred and sixty years or so of Book of Mormon history.[18]

We also know that the Lamanites waged four aggressive wars against the Nephites during the time that the sons of Mosiah were performing their missionary labors among them. The first such war, reported in Alma 2, occurred about 87 BC, in the fifth year of the reign of the judges (Alma 2:1). The dissenting Amlicites, who had just been defeated and driven out by Alma's army, joined "a numerous host of the Lamanites" who had entered Nephite land (Alma 2:24). As Alma's army rushed to defend Zarahemla against the attackers, the combined Lamanite and Amlicite forces "came upon them to destroy

---

18. We also know of one occasion during this period when a group of Nephites made plans to attack and destroy the Lamanites in the land of Nephi. Internal dissension disrupted the plan, however, and the attack never materialized. (See Mosiah 9:1–2.)

them" at the river Sidon (Alma 2:27). Finally, Alma's army prevailed and their attackers fled (Alma 2:35–38). It was in this war that Alma personally slew Amlici, the Nephite dissenter (Alma 2:31), and fought against the guards of the king of the Lamanites (Alma 2:32–33).

The second war occurred "not many days after," when "another army of the Lamanites came in upon the people of Nephi, in the same place" (Alma 3:20). Although this could have been led by one of the territorial kings, or even a king over all the land that we know nothing else about, it could also, ironically, have been Lamoni's father who was "king over all the land" of the Lamanites during at least part of the time that the sons of Mosiah were among them (Alma 20:8, 22:1). Wounded at the time, Alma did not personally lead the Nephite defense on this occasion, but sent an army that drove the Lamanite army out of the land (Alma 3:23). This war also occurred in the fifth year of the reign of the judges, or about 87 BC (Alma 3:25).

In the third war, Lamanite armies attacked about six years later, in the eleventh year of the reign of the judges (Alma 16:1) and, among other things, destroyed the city of Ammonihah (Alma 16:8, 25:1–2).

Finally, we are told in Alma 16:12 that the Lamanites did not attack again "until the fourteenth year of the reign of the judges," and this too would have been during the time that the sons of Mosiah were still performing their missionary labors (which began in the first year of the reign of the judges and continued for fourteen years—Alma 17:4, 6). Although we are given no description of the war that occurred in this year, we *are* told that the Lamanites, after the destruction of Ammonihah, "had many battles with the Nephites, in the which they were driven and slain" (Alma 25:3). It is reasonable to assume that these are the battles referred to as occurring in the fourteenth year, because the next large war against the Nephites did not occur until the fifteenth year of the reign of the judges—which was after the Ammonites' conversion and after they had already been attacked twice by the Lamanites and had subsequently been established in the land of Jershon.[19] It was during this latter period that many of the Lamanites "began to be stirred up in remembrance of the words which Aaron and his brethren had preached to them" and became converted (Alma 25:6).

Lamanite aggression was not only long-standing, but, as mentioned, it also occurred simultaneously with the missionary efforts of the sons of Mosiah. That those who later became converted were integrally involved in these attacks is certain (see again Alma 25:6 for an explicit mention of this), especially in light of the preeminent position that king Lamoni's father held among the Lamanites during at least part of the time that the Lamanites were launching these wars. We also know that before their conversion the

---

19. See Alma 24:20–25; 27:2–3; 28:1–3, 7.

Ammonites were allied with such Nephite dissenters as the Amlicites and Amulonites. In most, if not all, of the four wars waged by the Lamanites during the missionary labors of the sons of Mosiah, these Nephite dissenters played a major role. While there is no mention of Nephite dissenters aiding or provoking the Lamanite aggressions that occurred in the first few centuries of Nephite/Lamanite conflict, from the time of Alma and the sons of Mosiah forward, such dissenters played a central role in Lamanite aggression.[20]

Lamanite Attitudes

We know that Nephite dissenters who became Lamanites were more hardened in their hatred for the Nephites than other Lamanites were (see Alma 24:29–30; 43:6; 47:36), but this does not mean that these other Lamanites didn't *also* hate the Nephites. They did and they had a long history of doing so. Jacob, for example, writes in the earliest days of Lamanite "hatred" for the Nephites and does so while praising them for their superiority to the Nephites (Jacob 3:7). He also reports that the Lamanites "delighted in wars and bloodshed," that they "had an eternal hatred against us," and sought "by the power of their arms to destroy us continually" (Jacob 7:24). Later, Enos speaks of the Lamanites' "wrath" and of their desire to "destroy our records and us" (Enos 1:14). He also reports that "their hatred was fixed" and that they "were continually seeking to destroy us" (Enos 1:20). Years later Jarom reports that the Lamanites "loved murder" (Jarom 1:6), and a hundred and twenty years after that Zeniff describes the Lamanites as having an "eternal hatred towards the children of Nephi," and reports that they "taught their children that they should hate" the Nephites and "do all they could to destroy them" (Mosiah 10:17). King Benjamin also speaks of the Lamanites' early "hatred" toward the Nephites (Mosiah 1:14). Mormon corroborates the account, reporting that "the Lamanites were taught to hate the children of Nephi from the beginning" (4 Ne. 1:39).

All of this is related to "the wicked traditions" that the Lamanites had inherited from their fathers (see Alma 23:3, 24:7). Recall, for example, Zeniff's report of the Lamanite tradition that Laman and Lemuel had been repeatedly mistreated by Nephi (Mosiah 10:12–16) and that the Lamanites therefore explicitly "taught their children that they should hate them [the Nephites]" (Mosiah 10:17). Captain Moroni also explains the Lamanites' hatred as due to the "tradition of their fathers" (Alma 60:32), and Samuel the Lamanite at-

---

20. The absence of any mention of Nephite dissenters playing a role in the early centuries could well be due to the brevity of the reports the Book of Mormon gives us. While reports about war in the Book of Alma are lengthy, reports regarding conflict from earlier centuries are typically found in a single verse (see 2 Nephi 5:14; Jacob 1:10, 7:24; Enos 1:20; Jarom 1:6; Omni 1:10, 1:24; Mosiah 9, 10, 19–21; and W of M 1:13–14).

tributes the Lamanites' evil in his day to "the iniquity of the tradition of their fathers" as well (Hel. 15:4). The same theme is seen in Lamoni's father, the Lamanite king, who not only cited the tradition (Alma 20:10, 13), but also later proclaimed safety for the Nephite missionaries precisely in order that the gospel could be preached and that "his people might be convinced concerning the wicked traditions of their fathers" (Alma 23:3). More than two hundred years after the appearance of Christ, Mormon also tells us that the people now called Lamanites "were taught to hate the children of God, even as the Lamanites were taught to hate the children of Nephi from the beginning" (4 Ne. 1:39).

These attitudes were firmly in place at the time of the sons of Mosiah. The account tells us that one of these missionaries' explicit purposes in laboring among the Lamanites was "to cure them of their hatred toward the Nephites" (Mosiah 28:2). Ammon himself tells us that the Lamanites, prior to their conversion, were "racked with hatred against us" and were "in the darkest abyss" and in "the pains of hell" (Alma 26:9, 3, 13). And it is important to note that Ammon tells us this about the Lamanites *after* he had lived with them for fourteen years and had come to know and to love them in a personal way. This is not an ignorant and prejudiced report made in advance of his mission and without firsthand experience of the Lamanites. In addition, Mormon includes a description of the Lamanites at this time as:

> a wild and a hardened and a ferocious people; a people who delighted in murdering the Nephites, and robbing and plundering them; and their hearts were set upon riches, or upon gold and silver, and precious stones; yet they sought to obtain these things by murdering and plundering, that they might not labor for them with their own hands (Alma 17:14).

About the time of the missionary labors of the sons of Mosiah, then, the Lamanites had waged large-scale war against the Nephites from time to time, were engaging in a violent form of banditry ("robbing and plundering" the Nephites), and actually took delight in murdering Nephites.[21] It is also rel-

---

21. Sometimes, in the effort to make sure we are not being too hard on the Lamanites, it is easy to emphasize the simultaneous deficiencies of Nephite society. But it is possible to overreach in this direction as well. It is worth noting that at least some of the time, for example, the Nephites made efforts to "restore the Lamanites to the knowledge of the truth," as Jacob reports (Jacob 7:24). And Enos describes his own "many long strugglings" in prayer for the Lamanites and of his desire that "they might be brought unto salvation" (Enos 1:11–13). He also speaks of "*our* strugglings" to restore them "to the true faith" (Enos 1:14), indicating that he was not alone in his efforts to reach the Lamanites. Indeed, he reports that the people of Nephi *in general* sought "diligently" to restore the Lamanites to faith in God (Enos 1:20). In addition, the Nephite record-keepers knew they were keeping the plates precisely in order to benefit "our brethren the Lamanites" (Jarom 1:2), and one group of Nephites

evant in this context to remember that Ammon was threatened with death twice while among the Lamanites, and that he was spared only through the power of the Lord.[22]

In sum, prior to their conversion, the Lamanites were a people who for centuries had hated the Nephites, waged aggressive war from time to time to destroy them, sought to murder the Nephites and actually "delighted in" and "loved" murdering them, and sought to plunder and rob the Nephites to gain gold and silver without labor. Indeed, one wonders if the Lamanites at this time were not, in part, like the Gadianton robbers who first appeared fewer than forty years later (Hel. 2:1–4) and who ultimately proved the destruction of the Nephites (Hel. 2:13–14).[23]

Of course these are not the only characteristics that the Lamanites displayed over the centuries and during the time immediately prior to the mission of the sons of Mosiah. For example, the Lamanites do not appear to have waged war *annually* (even though both Jacob and Enos do use the word "continually" to describe the Lamanites' efforts to destroy the Nephites), and Jacob in his day explicitly recommended the chaste family conduct of the Lamanites to his Nephite brethren (Jacob 3:5–7). But such accounts of Lamanite attitudes and aggression—even if they do not capture the totality of Lamanite life—nevertheless seem accurate in the conduct they do describe. The story is consistent across prophetic reports and across centuries, is corroborated by such significant spiritual figures as Mormon and Ammon (who lived at length among the Lamanites), and is further supported by both Samuel (who was himself a Lamanite) and Lamoni's father (who was the *king* of the Lamanites). Whatever their virtues, the Lamanites presented over time a consistent pattern of hatred and aggression toward the Nephites.[24]

---

found themselves "filled with pain and anguish" for the welfare of the Lamanites' souls (Mosiah 25:11). Although the Nephites were riddled with their own brand of unrighteousness from the beginning, they were not without periods, or leaders, characterized by compassion and concern for their Lamanite brethren. In this they mirrored the efforts of later Lamanites to reach out and reclaim *Nephite* groups that had fallen into error and wickedness (e.g., see Hel. 6:1–6, 13–15).

22. See Alma 17:34–37, 19:14–20; Mosiah 28:7.

23. An interesting study of the Gadianton robbers is found in Daniel C. Peterson, "The Gadianton Robbers as Guerilla Warriors," 146–73. The seriousness of the threat posed by robbers of this sort is reflected in the severe penalties they received, both in the ancient Near East and in the Book of Mormon. See John W. Welch, "Law and War in the Book of Mormon," 46–102, esp. 86–91.

24. Some specifically question Zeniff's description of Lamanite attitudes and conduct (see, for example, J. Christopher Conkling, "Alma's Enemies: The Case of the Lamanites, Amlicites, and Mysterious Amalekites," 108–17), but it is difficult to dismiss Zeniff's account completely when so many others, including *Lamanites*, make

related reports. Indeed, we will see in Chapter 5 that another significant Lamanite—Anti-Nephi-Lehi, the Ammonites' king—also corroborates the view of Lamanite conduct as aggressive and murderous in character. John Sorenson attributes prejudice to some Nephite descriptions of the Lamanites on the grounds that the Book of Mormon recorders were not firsthand witnesses of what they describe; see Sorenson, "When Lehi's Party Arrived in the Land," 26; see also his *An Ancient American Setting for the Book of Mormon*, 90–91. But Sorenson cannot mean to extend that explanation to account for reports of Lamanite hatred, or of their efforts to destroy the Nephites over the years: these are matters with which the Nephites did, in fact, have firsthand experience. It does not follow from all this, of course, that the Nephites were an impressive contrast to the Lamanites in righteousness and that they had no wickedness of their own. The record testifies abundantly that they did. But in this chapter I am examining only the behavior of the Lamanites, not the Nephites. That is the population most germane to understanding the Ammonite sub-population.

Chapter 5

Were the Ammonites Pacifists? Part Two

To this point, we know that the Lamanites who converted to the gospel and became known as Ammonites included virtually none of the Nephite dissenters who lived among them. There is also good reason to believe that they were at least a significant subset of the total Lamanite population—both in size and in status. And the record is also clear that Lamanite hatred of the Nephites was deep and centuries old, and that the Lamanites had regularly (and by some accounts "continuously") waged war to destroy the Nephites. Moreover, they had "delighted in" and "loved" murdering Nephites, and had sought to plunder and rob them in order to achieve riches without labor. This is the reality into which the sons of Mosiah stepped as they embarked upon their mission to the Lamanite population.

The Ammonites' Conversion

What Did the Ammonites Repent Of?

Those Lamanites who later came to be known as the Ammonites eventually converted to the gospel and repented of their sins. This much is highly familiar, but it is important to be specific about their repentance. Exactly what did they think they had done wrong? Fortunately, the record tells us. As the king of the converted Ammonites (renamed Anti-Nephi-Lehi by his father) considered the defense of his people against anticipated Lamanite attacks, he took occasion to speak of the sins for which they had been forgiven, saying in part:

> And behold, I also thank my God, that by opening this correspondence we have been convinced of our sins, and of the many murders which we have committed. And I also thank my God, yea, my great God, that he hath granted unto us that we might repent of these things, and also that he hath forgiven us of our many sins and murders which we have committed, and taken away the guilt from our hearts, through the merits of his Son. And now behold, my brethren . . . it has been all that we could do, (as we were the most lost of all mankind) to repent of all our sins and the many murders which we have committed, and to get God to take them away from our hearts, for it was all we could do to repent sufficiently before God that he would take away our stain. (Alma 24:9–11)

Later, when Ammon tried to persuade the Ammonites to flee Lamanite danger by moving into Nephite lands, the king said further:

Behold, the Nephites will destroy us, because of the many murders and sins we have committed against them . . . we will go down unto our brethren, and we will be their slaves until we repair unto them the many murders and sins which we have committed against them. (Alma 27:6, 8)

In both cases, the king emphasizes the "murders" and even "the many murders" they had committed against the Nephites. These are the sins for which they had been forgiven. It is important to attend to this because, according to Nibley's reading of the matter, speaking of murder in this context is just a rhetorical way of claiming that *all* killing in war is murder. It would be as if Anti-Nephi-Lehi were saying, "It was wrong for us to fight for our country and to engage you in war. We had legitimate reasons for fighting, but all killing in war is murder, and because we killed in war, we committed murder. And we are grateful beyond measure for the Lord's goodness in forgiving us of these murders." If we want to claim that all killing in war is murder and that the Ammonites' attitude proves it—this is how we must take Anti-Nephi-Lehi to be speaking.

But it is evident that Anti-Nephi-Lehi is actually saying nothing like this. To see this, recall that the record tells us more than once that the Lamanites *delighted* in shedding Nephite blood. Far from being reluctant, the Ammonites' killings had in fact been wanton and deliberate, in both large-scale aggressive wars and in smaller-scale marauding and banditry.[1] Furthermore, one of the Lamanites' motives for attacking Nephites was to rob them—to take from them gold and silver so that they would not have to mine it for themselves. And finally, note that in all their conflicts, the Lamanites, not the Nephites, had been the aggressors, and that the wars had all occurred on Nephite lands.[2] So the wars Anti-Nephi-Lehi is

---

1. See the section "Lamanite Attitudes" in Chapter 4.
2. The story of Zeniff in Mosiah 9 is not an exception to this pattern. Recall that Zeniff was part of an armed force of Nephites that originally sought to conquer the Lamanites in the land of Nephi and to retake that land. Once this party reached the land of Nephi, however, Zeniff changed his mind and a battle ensued between those who wanted to continue with the original plan to attack the Lamanites and those who, led by Zeniff, wanted to seek a peaceful rapprochement with them and specifically *not* to engage in war. Indeed, Zeniff had developed a desire to *protect* the Lamanites. In the internal conflict that arose over this matter the majority of the Nephite warriors actually lost their lives. Zeniff at this point returned to Zarahemla and subsequently gathered others who desired to live in the land of the first inheritance. But nothing in the record suggests that Zeniff returned to the land of Nephi on this occasion with an army or that he threatened the Lamanites in any way. Indeed, recall that Zeniff had specifically *rejected* conflict as a way to approach the Lamanites and had actually entered battle against his Nephite brethren on the first expedition precisely in order to prevent such action. Nor does Zeniff mention anything about an army on this second excursion, even though he shows no hesitancy about reporting this sort of thing in general: the hostile and armed character of the initial expedition was one of the first things he mentioned about that episode. Thirteen peaceful

speaking of here were not wars involving legitimate disputes that simply escalated out of control, but rather aggressive wars and acts of plunder that were instigated and pursued in the first instance by the Lamanites themselves.

In light of these facts it is not surprising that Anti-Nephi-Lehi would use "murder" to describe the killings the Lamanites had committed. He is not speaking here of his people as an agglomeration of unfortunate, conscripted soldiers who had fought the Nephites with resignation and only out of a sense of duty to their homeland over complicated and legitimate disputes with their neighbors. It is not against *this* background that he refers to his people's actions as murder. Rather, he refers to his people's actions as murder against the background of their status as the aggressors in all of their conflicts with the Nephites, as marauders who had plundered the Nephites to obtain riches without labor, and as callous belligerents who had actually delighted in killing Nephites.

Ammon's encounter with Lamoni's father, the king over all the Lamanite land, illustrates the depth of Lamanite hatred for the Nephites. Upon seeing his son Lamoni with "this Nephite, who is one of the sons of a liar," the king "commanded [Lamoni] that he should slay Ammon with the sword," and when Lamoni refused, the king attempted to slay Ammon himself (Alma 20:10–20). Ammon had neither said a word nor performed a single disagreeable action; his status as "one of the sons of a liar" was sufficient to justify his death. So the record not only reports, but also shows, the contempt in which Lamanites held the Nephites and the ease with which they were willing to kill them. Such was the moral atmosphere among the Lamanites, and it is little surprise that Anti-Nephi-Lehi, in hindsight and from the perspective

---

years later, after Zeniff and his people had long been settled among the Lamanites on the lands granted to them by King Laman, "a numerous host of Lamanites" entered one of these lands and attacked and killed people of Zeniff who "were watering and feeding their flocks, and tilling their lands" (Mosiah 9:14). Zeniff and his people formed an army at this time and drove the Lamanites out of their land, slaying many of them. Thus began a series of subsequent conflicts—yet even here it is noteworthy that the clash was initiated by Lamanites (1) entering land that was legitimately occupied by the Nephites, (2) killing the Nephites who dwelt there, (3) stealing the Nephites' goods (in this case "flocks and the corn of their fields"), and (4) having then to be driven out by force of arms. Whatever else might be said about Zeniff, his story is not a departure from the overall pattern of wars occurring on Nephite rather than Lamanite lands due to Lamanite aggression. The only way to describe this episode as other than an unjust invasion into Nephite territory is to speculate that the Nephites may have expanded beyond the lands originally granted to them by King Laman. But the record tells us that the Nephite farmers who were attacked were "*on* the south of the land" that had been given to them (Mosiah 9:14), not that they were "*south* of the land" that had been given to them. Any reading of the text that implies expansion seems stretched, and thus there is no reason to suppose that the Lamanite invasion and killings on this occasion were anything other than illegitimate and unjust.

of a changed heart, could see such acts of hate-filled killing as thoroughly murderous in character.

The Nephites understood the Lamanites' killings to be murderous in exactly the same way. This is how Mormon describes their behavior, for example, telling us that they were "a ferocious people," and "a people who delighted in murdering the Nephites" (Alma 17:14). And when the Nephites subsequently gave the land of Jershon to the Ammonites for their safety, they did so because of the fear of the Ammonites to take up arms "on account of their many murders and their awful wickedness" (Alma 27:23). It is important to note that the Nephites had themselves been waging battle to defend themselves, and yet they did not consider their own killings to be acts of murder. They used "murder" specifically in regard to the Ammonites, and in exactly the same way that the Ammonites used the term to describe themselves. It refers to acts that are murderous in character, not to ordinary acts committed during conventional war.

All of this may be the reason that Anti-Nephi-Lehi never mentions the word "war" in his inspiring speech of thanksgiving for the Ammonites' forgiveness—the famous discourse in which he declares his people's intention to bury their swords permanently in the earth (Alma 24:7–16). Mormon refers to the weapons they buried as "weapons of war,"[3] and, indeed, they were swords used in the aggressive wars and acts of raid and spoil waged by the Lamanites. However, he also refers to these weapons twice as weapons of "rebellion" (Alma 23:7, 13), which may not be accidental. Indeed, the king himself may not have found the word "war," in its conventional sense, to be the best descriptor of Lamanite conduct given the plunder and banditry they had engaged in, and the hatred that had driven their large-scale assaults against the Nephites. Thus, while he never uses "war" in his speech of thanksgiving and commitment, he uses "murder" repeatedly.

Personal acts of murder. It is also important to note that Anti-Nephi-Lehi is speaking of the murders that his people had personally committed, not of acts attributable to the general class of Lamanites but which had not included the Ammonites themselves. The king is speaking only of those who had repented, and since the larger group of Lamanites (including the Amlicites and Amulonites) had *not* repented, they obviously were not included in his reference. Thus, when the new king speaks of "our" murders he is not seeking to hide the actions of himself and of his own people within the larger Lamanite population; rather, he is speaking specifically of the audience in front of him and of the murders that they themselves had committed against the Nephites.

This is also evident when Anti-Nephi-Lehi expresses fear of going to the land of the Nephites to find safety. He worries that the Nephites will

---

3. Alma 23:13; 24:19, 25; 25:14; 26:32.

destroy them "because of the many murders and sins we have committed against them" and proposes becoming slaves to the Nephites until those "many murders and sins" can be repaired (Alma 27:6, 8). This is important to notice because the king would have had no reason to fear retaliation if his people had not in fact been the ones who had committed the murders that he was discussing. In that case he could have simply explained to the Nephites that it was the larger body of Lamanites who had been committing aggression against them, but that this particular subset—now called Anti-Nephi-Lehies—had never been personally involved. That would have been the most natural position to take if it were true, and it would also have removed any concerns about Nephite retaliation. But Anti-Nephi-Lehi says nothing like this. Again, it is important to recall that in his speech, the king is specifically addressing only those who had repented, and thus all of his references to the murders that had been committed are references to those committed *by his audience*: himself and his people.

In the end the record seems clear. When the Ammonites repented, they were not repenting of acts of killing that had occurred in conventional war as we normally think of it. They were repenting of aggressive acts they had personally committed that had been motivated by hatred, greed, and a desire for Nephite blood. Since the character of such acts is so clearly murderous, it is not surprising that Anti-Nephi-Lehi would use the term "murder" to describe them, and it is not surprising that his people would feel the need to repent of them with such earnestness. When we read Anti-Nephi-Lehi's speech in context we see that his use of "murder" is not remotely tantamount to a blanket condemnation of all killing in all war, but rather a condemnation of the specific character of the killings that the Ammonites themselves had committed in conditions that were very much unlike conventional war. It was for such acts of aggression and murder that the Ammonites felt the need to repent.

How Did the Ammonites Repent?

As part of their repentance the Ammonites buried their weapons and entered a covenant that they would "give up their own lives" rather than use them again to shed blood. Anti-Nephi-Lehi says in part:

> Since God hath taken away our stains, and our swords have become bright, then let us stain our swords no more with the blood of our brethren . . . for perhaps, if we should stain our swords again they can no more be washed bright through the blood of the Son of our great God, which shall be shed for the atonement of our sins. . . . And now behold, since it has been as much as we could do to get our stains taken away from us, and our swords are made bright, let us hide them away that they may be kept bright, as a testimony to our God at the last day . . . that we have not stained our swords in the blood of our brethren since he imparted his word unto us and has made us clean thereby. . . . [Y]ea, we will

bury them deep in the earth, that they may be kept bright, as a testimony that we have never used them, at the last day. (Alma 24:12–13, 15–16)

Mormon adds:

[T]hey took their swords, and all the weapons which were used for the shedding of man's blood, and they did bury them up deep in the earth. And this they did, it being in their view a testimony to God, and also to men, that they never would use weapons again for the shedding of man's blood; and this they did, vouching and covenanting with God, that rather than shed the blood of their brethren, they would give up their own lives. (Alma 24:17–18; see also Alma 53:11)

Finally, as an outgrowth of their repentance, the Ammonites became "distinguished for their zeal toward God, and also toward men"; they were "perfectly honest and upright in all things"; and they were "firm in the faith of Christ, even until the end" (Alma 27:27).

How Did the Ammonites Behave After Entering Their Covenant?

The Ammonites' behavior after entering this covenant tells us much about them and about how they understood the covenant they had made. The account identifies five separate events.

First, soon after their conversion, the Ammonites allowed themselves to be slain by the Lamanites rather than take up arms against them. We are told that "they went out to meet [the Lamanites], and prostrated themselves before them to the earth, and began to call on the name of the Lord" (Alma 24:21), whereupon the Lamanites slew more than a thousand of them.

Second, on a later occasion, the Amalekites stirred up the Lamanites' anger against the Ammonites and they "began again to destroy them" (Alma 27:2). Mormon tells us that the Ammonites "again refused to take their arms, and they suffered themselves to be slain according to the desires of their enemies" (Alma 27:2–3). Ammon attributes the Ammonites' behavior on these occasions to "their love toward their brethren. . . . [F]or behold, they had rather sacrifice their lives than even to take the life of their enemy" (Alma 26:31–32). It was following these slaughters that the Nephites gave the land of Jershon to the Ammonites as a means of protecting them from further attack by the Lamanites (Alma 27:22).

Third, the Ammonites immediately began materially supporting the Nephite armies in their battles against the Lamanites and supported them throughout the lengthy war with "a large portion of their substance" (Alma 43:13; see also Alma 27:24).

Fourth, when the war became particularly dangerous, and the Ammonites observed the suffering and afflictions borne by the Nephites for them, "they were moved with compassion and were desirous to take up arms in the defence of their country" (Alma 53:13). Indeed, they were "about to take their weapons of war"

(Alma 53:14), and only the devoted efforts of Helaman and his brethren could persuade them otherwise. In light of the oath they had taken, Helaman "feared lest by so doing they should lose their souls." The Ammonites relented and abstained from entering the war as they had originally planned (Alma 53:14).[4]

Fifth, the Ammonite sons—those who had not been party to the original covenant of their fathers—entered a covenant of their own: "a covenant to fight for the liberty of the Nephites, yea, to protect the land unto the laying down of their lives; yea, even they covenanted that they never would give up their liberty, but they would fight in all cases to protect the Nephites and themselves from bondage" (Alma 53:17). These sons were the celebrated 2,000 stripling soldiers of Helaman recounted in Alma 56–58.[5]

All of these aspects of the Ammonites' conversion, and of their subsequent conduct, are illuminating. Their behavior indicates that though they repented both by completely eschewing any sort of conflict and by becoming zealous in faith and righteousness, they still, in this repentant, faithful, and righteous condition, supported however they could the efforts of a war they considered just.

Refutation of the Ammonites as Pacifist Examples

Against the background of Chapter 4, as well as all of the information we have covered here, we can consider anew the frequent claim that the Ammonites were pacifists. Again, as mentioned in Chapter 2, pacifism is opposition, on moral grounds, to all war of any kind. This is how Nibley and others use the term when describing the Ammonites, and some features of the account do seem to suggest this possibility. After all, the Ammonites:

1. sorely repented of the killings they had committed prior to their conversion;
2. permanently buried their weapons following their conversion;
3. entered a covenant that they would never stain their swords with blood again, under any circumstances;
4. allowed themselves to be slaughtered on two separate occasions rather than violate this covenant; and
5. were motivated in this self-sacrifice, Ammon tells us, by the love that they had for their Lamanite brethren.

---

4. Helaman retells this story in an epistle to Moroni in Alma 56:6–8.

5. John Welch dates the Ammonite conversion to about 80 BC, and their sons entered the war about sixteen years later at approximately twenty years of age (see John W. Welch, "Law and War in the Book of Mormon," 66), and thus they would have been young children at the time of their fathers' covenant. Stephen Ricks points out that the word *stripling* in Alma 53:22 and 56:57 is roughly parallel to the Hebrew word used in the Old Testament to refer to young men of military age; see Stephen D. Ricks, "'Holy War:' The Sacral Ideology of War in the Book of Mormon and in the Ancient Near East," 109.

Based on this set of features we might draw the conclusion that the Ammonites' spiritual conversion led them to the belief that all killing in warfare, no matter how conventional its nature, is equivalent to murder, and that for this reason they repented and eschewed any further conflict—even defensive war—in the aftermath of their conversion. If all acts of war are murder, and therefore are cause for repentance, it follows that all war must be wrong.

Seven Points that Refute the View of Ammonite Pacifism

It should be clear by now, however, that this interpretation of the Ammonites' conduct is based on too thin a reading of the account. When we complete the picture this pacifist understanding is untenable. Consider these seven points:

1. The prior actions of the Ammonites were of a murderous character.

First, we have seen that the acts of killing that the Ammonites repented of were either aggressive, large-scale attacks against the Nephites, or small-scale (but equally aggressive) acts of banditry and plunder. The Lamanites were emphatically not reluctant warriors forced to fight from time to time in conventional war over complicated disputes with their equally aggressive Nephite neighbors. On the contrary, in every case of conflict up to that time the Lamanites were the aggressive instigators, motivated by hatred and delight in Nephite blood. They sought at times not only to rob the Nephites, but to destroy them. Every battle between the Nephites and Lamanites occurred on Nephite land, and both the Ammonites and the Nephites explicitly refer to the Ammonites' prior actions as "murder." Moreover, the Lamanites more than once are described as "hardened," "racked with hatred," and as delighting in taking Nephite lives.[6]

This is why, as we have already seen, the Ammonites' repentance was not, as Nibley puts it, for "deeds of valor on the battlefield"—for normal, non-bloodthirsty acts of killing that had occurred in conventional war. The Ammonites' repentance was for aggressive acts of killing that Mormon, the Nephites, and the Ammonites themselves all described meaningfully as "murder." The belief that the Ammonites were repenting of normal wartime acts, and that they considered *these* acts to be murder, is mistaken.

---

6. Contrast this with the behavior of Captain Moroni who, on one occasion during wartime, could have slain a number of Lamanites who "were drunken," and yet refused to do so because "this was not the desire of Moroni; he did not delight in murder or bloodshed, but he delighted in the saving of his people from destruction" and therefore he "would not fall upon the Lamanites and destroy them in their drunkenness" (Alma 55:18–19). It is not clear whether the same could be said of all the Nephites as a group, but it was clearly characteristic of many of the leaders of Nephite armies through the centuries. Consider that Nephi, King Benjamin, Alma, Gidgiddoni, Mormon, and Moroni all led armies of one size or another and that all were significant spiritual leaders.

2. *The Ammonites had non-pacifist motivations for their conduct.*

Second, though the Ammonites eschewed war there is no record of them expressing a pacifist explanation for doing so. They never state that all killing in war is wrong and that all war is thus wrong. Instead, the Ammonite king voiced his worry that "perhaps, if we should stain our swords again they can no more be washed bright through the blood of the Son of our great God" (Alma 24:13). This was a reasonable fear. The Ammonites were a people who had been motivated by hatred and had committed murder in both aggressive, large-scale wars and in attempts to plunder gold and silver from the Nephites. Yet despite this history of violence, they had, with difficulty, won forgiveness (Alma 24:10–13). Given the harsh reality of their past, and the difficulty of their repentance, it is not surprising that they felt the need to maintain this forgiveness by repudiating not only murder, but anything remotely resembling it. This was their reason for repudiating the shedding of blood under any conceivable circumstances. John Welch relates the Ammonite situation to Deuteronomy 20:8, where the "fearful and fainthearted" are exempted from military service. He points out that the Talmud explains this verse as alluding "to one who is afraid *because of the transgressions he had committed*" in the past.[7] Welch adds, "because of their 'many murders,' the Ammonites deeply feared that any further shedding of blood might take them beyond the scope of forgiveness."[8] This seems exactly right. So while it is no doubt true, as Ammon reports (Alma 26:31–32), that the Ammonites were motivated by love of their brethren in refusing to take up arms against them, it is also true that they were motivated by the fear of losing the forgiveness they had obtained and that they had good reason to fear losing.[9]

So even when the Ammonites permitted themselves to be slaughtered, this self-sacrifice was not based on an abstract rejection of war in principle. It was, at least in significant measure, based on the desire to maintain their condition of forgiveness before the Lord. It was an act of penance—a testament to their repentance—not a testament to their rejection of war.

3. *The Ammonites provided support for the Nephite war efforts.*

Third, the Ammonites did not object to the *Nephites* waging war against their Lamanite attackers, nor did they object to the Nephites using military

---

7. Welch, "Law and War in the Book of Mormon," 63–64.
8. Ibid., 86.
9. There may be an additional reason for the Ammonites' entrance into such a covenant: their past conduct had exposed the Ammonites to a carnal appetite that Satan could easily exploit if they were once again to approach anything even remotely similar to their past behavior. Given such vulnerability "it was imperative for them to protect themselves spiritually from any attraction to the memory of past sins." See Elder Richard G. Scott, "Personal Strength through the Atonement of Jesus Christ."

means to protect *them* from Lamanite attack. Throughout the lengthy war, the Ammonites willingly provided substantial material support to the Nephite armies. This makes it evident that the Ammonites entered their covenant of non-bloodshed not because of a general repudiation of war in principle or of a conviction that others ought to do the same, but for reasons that they clearly believed to be peculiar to themselves. As repentant murderers, such a covenant made perfect sense for them, but nowhere in the record do they generalize its application to others. Indeed, in supporting the Nephites in their wartime activities, they did just the opposite.

4. *The Ammonites desired to enter the war.*

Fourth, recall that in this same long war the Ammonites reached a point where, out of a fervent concern and sympathy for the sacrifice of their Nephite protectors, they actually *wanted* to take up arms and assist the Nephites in active defense of their liberty and their lives. It was only the concerted efforts of Helaman and his brethren—not the self-reflection of the Ammonites themselves—that prevented them from fulfilling this desire. Again, while the Ammonites certainly loved their Lamanite brethren, this did not prevent them from wanting to take up arms against them when the situation seemed to warrant it.

5. *A pacifist rationale is absent in the Ammonites' decision not to enter the war.*

Fifth, it is instructive to note that when the Ammonites were finally persuaded not to enter the war, it was not on the basis of the idea that all killing (even in warfare) is sinful. Recall that this is Nibley's reading of why the Ammonites repented: they were contrite over all the killings they had committed in war because they now saw those killings as murder. But if this had been the Ammonites' view, it would have been the most obvious, not to mention the most compelling argument for Helaman to use to persuade them not to take up arms. But he did not do this. Instead, he appealed to the Ammonites explicitly and solely on the basis of their need to honor the idiosyncratic covenant they had made that "they never would shed blood more" (Alma 53:11). As the record says, the Ammonites were "overpowered by the persuasions of Helaman and his brethren, for they were about to break the oath which they had made. And Helaman feared lest by so doing they should lose their souls" (Alma 53:14–15). Obviously, the Ammonites would gladly have taken up arms if they had never made such a covenant in the first place, and under those circumstances Helaman would gladly have embraced their military contribution. It was only this covenant—not an attitude of pacifism—that prevented the Ammonites from entering the war.

6. *The Ammonites did not encourage pacifism in the Nephites.*

Sixth, if the Ammonites had truly been pacifists we would expect them to have turned the tables on Helaman at this point and to argue that *he* should not be waging war either. After all, if the Ammonites were opposed to war in principle then why wouldn't they encourage Helaman and his brethren to put down their own swords and explain to them the sinfulness of what they were doing? That would have been the natural stance to take if the Ammonites had truly believed that all killing in war was murder. The Ammonites, however, did no such thing. Not only did they willingly accept the Nephites' acts of killing in defense of their lives, there is no record of them trying to dissuade the Nephites from waging war at the very time that Helaman was trying to dissuade *them* from doing so. It seems inconceivable that this could occur if the Ammonites were genuinely pacifists.

7. *The Ammonites did not encourage pacifism in their sons.*

Seventh, not only is there no record of the Ammonites discouraging the Nephites from engaging in war, there is no sign that they objected to their own sons entering the war either. Never bound by the covenant of their fathers, these sons entered a covenant of their own that actually *committed* them to taking up the sword and shedding blood in defense of a righteous cause. They were as zealous in righteousness as were their fathers (Alma 56:46–48, 58:40), but because they did not share the same history as their fathers they did not enter the same covenant. Unlike their fathers, they were not repentant murderers and thus had no need to offer the penance that their fathers were offering.

What is most noteworthy about all this, however, is the failure of the Ammonite fathers to object to their sons' enlistment in the war, not to mention to the covenant these sons made that explicitly *obligated* them to take up the sword in conflict. If these fathers really thought that all killing in war was murder why didn't they do everything in their power to prevent their sons from enlisting and thereby prevent them from committing such wrongful acts of killing? This would have been by far the most natural course for a group of pacifist fathers to pursue if they genuinely considered all killing in war to be murder. Yet the Ammonites did nothing remotely resembling this.[10]

---

10. Points 6 and 7 further substantiate the earlier claim about the nature of the Ammonites' repentance. Since the Ammonites objected neither to the Nephites' waging of defensive war, nor to their sons' own determined entrance into it, it is obvious that the Ammonite fathers did not consider war itself to be something that was wrong and required repentance. This alone—even without the evidence discussed earlier in this chapter—demonstrates that their repentance was not for normal acts of killing conducted in conventional acts of war, as Nibley repeatedly asserts.

Idiosyncratic circumstances and covenant. When we consider points six and seven, the most reasonable conclusion we can draw is that the Ammonites simply did not generalize to others the covenant they had made for themselves regarding the non-shedding of blood. They did not generalize such a covenant to their Nephite protectors, and they did not generalize it even to their own sons. The most natural explanation for this seems to be what we have already seen: the Ammonites' refusal to take up arms was an act of righteousness that they saw as peculiar to themselves and to their circumstances. It was based on an attitude they embraced simply as personal penance for the murderous acts they had committed in the past. They did not generalize their principle of self-sacrifice to others, nor did they demand or even encourage others to act as they were acting. Their refusal to take up arms was not a repudiation of war *per se*, but merely a repudiation of war *for themselves*—a repudiation they embraced specifically as penance for the kind of killings they had committed in the past. Based on their conduct, we can surmise that if the Ammonites had considered their covenant generalizable to others, it would only have been to others who were also repentant murderers and who likewise needed to offer penance.

The idiosyncratic nature of the Ammonites' covenant is the most natural explanation for why other Book of Mormon leaders did not follow their example. The redoubtable Mormon is the one who included their story in his account of Nephite history in the first place and yet he did not consider the Ammonites' laying down their arms a prototype to be followed. He behaved nothing like that, nor did he enjoin his people to do so, urging them instead to "stand boldly before the Lamanites and fight for their wives, and their children, and their houses, and their homes" (Morm. 2:23). Nor did the Ammonites' contemporaries consider their actions an example to emulate. These included such significant figures as Alma, Captain Moroni, Lehi, and Helaman. And we also know that neither Nephi nor King Benjamin nor Gidgiddoni nor Lachoneus nor the later Moroni would consider the Ammonites a prototype to follow. None of them behaved as did the Ammonites.

All of this is significant, and the quick conclusion to draw from it is the one Nibley draws—namely, that the Ammonites were simply *better* and that they set the *highest* example. But this verdict on the matter could hardly be more mistaken. Everything in the record indicates that these spiritual figures could see what the Ammonites themselves appreciated but that some modern readers don't: the Ammonites' refusal to take up arms was not a rejection of war per se, but a rejection of war for themselves in *their* circumstances. Their conduct does not generalize to others because the covenant they entered was idiosyncratic—suited to their status as a people who were trying to overcome a past that included murder. Alma and other prophetic leaders could appreciate this and that is why, not being repentant murderers themselves, they did not behave in the same way.[11]

Conclusion

In sum, it is true that the Ammonites deliberately made themselves noncombatants and even suffered themselves to be slaughtered in consequence of that decision. It is also true that they supply what must certainly be among the most inspiring examples of repentance, contrition, humility, and sustained devotion to the Lord that can be found anywhere in scripture. In every way we feel on holy ground as we think of these devoted and sanctified people.

But it is also true that the Ammonites were not pacifists. Not only did they never express a pacifist attitude toward war—and even behaved in ways that explicitly contradicted such an attitude—but, in the two instances where they appeared to behave as pacifists, the resemblance turns out to be superficial because in neither case were they acting from pacifist motivations. It turns out that the Ammonites were opposed to war only for themselves, and for reasons peculiar to themselves, but they were not opposed, as a matter of principle, to war itself.

In the end, whatever arguments there may be for a pacifist view of war, the Ammonite example cannot be among them. In response to the question, "Were the Ammonites pacifists?" the record makes it clear that the answer is no.

---

11. In this connection note that the Ammonites' overt self-sacrifice is part of the reason we admire them: in Alma 24 and 27 they deliberately prostrated themselves before their enemies. But before concluding that it is significant that other prophetic figures did not follow this pattern of overt self-sacrifice—from Nephi to King Benjamin to Mormon—it is useful to remember that the Ammonites themselves did not follow this pattern in later circumstances. They had further opportunity to prostrate themselves before their enemies, but they never did so. This is a matter I take up in the section "The Ammonites' Strategy of Self-Sacrifice" in Chapter 10.

Chapter 6

On Righteousness, Discussion, and the Non-necessity of War

"Bad Guys and Other Bad Guys"

One view of the Book of Mormon is that it is the tale of perennial conflict between two warring factions, the Nephites who were righteous and the Lamanites who were not. From such a reading it is easy to draw the conclusion that war must be justified since the righteous Nephites so frequently engaged in it. But what if the Nephites were not in fact righteous? Indeed, what if the only reason the Lamanites ever attacked the Nephites was because the Nephites were *un*righteous? What would that do to the argument that war must be justified because the Nephites engaged in it?

This is an important matter, and it has not gone unnoticed. Indeed, in his writings Hugh Nibley frequently presses the claims that the Lamanites attacked the Nephites only when the Nephites were unrighteous, that the Lamanites attacked the Nephites only *because* the Nephites were unrighteous, and that such assaults would not have occurred had the Nephites only been obedient to the Lord. It is in this connection that Nibley emphasizes the Lord's early promise to Nephi that the wicked Lamanites "shall have no power over thy seed except they shall rebel against me also" (1 Ne. 2:23),[1] a promise which he takes to mean that Lamanite attacks against the Nephites "would never have taken place if [the Nephites] had not brought it on themselves."[2] He reports that although, according to the promise, there will be fighting if both the Lamanites and the Nephites are wicked, "there is going to be no fight" if the Nephites are righteous. That, he says, "was the agreement."[3] He notes elsewhere that, "From the beginning [the Nephites] received full assurance . . . that they had absolutely nothing to fear as long as they behaved themselves."[4] This view seems reflected in the Lord's statement that the Lamanites would be "a scourge" to the Nephites "to stir them up

---

1. See, for example, Hugh Nibley, "Warfare and the Book of Mormon," 283–84.
2. Hugh Nibley, "Freemen and King-men," 338.
3. Nibley, "Warfare and the Book of Mormon," 284. Eugene England picks up Nibley's point, saying that "conflict, including war, occurs only when both sides have sinned." See Eugene England, "Healing and Making Peace in the Church and the World," 8. England extends the point, asserting that when either side in a conflict stops fighting, the violence ends. I will take up this claim of England's in Chapter 11.
4. Hugh Nibley, *Since Cumorah*, 339.

in remembrance of me" (1 Ne. 2:24; 2 Ne. 5:25). Would the Nephites ever have received such scourging if they hadn't *needed* to be stirred up in remembrance?

It is in regard to this point that Nibley argues that Book of Mormon warfare—whatever the popular reading might be—was never actually between good guys and bad guys. Instead wars were always fought between bad guys and *other* bad guys. He calls it an illusion to think that it is "good guys fighting bad guys" in the wars between the Nephites and Lamanites,[5] and he observes: "We are apt to forget when we read about the heroic resistance of the Nephites to the overwhelming Lamanite power and the noble deeds of the 2,000 youths during the long war, that the gallant Nephites had brought the war upon themselves and were being punished by God for their sins. . . . Whenever Nephites and Lamanites collide it is because they are both bad."[6] Elsewhere he says, again: "It's always the wicked against the wicked in the Book of Mormon, never the righteous against the wicked."[7] Additionally he observes, "The old polarization broke down or vanished completely whenever the Nephites were truly righteous."[8]

In this connection Nibley also emphasizes Mormon's declaration that, "it is by the wicked that the wicked are punished" (Morm. 4:5) suggesting that God does not use the righteous, through war and conflict, to deal with the wicked. Rather, God lets the wicked deal with each other.[9] Nibley thus feels that when the Nephites and Lamanites fight "it is because they are both rebellious against God,"[10] and adds that, "at every confrontation of the Nephites and Lamanites in war, the Book of Mormon is at pains to point out that the conflict is to be attributed to the wickedness of both parties."[11] Regarding one long war Nibley notes that it was the Nephites' own wickedness "that brought the whole thing on"[12] and, applying the lesson to our own day, he also remarks that if we are good enough the Lord "will see to it" that the wicked punish the wicked, adding: "that is a promise that has never failed of fulfillment."[13]

---

5. Hugh Nibley, "In the Party but Not of the Party," 122.

6. Nibley, *Since Cumorah*, 348; see also Nibley, "Freemen and King-men," 337; Nibley, "The Prophetic Book of Mormon," 436–37; and Nibley, "Last Call: An Apocalyptic Warning from the Book of Mormon," 524.

7. Nibley, "Warfare and the Book of Mormon," 283.

8. Nibley, *Since Cumorah*, 340.

9. See, for example, Hugh Nibley, "Brigham Young and the Enemy," 238; Nibley, "Warfare and the Book of Mormon," 283; Nibley, "Scriptural Perspectives on How to Survive the Calamities of the Last Days," 493.

10. Nibley, "Warfare and the Book of Mormon," 284; see also Nibley, *Since Cumorah*, 342–43.

11. Nibley, *Since Cumorah*, 342.

12. Nibley, "Last Call," 524.

13. Nibley, "Brigham Young and the Enemy," 238.

Nibley takes this point about good guys/bad guys and the wicked punishing the wicked in the Book of Mormon very seriously. He explains, for example, that even the deadly confrontation between the prophet Alma and the war-monger Amlici (Alma 2:29–31) was not a case of "a good guy against a bad guy," because "when the war was over [the Nephites] mourned terribly because they were convinced that the war had been because of their wickedness."[14]

In all of this emphasis on Nephite unrighteousness Nibley intends to correct the simplistic reading of Book of Mormon wars as an ongoing conflict between the "good" Nephites and the "bad" Lamanites. Against such a caricature Nibley wants us to see that both sides are actually bad guys, that therefore it is bad guys who lose, and that they lose *because* they are bad.[15]

This collection of observations has obvious relevance to claims regarding pacifism. After all, if it is true that the Nephites were attacked by the Lamanites only because of the Nephites' own unrighteousness, we have a difficult time saying something like, "War *must* be acceptable because the Nephites were righteous and *they* fought." If the Nephites were not in fact righteous, what is the point in appealing to their conduct as a moral compass for our own? Furthermore, the idea that righteousness will prevent attack is highly appealing. Perhaps if we are righteous enough the Lord will arrange in our case, too, for the wicked to fight among themselves so that we also will be spared conflict. That seems to be Nibley's reading of the promise to the Nephites, and, if accurate, it is possible that a similar promise might generalize to us.

But all of this depends on the truth of Nibley's claims and on the logic of their application. Is it true, for example, that the Nephites faced assault only when they were unrighteous? Is it true that this was the nature of the Lord's promise to Nephi—that his seed would never be attacked if they were obedient to the Lord? Put another way: Is it true that since it is by the wicked that the wicked are punished, if the Nephites had only been more righteous the Lamanites would have just fought among themselves and left their Nephite neighbors alone?[16]

---

14. Nibley, "Warfare and the Book of Mormon," 283; see also Nibley, "Freemen and King-men," 338.

15. Nibley finds this caricature in Thomas F. O'Dea, *The Mormons*. See Nibley, *Since Cumorah*, 342.

16. This chapter will examine these factual claims, but notice that even if it is the case (1) that the Nephites were unrighteous whenever they were attacked, (2) that this unrighteousness was what brought their wars upon them, and (3) that this correlation between unrighteousness and assault was the meaning of the promise to Nephi, it still does not follow that the Nephites were therefore unjustified in defending themselves when under assault. To reach this conclusion is to draw a particular logical inference, and this I will examine in Chapter 7.

Differences in the Character of Nephite and Lamanite Unrighteousness

At first glance, it seems insightful to point out that the Nephites were unrighteous just as the Lamanites were, and that this was the reason the Nephites so often found themselves embroiled in war. According to such a view, in matters of obedience to God there was no substantial difference between the two peoples. As a result, the Nephites do not turn out to be the sympathetic figures we had supposed them to be.

One weakness of this view, however, is its failure to distinguish sufficiently between the *character* of Nephite and Lamanite unrighteousness. Because Nibley is not specific in describing the Nephite and Lamanite populations—and instead simply affixes the appellation "bad" to both of them—he creates the impression that these populations were similar in their unrighteousness. This is misleading. For example, until very late in the civilization's history military attacks always came from the Lamanites toward the Nephites and never the other way around.[17] As Moroni remarks in his missive to the wicked Ammoron in the middle of one long war, "Ye have sought to murder us, and we have only sought to defend our lives" (Alma 54:13).[18] And as Nibley himself significantly notes, "all Book of Mormon wars take place on Nephite property, not on Lamanite."[19] It is also relevant that Mormon describes the Lamanites during one period as "a wild and a hardened and a ferocious people; a people who delighted in murdering the Nephites, and robbing and plundering them" (Alma 17:14).

The difference between societies is displayed even in those cases where Nephite dissenters led the Lamanites into war against the Nephites (or at least in their prosecution of the war by such dissenters). Examples include Amlici

---

17. See the section "What Were the Ammonites Like Before Their Conversion?" in Chapter 4 and note 2 in Chapter 5. We know of one occasion when a group of Nephites made plans to attack and destroy the Lamanites in the land of Nephi, but the plans were never realized (see Mosiah 9:1–2). We also know that late in Book of Mormon history the Nephites began seeking vengeance rather than defense, and apparently this led to aggressive attacks against the Lamanites (although this is more implied than explicitly stated). If so, this is one exception to the overwhelming pattern of Lamanite aggression throughout the Book of Mormon, and it was at this time that Mormon stepped down and refused to lead the Nephites (see Morm. 3:8–16). See Chapter 5 for more on the pattern of Lamanite aggression.

18. Although the current edition of the Book of Mormon reads here "defend ourselves," Royal Skousen points out to me that the original manuscript reads "defend our *lives*"—a correction to the text which lends even greater importance and poignancy to the character of the Nephites' self-defense. See Royal Skousen, ed., *The Book of Mormon: The Earliest Text*, 473.

19. Hugh Nibley, "Warfare and the Book of Mormon," 294; see also Nibley, *Since Cumorah*, 298 and Nibley, "Freemen and King-men," 354. Again, see Chapter 5 for more on this.

(Alma 2), the Amalekites and Amulonites (Alma 24), the Amalekites (Alma 27), the Zoramites and Amalekites (Alma 43–44), Amalickiah (Alma 46–51), Ammoron (Alma 52–62), and Coriantumr (Helaman 1). In addition, unnamed Nephite dissenters were highly instrumental in Lamanite aggression in Alma 63:14–15, Helaman 4, and Helaman 11.

It is noteworthy that no examples occur in which agitators gained power by stirring the Nephites up to anger and prodding them into war against the Lamanites. There are multiple examples, however, of such dissidents doing exactly that with the Lamanites toward the Nephites. Seemingly representative of such agitation is this report:

> And it came to pass in the fifty and fourth year there were many dissensions in the church, and there was also a contention among the people, insomuch that there was much bloodshed. And the rebellious part were slain and driven out of the land, and they did go unto the king of the Lamanites. And it came to pass that they did endeavor to stir up the Lamanites to war against the Nephites; but behold, the Lamanites were exceedingly afraid, insomuch that they would not hearken to the words of those dissenters. But it came to pass in the fifty and sixth year of the reign of the judges, there were dissenters who went up from the Nephites unto the Lamanites; and they succeeded with those others in stirring them up to anger against the Nephites; and they were all that year preparing for war. And in the fifty and seventh year they did come down against the Nephites to battle, and they did commence the work of death; yea, insomuch that in the fifty and eighth year of the reign of the judges they succeeded in obtaining possession of the land of Zarahemla; yea, and also all the lands, even unto the land which was near the land Bountiful. (Helaman 4:1–5)

All of this highlights an important distinction between Nephite and Lamanite societies: Lamanite unrighteousness consisted at least partly in large-scale invasion, attack, and murder—including, on a smaller scale, acts of spoliation and plunder—while Nephite unrighteousness did not take this form. Moreover, Nephite dissenters had significant success in prodding Lamanites into war against the Nephites, but there is no example of the opposite occurring. Therefore, to simply say that both sides are bad guys, and to leave the matter at that, is to overlook completely at least this one large difference between them.

Were the Nephites Always Unrighteous When Involved in War?

Even if this difference in Nephite and Lamanite unrighteousness is left aside, however, the question still remains of whether or not the Nephites were always unrighteous when involved in war, regardless of how "righteousness" is defined. As we have already seen, Nibley says that all wars in the Book of Mormon were between bad guys and other bad guys, and that the Nephites faced assault from time to time only *because* they were unrighteous—since, as the scriptures state, it is by the wicked that the wicked are punished.

But this line of thinking is a mistake. Consider first the proposition that the righteous should expect no conflict with the wicked (or certainly that they should not have to spill any blood) because "it is by the wicked that the wicked are punished." Although this seems appealing in the abstract, the idea encounters problems within the first eight pages of the Book of Mormon when the Lord uses Nephi specifically to slay Laban. The Spirit says at this time, "Behold, the Lord slayeth the wicked to bring forth his righteous purposes," and, of course, it is through the righteous Nephi that he does so—a circumstance that clearly belies any supposition that the wicked will have no conflict except with others who are also wicked.[20]

Next, consider Captain Moroni's explicit discussion of the relationship between righteousness and suffering attack, and even death, in war. In a state of exasperation he says to Pahoran:

> Do ye suppose that, because so many of your brethren have been killed it is because of their wickedness? I say unto you, if ye have supposed this ye have supposed in vain . . . for the Lord suffereth the righteous to be slain that his justice and judgment may come upon the wicked. Therefore ye need not suppose that the righteous are lost because they are slain; but behold, they do enter into the rest of the Lord their God. (Alma 60:12–13)

Captain Moroni thus believed that the wicked are permitted to slay the righteous in order that "justice and judgment may come upon the wicked." This is a relationship between righteousness and assault that Nibley does not consider, although it is an explicit part of the record. Unlike Moroni, Nibley believes that the Lamanites attacked the Nephites only because, and only when, the Nephites were unrighteous. But if that were the case it would be absurd for Moroni to speak, as he does, of the deaths of the righteous as serving to ensure a just judgment against the wicked.[21] This is a connection between righteousness and assault that flatly contradicts the claim we are examining.

This view of Captain Moroni is not the only factor to weigh in analyzing the assertion. Consider, for example, this account:

---

20. Some are disposed to find fault with Nephi for his slaying of Laban, and thus are likely to think that this is, in fact, a case of the wicked punishing the wicked. I take up such criticism of Nephi in Chapters 8 through 11.

21. Nor would we expect him to describe those who had been slain in this particular case as righteous, or to state that they had entered into the rest of God: that is *not* what we would expect to happen if those who were slain were themselves wicked. One might say, of course, that Lamanite attacks occurred only when the general society of Nephites was unrighteous, but that individual soldiers could themselves still be worthy and thus merit Moroni's description. Nibley never makes this argument, however, and in any case it still leaves the larger problem—that Moroni identifies a role for the righteous in suffering assault from the wicked that is a straightforward denial of Nibley's view.

And the people did humble themselves because of their words, insomuch that they were highly favored of the Lord, and thus they were free from wars and contentions among themselves, yea, even for the space of four years.

But, as I have said, in the latter end of the nineteenth year, yea, notwithstanding their peace amongst themselves, they were compelled reluctantly to contend with their brethren, the Lamanites. Yea, and in fine, their wars never did cease for the space of many years with the Lamanites, notwithstanding their much reluctance.

Now, they were sorry to take up arms against the Lamanites, because they did not delight in the shedding of blood; yea, and this was not all—they were sorry to be the means of sending so many of their brethren out of this world into an eternal world, unprepared to meet their God. Nevertheless, they could not suffer to lay down their lives, that their wives and their children should be massacred by the barbarous cruelty of those who were once their brethren, yea, and had dissented from their church, and had left them and had gone to destroy them by joining the Lamanites. Yea, they could not bear that their brethren should rejoice over the blood of the Nephites, so long as there were any who should keep the commandments of God, for the promise of the Lord was, if they should keep his commandments they should prosper in the land. (Alma 48:20–25)

Here we have a time when Mormon describes the Nephites as humble, highly favored of the Lord, and at peace among themselves, and yet he also tells us that they suffered attacks from the Lamanites.

In another example, Jarom reports a time when the people of Nephi "observed to keep the law of Moses and the Sabbath day holy unto the Lord . . . and they profaned not; neither did they blaspheme . . . and the laws of the land were exceedingly strict." Nevertheless, despite these circumstances, the Lamanites still "loved murder . . . and came many times against us, the Nephites, to battle. But our kings and our leaders were mighty men in the faith of the Lord; and they taught the people the ways of the Lord; wherefore, we withstood the Lamanites and swept them away out of our lands" (Jarom 1:5–7). This presents an additional case where the Nephites were righteous and nevertheless suffered Lamanite attack.[22]

Yet another example is found in 3 Nephi where Mormon reports the historic occasion when all the converted Lamanites and Nephites were united as one. The Lamanites' curse, he tells us, "was taken from them" and they "were numbered among the Nephites, and were called Nephites." In these righteous and favored conditions Mormon tells us that the people still had to take up

---

22. One might wonder whether these people were righteous in the truest sense, since it was the Law of Moses that they obeyed and it is at least possible that they might have followed that Law as the Pharisees of the New Testament followed it—not as a way of actually being righteous, but as a way of *displaying* themselves as righteous. This possibility seems highly unlikely, though, based on Jarom's clear approval of the people and on his emphasis that the Nephite leaders were "mighty men in the faith of the Lord" who taught the people in "the ways of the Lord" (Jarom 1:7).

arms against the Gadianton robbers because of those robbers' determination to destroy them (3 Ne. 2:11–17). It is another example of people suffering attack despite their impressive, even singular, righteousness.

The remarks of Moroni in Alma 60:12–13, then, along with the episodes recounted in Alma 48:20–25, Jarom 1:5–7, and 3 Nephi 2:11–17 all disprove the sweeping claim that the Nephites were unrighteous whenever they were involved in war. In each of these cases people whom the Book of Mormon itself identifies as righteous suffered attack from enemies who wanted to destroy them. Indeed, the Nephites and the Lamanites *both* suffered attacks, and took up arms to defend themselves, in cases where the record clearly identifies them as righteous. So it is inaccurate to say that the Nephites "had absolutely nothing to fear as long as they behaved themselves."[23] The polarization which Nibley claimed vanished with Nephite righteousness[24] in fact diminished only when the Nephites and the Lamanites were both truly righteous (as in 4 Ne. 1:2). Despite Nibley's claim, there are clear instances in the Book of Mormon where the conflict genuinely was between good guys and bad guys, and thus we *cannot* take the phrase "it is by the wicked that the wicked are punished" to be a universal description of what happens in war. At least part of the time it is obviously something else, as the Book of Mormon itself attests multiple times.[25]

The Ancient Promise to Nephi

We find another counterexample to the claim we are considering in the case of King Benjamin, a righteous leader who was forced to fight at length to

---

23. Nibley, *Since Cumorah*, 339.
24. Ibid., 340.
25. Although the concept of righteousness is central to the point being discussed, it is obviously a somewhat subjective notion. It is not likely, for instance, that any two groups that qualify to be called righteous are identical in how they live the gospel. Each will have various strengths and weaknesses and these are unlikely to match up in any precise way. What such groups have in common, therefore, is not perfection, but a level of devotion to the Lord that at least passes a certain (high) threshold of faithfulness. Whatever their mortal weaknesses, the Book of Mormon reports multiple groups that managed to do this. Also, it may seem plausible at first glance that the Lamanites would have fought among themselves and left the Nephites alone if only the Nephites had been righteous. After all, many of the wars from Alma forward were fomented, and/or even led, by Nephite dissenters, and, as Mormon tells us (Alma 50:21), such dissensions *constituted* part of the Nephites' unrighteousness. This is not dispositive, however, because it is not clear that all wars suffered by the Nephites were incited by Nephite dissension. It is possible that this is the case, but it is at least relevant that none of the wars that occurred in the first few centuries are designated this way. As discussed in Chapter 4 (note 20), this may be due to the brevity of the reports that appear in this part of the record, but the absence of specific mention of dissenters makes it difficult to conclude that dissenters *always* played a role.

protect his people. The record tells us that "the Lamanites came down out of the land of Nephi" to wage war against King Benjamin's people, and that "King Benjamin gathered together his armies, and he did stand against them; and he did fight with the strength of his own arm, with the sword of Laban . . . until they had slain many thousands of the Lamanites . . . [and] had driven them out of all the lands of their inheritance" (W of M 1:13–14). Finally, at the end of his life, King Benjamin appealed to his people:

> And now, my brethren, I would that ye should do as ye have hitherto done. As ye have kept my commandments, and also the commandments of my father, and have prospered, and have been kept from falling into the hands of your enemies, even so if ye shall keep the commandments of my son, or the commandments of God which shall be delivered unto you by him, ye shall prosper in the land, and your enemies shall have no power over you." (Mosiah 2:31)

Note carefully what Benjamin is saying here. He is reporting both that his people had been righteous ("*as* ye have kept my commandments") and that the Lamanites had attacked them. Even though King Benjamin's people were faithful, they suffered assaults from their Lamanite brethren and were forced to defend themselves (the fifth time we have seen this).[26]

King Benjamin also states that his people had "prospered." That makes us want to know *how* they had prospered. According to Nibley, if Benjamin's people were righteous, and if they had prospered, then certainly as a blessing they must have been spared conflict. This conclusion is based on Nibley's reading of the Lord's early promise to Nephi that the wicked Lamanites "shall have no power over thy seed except they shall rebel against me also" (1 Ne. 2:23), a promise he takes to mean that the Nephites would suffer *no* conflict if they were righteous. But we have just seen that this was not the experience of King Benjamin and his people. They experienced plenty of conflict. The Lamanites came against Benjamin's people in large numbers, and the Nephites slew "thousands" of their attackers in defending themselves. So it can hardly be said that King Benjamin and his people had prospered in the sense that they were spared any attack whatsoever. Instead, King Benjamin tells us that his people had prospered in the sense that they were kept from falling "into the hands" of their enemies. In Benjamin's mind, for the Nephites to prosper meant that they prevailed in defending themselves, not that they were spared any attack at all.

---

26. This does not mean that Benjamin's people were perfect. We are told that "he had somewhat of contentions among his people" (W of M 1:12), but Mormon does not use this fact to explain the Lamanite attacks. He treats it as a separate affliction altogether. The account in Alma 48:20–25 is relevant here: remember that these people were attacked even when they were at peace among themselves, as Mormon goes out of his way to tell us. And in any case, *King Benjamin* was obviously satisfied with his people's righteousness, imploring them to continue living just as they had been.

It is in this context that King Benjamin now says to his people: "Even so if ye shall keep the commandments . . . of God . . . *ye shall prosper in the land, and your enemies shall have no power over you*" (Mosiah 2:31). Here the king significantly and explicitly invokes the ancient promise given to Nephi. Far from understanding the promise to mean, as Nibley asserts, that there would be no conflict at all if the Nephites were righteous, King Benjamin took it to mean that if his people were righteous and were attacked, they would *prevail*—they would be kept from "falling into the hands of their enemies." This was what it meant to say that "your enemies shall have no power over you."

King Benjamin is not alone in this reading. Captain Moroni also invoked the ancient promise, with the same understanding of its meaning. He said to Zerahemnah at the end of a long and bloody battle: "The Lord . . . has delivered you into our hands. . . . [Y]ea, ye see that God will support, and keep, and preserve us, *so long as we are faithful unto him*." He then added: "And never will the Lord suffer that we shall be destroyed except we should fall into transgression and deny our faith" (Alma 44:3–4). Since Moroni believed that the Nephites won this battle precisely *because of* their faithfulness, he obviously did not believe that the Nephites would be spared all battles whatsoever by being faithful. In Moroni's view the Nephites would not be spared torment and attack by being righteous—they would only be spared destruction.

Addressing this same issue, Alma queries the Nephites: "For has not the Lord expressly promised and firmly decreed, that if ye will rebel against him that ye shall utterly be destroyed from off the face of the earth?" (Alma 9:24). Unless Alma was referring to a promise not appearing in Mormon's abridgment of the Nephite record, the closest referent in meaning is the early promise to Nephi regarding rebellion and the Lamanites' power over the Nephites. If that is true, Alma read the promise just as King Benjamin and Captain Moroni read it—not in terms of being spared attack, but only in terms of being spared destruction. The same meaning is found in Amaron's report that the Lord spared the righteous "that they should not perish, but did deliver them out of the hands of their enemies" (Omni 1:7). Here too "deliverance" is equated with "not perishing."

Mormon read the ancient promise the same way. He tells us in one place that "those who were *faithful in keeping the commandments of the Lord* were delivered at all times" (Alma 50:22), even though those same people had been attacked and had suffered much from Lamanite aggression. Mormon also approvingly recounts how, with "much reluctance," Nephites took up arms against the Lamanites who persisted in attacking them. He tells us that these Nephites "did not delight in the shedding of blood" and that "they were sorry to be the means of sending so many of their brethren out of this world into an eternal world, unprepared to meet their God." Nevertheless, "they could not bear that their brethren should rejoice over the blood of the Nephites, so long as there were any who should keep the commandments of God." And why was it so important that they prevent this? Because, Mormon tells us, "the promise of the Lord was, if they should keep his commandments they should prosper in the land" (Alma 48:23–25), and obviously they would not be prospering if they were being massacred. The irony of this situation could hardly be more striking: Nibley takes the ancient promise to mean that if the Nephites had been righteous they would never have to go to battle, but here we have a case where righteous Nephites went to battle precisely in order *to fulfill* that ancient promise.

That is not the only example of such irony. Moroni also argues, to Pahoran, the governor of the Nephites at the time, that if the Nephites, in the beginning of their peril, "had gone forth against our enemies . . . yea, if we had gone forth against them in the strength of the Lord," they would have dispersed and beaten those enemies. Why? "For it would have been done, *according to the fulfilling of his word*" (Alma 60:15–16). Moroni is saying that the ancient promise would have been fulfilled if only the Nephites had been united in *fighting* the Lamanites at the beginning of their conflict. Far from believing that the ancient declaration promised *no* fighting, Moroni explains that that declaration of conditions would have been fulfilled if only the people *had* fought.[27]

---

27. Note that Moroni says that the Nephites would have withstood their enemies "according to the fulfilling of his word," but that he does not cite what specific "word" of the Lord he has in mind in saying this. Despite this lack of specificity, there are eight reasons that cumulatively provide a compelling case for concluding that he has in mind the ancient promise to Nephi. First, as discussed previously in this section, Moroni himself earlier tied Nephites' deliverance specifically to their faithfulness (Alma 44:3–4)—which is exactly the connection found in that early promise—indicating that Moroni was familiar with this ancient word from the Lord. Second, Moroni speaks specifically in this passage about the word of the Lord being *fulfilled*—which presupposes that the "word" he has in mind must be a promise or prophecy of some kind: in some way it must be regarding the future. Third, that promise/prophecy must have application to war, and likely to relations between the Nephites and the Lamanites, since the context of Moroni's statement entails both. Fourth, it is difficult to find a statement by the Lord—besides the early promise to Nephi—that meets these criteria: a promise/prophecy about war that involves the Nephites and Lamanites. What other statement satisfies all three conditions? Fifth, even if some other statement or phrase does seem to meet these conditions, it is doubtful that it can come close to matching the prominence enjoyed by the promise to Nephi: some version of that promise is explicitly reported twenty different times in the Book of Mormon. It is mentioned by seven different figures, in seven different books, in six different centuries. As promises about Book of Mormon peoples go, this one dominates the record. Sixth, precisely because of its prominence, it is easy to imagine Moroni referring to this promise without citing it explicitly—something he would be far less likely to do if he were referring to some other, less prominent,

It is apparent, then, that King Benjamin, Alma, Mormon, and Moroni (twice) all understood the ancient promise the same way. They believed it to mean that the Nephites would prevail and would avoid destruction if they were righteous. They did not understand it to mean that the Nephites would avoid conflict altogether. Indeed, we have seen that the Nephites were actually willing to go to battle in order to fulfill the ancient promise.

All of this is reinforced by Mormon's report that the Nephites were taught (1) to defend themselves "even unto the shedding of blood if it were necessary," and (2) "never to give an offense" (Alma 48:14). It was in response to both efforts, Mormon tells us, that "God would prosper them in the land" and "warn them to flee, or to prepare for war" in order to deliver them from their enemies (Alma 48:15–16). Here, again, God's prospering of the Nephites is framed specifically in terms of delivering them from conquest, not from any attack whatever; moreover, such prospering is built on the *expectation* that the Nephites would defend themselves with the sword when doing so was necessary to preserve their lives.

These considerations do not prove Nibley's reading of the ancient promise to be wrong, of course. Technically, all they prove is that he reads the promise differently than King Benjamin, Alma, Moroni, and Mormon read it. But this is reason enough to regard the reading as highly implausible and thus as providing no support for the idea that the Nephites would have been

---

statement from the Lord. (This is particularly true since Moroni is writing in this passage specifically to Pahoran, governor of the Nephites at the time, and someone who could be presumed to be as familiar with Nephite teachings as was Moroni himself.) Seventh, it is evident that the ancient promise was "in the air" specifically around the time of Captain Moroni: Alma, head of the Church during at least part of that time, referred to it frequently (Alma 9:13–14, 24; Alma 36:1; Alma 36:30; Alma 37:13; Alma 38:1). Given its prominence in Alma's mind, it would not be surprising if other leaders around that time were familiar with the promise and referred to it in an oblique way to one another. Finally, following Moroni's statement that the Nephites would have been able to defeat the Lamanites if only the Nephites had been united in fighting them (Alma 60:15–16), he tells us that the Nephites were instead being overrun, killed, and some of them taken captive, "and this because of the great wickedness of those who are seeking for power and authority, yea, even those king-men" (Alma 60:17). So Moroni connects the dire consequences the Nephites were experiencing directly to the wickedness found among them—which, again, is specifically the connection identified in the ancient promise. This too suggests that the "word" Moroni refers to in verse 16 is indeed that early statement from the Lord. Separate mentions of the promise, in one version or another, are at least these: 1 Nephi 2:20–24; 4:14; 2 Nephi 1:9, 20; 2 Nephi 5:20, 25; Jarom 1:9; Omni 1:6; Mosiah 1:7; 2:22, 31; Alma 9:13–14, 24; 36:1, 30; 37:13; 38:1; 48:25; 50:20–21; 3 Nephi 5:22. My thanks to Skousen for indicating the need for this discussion and for his invaluable help in identifying relevant passages.

spared any conflict whatever if only they had been righteous. Nothing in the record, including the promise to Nephi, holds out such an expectation.[28]

Can Conflict Always Be Avoided by Discussion?

According to Boyd Petersen, Hugh Nibley believed that, because "every conflict must sooner or later be settled by discussion," we should just "'have the discussion now' and avoid the senseless conflict."[29] Nibley is right, of course, that people in conflict eventually end up talking, and he is obviously right to wish this to happen before the conflict even begins. But just because conflict always ends in discussion it does not follow that it could always be avoided by discussion. If it could, then pacifism is obviously required—if discussion can always avert conflict, then it *should* always avert conflict; defensively taking up arms against an aggressor would indicate a moral failure to be sufficiently willing to talk.

Unfortunately, while the idea of always being able to avoid conflict through discussion is highly appealing, the claim rests on at least two false assumptions. The first of these is the idea that aggressors themselves are universally willing to talk before they begin their aggression. If this were true, then discussion would likely be enough to avoid conflict. But how reasonable is this assumption in view of the many leaders who are bent on aggression and who are only willing to talk when it is in terms of surrender—as either victors or losers of conflict? Consider the experiences of Captain Moroni, who was always open to discussion to avoid conflict.[30] In one instance, after gaining military advantage over Zerahemnah, Moroni (to cite Nibley), "immediately called a halt to the fighting. . . . He had his men fall back and went out to meet Zerahemnah" to talk.[31] At this point Moroni offered Zerahemnah and his army the chance to lay down their arms and preserve their lives if only they would enter an oath never to take up arms again—otherwise, "I will command my men that they shall fall upon you, and inflict the

---

28. Perhaps Nibley has an argument somewhere that (1) acknowledges the difference between his own reading of the promise and the reading common to these Book of Mormon figures, and that (2) shows his reading to be a purer interpretation of it than theirs is. If so, I have not seen it. For more on the ancient promises to Nephi and Lehi see Appendix 2.

29. As reported in Boyd Jay Petersen, *Hugh Nibley: A Consecrated Life*, 221.

30. Nibley emphasizes this aspect of Moroni's conduct. Hugh Nibley, *Since Cumorah*, 298–301; "Leaders to Managers: The Fatal Shift," in Hugh Nibley, *Brother Brigham Challenges the Saints*, 499–501; "'Exemplary Manhood,'" in Hugh Nibley, *Brother Brigham Challenges the Saints*, 513–14; "Freemen and King-men," in Hugh Nibley, *The Prophetic Book of Mormon*, 353–54.

31. Hugh Nibley, *Since Cumorah*, 298–99.

wounds of death in your bodies, that ye may become extinct" (Alma 44:6–7). Understandably, Zerahemnah paused to consider Moroni's offer, which at this point in the battle was an impressive testament to Moroni's character. This opening to talk, however, did not come because of Zerahemnah's own desire for discussion—Moroni was only able to reach this point with Zerahemnah after defeat and after Moroni's threat of continued conflict. How willing was Zerahemnah to talk before all of this? Apparently, not at all.

This brings us to Nibley's second assumption: that talk before conflict and talk after conflict are equivalent. But as we have just seen in the case of Moroni and Zerahemnah, this assumption could not be more false. After all, Zerahemnah's remarks at this point in the conflict were thoroughly defiant. He refused to take the oath "which we know that we shall break" and added that "we do not believe that it is God that has delivered us into your hands; but we believe that it is your cunning that has preserved you from our swords" (Alma 44:9). Because of this defiance Moroni resumed the battle, and the Lamanites "did fall exceedingly fast before the swords of the Nephites" (Alma 44:18). The battle again raged on until Zerahemnah, now injured himself, was willing to talk again—but differently this time. He cried "mightily unto Moroni, promising that he would covenant and also his people with them, if [the Nephites] would spare the remainder of their lives" (Alma 44:19). As a result of *this* talk, in which the Lamanites entered the covenant of peace that Moroni had required, Moroni took their weapons of war and permitted them to depart into the wilderness (Alma 44:20).

This incident is instructive. For while it is true that Moroni and Zerahemnah had talks twice in the course of this encounter, it is also true that these discussions were not remotely the same—and it would be disingenuous to characterize them as if they were. The discussion after the continued conflict was different from the one before because *Zerahemnah* was different after the conflict than he was before: although the battle did not change his heart, it did change his attitude toward fighting. Faced with destruction, he was now for the first time willing to lay down his arms and to seek peace.

For this reason it would simply be an equivocation on terms to call both of these talks "discussions" without qualification, and to suppose that the one was in the same category as the other and therefore that the second talk for peace could and should have been conducted earlier than it was. The truth is that no discussion was meaningful in the absence of Zerahemnah's willingness to *make* it meaningful. As long as he was determined to wage war, it was not possible for anything less than war to dissuade him; no amount of talk by itself was sufficient.

Everyone, of course, wishes that war could be avoided by something as straightforward and painless as discussion, but the reality is that it is not always as simple as that—as the peace-loving but battle-weary Moroni could tell us.

War and Necessity

In Nibley's view, because of their experiences both Mormon and Moroni saw war as being "nasty, brutalizing, wasteful, dirty, degrading, fatiguing, foolish, and immoral," and "above all unnecessary."[32] Such a view obviously supports pacifism: if, among other things, the violence of war is *unnecessary*, then it is obviously immoral to participate in it. It would not be right to cause the devastation that war entails if it were avoidable.[33] What, though, can it mean to say that Mormon and Moroni held this view, when they personally led men into battle on numerous occasions? Would they have done that if they really thought it to be *unnecessary*?

One way to answer this question would be to understand Nibley as saying that Mormon and Moroni simply believed that war would never occur if all people were righteous. After all, since righteous people do not attack others, it follows that if everyone were righteous there would never be any acts of war, and war would therefore be both unncessary and nonexistent.

It is difficult to attribute this interpretation of Mormon and Moroni to Nibley, however, because the claim is an obvious tautology—it is true by definition—and thus adds nothing to our understanding. It hardly requires a Mormon or a Moroni to appreciate that no war would occur if everyone were righteous, so it is hard to imagine that this is the point Nibley means to make about them. A far more likely interpretation of the claim is that it intends to assert one or both of the points that have been already addressed: that if people are righteous they will never suffer attacks from those who are unrighteous and that conflict can always be avoided through discussion. Either of these claims would support the idea that war is unnecessary. However, since each of these views has been examined and shown to be inaccurate, there is no basis whatever for imagining that Mormon and Moroni held either of these beliefs and thus no reason to conclude that they thought war to be unnecessary because of them.[34]

---

32. Hugh Nibley, *Since Cumorah*, 292.

33. This reasoning is valid; what is in question is the truth of the premise that war is unnecessary. This is the question (largely) of whether a war's benefits can outweigh its costs, a matter we looked at in Chapter 3. See particularly the section "The Cost of Not Waging Defensive War."

34. In making his claim about Mormon and Moroni Nibley could also have in mind another of his assertions—namely, that God fights the battles of the faithful and thus they don't have to fight battles of their own. But as with the claims examined

In the final analysis, we simply have no reason to think that Mormon and Moroni believed war to be unnecessary. The best evidence of this is their very engagement in it. After all, if they did believe war to be unnecessary, they demonstrated quite the opposite through their active and frequent participation in conflict. Thus, while it is obvious that Mormon and Moroni considered war, in every case, to be thoroughly tragic and sad, their behavior itself demonstrates that, in the circumstances they faced, they emphatically did not believe it to be unnecessary.[35]

Conclusion

In short, it is not true that the Nephites faced assault only when they were unrighteous, and thus (obviously) it is not true that if only the Nephites had been righteous, the Lamanites would always have just fought among themselves and left their Nephite neighbors alone. Nor is it true that the Lord promised that the Nephites would never be attacked if only they were righteous. Although this seems a reasonable conclusion when the Lord's words to Nephi are read in isolation (e.g., 1 Nephi 2:24 and 2 Nephi 5:25), it seems completely untenable when the text is examined as a whole. After all, significant spiritual leaders who actually lived under the promise did not interpret it that way, including King Benjamin, Alma, Moroni, and Mormon.

An argument for pacifism, therefore, cannot rest on the idea that the Nephites never *really* had to fight (i.e., that they would never have suffered assault in the first place if only they had been righteous). The truth is that they experienced enemy attacks even when they were obedient to God. Because of this, there is no basis that can be drawn from the Book of Mormon for supposing that violent conflict can be avoided through righteous living, and thus there is no basis for supposing that we can embrace pacifism based on an expectation of that sort. Far from supporting such a hope, the Book of Mormon actually confutes it.

Nor can such hope rest on the idea that discussion is sufficient to avert conflict or on the proposition that both Mormon and Moroni thought war to be unnecessary. Neither of these views is accurate and thus neither can support pacifist claims.

---

in this chapter, this one is also mistaken (as we will see in Chapter 7). There is thus no reason to suppose that Mormon and Moroni held this view, any more than there is reason to suppose that they held the mistaken views examined in this chapter. Nothing in Nibley's assertions succeeds in supporting the claim that Mormon and Moroni believed war to be unnecessary.

35. One reply to this would be to argue that Mormon and Moroni *later* came to believe that war was unnecessary. This is a matter I will take up regarding Mormon in the section "The Narrative Approach and Mormon" in Chapter 9.

Chapter 7

Self-Defense and the Lord's Involvement in War

The previous chapter demonstrated that the Nephites were not always unrighteous when the Lamanites attacked them. Despite claims to the contrary, the Book of Mormon contains multiple accounts of the righteous suffering assault despite their obedience to God. But this alone does not mean that the righteous are justified in defending themselves when under attack. It could still be the case that self-defense is wrong, irrespective of one's state of righteousness. This seems to be Nibley's point of view.[1] In his biography of Nibley, Boyd Petersen includes what he calls Nibley's "chilling warning"[2] about war: "If we persist in reversing the words of the Savior, 'Who takes up the sword shall die by the sword' (cf. Rev. 13:10) to read, perversely, 'who does *not* take up the sword shall perish by the sword,' we shall deserve what happens to us."[3] This remark appeared in a 1971 letter to *The Daily Universe* and seems to consider perverse any call to defensive war. After all, if it is perverse to speak of taking up the sword to defend one's life, it would seem perverse to speak of defense for *any* purpose.[4] Petersen clearly seems to read Nibley's statement as prohibiting defense in this way and, if Nibley's claim is right, it obviously lends support to the pacifist view.

Self-Defense and the Righteous

So, is it right, or wrong, for the righteous to defend themselves when under assault? The first thing to notice about this question is something we saw in Chapter 6 (though it was not emphasized there):[5] In every case we looked at in which the righteous suffered attack from their enemies those righteous people defended themselves. This was true in the case of Captain Moroni's people (Alma 60:12–13 and Alma 48:20–25), the wars reported by Jarom

---

1. In speaking of such self-defense I obviously have in mind defensive acts that are violent in character (e.g., wielding a sword or a gun against an attacker). No important issue is raised by defensive acts that do not take this form (e.g., acts of running, hiding, digging trenches, building forts, and so forth).
2. Boyd Jay Petersen, *Hugh Nibley: A Consecrated Life*, 216; the description is Petersen's.
3. Hugh Nibley, "Renounce War, or a Substitute for Victory," 269.
4. Nibley, "Renounce War, or a Substitute for Victory," 267–69.
5. See the sections "Were the Nephites Always Unrighteous When Involved in War?" and "The Ancient Promise to Nephi."

(Jarom 1:5–7), the combined Nephites and Lamanites following Christ's birth (3 Ne. 2:11–17), and King Benjamin's people (W of M 1:13–14). Not only did these various groups suffer attack when they were righteous, they also defended themselves when they were righteous.

Consider also the Nephite leaders who took up the sword to defend themselves and their people. There is no question about the righteousness and devotion of such men of God—prophets[6] even—and yet they defended themselves militarily. Here is a partial list:

> Nephi: "And I, Nephi, did take the sword of Laban, and after the manner of it did make many swords, lest by any means the people who were now called Lamanites should come upon us and destroy us" (2 Nephi 5:14). And Jacob tells us that Nephi himself "wielded the sword of Laban" in defense of the people (Jacob 1:9).

---

6. It is sometimes thought noteworthy that no book of scripture, including the Book of Mormon, ever specifically uses the designation *prophet* with regard to Nephi (or to some others, for that matter). Other spiritual figures are explicitly identified as prophets—including Abinadi (Mosiah 7:26; Alma 5:11), Alma (Alma 8:20; 10:7), Samuel the Lamanite (3 Ne. 1:9; 8:3; 20:23; Morm. 2:10), Gidgiddoni (3 Ne. 3:19), Lachoneus (3 Ne. 3:19), and Ether (Eth. 12:12)—but neither Nephi nor the brother of Jared nor Mormon nor Moroni ever seems to be explicitly so designated. The same is true of Lehi. Although there are multiple references to Lehi's prophesying and to his visions, nowhere that I see is he specifically designated as a prophet (1 Ne. 1:20 comes the closest). But this array of scriptural facts seems insignificant for two reasons. First, the observation overlooks Nephi's remark that the Nephite records would be kept by prophets (1 Ne. 19:4)—a class which obviously includes himself, Mormon, Moroni, and others. Second, the designation *prophet* is not the defining characteristic of those who qualify for that status in any case. While it is true, for example, that the patriarch Abraham is specifically called a prophet (Gen. 20:7), nowhere in scripture, it seems, are Isaac and Jacob designated this way (3 Ne. 20:25 comes the closest), and neither is Joseph, son of Jacob. The same seems true of both Enoch and Adam. But it is hard to imagine an argument that could convince us that Joseph and Enoch were not prophets, much less Adam. It is also useful to notice that neither Joel nor Daniel is identified as a prophet until the New Testament (see Acts 2:16; Matt. 24:15; D&C 116:1; JS–Matt. 1:12, 32) and that Ezekiel is not so identified until the Doctrine and Covenants (D&C 29:21). But it is not these late announcements that tell us they were prophets, but what they did and how the Lord used them. Jehu, who gave us no canonical teachings, is reported to be a prophet in the Old Testament (1 Kgs. 16:7, 12), while Mormon, who gave us a whole volume of canonical teachings (including his own), is not specifically so designated anywhere in scripture. But it is difficult to see how this difference gives us any reason to conclude that the one was a prophet while the other was not. There seems to be no basis for this and that is why it appears perfectly reasonable to refer to Nephi, Mormon, and Moroni as prophets.

King Benjamin: "And it came to pass also that the armies of the Lamanites came down out of the land of Nephi, to battle against [King Benjamin's] people. But behold, king Benjamin gathered together his armies, and he did stand against them; and *he did fight with the strength of his own arm*, with the sword of Laban" (W of M 1:13).

Alma: "And it came to pass that Alma fought with Amlici with the sword, face to face; and they did contend mightily, one with another" and Alma "was strengthened, insomuch that he slew Amlici with the sword" (Alma 2:29, 31).

Moroni: "A strong and a mighty man . . . a man who did labor exceedingly for the welfare and safety of his people . . . a man who was firm in the faith of Christ" (Alma 48:11–13), and a man whose battles and wartime activities dominate twenty chapters of the Book of Mormon (Alma 43–63).

Mormon: "And notwithstanding I being young, was large in stature; therefore the people of Nephi appointed me that I should be their leader, or the leader of their armies. Therefore it came to pass that in my sixteenth year I did go forth at the head of an army of the Nephites, against the Lamanites" (Morm. 2:1–2).

Moroni, son of Mormon: "And we also beheld the ten thousand of my people who were led [in battle] by my son Moroni" (Morm. 6:12).

If self-defense is a perversion of the Lord's teaching, every one of these Nephite leaders is guilty of such perversion.

Furthermore, according to the record, the Lord actually *helps* victims defend themselves. To consider just one instance recall Helaman's rejoicing at the survival of his stripling warriors and at the victory his army had won with them: "But behold, we trust in our God who has *given* us victory" (Alma 58:33). Far from disapproving of Helaman's military efforts to defend Nephite society, the Lord actually helped him do so. In such cases, if self-defense is a perversion of the Lord's teachings, then the Lord himself is guilty of just such perversion.

Self-Defense and the Unrighteous

But what about the unrighteous? After all, even though we have seen cases where the Nephites were righteous, a common case throughout the Book of Mormon is the *un*righteousness of Nephite society. The Nephites often really were bad guys when they were involved in war and, according to Nibley, the conclusion that should be drawn from this is that the wicked Nephites shared the guilt for the wars that embroiled them—they were not innocent.[7] Although this assertion could be challenged, to simplify matters let's accept it for the moment. The question then is, does anything further follow from this? For

---

7. Hugh Nibley, "Freemen and King-men," 337, 339.

example, in those cases where the Nephites were bad—and therefore brought wars upon themselves—does it follow that they should not have fought back when they were attacked? Did their unrighteousness render self-defense *wrong*?

We need look no further than to the same prophets we have already met to answer this question. Mormon, for instance, tells us that Nephite wars were caused by their own sins (Alma 50:21) and yet, during one of their most wicked periods, Mormon himself urged the people to battle: "I did speak unto my people, and did urge them with great energy, that they would stand boldly before the Lamanites and fight for their wives, and their children, and their houses, and their homes" (Morm. 2:23). Thus, despite the Nephites' abject unrighteousness at the time, Mormon still urged the people to defend themselves militarily and personally led them into battle.

The same is true in the case of Captain Moroni. It is precisely regarding the time of Moroni that Mormon reports that the Nephites' own wickedness had brought their wars upon them (Alma 50:21), and yet the stalwart and faithful Moroni worked with all of his soul to lead those very people in defending themselves. He urged them to greater faithfulness *and* to diligence in defending their liberty.

More than that, it was during this period of time that the Book of Mormon states that the Lord himself helped the Nephites in their defense. As the people responded to the urgings of Moroni and others to repent (Alma 7:7, 17–19), the record tells us that the Lord would warn them "to flee, or to prepare for war, according to their danger" and that he would actually tell them "whither they should go to defend themselves against their enemies" (Alma 48:15–16). So in addition to spurring the Nephites to repentance, Mormon and Moroni also urged the Nephites to defend themselves, and we have explicit record of the Lord helping them do so.

All of this indicates that it is a mistake to focus on the dimension of righteousness and unrighteousness in framing the matter of self-defense. Far more salient is the distinction between aggressors and victims. Even when they were unrighteous the Nephites were the victims of Lamanite aggression, and *this* justified the Nephites in fighting back, whatever their own state of righteousness might have been. This seems the clearest moral that emerges from the frequent conflict between Nephite and Lamanite populations and it reinforces the distinction between aggressors and victims discussed earlier.[8] By emphasizing the matter of Nephite unrighteousness, Nibley attends to a dimension that makes little, if any, difference regarding the propriety of fighting, and simultaneously overlooks a dimension that makes an immense difference on that matter. In the

---

8. See the sections "Anti-Violence Based on Wrong Action" and "The Relational Foundation of Right and Wrong" in Chapter 2.

end, the important distinction regarding the legitimacy of fighting is not between the righteous and the unrighteous, abstractly conceived, but specifically between those who mount aggression and those who are victims of it.

Scriptural Expressions about Defense

The scriptural episodes of self-defense we have examined are not the only incidents that contradict a general condemnation of defensive war. The Lord himself told the Nephites, for example, that "inasmuch as ye are not guilty of the first offense, neither the second, ye shall not suffer yourselves to be slain by the hands of your enemies" and also that "ye shall defend your families even unto bloodshed" (Alma 43:46–47). In the same spirit Mormon approvingly writes that the righteous Nephites "were sorry to take up arms against the Lamanites . . . nevertheless, they could not suffer to lay down their lives, that their wives and their children should be massacred" (Alma 48:23–24). He also reports that "the Nephites were taught to defend themselves against their enemies, even to the shedding of blood if it were necessary," and that they were never to raise the sword "except it were to preserve their lives" (Alma 48:14).

Mormon provides the same explanation for why the Nephites went to war to defend themselves and the people of Ammon against a Lamanite attack: to preserve their rights, privileges, liberties, and lives (Alma 43:7–12). Later, Pahoran explains that the Nephites would not shed blood if only the Lamanites would stay in their own land and not "take the sword against us." He adds that they would subject themselves to the Lamanites if God "should command us to do so." But, he says, "he does not command us that we shall subject ourselves to our enemies," and if words are not sufficient to resist evil rebellions and dissensions, "let us resist them with our swords" (Alma 61:10–14). All of this is enthusiastically agreed to by Captain Moroni and approvingly reported by Mormon. Mere verses later Moroni tells us that he fought in defense precisely because, "It is *according to [the Lord's] commandments*," and he explains that, "I do take my sword to defend the cause of my country" (Alma 60:28).

This theme continues in the Doctrine and Covenants. To the Prophet Joseph Smith the Lord said: "This is the law that I gave unto mine ancients, that they should not go out unto battle against any nation, kindred, tongue, or people, save I, the Lord, commanded them" (D&C 98:33). This statement indicates that there are occasions when the Lord will actually command his people to take up the sword in order not to perish by it. He then explains that if any nation proclaims war, the threatened nation must lift a standard of peace three times. But if it is not accepted, the Lord "would give unto them a commandment, and justify them in going out to battle" (D&C 98:36).

Finally, speaking of the prediction that in the last days it will be "army against army," the Prophet remarks: "It may be that the Saints will have to beat their ploughs into swords, for it will not do for men to sit down patiently and see their children destroyed."⁹ Moreover, not only did Joseph establish the Nauvoo Legion, but he also wielded a handgun to defend himself and his brethren while under attack in Carthage jail. In light of all this it is clear that there is more to the story than some, like Hugh Nibley, suggest when quoting Joseph Smith as saying, "I never did harm any man since I was born in the world. My voice is always for peace."¹⁰ It is true that the Prophet's voice was always for peace, but it is false to suppose that he did not simultaneously countenance self-defense. Obviously, he did. The same can also be said of King Benjamin, Moroni, Pahoran, and Mormon. Their voices were for peace, and yet circumstances still forced them to lead thousands of men into war in self-defense.

The weakness of a total repudiation of defensive war for adherents to the gospel, then, is that it claims far too much. It cannot be true that every appeal to defensive war is perverse when prophets—not to mention the Lord himself—so often make this very appeal. And the situation is no different whether the people are righteous or unrighteous: if they are under attack, they are permitted—even encouraged—to defend themselves. The scriptural record on the matter is clear.

God's Role in the Battles of the Righteous: The Importance of Context

Another claim that could be used to support pacifism is the view that God himself fights the battles of the righteous. Nibley puts the point this way: "The saints were told time and again to stand still and let God fight their battles,"¹¹ and he cites three scriptural passages to reinforce this view:

1. "And I, the Lord, would fight their battles" (D&C 98:37)
2. "As I said in a former commandment, even so will I fulfill—I will fight your battles" (D&C 105:14)
3. "Thou wilt fight for thy people as thou didst in the day of battle, that they may be delivered from the hands of all their enemies" (D&C 109:28)

There are additional passages as well that Nibley could have cited, which all bear the same message:

4. "The Lord your God which goeth before you, he shall fight for you" (Deut. 1:30)
5. "The Lord fought for Israel" (Joshua 10:14)
6. "The battle is not yours, but God's" (2 Chron. 20:1–29)

---

9. Joseph Fielding Smith, comp., *Teachings of the Prophet Joseph Smith*, 366. This is taken from Thomas Bullock's report, which is the most complete record of this sermon. See Andrew F. Ehat and Lyndon W. Cook, *The Words of Joseph Smith*, 367.

10. Hugh Nibley, "Brigham Young and the Enemy," 212–13.

11. Hugh Nibley, "If There Must Needs Be Offense," 271.

This is an impressive collection of promises, and the pacifist reading of them is apparent: God's people need do no fighting to defend themselves because they will be protected by the Lord without having to do so.

Again, though, while this is a very appealing idea, it contains a serious weakness. For example, in the first scriptural passage (D&C 98:37), the meaning of the verse changes entirely when read in context. In the verses immediately preceding it, the Lord says:

> And again, this is the law that I gave unto mine ancients, that they should not go out unto battle against any nation, kindred, tongue, or people, save I, the Lord, commanded them. And if any nation, tongue, or people should proclaim war against them, they should first lift a standard of peace unto that people, nation, or tongue; and if that people did not accept the offering of peace, neither the second nor the third time, they should bring these testimonies before the Lord; then I, the Lord, would give unto them a commandment, and justify them in going out to battle against that nation, tongue, or people (D&C 98:33–36).

It is only after saying all this that the Lord then adds "and I, the Lord, would fight their battles" (D&C 98:37). So this reference to God fighting battles for the righteous actually appears in the context of battles that are already being waged *by* the righteous. Thus, far from asserting that God's people will be kept from battle, the scriptural context actually assumes that God's people will be involved in conflict.

The second two scriptural declarations make no claim of their own, but simply refer to events of the past. In each we are told only that the Lord will fight battles as he has done before, but we are not told what historical events the Lord has in mind. Fortunately, the fourth and fifth passages do refer to specific events. The fourth (Deut. 1:30) reports the words of Moses to Israel at the time the Israelites were commanded to enter the promised land and make it their own. While this appears to support the view that God will do all the work, according to the record the children of Israel themselves waged war at length to take the promised land. While the text reports that the Lord went before them and fought for them, just as Moses promised, he did not fight for them in the way that the pacifist view we are considering would have to suppose. The record tells us that the Lord helped the children of Israel *in* their battles, not that he protected them from having to *fight* such battles.

The fifth scriptural passage is a perfect example of this pattern. It is taken from Joshua 10 and refers to the time that the Amorites attempted to destroy the Israelites. We are told that the Lord "discomfited" these armies and even "cast down great stones from heaven" upon them, and that he "fought for Israel" (Josh. 10:10–14). To this point the record makes it seem as if the Lord has done all the fighting, but then Joshua commands his armies to pursue these enemies, "for God hath delivered them into your hand," and his armies slay the Amorites "with a very great slaughter" (Josh. 10:19–20). Wars continue throughout the remainder of the chapter, summarized with: "And Joshua smote them from Kadesh-barnea even unto Gaza, and all the country of Goshen, even unto Gibeon. And all the kings and their land did Joshua take at one time, *because the Lord God of Israel fought for Israel*" (Josh. 10:41–42).

Ironically, it is explicitly in the context of Israel's *fighting* that we are told that the Lord "fought for Israel." Thus, the record's report of God's fighting does not negate the same record's report of God's people fighting. It clearly says that they did. This instance, along with the others we have seen, demonstrates that a phrase such as "God fights the battles of the righteous," when read in context, cannot mean what Nibley suggests that it means—at least not in the cases we have looked at so far.

How God Most Often Fights the Battles of the Righteous

So what do the scriptures mean when saying that God will fight the battles of the righteous? A clue is found in the Book of Mormon. Consider, for example, the report that "the Lord did strengthen the hand of the Nephites" as Alma's army waged battle with the Amlicites (Alma 2:16–19), and the subsequent report that both Alma's army and Alma himself were "strengthened by the hand of the Lord" (Alma 2:27–31) as the same force later contended with a combined army of Amlicites and Lamanites. Consider also Moroni's contention to Zerahemnah, at the end of a long battle, that the Lord had supported, kept, and preserved the Nephites in conflict because of their faithfulness. He adds that God "has strengthened our arms that we have gained power over you" (Alma 44:3–5). Similarly, Helaman attributes the protection of his stripling sons to "the goodness" and "miraculous power of God" (Alma 57:25–26). Mormon also reports that King Benjamin and his people contended against their enemies "in the strength of the Lord" until "they had slain many thousands of the Lamanites" (W of M 1:14). Finally, after defeating the Gadianton robbers in the greatest slaughter in their history to that time, the Nephites praised God because of "the great thing which he had done for them, in preserving them from falling into the hands of their enemies" and "because of the great goodness of God in delivering them out of the hands of their enemies" (3 Ne. 4:11, 31, 33).

In each of these cases the Nephites' strength and success in waging battle are attributed directly to the Lord. Therein, it would seem, lies the answer to the meaning of the phrase "God fights the battles of the righteous," at least in the cases we have seen so far. In these typical instances the Lord fights battles for the righteous simply by helping them *in* their battles. He fights for them, it is true, but he does not replace them or substitute for them. Thus the people of Gidgiddoni could praise God for preserving and delivering them from the hands of their enemies even though they had been forced to wage a protracted and massive war themselves in order to achieve this outcome

(3 Ne. 4:11–33). The same is true for each of the other examples above: the people had to fight, but the Lord helped them do so. All of this is reinforced when Mormon tells us of a time when he was personally leading the Nephites in war and "the strength of the Lord was *not* with us; yea, *we were left to ourselves*, that the Spirit of the Lord did not abide in us; *therefore we had become weak like unto our brethren*" (Morm. 2:26).

In this connection it is also worth noting that Mormon tells us approvingly that the Nephites believed that if they were righteous "God would prosper them in the land" (referring to the ancient promise we examined in the previous chapter[12]). And how exactly would he prosper them? Knowing how Mormon read the ancient promise the answer is no surprise. The Lord would prosper the Nephites, he says, by warning them "to flee, *or to prepare for war*, according to their danger." Moreover, the Lord would actually tell them "whither they should go to defend themselves against their enemies" (Alma 48:15–16). This, Mormon tells us, is how the Lord "would deliver them" (Alma 48:16), and he even preserves two examples: the Lord revealing enemy troop movements to Alma, the high priest over the Church, to help the Nephites wage war in defending themselves (Alma 16:5–8; 43:22–24).

The same sense of God's deliverance is found in the account of the Chief Captain Gid, who was in charge of Lamanite prisoners of war. When these warriors learned that an army of Lamanites was marching toward the city Cumeni, they took courage and rebelled against Gid's force, attacking them. In consequence, Gid slew most of these captives and then marched to Cumeni to help preserve the city against the Lamanites' assault. And then, despite having been bathed in extensive battle to accomplish this end, Gid exults: "Behold, we are again delivered out of the hands of our enemies. And blessed is the name of our God; for behold, it is he that has delivered us; yea, that has done this great thing for us" (Alma 57:35). Helaman, who received Gid's report, tells us of his own joy "because of the goodness of God in preserving us" (Alma 57:36).

We find the same attitude in Pahoran, who reports of the Lord that "he doth not command us that we shall subject ourselves to our enemies, but that we should put our trust in him, and he will deliver us" (Alma 61:13). He then proceeds to lay out a plan of *military attack* both against Nephite dissenters and the invading Lamanites (Alma 61:14–21). At the end of explaining his military plans, he asks Moroni to "strengthen Lehi and Teancum in the Lord" and to tell them not to fear, "for God will deliver them" (Alma 61:21). In Pahoran's mind, God's deliverance does not remotely imply that the Nephite armies will not have to fight.

---

12. See the section "The Ancient Promise to Nephi" in Chapter 6 and Appendix 2.

The Nephites' conflict with the Gadianton robbers in Third Nephi displays this same sense of "deliverance." There Lachoneus first tells the people that they cannot expect the Lord to deliver them from those robbers if they do not repent and cry unto the Lord (3 Ne. 3:15); and then, after protracted war and many thousands of deaths, when the Nephites finally do prevail, their victory is attributed to "the great goodness of God in delivering them out of the hands of their enemies" (3 Ne. 4:33). God delivered them, it is true, but not in the absence of serious and sustained fighting of their own.

In all of these cases, the only meaning of "God fighting the battles of the righteous" or of God "delivering" his people from their enemies is of God helping the righteous *in* their battles. He helps them *prevail*. He does not prevent such battles from occurring in the first place or deliver his people in a way that they themselves never have to fight. At least this is the nature of the record regarding Joshua, the children of Israel generally, and King Benjamin, Alma, Moroni, Gid, Helaman, Pahoran, Gidgiddoni, and Mormon.

Literal Cases of God Fighting the Battles of the Righteous

There are a few examples, however, in which Nibley's understanding does seem to apply. The sixth scriptural passage mentioned above (2 Chron. 20) describes such a time. Multiple nations were gathered against Judah, and the Lord arranged for these people to war among themselves and to destroy each other. The Lord had told Judah, "the battle is not yours, but God's" (2 Chron. 20:15), and at the end we are informed that "the fear of God was on all the kingdoms of those countries, when they had heard that the Lord fought against the enemies of Israel" (2 Chron. 20:29).

Similarly, the record tells us that the children of Israel had to take no arms when the pursuing Egyptians were drowned in the Red Sea (Ex. 14). In that case, too, when we are told of the Lord's promise that "the Lord shall fight for you" (Ex. 14:14), we are obviously to take this promise in the strict and literal sense.

Another example is found in the Lord's protection of Alma and his small band in Mosiah 24. In that incident the Lord caused a "deep sleep" to come upon their Lamanite captors and then warned Alma to flee, telling him that "I will stop the Lamanites in this valley that they come no further in pursuit of this people" (Mosiah 24:23). Here, too, in an important sense the Lord literally fought the battles of these righteous people.

We see a fourth example in the account of Elisha in 2 Kings 6. We are told that the king of Syria, angered at Elisha for helping protect the king of Israel from him, surrounded the city where Elisha lived. When Elisha's servant expressed alarm at the sight of the Syrian army, Elisha "prayed, and said, Lord, I pray thee, open his eyes that he may see. And the Lord opened the eyes of the young man; and he saw: and, behold, the mountain was full of horses and chariots of fire round about Elisha" (2 Kgs. 6:17). At this point Elisha asked the Lord to smite the Syrians with blindness, whereupon he led them away to Samaria. Once in Samaria, the Lord restored their sight, the king of Israel feasted them at Elisha's direction, and the Syrians were then sent away to "their master" (2 Kgs. 6:18–23). This is a clear example in the record of the Lord literally protecting his people (in this case, Elisha) from suffering harm.

A final example is the account of the people of Enoch as described in Moses 7:13–16. In that account, when their enemies came against them, Enoch "spake the word of the Lord, and the earth trembled, and the mountains fled . . . and all nations feared greatly, so powerful was the word of Enoch" (Moses 7:13). Although the account is brief and incomplete, the power of God is the element that is emphasized in the record, and that power is wonderfully miraculous. In this case, too, God fought battles for his people, and it appears that he did so literally.[13]

What Accounts for the Difference?

There is some variation, then, in how scriptural texts use the expression "God fights the battles of the righteous,"[14] and this presents us with a puzzle. On one hand there are examples of the Lord literally fighting battles for his people. On the other hand there are far more examples of the Lord not helping in this way at all, but only helping his people *in* their battles—with the scriptures still referring to such assistance as "fighting battles" or as "delivering" his people. So how are we to account for the difference? Why does the Lord help in one way in a few cases, and yet help in another way in far more?

Differing Circumstances

One possibility has to do with differing circumstances. In Alma's case, for example, it is relevant that his people numbered only about four hundred and fifty (Mosiah 18:35), that they were newly formed and had no army (or anything close to it, in all likelihood), and that they were being occupied at

---

13. Note, however, that Enoch's experience further weakens Nibley's earlier claim, examined in Chapter 6, that the Nephites would have faced no attack at all if they had been righteous (and presumably that others would not face wars if they satisfied the same condition). After all, the people of Enoch were unparalleled in righteousness, and yet God fought battles for them *precisely because they were under attack*. So, despite what Nibley's claim would predict, these people's pre-eminent righteousness did not prevent them from suffering assault from their enemies.

14. This should not be surprising since this is not the only example. The scriptures also use the term "faith" in multiple ways, for instance, and only context can tell us which usage a given passage intends. A treatment of two such usages of "faith" is found in my "Faith as a Holy Embrace," 107–27.

the time by a large army of Lamanites. This constellation of circumstances is not the norm in other incidents of enemy confrontation in scripture, and may explain the Lord's out-of-the-norm action in this case. The same may be true regarding the destruction of the Egyptians at the Red Sea. The Israelites at the time, though large in numbers, had barely left Egypt after centuries of living in slavery and had certainly formed nothing like an army. This was not the case decades later, however, when they were expected to prepare for war, to enter battle, and to take the promised land from those who currently occupied it.[15] The circumstances at the Red Sea were dissimilar, and this may explain the difference in the nature of the Lord's intervention and in the nature of his expectations of his people in that case.

Degree of Righteousness?

Another possibility is that the Lord intervenes differently in different cases based on the degree of righteousness possessed by the population in question. Perhaps the Lord helps righteous people in general by helping them in their battles, while he helps people who are the *most* righteous by fighting their battles for them literally.

While this may seem like a promising explanation at first glance, the problem with it becomes apparent when we consider the Ammonites. It is easy to see the Ammonites as among the best people in the Book of Mormon, but it is important to note that God did not fight battles in a literal way for *them*. On two occasions he permitted many of the Ammonites to be slaughtered, and in all other cases he left them to rely on the Nephites and their own sons for a defense of their lives. Indeed, Mormon tells us that the Ammonites suffered death "in the most aggravating and distressing manner" in the same

---

15. See the section "God's Role in the Battles of the Righteous: The Importance of Context" earlier in this chapter. Also, recall that these nations were wicked and that the land would not have been given to the children of Israel in the first place had this not been the case. Nephi reports: "And after they [the Israelites] had crossed the river Jordan he did make them mighty unto the driving out of the children of the land, yea, unto the scattering them to destruction. And now, do ye suppose that the children of this land, who were in the land of promise, who were driven out by our fathers, do ye suppose that they were righteous? Behold, I say unto you, Nay. Do ye suppose that our fathers would have been more choice than they if they had been righteous? I say unto you, Nay. Behold, the Lord esteemeth all flesh in one; he that is righteous is favored of God. But behold, this people had rejected every word of God, and they were ripe in iniquity; and the fulness of the wrath of God was upon them; and the Lord did curse the land against them, and bless it unto our fathers; yea, he did curse it against them unto their destruction, and he did bless it unto our fathers unto their obtaining power over it" (1 Ne. 17:32–35).

breath that he tells us they were "highly favored" of the Lord (Alma 27:29–30). So that forces us to ask, did even the Ammonites fail to measure up?

The Ammonites, however, are not the only problem. There is also the rarefied instance of the completely unified and purified Nephites and Lamanites of 3 Nephi, who, as we saw in the previous chapter, were also forced to take up arms against the Gadianton robbers in defense of their lives (3 Ne. 2:11–17). If the possibility we are considering here is true—that the most righteous, at least, will never have to fight—then why did God not come to *their* defense and spare *them* the need to take up arms to defend themselves?

Such cases make it implausible to imagine that we can account for these differences in scriptural cases by appealing to degrees of righteousness. That approach forces us to characterize the most dramatic and compelling examples of righteousness in the Book of Mormon as not dramatic and compelling enough. Though a possible view, it does not seem plausible, much less persuasive or compelling.

The Central Question

But even if we were to consider the claim compelling, it would still do little to help us with the central question of the view we are examining: whether or not it is true that all war, including defensive war, is unjustified. To see this, think again of Enoch's people. If we consider them among the best people of all, and if we suppose that the Lord will single-handedly fight battles only for people who are their spiritual equals, then what does that suggest about everyone else? Does it follow that no one else can ever defend themselves? And does it follow that the Lord will *help* no one else defend themselves? As we have seen in this chapter, the answer to both questions is no. There are abundant examples of people less faithful than the people of Enoch righteously defending themselves, and there are abundant examples of the Lord actively helping them do so.

Thus, even if it were true that the most righteous genuinely never have to fight, it would not follow that less righteous people never have to fight or that they would be wrong in doing so. Among others we have considered in this chapter, the Ammonites and the Nephites and Lamanites of 3 Nephi 2 demonstrate this.[16]

In the final analysis, the most we seem able to say about God fighting the battles of the righteous is that he sometimes does so literally (most likely based on the peculiarity of the circumstances at the time), but most of the

---

16. It should be remembered that it has not been shown in the first place that those who are the most righteous never have to fight. We have seen a handful of cases, it is true, in which people did not have to defend themselves, but (1) those cases are significantly in the minority, and (2) it is simply implausible that degree of righteousness was the factor that made them different in any case.

time he does not. The implication that the righteous never have to fight because God will do all the fighting for them does not find support in scripture. At a minimum, the promise of God's protection is a far more complicated and subtle matter than the claim we are considering suggests.

Predisposition and Its Effects

As seen over the last four chapters, Nibley's mistakes include his claims regarding the Ammonites, the Nephites' status when under attack, the Lord's early promise to Nephi, the ability of discussion to prevent conflict, the attitude of Mormon and Moroni toward the necessity of war, the propriety of self-defense (by both the righteous and the unrighteous), and the nature of the Lord's involvement in war. Such a pattern suggests that Nibley, particularly in his later writings,[17] read the Book of Mormon with a predisposition toward a pacifist point of view and thus tended to read in a way that simply confirmed this perspective, thereby leading to the errors we have seen.[18] That same predisposed reading of the text also manifests itself in brief asides that Nibley makes from time to time. These remarks, while clever, actually mischaracterize important matters regarding violence. They simply reveal, again,

---

17. In *An Approach to the Book of Mormon*, published in 1964, Nibley devoted thousands of words to wars in the Book of Mormon, and displayed a general attitude of necessity and resignation regarding such conflicts. In 1967, however, he published *Since Cumorah* in which he first emphasized that Book of Mormon wars were always between "bad guys and other bad guys" and in which he expressed greater impatience toward war generally. Then, in 1971, Nibley published an *Ensign* article in which he actually set out a justification for defensive war. He noted there the distinction between the general prohibition against war and the Lord's commandment for it in specific instances, and he also observed that a crucial variable in war is the "spirit" in which things are done—noting first the nobility of Captain Moroni, even in his wartime conduct, and second, the difference between David and Goliath, even though both engaged in fighting; see "If There Must Needs Be Offense," 270–77. Following this 1971 article, however, it is difficult to find a statement from Nibley that is as friendly to such distinctions as he is in this paper. Observations from this point on, including to the end of his life, emphasize the wickedness of war, and in general display his pacifist impulse.

18. It is true, of course, that unexamined assumptions and predispositions play some role in all intellectual inquiry, including in our study of the Book of Mormon. But since some assumptions are far more overt than others, not all are equally difficult to identify and examine. Nibley, for example, knew that his pacifist thinking about the Book of Mormon was a minority point of view, and this might easily have led him to take up the topic in a systematic and comprehensive way. He could have identified all of the elements of the text that suggest a non-pacifist interpretation and then attempted to rebut them methodically and with care. Although that would have been a natural course, and although it would have provided a nice examination of his assumption, nowhere does Nibley do this.

the risks of reading with bias. Examples include off-the-cuff comments regarding Teancum, Alma, Ammon, and "Orwellianism."

Teancum and Amalickiah

In his "Warfare and the Book of Mormon," Nibley begins by quoting Clausewitz, the great historian and commentator on war, that "the ruthless user of force who shrinks from no amount of bloodshed must gain an advantage if his opponent does not do the same." He then remarks that "Teancum and Amalickiah typify this principle."[19] This, of course, is a reference to Amalickiah's fomenting of large-scale aggressive war against the Nephites (Alma 46–51), and to Teancum's role in waging battles in defense—as well as to his stealth in slaying two Lamanite army leaders, including Amalickiah (Alma 51, 62). Nibley lumps these two Book of Mormon figures together, saying that jointly they exemplify the mutual ruthlessness of war.

But characterizing the matter this way seems to do violence to the record, not to mention to Teancum. In treating Teancum equivalently to Amalickiah we must either overlook or disregard three obvious features of the record: (1) Amalickiah was treacherous and murderous in character (Alma 46–47), while Teancum possessed a Christlike nature—as demonstrated, to name one example, by his attitude of forgiveness in extremely trying circumstances (Alma 50:25–36); (2) Amalickiah started and perpetuated a war of aggression that resulted in many thousand deaths (Alma 46–51), while Teancum fought only in defense *against* aggression (Alma 51–53, 61); and (3) Amalickiah kept the company of ambitious, wicked, and murderous men (Alma 46:3–5, 10; 47:1–3), while Teancum kept the company of Moroni and Lehi (Alma 50, 52, 61, 62). It is little wonder that Mormon describes Amalickiah as a "very wicked man," of "cunning device" (Alma 46:9–10), and as "a very subtle man to do evil" (Alma 47:4), while he goes out of his way to praise Teancum (Alma 62:37).

Treating Teancum and Amalickiah as analogous thus relies on a single superficial similarity between the two while disregarding the monumental differences that existed between them. This is unfortunate because, swift as it is, the comment invites agreement, not evaluation, and serves to blur the very distinctions that matter most in making judgments about individuals' involvement in war.

Alma and Amlici

A similar obscured reading of the Book of Mormon occurs when Nibley asserts that the fight (Nibley calls it a "duel") between the prophet Alma and the conspiring and evil Amlici was not a clear case of the righteous in battle against the wicked—or, as Nibley picturesquely puts it, "a good guy against

---

19. Hugh Nibley, "Warfare and the Book of Mormon," 283.

a bad guy"—because the Nephites later admitted that the war had occurred because of their own wickedness.[20]

While this claim regarding Alma and Amlici is interesting, making it requires a leap of logic and a distorted reading of the text. After all, even if we stipulate that Nephite society was unrighteous at the time of the conflict between the two men, it does not follow that each citizen of Nephite society (including Alma) was unrighteous. It is for this reason, apparently, that Nibley draws attention to Alma's status as a representative of Nephite society,[21] implying that, despite whatever his own level of righteousness may have been, Alma's participation in this war was a result of the unrighteousness of the two battling societies. Relying on this, Nibley can feel comfortable in denying that Alma himself counts as "a good guy" in the situation.

The first problem with this approach, however, is its failure to recognize the full scope of Alma's surrogate role. After all, in addition to being a representative *of* Nephite society, Alma also served as a representative of the Lord *to* Nephite society. It is difficult to see any sense in which Alma failed to qualify as a "good guy" in this aspect of his proxy status, and, if we think his proxy status is relevant (as Nibley does), then we must account for *this* part of it in any judgment about what to call Alma in the situation (i.e., whether "good guy" or not).

But even more important, it is still worth asking what it means to say that the populace Alma represented was unrighteous. Recall, for example, that Nephite unrighteousness differed significantly from Lamanite unrighteousness, and that it posed no threat to the Lamanites.[22] Remember too that the Lord himself strengthened the Nephites in their defense at this time, as well as specifically strengthening Alma in his battle with Amlici (Alma 2:28–31). Finally, recall that the Lord explicitly justified the Nephites, in general, in defending themselves from Lamanite attack.[23] These facts make it apparent that it is unnecessarily and misleadingly narrow to limit our description of Nephite society to a single general designation of unrighteousness—i.e., "bad." Because its members fought only defensively, and because the Lord actually assisted them in doing so, we could with equal accuracy describe Nephite society as "no-threat-to-their-neighbors," as "strengthened-by-the-Lord-in-fighting," and as "justified-by-the-Lord-in-fighting." It is a distortion

---

20. Nibley, "Warfare and the Book of Mormon," 283; see also "Freemen and Kingmen," 337–38.

21. Nibley, "Warfare and the Book of Mormon," 282.

22. See the section in Chapter 6, "Differences in the Character of Nephite and Lamanite Unrighteousness."

23. See the sections earlier in this chapter, "Scriptural Expressions about Defense" and "How God Most Often Fights the Battles of the Righteous."

of the record to think of the Nephites only as "bad guys" and thus to think that Alma failed to be a good guy because he represented them.

At the same time, it is significant that such descriptions could *not* be applied to Amlici and his society. They did in fact present a serious threat to their neighbors and they enjoyed nothing like justification from the Lord in fighting. The contrast is stark, and demonstrates in obvious fashion the radical asymmetry that existed between Alma and Amlici. The casual disregard of this asymmetry appears clever on the surface, but at a deeper level it actually does nothing so much as dishonor both Alma and Nephite society.

This is why, in addition, it seems insulting (doesn't it?) to refer to the clash between Alma and Amlici as a "duel" in the first place. That term both trivializes the nature of their conflict and implies that the two were somehow equals—when, morally and spiritually speaking, they could hardly have been more different. The expression is clever but far from accurate.

Ammon

Similar indifference appears in Nibley's remarks about Ammon. Well known is the account of Ammon and his companions embarking on their mission to the Lamanites while other Nephites, completely skeptical of any success, "laughed them to scorn," thinking it better to wage war against the Lamanites than to attempt to teach them the gospel (see Alma 26:23–26). Nibley emphasizes that Ammon preached to the Lamanites rather than seeking to destroy them, and that he suffered all manner of tribulation along the way.[24] It is with this in mind that Nibley tells us that Ammon "renounced all military solutions to the Lamanite problem,"[25] and tells us that "that is the way you deal with the bad guys."[26]

But surely it is relevant in any discussion of Ammon to acknowledge that he did not "renounce all military solutions" *whatever* and that he did not believe that preaching the gospel was "the way you deal with the bad guys" *uniformly*. Ammon embraced violence at the waters of Sebus, doing nothing close to teaching the gospel in that situation (Alma 17:25–39). He killed some of the plunderers and permanently maimed others, and would have caused even greater damage had they not begun "to flee before him." And Ammon later threatened to kill the father of King Lamoni two separate times, first in self-defense and then in order to extract a promise from him (Alma 20:7–28). Surely all of this must be mentioned in any discussion of Ammon's attitude toward "military solutions" and toward "the way you deal with the

---

24. Hugh Nibley, "Scriptural Perspectives on How to Survive the Calamities of the Last Days," 486-87; also Hugh Nibley, "'Exemplary Manhood,'" 515-16.

25. Nibley, "Scriptural Perspectives on How to Survive the Calamities of the Last Days," 492.

26. Ibid., 487.

bad guys." Instead, Nibley's description obscures the truth about Ammon's conduct and encourages the drawing of a false conclusion from it.[27]

"Orwellianism"

A similar example occurs when Nibley uses the term "Orwellian" to describe a reference to military personnel as "peacemakers."[28] Behind a complaint of this sort is the assumption that, since war and peace are contradictory states, it is duplicitous to refer to warriors as entering conflict to establish peace.

A reading of the Book of Mormon, however, demonstrates that this is commonly how righteous warriors in that book are described. Mormon, for example, approvingly reports a time when Captain Moroni's armies "gathered themselves, and armed themselves, and entered into a covenant *to keep the peace*" (Alma 46:31). And in another example from Moroni, we see in a single chapter both his steadfast commitment to seeking peace at every opportunity *and* his steadfast commitment

---

27. It also seems significant that Nibley misreads part of the account. One verse reads: "Now six of them had fallen by the sling, but he slew none save it were their leader with his sword; and he smote off as many of their arms as were lifted against him, and they were not a few" (Alma 17:38). Nibley interprets this passage to mean that Ammon actually slew no one but the leader—"he only contended with the leader to death"—suggesting that this demonstrates Ammon's restraint; see Hugh Nibley, "The Book of Mormon: Forty Years After," 540. But Nibley's reading is mistaken. In addition to the expression "had fallen" (v. 38)—which, though not explicit, certainly implies death—two verses earlier we are explicitly told that Ammon "slew a certain number of them" (v. 36), and later we read Ammon's report to the king, framed in the form of a question: "Is it because thou hast heard that I defended thy servants and thy flocks, and *slew seven of their brethren* with the sling and with the sword, and smote off the arms of others, in order to defend thy flocks and thy servants; behold, is it this that causeth thy marvelings?" (Alma 18:16) So it is obvious that Ammon killed more of the band than just their leader. The verse Nibley relies on means only that Ammon slew six of the marauders *with a sling*, and that the leader was the only one who died by the sword. Nibley's misreading is significant because it is difficult to see how anything but a predisposition to Ammon in a particular way could explain the failure to understand what the account says of him more than once.

28. This occurred in a letter to the editor of *This People* magazine, where Nibley is listed as one of the authors of the letter; see "Letters to the Editor," *This People*, February/March, 1987, 8–9. The letter called "Orwellian" the title of an earlier article in the magazine, "Blessed Are the Peacemakers: LDS in the Military;" see JoAnn Jolley, "Blessed Are the Peacemakers: LDS in the Military," *This People*, June/July, 1984, 66–73. Although I recall both issues of the magazine and their contents, neither is currently found in the Harold B. Lee Library of Brigham Young University, so I am relying on the bibliographic information provided by Nibley's biographer; see Boyd Jay Petersen, *Hugh Nibley: A Consecrated Life*, 219, where he also refers to the episode.

to waging war to achieve it (Alma 44). And it was *his* army that entered the covenant "to keep the peace" in the first place and that armed itself to do so.[29]

In another example, Mormon praises Gidgiddoni (whom he calls "a great prophet"—3 Ne. 3:19) and other leaders who established "great peace in the land" (3 Ne. 6:6). Among their methods for doing so, Mormon reports that "Gidgiddoni commanded that his armies should pursue [the Gadianton robbers] as far as the borders of the wilderness, and that they should not spare any that should fall into their hands by the way" (3 Ne. 4:11–13). Later, Gidgiddoni surrounded the Gadianton invaders so that they could not retreat from battle; as a result many were taken prisoner, "and the remainder of them were slain" (3 Ne. 4:27).

Mormon also tells us of Pahoran and Moroni who "restored peace to the land of Zarahemla" (Alma 62:11). They did this in part by putting to death rebellious and hostile Nephites, inflicting "death upon all those who were not true to the cause of freedom" (see Alma 62:9–11).[30] This is how they restored peace to that part of the land.

As a final example, think of King Benjamin who, the record tells us, "did once more establish peace in the land" (W of M 1:18). As we saw in Chapter 6, many elements were involved in his efforts, but among them, King Benjamin: "gathered together his armies;" fought "with the strength of his own arm;" contended "in the strength of the Lord;" slew with his army "many thousands of the Lamanites;" and contended against the invading armies until they had "driven them out of all the lands of their inheritance" (W of M 1:13–14). King Benjamin was a warrior of the first rank and the record informs us that the context of all of his war efforts was the desire to establish peace.

Such examples from the Book of Mormon suggest that, whatever its cleverness, it is fallacious to designate as "Orwellian" any description of military personnel in terms of seeking peace. Since that description appears multiple times in the Book of Mormon, are we to call the Book of Mormon itself Orwellian?[31]

---

29. Nibley sometimes sees this point, or something close to it. See, for example, "Freemen and King-men," 352, but it receives no attention in this public letter.

30. I take it that not being true to the cause of freedom included actually fighting against it, as verse 9 suggests. That the king-men did so is explicitly stated in Alma 60:16.

31. Nibley alerts us to the seductiveness of "rhetoric," explaining that one of Satan's favorite tricks is to manipulate our minds "with false words and appearances." He adds that "every rhetorician knows that his most effective weapons by far are *labels*" and that the opposition can be demolished "with simple and devastating labels such as communism, socialism, or atheism, popery, militarism, or Mormonism, or give his clients' worst crimes a religious glow with noble labels such as integrity, old-fashioned honesty, tough-mindedness, or free competitive enterprise." See Hugh Nibley, "What is Zion? A Distant View," 53–54; emphasis his. Most find it difficult to live up to

Conclusion

Despite first appearances, the claim that Book of Mormon wars were always between bad guys and other bad guys ultimately lends no support to the pacifist view. In the first place, we saw in Chapter 6 that the claim is simply inaccurate; and in the second place, we have seen in this chapter that the Nephites were justified in defending themselves *whether they were righteous or not*. In both cases, scripture records prophets and other men of God urging the Nephites to defend themselves from Lamanite assault.

The claim that appeals to self-defense are a perversion of the Lord's words fares no better. It cannot be true that every appeal to defensive war is perverse when scripture includes so many appeals of exactly this sort. Most glaringly, it seems impossible to maintain this claim in the face of the Lord not only commanding his people to defend themselves, but also actually helping them do so.

Moreover, the idea that God will straightforwardly do all the fighting for the righteous—and thereby relieve them of the need to take up arms themselves—is not supported in the scriptural canon. The reality on this matter is much more nuanced and is far from supporting a pacifist conclusion about war.

Finally, there is no sound reason for treating Teancum as though he were in any way similar to Amalickiah, for failing to describe Alma as a "good guy" in his lethal conflict with Amlici, for failing to see the full truth about Ammon when using him to support anti-violence claims, and for suggesting that it is automatically illegitimate to explain war in the name of seeking peace. Such elements make their appearance in Nibley's commentary, but the scriptural record itself shows them all to be mistaken.

There is a pattern of error, then, in the claims made by Nibley, and certainly a pattern this pronounced cannot be due to mere inaccuracy in reading; it must be due to a point of view that actually influenced his study. Reading in this way has certain costs, and we have observed some of them in these chapters. While various claims made by Nibley might seem to support a pacifist conclusion, in the end they all fail.

Nibley, of course, is not the only LDS author to show a strong pacifist impulse and to believe that the scriptures support such a view. Many others have carried on Nibley's legacy in mining and reinterpreting the scriptures to argue for pacifism. The next five chapters—8 through 12—will consider recent treatments by other LDS authors on the matter of war and peace.

---

every standard they espouse, and that is what is evident here: Nibley's use of the label "Orwellian" in this context is not different from the rhetoric he condemns.

Chapter 8

A "Narrative" Reading of the Book of Mormon: Part One

With an ordinary, though careful, reading of the text it seems impossible to draw a pacifist message from the Book of Mormon. As we have seen, the Anti-Nephi-Lehies were not the pacifists they are frequently thought to have been. Furthermore, examples of prophets and other significant spiritual leaders taking up the sword to defend themselves from Lamanite assault are ample, from Nephi, King Benjamin, and Alma to Gidgiddoni, Mormon, and Moroni. Previous chapters have also identified multiple examples of not only the Lord's approval of his people defending themselves militarily, but also of his actual assistance to them in doing so. On the face of it, the text of the Book of Mormon seems to close off the possibility of anything like a pacifist reading.

A Narrative Interpretation

But could there be a novel interpretation of the text that gives new life to the possibility? One candidate for such an interpretation is through a narrative reading of the Book of Mormon, such as argued by Joshua Madson.[1] This approach emphasizes the global character of the telling of events in the book. For example, it recognizes that the story has a beginning, a middle, and an end, and that the end of the book—that is, the culmination of the book's full historical and spiritual sweep—is essential to telling us the story's overall theme. A narrative approach of this sort seems appealing since Mormon himself, "the primary narrator, confirms that there is an intent and theme to his work," from which it naturally follows that the book is "a narrative by design" and that it is thus explicitly intended to be read "as a whole."[2] In a book of this kind we are to look for its moral message in the *whole* book rather than in whatever propositions appear here and there throughout. We are to look "to the meaning of the story" itself, seeing that as primary, and understanding that "statements and propositions ultimately serve the story and are to be understood in light of the import of the larger narrative."[3]

---

1. See Joshua Madson, "A Non-Violent Reading of the Book of Mormon," 13–28.
2. Ibid., 15.
3. Ibid., 22.

As we read the Book of Mormon, then, we cannot take various statements or episodes to have meaning apart from how they fit into the larger story; if we do, we are likely to be misled. This is true even of statements by spiritual figures explicitly identified as prophets. What they say is not dispositive. If they either assume, or explicitly assert, a proposition that is not consistent with the overall theme of the larger narrative—or if they *act* in a way that is not consistent with it—then those spiritual figures are best thought of as imperfect beings who, though doing their best, have simply misunderstood what God genuinely intends.[4]

In understanding the Book of Mormon narrative it is particularly important to appreciate the appearance of Christ in Third Nephi. As Madson writes, "At the center of the Book of Mormon we find a resurrected Christ who interrupts the narrative and compels us to reinterpret the entire history and future of the Lehite civilization."[5] The Lord's teachings on this occasion are "the interpretive key to understanding the Book of Mormon's overall narrative,"[6] and they are viewed as critical to the pacifist conclusion, because here Jesus "denounces all sacrificial violence, including war" and identifies converted Lamanite pacifist behavior as "a perfect imitation of Christ" and the essence of genuine conversion.[7] With this approach it is argued that during his personal appearance Jesus made declarations about how we are to live that are "corrective" of any opposing claims that may be found or implied elsewhere in the Book of Mormon.[8] Thus, "justifications for violence, taken from teachings and actions in the first three acts of the Book of Mormon, no longer trump the corrective teachings of Jesus in Act 4."[9] In this narrative approach we value Jesus' teachings above all other claims in the text and see any assertions in support of violence to be "inherently suspect" because such claims "are not in harmony with the life, words, and death of Jesus of Nazareth."[10]

---

4. A very general description of the narrative approach to scripture, based on the form it takes in Biblical studies, is found at http://www.patheos.com/blogs/rogereolson/2011/10/narrative-theology-following-up-on-my-review-of-smiths-book-about-biblicism/.
5. Ibid., 24.
6. Ibid., 24. See also, 25.
7. Ibid., 25.
8. Ibid., 15, 28.
9. Ibid., 28.
10. Ibid., 16, fn. 6. Reference to "the life, words, and death of Jesus of Nazareth" implies a pacifist view of the Lord. Taking up this matter is not important in this chapter, but we have already examined incidents, in Chapters 6 and 7, that suggest natural questions about such a claim. I explicitly take up the matter of Jesus' pacifism in the section "Inadequate Conception of Jesus' Personality" in Chapter 10 and in the

According to this view, another key element in understanding the overall narrative of the Book of Mormon is how it ends. Since one very large aspect of the book's conclusion is the destruction of Nephite civilization, it is natural to presume that we are to see the moral of the book in this dramatic outcome. If so, then the message would seem to be that conflict is both evil and futile—i.e., that "those who live by the sword die by the sword, and that violence begets violence."[11] Nephite history itself thus stands as a testament against resorting to violence "by showing the eventual results of living in such a manner,"[12] where what we see in "Nephite destruction" are "the consequences of choosing violence."[13] According to this view, the Book of Mormon argues for pacifism by the very nature of the narrative it provides: the Nephites resorted to violence, and that dependence on violence was the cause of their eventual destruction. It follows that resorting to violence is wrong. *Quod erat demonstrandum.*[14]

The final key element in understanding the overall narrative of the Book of Mormon is how it begins, with the slaying of Laban by Nephi. This, we are told, was the beginning of Nephite civilization, which means that the civilization was "founded upon a violent act"[15] and that this "founding murder"[16] set Lehite society on a violent path. Thus, "in effect, any threat to future Nephite society could be recast into the foundational framework," so that later Nephites were justified "in killing Lamanites or others now demonized as enemies and existential threats."[17] It is this path that we see unfold over the centuries, ultimately leading to the Nephites' demise.

Four key claims, then, seem to lie at the core of this narrative reading of the Book of Mormon: because Mormon had an intent and theme in creating the record, and because that theme turns out to be pacifist in character, it was Mormon's intent to create that pacifist theme in his book; because of its violent ending, the story of Nephite civilization is a story with a pacifist moral; Christ's personal teachings in Third Nephi are pacifist in character; and finally, Nephite civilization failed to live up to the pacifist ideal because

---

section "Old Testament Violence and the Prince of Peace" in Chapter 11. I consider the meaning of Christ's behavior in the events leading up to and including his death in the section "Christ's Death" in Chapter 11.

11. Ibid., 27.
12. Ibid., 16, fn. 6.
13. Ibid., 16.
14. Assumed in this argument is what I take to be the unobjectionable premise that (other things equal, at least) it was undesirable for the Nephite civilization to end.
15. Ibid., 17.
16. Ibid.
17. Ibid., 19.

Nephi himself set the society on a violent path at its inception. These four claims combine to compel a pacifist reading of the Book of Mormon and this pacifist reading then gives rise to an important corollary: any *non*-pacifist elements of the text, whether in the form of words or actions, are simply mistaken. We are to see such features in light of the overall theme of the book and to reinterpret them accordingly, regardless of how they have been traditionally understood. Reading the text in this narrative way we are able to appreciate "the anti-war message of the Book of Mormon" and to see that it is "in fact an anti-war text."[18]

Intellectual Soundness

Two Examinations

Such a narrative interpretation of the Book of Mormon is theoretically possible, of course. But theoretical possibility is not equivalent to intellectual soundness. To determine soundness we need to examine the approach in two ways. The first is to consider the central corollary of the narrative approach: the idea that non-pacifist elements of the text are mistaken and should be reinterpreted. This is an effective place to begin because it helps us appreciate what is at stake—exactly how much of the record must be reinterpreted in light of narrative claims. Further, we are able to consider whether the reinterpretations that follow from narrative claims seem plausible or implausible. These are questions we will take up in the remainder of this chapter through consideration of three examples: Captain Moroni, the Lord as portrayed in the Book of Mormon, and Nephi.

The second investigation is to discover whether the central claims of this narrative interpretation make sense of the text according to the interpretation's own assumptions. Madson assumes, for instance, that his claim about the pacifist character of Christ's teachings in Third Nephi requires support from the text. As we will see in the next chapter, he appeals to other scriptural passages to substantiate his reading of Third Nephi, which means that he considers such textual support to be important. If we make the same assumption, then the natural course is to examine those scriptural passages to determine the degree to which, if any, they provide the support claimed for them. In asking this question we are doing nothing more than examining this particular narrative reading according to its own assumptions. It is a question we will be asking in the next chapter about each of the four central claims of this narrative approach.

---

18. Ibid., 14.

Examining the Corollary of the Narrative Approach: The Example of Captain Moroni

Again, the corollary of the narrative approach we are examining is that non-pacifist elements of the Book of Mormon text must be reinterpreted. They must be understood in a way that instantiates the overall theme of the book rather than in a way that opposes it.

An example of this sort is found in the case of Captain Moroni. We have seen previously that during Moroni's time the Book of Mormon explicitly justifies going to battle by appealing to the Nephites' need to defend their lives, families, lands, country, rights, and religion (Alma 43:47). On the face of it, this seems like a strong set of reasons for going to war, and, found in the Book of Mormon as it is, this rationale seems to carry a lot of weight, not to mention divine approval.

But if (in accordance with the narrative approach) we read this incident in light of the theme of the Book of Mormon as a whole, we do not actually learn from it that war is justified in one circumstance or another. Instead, we learn from the incident that it was exactly this way of thinking, repeated many times over the centuries, which actually led to the destruction of Nephite society. Thus, rather than reading the account of Captain Moroni in isolation from the rest of the text, we must read such "pro-war" elements in light of "the good news" of Jesus' pacifist message regarding violence and conflict.[19] When we do this we no longer study Moroni's battles "ignorant of Jesus's teachings,"[20] and we recognize that "it is not to Captain Moroni . . . that we should look for our views on war" at all, but to "the larger narrative and subsequent acts, especially as they resolve or explain the problem of violence." Doing so, we realize that "certain parts—or acts—of this story are no longer morally determinative for us today."[21]

In short, according to this narrative view, the Book of Mormon itself nullifies Captain Moroni's conduct as an example for us to emulate. His behavior actually illustrates what we should *not* do.

Reverberations

While this kind of reading of Captain Moroni might seem appealing to some, it is important to appreciate the consequences it leaves in its wake. First is the question it creates regarding Mormon's attitude toward Captain Moroni. Mormon describes Captain Moroni as a man of "perfect understanding," for example, and as "firm in the faith of Christ" (Alma 48:11, 13). He tells us that

---

19. Ibid., 27.
20. Ibid.
21. Ibid., 15–16.

"if all men had been, and were, and ever would be, like unto Moroni, behold, the very powers of hell would have been shaken forever; yea, the devil would never have power over the hearts of the children of men" (Alma 48:17). It seems unlikely that Mormon, who himself saw the Lord at age fifteen (Morm. 1:15), continued to receive and record detailed revelations from the Lord throughout his life (3 Ne. 30; Moro. 8:7–9), and to teach doctrines of the gospel that have the authority of scripture (Helaman 12; Morm. 7; Moro. 7–9), could be so misguided in judging the character of Moroni, and specifically in the context of Moroni's wartime efforts. To see Moroni as wrong in his conduct is simultaneously to see Mormon to be wrong in admiring him.[22]

A similar matter arises in regard to President Gordon B. Hinckley. In his general conference address on the day the United States began its attacks in Afghanistan in response to the events of September 11, 2001, President Hinckley emphasized that although we are people of peace, "there are times when we must stand up for right and decency, for freedom and civilization, just as Moroni rallied his people in his day to the defense of their wives, their children, and the cause of liberty (see Alma 48:10)."[23] Appealing specifically to Moroni as he does, it is clear that President Hinckley did not believe that Captain Moroni's conduct is no longer normative for us. Rather, he plainly *did* consider it relevant and normative for us in our day. Thus, to read the Book of Mormon as a narrative, to read it as an anti-war text, and to see Moroni as wrong, is to see President Hinckley to be wrong as well.

This is just a sample; the same observations could be made of Nephi, Jacob, Alma, the Ammonites, and others with the same conclusions.[24] This

---

22. It might be thought that Mormon changed his mind toward the end of his life and that it was then that he developed a pacifist attitude and a non-violence theme for the Book of Mormon. Thus, while he might have admired Captain Moroni at one point in time, Mormon later came to eschew violence, and *that* is the ultimate message we should take from him. In Chapter 9, however, we will see that such a claim is mistaken, and thus it cannot be used to explain away Mormon's admiration for Captain Moroni.

23. President Gordon B. Hinckley, "The Times in Which We Live."

24. According to the Book of Mormon, Jacob, for example, saw the Lord (1 Ne. 11:3), experienced the most dramatic miracles (Jacob 4:6), labored diligently and tirelessly for the spiritual welfare of the people (e.g., Jacob 1:5–8; 7:24), provided many teachings canonized as scripture (2 Ne. 9; Jacob 2–4), and yet spoke affectionately both of Nephi's efforts to defend his people using the sword of Laban (Jacob 1:10) and of the tragic necessity of the Nephites defending themselves from Lamanite assault. But if, as this narrative approach claims, Captain Moroni was wrong in seeing self-defense to be necessary, then so was Jacob, whatever his spiritual status might have been. Alma's case is similar. The record tells us that he saw an angel (Mosiah 27:10–17; Alma 36:5–11), had a vision of God (Alma 36:15–24), presided over the Church as high priest (Mosiah 29:42), taught many significant spiritual truths that are part of the scriptural

type of narrative reading of Captain Moroni thus reverberates with implications for how we must see a host of spiritual figures. On the face of it, the Book of Mormon presents these leaders as being right in their conduct and attitudes toward conflict, but if, on a narrative reading, we must reverse our judgment of Moroni, then we must also reverse our judgments of them.

Implausibility, the Narrative Reply, and Resulting Questions

Some will find such implications completely implausible and see them as sufficient reason to reject the narrative approach straightaway, thinking that no interpretive scheme can be right that produces outcomes of such seeming improbability and number. What is the likelihood that the record actually repudiates the teachings and conduct of so many spiritual figures, of such importance, who, on the face of it, are so obviously presented in the record as being *right*?

Others will not see the matter this way. After all, as mentioned previously, the narrative approach explicitly denies that there is anything inherently dispositive about the statements, assumptions, or actions of human beings, including prophets. Those who embrace this approach will say that it is not surprising that prophets, from Jacob to Gordon B. Hinckley, could be mistaken on any given matter. Being human and imperfect, it is not possible that they can escape biases altogether. This should neither surprise nor concern us; it is a reality of life. The good news is that the scriptures, taken as a whole, both correct the individual mistakes of men *and* allow us to identify what those mistakes are so that we need not be misled by them.

---

canon (Alma 5, 7, 9, 12, 13, 32, 36–42), and led Nephite armies in war, personally engaging in combat himself (Alma 2:16–36). Moreover, he was actively involved in *helping* Captain Moroni wage war (e.g., Alma 16:6–8; 43:23–24), a matter that will be treated further in due course (see the section "The Problem with the Narrative Answer" later in this chapter). If Captain Moroni was wrong in his violent conduct, then how much more was Alma—who did wrong not only in the face of his spiritual status but also in the face of his significant spiritual experience? In addition to all of this, in the middle of Alma's very personal involvement in war—between his personal experience in wielding the sword in Alma 2 and his active help of Captain Moroni in Alma 16 and 43—it is noteworthy that an angel of God specifically described Alma as "a prophet of the Lord; yea, a holy man, who is a chosen man of God" (Alma 10:7). And yet, if Captain Moroni was wrong in the way he behaved, then, since Alma behaved precisely as Captain Moroni did, Alma was wrong in his conduct as well—even though praised by an angel as "holy" and as "a chosen man of God." And as seen in the previous four chapters, similar analyses would apply to the attitudes and/or conduct of such significant spiritual figures as Nephi, King Benjamin, the Ammonites, Lachoneus, Gidgiddoni, and the later Moroni (as well as to others receiving approval in the record, including Helaman, Lehi, Gid, and Teancum).

An appeal to bias in this way is not sufficient, however, since for many this kind of claim for support raises questions of its own. After all, appealing to bias forces the conclusion that while these prophets were men of God (and presumably, therefore, that they can be trusted with regard to their teachings), they cannot be trusted with regard to their teachings and actions regarding conflict. This seems intellectually problematic. If Book of Mormon prophets (for example) are wrong, what exactly is the textual evidence for the claim?[25]

---

25. The converse of this question, of course, is: What is the evidence for the claim that they are *right*? The two questions are not symmetrical, however, and do not carry equal burdens of proof. For example, Latter-day Saints who take the Book of Mormon seriously for spiritual reasons take the logical default position that the Book of Mormon is what it presents itself to be: (1) a historical record of God's dealings with his people in the Americas, as recorded by prophets who were genuinely called and inspired by him; (2) a record assembled and annotated by another prophet of God, who was specifically called to this work and who deliberately included the teachings and actions that appear in the book; (3) a record explicitly created to contain the fullness of the Gospel and to be the means of gathering Israel in the last days; and (4) a second witness to the reality of Christ and to his status as the Savior of the world. Relevant to their taking this default position is the fact that neither Mormon (the architect of the record), Joseph Smith (the translator of the record and the prophetic head of this final dispensation), nor any prophet or apostle in nearly 200 years of Church history has ever suggested that the book *isn't* what it presents itself to be. Moreover, the Doctrine and Covenants reports the Lord himself saying about the Book of Mormon that "as your Lord and your God liveth it is true" (D&C 17:6). For all of these reasons the obvious default position for Latter-day Saints is to take the book to be what it presents itself to be. What seems to follow from this position is the corollary that the prophetic teachings and actions that appear in the book are reliable—that they are accurate in revealing the nature of the Lord and how he wants us to live. On the face of it, at least, it seems implausible that the Lord would use the Book of Mormon as the primary means for gathering Israel in the last days if its prima facie teachings were mistaken on a matter as common in the book, and as fundamental, as conflict. It is even more implausible to suppose that, even if it *were* mistaken in this way, the Lord would not find a way to communicate this mistakenness (either when talking about the Book of Mormon in the Doctrine and Covenants or subsequently) in order to prevent the Saints from being misled by it. For all of these reasons Latter-day Saints who take the book seriously for spiritual reasons see the burden of proof falling on those who want to argue that we should *eschew* these logical default positions. But the same would also be true for anyone who took the Book of Mormon seriously enough to study it but who did not, for one reason or another, take it to be what it presents itself to be—i.e., an actual historical record. Because they too would recognize that the book at least presents itself to be a historical record, complete with prophetic figures who teach and behave in certain ways, even for them the question would be what textual arguments could be given for

Put another way, what rationale can be found in the record for claiming that its prophets are to be trusted on some topics, but not on others, particularly when both are part of the scriptural canon? And even if there *is* a distinction between times when prophets can be trusted and times when they cannot, what is the distinguishing principle between them? How do we tell which times are which?

These are significant questions, and the narrative interpretation includes natural answers to them. The short reply of the narrative view to the first question is this: We know that various prophets in the Book of Mormon are wrong because at various times their statements and/or actions contradict the overall pacifist moral of the book (as well as the central, corrective pacifist teachings of Jesus that appear in it). That is how we know they are wrong and that's what gives us the rationale for trusting them at some times and not at others. The short answer of the narrative view to the second, related question is this: We obviously know exactly where such prophetic figures are wrong because it is simply wherever they are non-pacifist and thus generate this contradiction. That is the principle that guides us in determining when prophets in the Book of Mormon are reliable and when they are not.

So the narrative interpretation not only asserts that various spiritual figures are wrong, but also gives us the formula for detecting when this occurs. This means that we can feel safe in taking such prophets at their word on other matters they teach, but the book itself, when read carefully, carves out this class of teachings as at least one category in which they are mistaken.[26] Thus, on the topic of conflict and violence at least, we can safely disregard the example of Captain Moroni as well as the attitudes and actions of Mormon

---

reading the book differently than the way it seems for all the world to want itself to be read. What elements of the text persuade us that the actual message of the book can only be read between the lines and that that message is widely divergent from what the book so evidently *seems* to say? Even for such readers, then, the burden of proof would fall on those trying to argue from the text that the book's prophets should be read as wrong, or at least as unreliable, since the prima facie message of the book seems to be just the opposite. Such seems to be the approach of this narrative view. It acknowledges that the book is standardly read a certain way and simply tries to advance good reasons, from the text itself, for abandoning that reading and replacing it with another. It accepts the burden of proof, and in these two chapters we are simply examining the degree to which, if any, it meets this burden.

26. I say "one category" because if one were to adopt a narrative approach, and argue that the book displays a particular narrative theme regarding some topic other than violence, then the trustworthiness of any statement and/or action by any prophetic figure on *that* topic would also be judged by its degree of conformity to the identified theme. Discrete teachings and episodes are always subordinate to the larger narrative structure, whatever it is, and are judged against it.

and President Gordon B. Hinckley, not to mention Nephi, Jacob, King Benjamin, Alma, Lachoneus, Gidgiddoni, and the later Moroni. On this topic they all teach incorrect principles or behave wrongly.

The narrative approach thus yields large consequences regarding various prophetic figures. On the face of it, such a general repudiation of so many prophets' actions and attitudes seems wildly implausible. It does not seem likely that so many significant spiritual leaders could all be so fundamentally wrong. The only way to make such a circumstance seem plausible is to provide a compelling scriptural case for the claim on which it rests, namely, that the Book of Mormon does indeed have the pacifist moral that the narrative view claims for it. If this is truly the case, then the conclusion follows that the prophets we have seen are genuinely mistaken. If this is not the case, however, then the conclusion does not follow at all and there would be no reason whatever to imagine that such spiritual figures taught or behaved wrongly.

All of this brings us to a further intellectual question raised by the narrative claim that prophets are subject to bias and can be wrong. The question is, How is it possible for all of these prophets to get it wrong, over a period of centuries, *on the same issue?* We would imagine that if prophets are vulnerable to biases and can therefore be wrong in their official acts and pronouncements, then they would be likely to have different biases and thus to be wrong in different ways. Thus, in addition to explaining how we know that such spiritual figures *are* wrong part of the time, and to explaining how we can tell the difference between when they are right and when they are wrong, the narrative approach must also explain why it is that a large number of Book of Mormon prophets all happen to be wrong on exactly the same topic.

The explanatory task of the narrative approach we are examining is large and the stakes are high. Can this approach succeed in providing plausible and persuasive answers to these intellectual questions, and can it thus succeed in revolutionizing our thinking, both about the message of the book and thus about the prophetic figures who populate its pages? Before turning our attention to addressing this fundamental question it is important to examine two more manifestations of the claim that all non-pacifist elements of the Book of Mormon must undergo reinterpretation.

Examining the Corollary of the Narrative Approach: The Example of the Lord's Own Conduct

Another serious implication of the narrative interpretation we are examining is that not only must we see a host of prophets to be wrong in their utterances or in their conduct, but also, on the face of it at least, we must see the Lord himself to be wrong in the same ways. This is evident when we consider all the times that significant spiritual figures in the Book of Mormon describe the Lord as having strengthened them and helped them in battle. Captain Moroni does this (Alma 44:3–5), as do Helaman (Alma 57:25–26, 36), King Benjamin (W of M 1:14), and Alma (Alma 2:16–19, 27–31). Mormon himself approvingly reports Nephites' attribution of their success in defending themselves to God (3 Ne. 4:11, 31, 33), and he assumes the same experience of divine help when he reports a time when "the strength of the Lord was *not* with [them]" (Morm. 2:26). Divine help of this sort is also evident on the occasion when Ammon was in a vulnerable condition and was protected from being killed by the sudden death of his assailant (Alma 19:22–23). The record attributes this protection and the assailant's death to the Lord, quoting his words to Mosiah: "I will spare [Ammon], and it shall be unto him according to thy faith" (Alma 19:23).

The idea that God helped his people in battle is also presupposed in every instance in which a spiritual leader speaks of conflict in terms of the ancient promises to Nephi and Lehi that we examined previously. This was true of Nephi, Lehi, Jarom, Amaron, King Benjamin, Alma, and Mormon.[27] Their references to God's help in military matters comprise a consistent theme in the text.

The clear report of a host of spiritual leaders in the Book of Mormon, then, is that the Lord helps people defend themselves in war.[28] Moreover, we see occasions where the Lord explicitly *teaches* the people to engage in self-defense, telling the Nephites, for example, that "ye shall not suffer yourselves to be slain by the hands of your enemies" and also that they should defend their families "even unto bloodshed" (Alma 43:46–47).

But all of this leads to the following problem: If the overall theme of the Book of Mormon is pacifist, and if any *non*-pacifist teaching or behavior is therefore wrong, then all of these instances of the Lord's *own* teachings and actions must also be wrong. For example, if the Lord helped Alma slay Amlici in battle, as the record tells us he did (Alma 2:29–31), then according to the narrative interpretation he was wrong to do so. The same would also be true of incidents involving King Benjamin, Helaman, and every other leader where the Lord is reported to have strengthened his people in combat. If the Lord was involved, then the overall moral of the Book of Mormon identifies that involvement as wrong and stands as a correction of it.

This point becomes even more ironic when we consider the narrative claim that Jesus' teachings in Third Nephi are pacifist in character, and that those teachings, too, correct any non-pacifist elements of the text. The logical consequence of this is that Jesus' pacifist teachings in Third Nephi amount

---

27. For more on the ancient promises to Nephi and Lehi see the section "The Ancient Promise to Nephi" in Chapter 6, as well as Appendix 2, "The Promises to Nephi and Lehi."
28. See Chapter 7 for a more complete discussion of this.

to a correction of himself. So it is not just the overall theme of the Book of Mormon that corrects various teachings and actions of the Lord in regard to Book of Mormon peoples; the Lord's own teachings do the same. This idea, to say the least, will give most readers pause. Under what circumstances is it reasonable to imagine Jesus being wrong and thus needing to correct himself?

The Narrative Answer

Although this question seems problematic on its face, the narrative reply to it is both simple and straightforward: the many prophetic figures who report the Lord's involvement in war are simply wrong. This conclusion follows logically from the central narrative claim that statements or actions of spiritual leaders are authoritative only to the degree that they instantiate the overall theme of the larger narrative. Such leaders are imperfect beings who are attempting to understand God and his wishes, but they can be wrong about these matters.

It is useful to think about Alma in this regard. While he reports that the Lord strengthened him and his army in battle, couldn't we point out that it is common for people to make claims of this sort when they win? After all, throughout history virtually all victors in war took their triumphs as evidence that their god was on their side and supporting them. Captain Moroni, King Benjamin, Helaman, and Mormon all make remarks about the Lord's divine assistance in the Nephites' battles; what, though, makes us think they are not doing so out of wishful thinking, spiritual bravado, false humility, or some other mortal predilection for explaining the events of human life?

If Alma, King Benjamin, and others can be mistaken about the Lord's support in their combat, it follows that we have no reason to suppose that the Lord's teachings in Third Nephi, or the Book of Mormon as a whole, are in any way correcting the Lord's own conduct. These possibilities arise in our minds only if we assume that reports of the Lord's involvement in violence are accurate. But according to the narrative interpretation, and its pacifist conclusion, this is precisely what these reports are not. So it is not that the Lord himself is wrong; it is that Book of Mormon reports *about* him are wrong.

The Problem with the Narrative Answer

On the surface this might seem like a promising answer to the problem, but a recurring element in the scriptural record demonstrates it to be inadequate. This recurring element is that scriptural figures don't simply report that they received the Lord's help in battle, but claim to quote the Lord's own words to that effect. Thus, as mentioned earlier, Mormon records the Lord telling him that "because this people repented not *after I had delivered them*, behold, they shall be cut off from the face of the earth" (Morm. 3:15). Here Mormon quotes the Lord's personal report that he had helped his people in conflict. Mormon also quotes the words of the Lord earlier in the record, that "inasmuch as ye are not guilty of the first offense, neither the second, ye shall not suffer yourselves to be slain by the hands of your enemies," and further that "ye shall defend your families even unto bloodshed" (Alma 43:46, 47). The record also rehearses the Lord's words to King Mosiah, regarding the protection of his son—"I will spare him"—a protection which came in the form of the divine slaying of a Lamanite who was intent on killing Ammon (Alma 19:18–23). These are not vague references to "the Lord's help" in defeating aggressors; they are presented as quotations of the Lord's own words.

This problematic element also appears in the Doctrine and Covenants. The Lord said to the Prophet Joseph Smith: "This is the law that I gave unto mine ancients, that they should not go out unto battle against any nation, kindred, tongue, or people, save I, the Lord, commanded them" (D&C 98:33). This statement, which presents the Lord speaking in the first person, presupposes that there are occasions when he will command his people to enter conflict. He explains that a nation under threat must lift a standard of peace three times, but if it is not accepted, he then "would give unto them a commandment, and justify them in going out to battle" (D&C 98:36). The Prophet is not reporting a general proposition or feeling to the effect that God helps his people in their battles; he is presenting the message as the Lord's own words on the matter.

Alma's experience is also instructive. Mormon tells us that the Nephites prospered with the help of the Lord, who warned them "to flee, or to prepare for war, according to their danger" and said that he would "make it known unto them whither they should go to defend themselves against their enemies" (Alma 48:15–16). In fulfillment, the record reports two occasions on which the Lord revealed enemy troop movements to Alma. In the first case, Alma was asked to help locate Nephites who had been taken captive by Lamanite armies after those armies had destroyed the people of Ammonihah. After inquiring of the Lord, Alma returned with this detailed report: "Behold, the Lamanites will cross the river Sidon in the south wilderness, away up beyond the borders of the land of Manti. And behold there shall ye meet them, on the east of the river Sidon, and there the Lord will deliver unto thee thy brethren who have been taken captive by the Lamanites" (Alma 16:6). Following these instructions, the Nephite armies found the Lamanite invaders and engaged them, successfully rescuing those who had been taken captive (Alma 16:8).

In the second case, Lamanite armies had shrunk from battle in the land of Jershon and had planned an assault on the land of Manti. Captain Moroni sent messengers to Alma to ask him to "inquire of the Lord" about the Lamanites' designs so that he could intercept their armies and thwart their plans (Alma 43:23). The record says that "the word of the Lord came unto

Alma" and that he informed the messengers that "the armies of the Lamanites were marching round about in the wilderness, that they might come over into the land of Manti, that they might commence an attack upon the weaker part of the people" (Alma 43:24). Armed with this information, Moroni formulated a strategy that resulted in a successful defense of the people and an extremely important victory against the Lamanites (Alma 43, 44). The people of Nephi "were exceedingly rejoiced, because the Lord had again delivered them out of the hands of their enemies" (Alma 45:1).

These incidents are significant because they are so detailed. It might seem possible to speak of human error if all we consider are general reports of the Lord's help in wartime activities, but how can Alma be mistaken in his detailed prophecies about enemy troop movements, especially when they are fulfilled to the letter? Similarly, we must wonder about direct revelations reported by Mormon, King Mosiah, and Joseph Smith. Even supposing that prophets can be mistaken in their judgment about the Lord's help in one circumstance or another, is it as easy to suppose that they can be mistaken in what they present as the Lord's own words? And if so, then what is the reason for accepting *any* of the revelations, whether in the Book of Mormon or in the Doctrine and Covenants?

Speculation about revelation vs. the central question. Of course, it would be possible to argue that these reports of Alma's revelations were written long after the actual events occurred, and therefore that they were subject to modification and even exaggeration prior to their transmission in written form. It could also be possible to argue that they are untrustworthy because they have passed through multiple hands—including Mormon's and Joseph Smith's—in a manner that is entirely unverifiable. But objections of this sort seem purely a priori; since there is nothing in the text or other records to suggest such tampering, the worry must be grounded in a general and pre-existing skepticism regarding revelation in principle. In that case nothing in the Book of Mormon that appeared to illuminate revelatory processes would ever be persuasive because everything of that sort is met with doubt and a set of alternative possibilities, regardless of their plausibility, simply because that is what skepticism demands.[29]

---

29. That is why addressing such skepticism is not the purpose of this book. The task is not to corroborate the truth claims of The Church of Jesus Christ of Latter-day Saints (there are other sources to consult regarding that), but only to identify the message of the Church's scriptural canon regarding conflict. All parties can participate in this effort, whether they affirm, ignore, or deny these truth claims. Everyone can appreciate that the scriptural texts say *something*, and therefore, from within that framework, employ normal intellectual standards of plausibility and consistency in determining what that something is. Thus, all readers can appreciate the difficulty that the accounts of Alma's

It is true, of course, that the Lord speaks to his prophets after the manner of their own language. Nevertheless, while recognizing this invites us to bring a little bit of care to the Lord's printed revelations, it does nothing to suggest that such revelations are generally untrustworthy and that we are therefore justified in a deep and comprehensive skepticism about their accuracy or meaning.[30] We assume, for instance, that the messages received and reported by Alma were in some measure a function of Alma himself, and that their form naturally reflects both Alma's own language and Alma's capacity to articulate those messages to others. In a sense—simply by virtue of the particular mortal language they speak, for example—prophets are participants in the revelations they receive.

For some this raises a broader question about the nature of revelation, including in cases where the revelation is identified as a direct quotation from the Lord. Perhaps there is some way, which we don't fully understand, in which receivers *always* determine the form a revelatory expression takes—some way that goes beyond merely delimiting the mortal language in which the message is couched. This is implied by instances in which a revelation later undergoes some revision or in which more than one expression is given for the same idea.[31]

---

revelations pose for the claim that prophets' reports are unreliable. Completely aside from any other issues one might have in mind, these instances in the text contradict that claim *about* the text. The same approach is appropriate for every other conclusion drawn in this and other chapters. Regardless of one's attitude toward ultimate truth claims, it is at least possible to reach conclusions (of one degree of strength or another) about what texts themselves say, based on normal standards of analysis.

30. In Chapters 10 and 15 I will explain why a portion of Doctrine and Covenants 98 exceeds our understanding and why it must be read with the greatest tentativeness. But this is an exception to the pattern. While all revelations are incomplete—each could contain far more than it does—and while this reality mandates an attitude of deep humility in studying them, it does not mandate skepticism or generalized mistrust. For a broad discussion of the mandate for humility in gospel study (as well as in academic exploration), see my "The Spirit and the Intellect: Lessons in Humility," *BYU Studies*, 50/4 (2011): 75–107.

31. Well-known examples of this are the Book of Mormon itself and the thread that appears in D&C 128:17–18; 2:1–3; and JS-H 1:36–39. (The best summary of revisions in the Book of Mormon is Royal Skousen's "Changes in the Book of Mormon," *Interpreter: A Journal of Mormon Scripture*, 11 (2014): 161–76.) An interesting contemporary case regarding linguistic elements in revelation is found in Elder Neal A. Maxwell's report of this divine message: "I have given you leukemia that you might teach my people with authenticity." The message takes the form of English, it is expressed as coming from the Lord in the first person, and it employs the sophisticated term "authenticity"—a choice of vocabulary suited to Elder Maxwell, but not to everyone. As we think about the nature of revelation—especially in cases where the divine communication is reported as an expression occurring in specific,

Be that as it may, none of this is material to the central question, which discrete words—one linguistic question is this: If Elder Maxwell were to describe this experience to a group of children, would he be restricted to these exact words to communicate his meaning, or could he legitimately find simpler expressions to communicate the meaning to them? And if he *could* legitimately use simpler expressions, and if he could construct a different sentence out of them, would it be legitimate for him to place the revised sentence in quotation marks? Would we see *those* words as coming from the Lord? Further, if Elder Maxwell later came to understand much more about leukemia, and to understand it *accurately*, would it disturb us if he then expressed the message in terms of white blood cells, DNA mutations, and retroviruses? Even if it would not disturb us to see him express the revelation in different words as a function of his audience, would it nevertheless disturb us to see him express it in different words as a function of his own expanded understanding of the conceptual context that lay behind and informed the words in the first place? And would we think it legitimate for him to place this expanded expression in quotation marks? Would *he* think it legitimate? Such questions are relevant to the general process of revelation, including to Joseph Smith and his practice, at times, of expressing revelations he had received in revised ways. This is not the place to explore the many layers and subtleties involved in understanding the exact character of translation (which is the transmission of meaning from one human being to another), much less the exact character of revelation (the transmission of meaning from a divine being to a mortal being). Nevertheless, it is fair to say that the way we would employ quotation marks—including declining to use them at all—tells us much about what we have either concluded, or assumed, about the character of meaning and meaning transmission, whether in translation *or* in revelation. In any case, it does not seem merely accidental that some revelations are presented in the form of discrete words rather than of feelings only. This is the form found throughout the Doctrine and Covenants, and it is common in the Book of Mormon as well. President Henry B. Eyring's biography reports several incidents of this sort in his life, and both President Marion G. Romney and President Boyd K. Packer report experiences in terms of actual hearing: "I've heard His voice many times" and "I know His voice when I hear Him," respectively. All of this indicates that there is a difference between revelations that take the form of spiritual feelings only and revelations that are reported in the form of discrete words. Because the scriptural canon and other LDS literature contain examples of both, it seems implausible that the latter is simply reducible to the former. (For the quotations, in the order in which they appear above, see: See Bruce C. Hafen, *A Disciple's Life: The Biography of Neal A. Maxwell*, 562; Robert I. Eaton and Henry J. Eyring, *I Will Lead You Along: The Life of Henry B. Eyring*, 100, 163, 174–75, 275; Marion G. Romney in George W. Pace, *Our Search to Know the Lord*, 223; and Boyd K. Packer, "Jesus is the Christ," *Church News*, December 25, 2010, 3. For one discussion of the complexities of translation in general, and of spiritual terms and concepts in particular, see Van C. Gessel, "Coming to Terms: The Challenge of Creating Christian Vocabulary in a Non-Christian Land," *BYU Studies*, 50/4 (2011), 33–59. For one discussion of the

is whether Alma *misunderstood* the Spirit when he received direction that would help the Nephites defend themselves militarily. That is the claim of the narrative argument—that prophets are mistaken when they report the Lord's involvement in such actions. Thus, whatever speculations there may be about the process of revelation that permitted Alma to present a first-person report of the Lord's own words, the primary question is whether Alma's revelatory understanding was *wrong*, as the narrative view claims. But according to the book itself, it is difficult to see how he could have been. Regardless of the processes that were involved in Alma's divine communications, the record reports that they generated messages that were both detailed and correct in the instructions they gave. It is a clear example of the text presenting to us prophetic figures who seem to understand the Spirit and its workings well, not poorly, and thus whose claims about the Lord's involvement in one matter or another are due an attitude of respect, not suspicion.[32]

This seems the more obvious when we recall the text's accounts of Alma's significant experiences with the Spirit at other times and on other matters. In light of such accounts, what confidence can we have in concluding that Alma would routinely misunderstand the Spirit in the cases where some would like to conclude that he must? It is simply implausible, and the same analysis would apply to additional prophetic figures as well, including Mormon and Joseph Smith. Everything in the record about their spiritual experiences presents these prophetic figures as acquainted, not unacquainted, with the workings of the Spirit and thus gives us every reason to trust, not mistrust, their reports of spiritual feelings. Indeed, Joseph Smith was deliberate about not claiming revelation on a matter when he had not in fact received it; in such cases he "followed the dictates of his own judgment," but "never gave anything to his people as a revelation, unless it was a revelation."[33]

Summary

It is not the case, then, that we can summarily dismiss elements in the Book of Mormon that report the Lord's assistance to his people in times of conflict. The narrative approach assumes that we can dismiss them, but strong reasons to

---

Prophet's revelatory translation of the Book of Mormon in particular, see Brant A. Gardner, *The Gift and Power: Translating the Book of Mormon*.)

32. Again, this follows from the text regardless of whether one affirms, ignores, or denies *ultimate* truth claims.

33. "The Prairies, Nauvoo, Joe Smith, The Temple, the Mormons, etc.," *Pittsburgh Weekly Gazette*, 15 September 1843, in *The Papers of Joseph Smith, Vol. 1: Autobiographical and Historical Writings,* ed. Dean C. Jessee 443, cited in Matthew Roper, "Joseph Smith, Revelation, and Book of Mormon Geography," *The FARMS Review*, 22/2, 2010, 83–84.

reject this assumption are not difficult to find. In the end the idea of prophets' mistakenness—at least in the way the narrative approach requires—is not supported in the text. The claim thus does nothing to solve the problem of how, on a narrative reading, much of the Lord's own conduct throughout the Book of Mormon is actually condemned, both by the overall pacifist theme that is claimed for the Book of Mormon as a whole, and by the pacifist theme that is claimed specifically for the Lord's own teachings in Third Nephi. That problem remains. The narrative approach thus creates a gaping intellectual inconsistency for which it seems unable to provide a solution.

Examining the Corollary of the Narrative Approach: The Example of Nephi

Nephi is a pivotal figure in this interpretive scheme because, according to this view, by killing Laban at the very beginning of their history Nephi planted the concept of justified violence at the center of Nephite culture. It was an idea that then shaped attitudes and behavior for centuries, eventually resulting in the civilization's wholesale destruction. Recall Nephi's report that he was "constrained by the Spirit" to kill Laban (1 Ne. 4:10), that the Lord had "delivered" him into Nephi's hands for this purpose (1 Ne. 4:11, 12), and that it was the Spirit that explained: "Behold the Lord slayeth the wicked to bring forth his righteous purposes. It is better that one man should perish than that a nation should dwindle and perish in unbelief" (1 Ne. 4:13). All of this presents a justification for this violence and thus explains why Nephi would act as he did.[34]

On the narrative account, however, there is no reason to take Nephi at his word about the justification, much less the righteousness, of his slaying of Laban. If the Book of Mormon is actually intended to deliver a message of pacifism, then we must see Nephi in much the same way that we see Captain Moroni—as someone who did wrong, not as someone who did right. We must see Nephi's conduct as unrighteous and his reporting of the events surrounding it as dishonest. After all, if it was wrong to slay Laban, then the Spirit couldn't have been the instigator of Nephi's doing so, despite what Nephi tells us. Thus, we are told by the narrative interpretation that Nephi's account is the "mythic"[35] narrative at the foundation of Nephite culture,[36]

---

34. Some find the reasoning here to be irksome. This is a matter I take up in Chapter 11 in the section "The End Justifying the Means."
35. Joshua Madson, "A Non-Violent Reading of the Book of Mormon," 23.
36. Ibid., 19–20.

that it was a "lie of sacred violence,"[37] and that the Book of Mormon itself is a "one-sided propaganda piece, written by and for Nephites."[38]

These are bold claims, expressing multiple ways of describing as dishonest the writings of both Nephi and the Nephite record-keepers generally. And "dishonest," rather than "mistaken," seems the appropriate word to use since, in light of the details he shares, it does not seem possible that Nephi was merely in error. Moreover, it is noteworthy that if Nephi was a liar in this situation, he was also a murderer. After all, if the Spirit did not instruct Nephi to do as he did, then Nephi killed Laban of his own volition, and this made it murder.

Nor was this just any murder. According to the narrative view, Nephi's act, and his account of it, established a rationale for violence that became central to Nephite society. More than once, therefore, Nephi's slaying of Laban is called the "founding murder"[39] of Nephite culture. In the wake of this precedent set by Nephi himself, why would subsequent generations *not* demonize Lamanites and consider them existential threats? And why would they *not* resort to violence in responding to the menace they presented? Nephi's example from the very beginning defined such attitudes and actions not only as justifiable, but as necessary and even righteous. It is tragic, according to the narrative view, that an event such as this formed the conceptual framework for succeeding generations of Nephites as it created a path for them that was both monumentally regrettable and completely unnecessary.

The Question of Plausibility

But is such a reinterpretation plausible? The first step in addressing this question is to note that Nephi's violence did not end with Laban, but seems to have stretched over his lifetime. Jacob tells us that Nephi "wielded the sword of Laban" in defense of the people (Jacob 1:9) and Nephi himself speaks of having "enemies" through his life (2 Ne. 4:22) and of making "many swords" in order to protect the Nephites from Lamanite attack (2 Ne. 5:14). But that raises this question for the narrative approach: If the Lord is actually pacifist, and if that is the standard of genuine discipleship, then why didn't he ever explain this to Nephi at *some* point over the course of Nephi's life? The text tells us that he

---

37. Ibid., 26.

38. Ibid., 19. In the same vein we are told that Nephi "asserts" that it was God's command (p. 18), that it was only a "claim" of Nephi's (p. 27), that Nephite political narratives "hid the truth" and "disguised" the violence at the foundation of Nephite culture (pp. 19–20), and that in doing so they made "their violence become God's violence" (p. 19).

39. Ibid., 17, 27.

gave Nephi a multitude of divine manifestations and taught him a multitude of eternal truths, so why was he unable to teach him *that*?[40]

Furthermore, it is hard to explain the numerous accounts of Nephi's divine manifestations on one hand, while accommodating both his murder of Laban and his continued violent conduct on the other. The Lord does not normally bless liars and murderers with revelations, visions, angelic visitations, and his own presence. The textual contradiction is thus both transparent and severe, especially given the Book of Mormon's repeated insistence that blessings follow righteous, not unrighteous behavior. If pacifism is the Lord's true standard it is impossible to see Nephi as righteous; and if Nephi is righteous, how is it possible to see pacifism as the Lord's true standard?[41]

Finally, if a proper reading of the text is that Nephi was a liar and a murderer, and if we are therefore to dismiss (as we would have to) the accounts of his divine manifestations, then we must also dismiss the numerous teachings of Nephi appearing in the text that are based on those manifestations. Put differently: To repudiate the text regarding Nephi's righteousness is to repudiate the text regarding his miraculous experiences, and to do this is to repudiate the text regarding the authenticity of his teachings.[42] The pacifist conclusion nullifies everything of consequence about Nephi.

The narrative approach to Nephi thus seems no more plausible than its approach to Captain Moroni and to the Lord. To see Nephi as a liar and a murderer is to create significant paradoxes in the text and to require a massive reinterpretation both of Nephi's spiritual experiences and of his doctrinal teachings. It is difficult to see what remains, if anything, of importance in Nephi's first-person record in First and Second Nephi.

---

40. Nephi's manifestations include seeing in vision events of the Savior's birth, life, and death (1 Ne. 11:1–33), the future of Nephite, Lamanite, and Gentile peoples on the promised land (1 Ne. 12–14; 2 Ne. 26:2–22), and the numerous matters pertaining both to this earth and to celestial life seen by John the Revelator (1 Ne. 14:18–30; 2 Ne. 4:23, 25). In addition, the Lord appeared to him personally (2 Ne. 11:3); he was taken to high mountains and shown things "too great for man" (2 Ne. 4:25); he entertained angels (2 Ne. 4:24); he held conversation with the Father and Son (2 Ne. 31:10–15); and he both prophesied at length and spoke the words of the Lord (2 Ne. 25–26, 28–30).

41. In the next chapter I will address the specific narrative argument purporting to justify a reinterpretation of Nephi's conduct; see the section "The Narrative Approach and Nephi's Inauguration of Nephite Culture."

42. For one reason or another Nephi's teachings may still be considered true, but they are inauthentic in the sense that they are not based on the manifestations they claim to be based on. We must repudiate that aspect of Nephi's teachings.

Conclusion

The narrative approach includes a number of central claims about the Book of Mormon as a pacifist document, as well as an important corollary that follows from them, namely, that non-pacifist elements of the book must be reinterpreted in light of the overall pacifist moral that is inherent in the text. Such non-pacifist elements are actually dominant in the record and include the conduct and teachings of Captain Moroni, the Lord himself, and Nephi. The stakes are high since the narrative view resolves these difficulties by condemning Captain Moroni and Nephi, and, as a logical consequence of the view, considering multiple Book of Mormon reports about the Lord to be false. We also seem compelled to reject the accounts of Nephi's many divine manifestations and to dismiss as inauthentic (at least) the extensive teachings of Nephi based on those manifestations. The implications of the narrative view are not small.

To justify such a massive overhaul of the text the narrative approach must substantiate its central contentions, namely, that: Mormon had a pacifist intent in creating the Book of Mormon; the Nephites' violent ending itself conveys a pacifist moral; Christ's personal teachings in Third Nephi are pacifist in character; and Nephi set his future society on a violent path due to his slaying of Laban. Examining these claims directly is the task of the next chapter.[43] To the degree the narrative view can substantiate these contentions it can justify the revolutionary reinterpretations it entails about the Book of Mormon and about prophetic utterances generally. To the same degree it will demonstrate that its answers to the core questions identified earlier are correct: the Book of Mormon is genuinely wrong in many places (but right in others); there is a reliable way to tell which times are which; and there is a simple explanation for why Book of Mormon prophets all manage to be wrong on the same topic.

So, are narrative claims sound enough to achieve all this?

---

43. Since textual interpretation always requires judgment, some might be content to transform the interpretation of the text even if the narrative view can substantiate only one or two of these claims. Others might be willing only if it can support all of them. The point becomes moot, of course, if it cannot support any of them.

Chapter 9

A "Narrative" Reading of the Book of Mormon: Part Two

The Narrative Approach and Mormon

One key element of the narrative approach is the role played by Mormon. We are told that "the Book of Mormon is a narrative by design and is meant to be read as a whole. Mormon, the primary narrator, confirms that there is an intent and theme to his work."[1] But if we are to take as the central message of the Book of Mormon the rejection of all violence, and if it was Mormon who assembled the record precisely in order to convey this message, then we must confront two significant features of Mormon's conduct.

Mormon's Messages and Engagement in Conflict

The first feature we must confront is inconsistency in Mormon's messages. It is noteworthy, for instance, that it is Mormon who expresses the justification for the Nephite military action under Captain Moroni in Alma 43, appealing, with approval, to their need to defend their lives, families, lands, country, rights, and religion (Alma 43:47). Similarly, it is significant that Mormon expressed justification for fighting during his own lifetime in a comparable way. He tells us that he urged his people "with great energy, that they would stand boldly before the Lamanites and fight for their wives, and their children, and their houses, and their homes" (Morm. 2:23). Both instances are significant since, if it is true that Mormon fashioned the Book of Mormon to be an anti-war text, then in both cases he is explicitly contradicting that intent. He is justifying people in fighting and even urging them to fight at the same time he is creating a book with the "intent and theme" that people should not fight.

It is also relevant that it is Mormon himself who describes Captain Moroni as a man of "perfect understanding" and as "firm in the faith of Christ" (Alma 48:11, 13), and who expresses the wish that "all men" were like him (Alma 48:17). This description is significant because it is hard to imagine Mormon praising Captain Moroni so highly on one hand—and specifically in the context of his extensive wartime conduct—while simultaneously creating a book intended to condemn exactly the way Moroni behaved on the other. The same paradox hovers over the

---

1. Joshua Madson, "A Non-Violent Reading of the Book of Mormon," 15.

text every time Mormon specifically praises or refers approvingly to the wartime activities of any Book of Mormon figure, from King Benjamin to Moroni to Gidgiddoni. If Mormon is genuinely creating a text intended to convey a pacifist theme, it is natural to wonder why, rather than praise Moroni without reservation, he wouldn't find a way to condemn Moroni's violence at least somewhere along the way. Surely, it is relevant that Mormon never condemns the violent behavior of Nephi, King Benjamin, Gideon, Alma, Moroni, Lehi, Teancum, Gid, Helaman, the two thousand stripling warriors, Gidgiddoni, his son Moroni, or even himself. But isn't this exactly what he would do if he had a pacifist intent in creating the record? The odds, so it would seem, do not favor Mormon creating a book intended to condemn all war, while simultaneously—*in* the book—approving of, and even praising, Nephite figures who wage it.

The second serious anomaly is Mormon's own engagement in conflict to the very end of his life. It seems unlikely that Mormon would write a book urging one point of view while at the same time failing entirely to embrace that view in his own conduct. On such a reading it seems we must see Mormon to be self-contradictory, either because he was unable to follow his own pacifist advice, or because he was *unwilling* to follow it. Furthermore, it seems we must conclude that while the text presents Mormon as of sufficient spiritual capacity that he could see the Lord at age 15 (Morm. 1:15) and be entrusted with creating the record that would be critical to accomplishing the Lord's work of salvation in the last days,[2] he was not of sufficient spiritual capacity to live up to the pacifist standard that he really held and desired to pass on to us. The inconsistency in Mormon's conduct is as serious as the inconsistency in his messages.

An Unsuccessful Solution

All of this seems problematic. Yet it might be said that the difficulties disappear if we simply see Mormon as changing his mind over time. After all, it is toward the end of the book that Mormon observes that "it is by the wicked

---

2. It is important to appreciate the significance of this responsibility in order to appreciate Mormon himself. Nephi explains that in the last days the Lord will restore his "lost and fallen people" by performing "a marvelous work and a wonder among the children of men," which work consists in bringing forth the Book of Mormon— "which words shall judge them at the last day, for they shall be given them for the purpose of convincing them of the true Messiah" (2 Ne. 25:17–18). The Book of Mormon contains the fullness of the Gospel (JS-H 1:34; 1 Ne. 15:13; D&C 20:9; 27:5; 42:12; 135:3); it is a witness to the truth of the Bible (Morm. 7:8–10; D&C 20:11); its appearance is a sign of the beginning of the Father's work in gathering Israel in the last days (3 Ne. 21:1–7); and it plays a role in the judgment (D&C 20:8–16; 2 Ne. 25:17–18). The canon thus presents Mormon as a most significant figure, one whose prophetic influence is surpassed by few in the scriptural record.

that the wicked are punished" (Morm. 4:5) and that he tells his latter-day readers, "ye must lay down your weapons of war" (Morm. 7:4).[3] Thus, whatever Mormon's conduct and statements might have been prior to this time, we should think of Mormon in light of the anti-war views he espoused at the end.

While promising at first glance several considerations render this interpretation unpersuasive. For example, the observation that "it is by the wicked that the wicked are punished" suggests nothing like the claim that every party to war is unrighteous and thus that war itself can never be a righteous act.[4] Mormon cannot be read to be making a claim of that sort. Also, when Mormon says that "ye must lay down your weapons of war" he goes on to say that we should not take them up again "save it be that God shall command you" (Morm. 7:4). Mormon thus explicitly acknowledges that God can and will command his children to enter conflict in certain circumstances. It is difficult to see, then, how this statement can be taken to support the idea that Mormon changed his mind about violence and rejected it altogether.

Furthermore, it is hard to say that Mormon's change of mind is demonstrated by his statement that the wicked are punished by the wicked, and by his command that we lay down our arms, since he himself continued fighting after making both of these statements. He took up leadership of the Nephite armies (Morm. 5:1), led them in war (Morm. 5:3–7; 6:1–15), and finally perished in battle at Cumorah, *dying* with a sword in his hand (Morm. 8:2–3, 5). The text itself, therefore, gives us two options: either Mormon did not in fact end up changing his mind about violence and rejecting it altogether, or he continued to take up the sword to the very end of his life *even though* he had changed his mind. But if the latter is true, then we must still grapple with Mormon's contradictory behavior and see him as either unable to live up to the pacifist standard he had embraced or as hypocritical and unwilling to live up to it. Either way we are left with a view of Mormon that is not credible in light of the rest of the record and what it reveals about him.

Faced with such objections it might seem that a reasonable fallback position would be to concede that Mormon did not deliberately weave a pacifist theme into the book, but that it is present in the story nonetheless. Whatever Mormon's intentions, Book of Mormon history still demonstrates the evil of resorting to violence, and thus, in the end, there is no need to argue that Mormon changed his mind.

But this answer creates intellectual problems of its own. If we say that the message of the book is found in the story even though Mormon himself did not place it there, then Latter-day Saints cannot rest a claim about the

---

3. Madson relies on these verses at ibid., 16.
4. This matter is discussed at length in Chapter 6.

pacifist character of the book even partly on Mormon's prophetic credentials and on the claim that he had an intent and theme in creating the record. That source of support evaporates. Furthermore, since we know that Mormon did in fact have an intent in creating the book, we know both that the record does indeed have a deliberate theme *and*, at least if Mormon is consistent rather than contradictory, that theme could *not* be pacifist.[5]

Mormon, then, is a problem for the narrative approach. We can appeal to him for support for pacifist claims if we see him as contradictory and deficient in character, but we cannot appeal to him for support if we see him as consistent and admirable. That's the choice. But in no case can we treat Mormon as unimportant to the narrative approach and its pacifist claims.

The Narrative Approach and the End of Nephite Civilization

Putting aside the problem with Mormon, does Book of Mormon history as a whole communicate a pacifist theme? As mentioned early in Chapter 8, one very large aspect of the Book of Mormon story is how it ends—in the complete destruction of Nephite civilization—and, according to this narrative view, such an ending stands as a testament against resorting to violence "by showing the eventual results of living in such a manner."[6] In Nephite devastation we see "the consequences of choosing violence"[7] and that resort-

---

5. Regarding the claim that Mormon had a deliberate intent in creating the Book of Mormon, note Mormon's explanation that the book's purpose was that the "unbelieving Jews," "all the house of Israel," and the seed of the Lamanites might be "persuaded that Jesus is the Christ, the Son of the living God" (Morm. 5:12–15). In this connection the title page of the Book of Mormon tells us it was written "to show unto the remnant of the house of Israel what great things the Lord hath done for their fathers; and that they may know the covenants of the Lord, that they are not cast off forever," and also to convince "Jew and Gentile that Jesus is the Christ, the Eternal God, manifesting himself unto all nations." And the Doctrine and Covenants tells us that one direct purpose in creating and preserving the Book of Mormon was that "the promises of the Lord might be fulfilled, which he made to his people" and that "the Lamanites might come to the knowledge of their fathers, and that they might know the promises of the Lord, and that they may believe the gospel and rely upon the merits of Jesus Christ, and be glorified through faith in his name" (D&C 3:19–20). Neither this statement, nor any other scriptural statement, frames the intent of the Book of Mormon in terms of violence. Whatever theme there might be about violence per se must be drawn from the story itself. It turns out that there is, indeed, such a theme, and it will be treated later in this chapter in the section "A Genuine Theme Regarding Book of Mormon Violence: The Ancient Promise to Nephi."

6. Ibid., 16, fn. 6.

7. Ibid., 16.

ing to violence is therefore both futile and wrong. Even if we cannot rely on Mormon for support, according to the narrative view we are still compelled to draw a pacifist conclusion from the history of Nephite civilization itself.

Two Problems

However, while such an argument might seem persuasive on the surface, there are two significant problems with this way of looking at the matter.

The Prophet Joseph Smith. The first problem with seeing a pacifist theme in Book of Mormon history is the Prophet Joseph Smith's failure to discern it. Recall the Prophet's observation that "it may be that the Saints will have to beat their ploughs into swords, for it will not do for men to sit down patiently and see their children destroyed,"[8] and recall his use of a handgun to defend himself and his companions while being murdered in Carthage jail. And remember the scriptural declaration in the Doctrine and Covenants that people "are justified in defending themselves, their friends, and property, and the government, from the unlawful assaults and encroachments of all persons in times of exigency" (D&C 134:11). Based on such instances, and more, it is not possible to see Joseph Smith himself as a pacifist. And this means that if the Book of Mormon displays a pacifist intent and theme, the translator of the record, for one, was unable to see it.

Such a conclusion will give most readers pause. It is hard to see on what basis we could feel comfortable in concluding that Joseph Smith, of all people, failed to comprehend a key message of the Book of Mormon. And even if we imagined that the Prophet did fail to discern this message on his own, based on the documentary record we would imagine that the Lord would explain it to him at some point. The catalogue of the Prophet's divine manifestations is stunning, ranging from seeing the Father and Son more than once and viewing the visions of eternity to entertaining prophets such as Abraham and Noah and seeing in vision events of the Book of Mormon itself.[9] It is difficult to see how one could embrace the many accounts of the Prophet's divine manifestations and simultaneously imagine that along the way the Lord would not teach him the pacifist intent and theme of the book he had commissioned him to translate.[10]

---

8. Joseph Fielding Smith, comp., *Teachings of the Prophet Joseph Smith*, 366. The statement appears in the report that Thomas Bullock made of this sermon. His notes give us the most complete record. See Andrew F. Ehat and Lyndon W. Cook, *The Words of Joseph Smith*, 367. This passage also appears in Chapter 7, the section "Scriptural Expressions about Defense."

9. See Appendix 3 for a brief review of less familiar reports of the Prophet's spiritual manifestations.

10. This is similar to the point made regarding Nephi in the section "Examining the Corollary of the Narrative Approach: The Example of Nephi" in Chapter 8.

Of course another possibility is that Joseph Smith actually did see the pacifist message in the Book of Mormon—either on his own or because the Lord taught it to him—but that he simply failed to embrace it. But then our situation is similar to the situation with Mormon: the Prophet was either unable, or unwilling, to follow the pacifist message he was delivering to the world, which means that the Prophet, like Mormon, was either weak or hypocritical.

But it is hard to see how this is anything but grasping at straws. Joseph Smith endured a life replete with persecution and other massive trials of all kinds—including the deaths of multiple children and, in the end, his own murder—all for the sake of the gospel he was sharing with the world. Along the way the record tells us that he received the promise of eternal life (e.g., D&C 88:2–4; 132:49–50) and heard explicit approbation from the Lord for his "sacrifices in obedience to that which I have told you"—sacrifices that the Lord compares to Abraham's sacrifice of Isaac (D&C 132:50). To believe that Joseph Smith was either weak or hypocritical is thus to believe that while he was of sufficient spiritual capacity that he could enjoy a nearly endless number of divine manifestations and receive both the promise of eternal life and the explicit approval of the Lord for his sacrifices, he was not of sufficient spiritual capacity that he could live up to the standard he was delivering to the world through the Book of Mormon.

A genuine theme regarding Book of Mormon violence: The ancient promise to Nephi. The second problem with seeing a pacifist theme in Book of Mormon history is best revealed by asking the question: If (as the narrative view claims) Nephite civilization ended because the Nephites resorted to violence, then why didn't the civilization end far earlier?[11] Why weren't the Nephites destroyed the *first* time they resorted to violence—or at least one of the countless times thereafter that they defended themselves? The narrative view relies on the single period in which Nephites' employment of violence ended in their annihilation, compared to the dozens of incidents (countless, really) in which the Nephites' resort to violence actually preserved their society. It is difficult to see how that collection of realities leads to a pacifist conclusion.

This raises the question of what accounts for the difference—the difference between the times the Nephites succeeded in defending themselves and the time, at the end, when they failed. The answer is found in the early promise made to Nephi that his posterity would prevail against their enemies *if they remembered the Lord* (1 Ne. 2:20–24). As seen in Chapter 6, this promise did not entail that the Nephites would be protected from any assault whatever by keeping the commandments, but that they would be protected from conquest and rule by the Lamanites by doing so.

---

11. I am indebted to Kimberly White for this way of framing the matter.

Although this promise was fulfilled throughout the history of Nephite civilization, all of this changed at the end. At this time Mormon spoke despairingly of the Nephites' lust to "avenge themselves" against the Lamanites (Morm. 3:9, 11) and of the Nephites' "wickedness and abomination" (Morm. 3:11)—reasons for which he "utterly refused" to lead the Nephites any longer in battle (Morm. 3:11, 16). In subsequent wars Mormon reports that "the Nephites repented not of the evil they had done, but persisted in their wickedness continually" (Morm. 4:10) and tells us (evidently regarding both the Lamanites and Nephites) that "there never had been so great wickedness among all the children of Lehi, nor even among all the house of Israel" (Morm. 4:12).

Not long after, Mormon reports that the Nephites never again had success against Lamanite attack (Morm. 4:18). The devastation continued even after Mormon relented and once again took leadership of the Nephite armies—doing so "without hope ... for they repented not of their iniquities" (Morm. 5:2). In a concluding psalm of anguish, Mormon again emphasizes the Nephites' failure to repent and remember the Lord, crying "O that ye had repented before this great destruction had come upon you" (Morm. 6:17, 22).

Moroni concludes the record with the report that, following the final battle at Cumorah, "the Nephites who had escaped into the country southward were hunted by the Lamanites, until they were all destroyed," adding that "great has been their fall; yea, great and marvelous is the destruction of my people, the Nephites. And behold, it is the hand of the Lord which hath done it" (Morm. 8:2, 7–8).

With this tragic conclusion in mind, the story line of the Book of Mormon seems clear regarding conflict and violence. Throughout most of their history, when the Nephites suffered Lamanite assault, they either repented of their sins and turned to righteousness,[12] or they were righteous already;[13] and in each case they were eventually able to defeat the Lamanite invaders and avoid destruction. At the end of their history, however, the Nephites were wicked *and* they refused to repent. And this time, as a consequence, they were destroyed—which is precisely what the Lord had earlier foretold

---

12. Though not well-known, an excellent example of this is seen in Lachoneus, who was governor of the Nephites during a time of particular peril due to threat from the Gadianton robbers. Lachoneus taught the people to "cry unto the Lord," telling them that "except ye repent" they would not be delivered from those robbers (3 Ne. 3:12, 15). Later, after the Nephites had prevailed, they rejoiced, knowing that "it was because of their repentance and their humility" that they had been saved from destruction (3 Ne. 4:33).

13. See the section "Were the Nephites Always Unrighteous When Involved in War?" in Chapter 6, and the following passages: Alma 48:20–25; 60:12–13; Jarom 1:5–7; 3 Nephi 2:11–17; and W of M 1:13–14 in conjunction with Mosiah 2:31.

through Samuel the Lamanite when he warned that "utter destruction" would come upon the Nephites "except ye repent" (Hel. 13:10). He had assured that everything would be different if they would "repent and return unto the Lord your God," but "wo unto him that repenteth not" (Hel. 13:11). Mormon expressed the same worry, fearing "lest the Lamanites shall destroy this people; for they do not repent" and proclaiming that "I know that they must perish except they repent" (Moro. 9:3, 22). The Nephites did not in fact repent, and they thus experienced the tragic fate that Samuel and Mormon had foretold.

A compelling candidate for the theme of the Book of Mormon regarding conflict, then, is found in the divine promise with which the story begins: If the Nephites repent and remember the Lord they will be spared, but if they do not repent and remember the Lord they will be destroyed. And this, of course, is exactly the pattern that the record displays. The Lord helped the Nephites defend themselves throughout their history, and when, at the end, he no longer helped them and they were destroyed, it was precisely for the reasons that the original promise specified.

This means that if the Book of Mormon is to be read as a narrative, it actually seems best read as a book bracketed by a divine promise. It is an account of a civilization that ends in direct fulfillment of the very conditions under which it began. As narrative structures go it is hard to surpass this one. Unfortunately for the narrative view we are considering, it is a structure that, far from supporting a pacifist conclusion, actually precludes it.

The Narrative Approach and the Savior's Teachings in Third Nephi

A third key feature of the narrative approach is its account of the Savior's visit in Third Nephi. As we saw early in Chapter 8, this visit "compels us to reinterpret" the events of the entire Book of Mormon and serves as an "interpretive key" to our understanding of the book's overall narrative. It helps us understand "the broader narrative, including the earlier acts of violence and the final apocalypse to come." Indeed, the Lord's pacifist sayings at this time supersede and thus correct any different pronouncements or attitudes that appear anywhere else in the book. They are central to reaching a pacifist conclusion.[14]

The Lord's teachings that accomplish all this are found in this passage.[15]

> And ye shall offer up unto me no more the shedding of blood; yea, your sacrifices and your burnt offerings shall be done away, for I will accept none of your sacrifices and your burnt offerings. And ye shall offer for a sacrifice unto me a broken heart and a contrite spirit. And whoso cometh unto me with a broken heart and a contrite spirit, him will I baptize with fire and with the Holy Ghost, even as the

---

14. Joshua Madson, "A Non-Violent Reading of the Book of Mormon," 24–25.
15. Ibid., 15, 28.

Lamanites, because of their faith in me at the time of their conversion, were baptized with fire and with the Holy Ghost, and they knew it not. (3 Ne. 9:19–20)

The narrative approach makes two major claims based on this passage that are central to the assertion that these sayings are pacifist in character.

Forbidding the Shedding of Blood

The first claim rests on the Lord's statement that "ye shall offer up unto me no more the shedding of blood." From this declaration not only is a prohibition against animal sacrifice assumed, but also against war. Here, we are told: "Jesus denounces all sacrificial violence, including war,"[16] and since this rejection of violence comes from the Lord himself, it is thoroughly dispositive.

However, by itself it is difficult to see how the Lord's statement supports this conclusion about war. He says, for example, that "ye shall *offer up to me* no more the shedding of blood," which presupposes that the blood the Lord is speaking of is expressly the blood that *had* been offered up to him. Given this, and given the language of offering, this reference is clearly to the blood of animal sacrifices performed according to Mosaic law. No Nephite leader went to war in the name of making an "offering," and thus it is difficult to see how any of their actions can be understood in those terms.[17]

Moreover, immediately after making this prohibition the Lord explicitly states: "Yea, your sacrifices and your burnt offerings shall be done away, for I will accept none of your sacrifices and burnt offerings." It is noteworthy that the Lord begins here with the expression, "yea," which reemphasizes the statement that preceded it and then proceeds to specify that he is speaking directly of sacrifices and burnt offerings. Everything in this passage thus indicates that it is specifically Mosaic animal sacrifices that are meant by this prohibition of the "shedding of blood;" nothing suggests the application to be broader. Additionally, this passage acts as a fulfillment of an earlier prophecy about the future of Mosaic sacrifices and prescriptions. It was this shedding of blood—and no other—that Amulek had prophesied would cease following the Lord's atonement (Alma 34:13). Everything in the text, therefore, including the Lord's own words, indicates a reading of this passage that undercuts the narrative interpretation.

---

16. Ibid., 25.

17. The narrative approach has its own way of seeing wars as a species of "sacrificial violence," but there is no evidence that the Nephites ever conceived of their conduct in this way and thus there is no reason to suppose that, in making these remarks, the Lord was communicating a message to them about their wartime behavior: There is no evidence that they would comprehend a message framed in this way. For a discussion of the narrative approach's view of war as sacrificial see the section "Use of Girard's Work on Cultural Scapegoating" later in this chapter.

Lamanite Example of Genuine Conversion

A second claim derived from this passage rests on this part of the text: "And ye shall offer for a sacrifice unto me a broken heart and a contrite spirit. And whoso cometh unto me with a broken heart and a contrite spirit, him will I baptize with fire and with the Holy Ghost, *even as the Lamanites*, because of their faith in me at the time of their conversion, were baptized with fire and with the Holy Ghost" (3 Ne. 9:20). The reference to the Lamanites is central here because, according to this narrative approach, the Lord is referring to Lamanites who had been converted to the Lord and, as a result of their conversion, had laid down their weapons and abandoned all possibility of war. Furthermore, we are told that "this was not an isolated event but a pattern" in Lamanite conversions.[18] Thus, Christ's message here is that true conversion is a change of heart that includes a rejection of violence. Such renunciation, therefore, is the standard of genuine discipleship and the Lord's commandment in this passage tells us it is a standard he expects us to meet.

To support this claim about the example of Lamanite conversion, reference is made to the Ammonites, as well as to two additional passages. One passage is the account of Lamanites who were converted through the miraculous events surrounding the imprisonment of Nephi and Lehi in Helaman 5. As the Lamanites began to develop faith in Christ, "the Holy Spirit of God did come down from heaven, and did enter into their hearts, and they were filled as if with fire" (Hel. 5:45). It is easy to imagine that Jesus was referring to this group in speaking of Lamanites who had been "baptized with fire and with the Holy Ghost." Three hundred accepted the teachings of Nephi and Lehi at this time, and they then taught others in the surrounding area of their transcendent experiences "insomuch that the more part of the Lamanites were convinced of them" (Hel. 5:50). The record then tells us that those who were converted "did lay down their weapons of war, and also their hatred and the tradition of their fathers" (Hel. 5:51).

The other passage used to support this claim comes from the prophet Samuel. In calling the Nephites to repentance, he reminded them of the steadfastness of the Lamanites who had been converted to the Lord, including the observation that "they have buried their weapons of war, and they fear to take them up lest by any means they should sin; yea, ye can see that they fear to sin—for behold they will suffer themselves that they be trodden down and slain by their enemies, and will not lift their swords against them, and this because of their faith in Christ" (Hel. 15:9).

The most plausible reading of all of these events seems to be that the laying down of weapons among the Lamanites began with the widespread

---

18. Ibid., 25.

conversion that occurred at the time of Nephi and Lehi and continued thereafter as conversions spread. This pattern, in conjunction with the identical behavior of the Ammonites, is thought to identify the pacifist character of genuine conversion to the Lord and to exemplify the Lord's command to have a broken heart and a contrite spirit.

Three problems with these Lamanite examples. There are three difficulties with this appeal to Lamanite conversion, however. The first is that the example of the Ammonites does not support it. As discussed in Chapters 4 and 5, the Anti-Nephi-Lehies refused to defend themselves, not out of a philosophical or spiritual rejection of violence per se, but out of an attitude of abject penance for the sustained acts of aggression and murder they had committed against the Nephites over time.

As for the later Lamanites who laid down their weapons as conversions spread, the record supplies a mere two verses. Combining them, we learn that these Lamanites had faith in Christ and that they were afraid (just like the Ammonites had been) of committing sin if they were to kill again. That is everything we are told about their views on war, although a wider look at the text paints a picture of their pre-conversion conduct that is highly reminiscent of the Ammonites prior to their own conversion. We are told, for example, that the Lamanites experiencing this change of heart had believed "the wicked and abominable traditions of their fathers" (see Hel. 5:19; 15:7) and shared a "hatred" for the Nephites (Hel. 5:51). Indeed, Nephi and Lehi were consigned by their Lamanite captors to prison and then to death, in the first place, for doing nothing more than preaching the gospel. We are also told that these Lamanites had earlier "come down against the Nephites to battle, and they did commence the work of death," and that "they succeeded in obtaining possession" of Nephite lands (Hel. 4:5)—many of which they succeeded in retaining despite Nephite attempts to win them back (Hel. 4:6–10). This is why, when the initial group of Lamanites was converted, the record tells us that "they did yield up unto the Nephites the lands of their possession" (Hel. 5:52).

Thus, not only did these Lamanites feel compelled to lay down their weapons at the time of their conversion, they also felt compelled to give back to the Nephites the lands that they had been able to win by killing Nephites with those weapons. As with the Lamanites at the time of the Ammonites' conversion,[19] this seems to be a people for whom life was cheap and who found themselves using their weapons to wage war and kill Nephites in order to conquer and possess Nephite lands.

---

19. Regarding similar descriptions of the Ammonites see the section "What Were the Ammonites Like Before Their Conversion?" in Chapter 4.

All of this indicates that these Lamanites were not innocent victims of war who laid down their weapons as a philosophical repudiation of violence in principle. They laid down their weapons as a repudiation of, and likely as penance for, the widespread killing that they themselves had inflicted upon the Nephites.[20] That is what we see in the Ammonites, and every indication is that the same factors are at play with these later Lamanites. Thus, while the narrative approach appeals to these Lamanite accounts for support, they do not actually provide the confirmation that is sought.

The third problem with the appeal to a general Lamanite pattern of conversion-as-pacifism appears in Third Nephi. There we are told of a singular group of Lamanites whose righteousness was such that their curse "was taken from them" and who joined with the Nephites and became one with them. Yet these Lamanites took up arms to defend themselves as a people from the destructive aims and actions of the Gadianton robbers who dominated the land at the time (3 Ne. 2:11–17). There is no question about the spiritual refinement and even preeminence of these Lamanites, and yet their response to aggression was nothing close to pacifist.

In short, the text does not support the claim that the Lamanites demonstrate the pacifist character of genuine conversion. Not all Lamanite converts laid down their weapons, and those who did lay down their arms fail to support pacifist claims in any event because they evidently did so for other than pacifist reasons. All of this means that there is no reason to see Jesus' teachings in Third Nephi as pacifist. No argument for the view succeeds. And this means that there is no reason to see these teachings as "corrective" of any other elements in the text.

The Narrative Approach and Nephi's Inauguration of Nephite Culture

A final key concept in the narrative approach is its account of Nephi's slaying of Laban. According to this view, rather than seeing Nephi as being obedient to the command of the Lord, we must see his slaying of Laban as an act of murder and his account of the episode as an act of mendacity.[21]

---

20. Part of their repudiation might also have been of their tendency to allow Nephite dissenters to stir them up against the Nephites. Such dissidents were a major part of Lamanite aggression from the time of Alma and the sons of Mosiah forward. In this particular case, the Lamanites succumbed to Nephite agitation only after first resisting it. But succumb they did (Hel. 4:1–4). For more on Nephite agitation of the Lamanites see the section "Differences in the Character of Nephite and Lamanite Unrighteousness" in Chapter 6.

21. See the section in Chapter 8, "Examining the Corollary of the Narrative Approach: The Example of Nephi."

Understood this way the event was thoroughly tragic because it fashioned the conceptual framework about violence that would determine Nephite attitudes for the duration of their civilization. Succeeding generations were captive to Nephi's founding narrative of justified violence.

Use of Girard's Work on Cultural Scapegoating

Central to this interpretation is a reliance on René Girard's work on cultural scapegoating. As applied to the Book of Mormon the core idea of this view is that cultures perpetuate violence and escalate it until they either face and heal the violence in themselves, or find a scapegoat on which to release their violence, and temporarily conceal it, until it erupts again.[22] The standard form such scapegoat-

---

22. Since the way LDS authors use Girard's work is what matters for my purposes, my characterization and treatment of Girard focus on the use that Madson, and Eugene England for that matter, make of him. Madson refers regularly to sources that rely on Girard, as well as to Girard directly, whose works include *Violence and the Sacred*, and *Things Hidden since the Foundation of the World*. England's reliance on Girard is explicit both in his "Healing and Making Peace, in the Church and the World," and "Why Nephi Killed Laban: Reflections on the Truth of the Book of Mormon," 1–22, and 131–55, respectively. At its most basic level Girard's theory of scapegoating violence is descriptive in character: it is a theory that seeks to explain the founding, preserving, and unifying of cultures. Roughly speaking, key concepts include the role of imitation ("mimesis") in creating the desire to acquire objects of one sort or another, the conflict this creates between imitators and those they imitate in seeking the desired object, the ensuing hostility and threat of violence between such individuals, the (subconscious) dispersion—or venting—of this hostility onto an agreed-upon victim-scapegoat rather than onto each other, and the resulting (temporary) alleviation of hostility between the individuals themselves (the hostility is not healed, but is instead dispersed through scapegoating violence of some sort toward another). These and related concepts explain how cultures form and preserve themselves, including the creation of mythologies and rituals relating to the scapegoat(s) around which communities have formed themselves. (This view of conflict, violence, and scapegoating informs Girard's view of the Atonement, which he seems to see not as an act that permitted the reconciliation of fallen beings with God, but as God's revelation of the futility of scapegoating mechanisms to end violence and create lasting peace.) Though descriptive in character as an explanation of violence and of its dispersion (and of how this relates to important cultural phenomena), Girard's concepts lead him to a Christian pacifism that condemns violence as well. Madson and England employ Girard's explanation of violence in a similar spirit, presupposing that the violence being explained is morally wrong. As an effort to vent violence rather than to heal it, it is an effort to flee the truth rather than to face it—all at the expense of a victim who happens to be convenient for these purposes and thus who can be (subconsciously) exploited. Seeing Nephi's conduct as an instantiation of such sacrificial violence thus makes it natural to condemn him and to question the accuracy of his account. (Whether Nephi's conduct actually meets all of

ing takes is in an act of violence that justifies itself in the name of redemption or necessity—an act of killing, for example, that is committed in the name of saving an entire nation. In this respect the violence is actually sacrificial in nature because it trades the demise of the few in order to preserve the many.

All of this is meaningful because the narrative argument supposes that Nephi's slaying of Laban is a clear example of just such scapegoating. As a killing that was justified specifically in the name of the spiritual protection of an entire nation, it was an act of violence that was seemingly sacrificial in character. The narrative view finds it natural, therefore, to condemn Nephi's act because it maintains that that event was a classic example of Girard's argument. As an act of scapegoating violence, the slaying of Laban was wrong. Appeal to the theory of scapegoating thus gives us reason to look past the apparent meaning of the Book of Mormon text and to see things in a more subtle light. It is a light that reveals Nephi's act to be murder and thus explains why he would lie about it.

The Problem with the Scapegoating Explanation

There is a problem with this way of thinking about the matter, however. The argument's reasoning jumps from the observation that the slaying of Laban was an act of violence that justified itself, to the conclusion that the slaying of Laban was therefore an act of scapegoating (an act that seeks to hide, rather than to heal, the violence in oneself) because it assumes that all acts of violence that justify themselves are acts of scapegoating.

But it is obvious that we cannot simply assume this. The claim calls for demonstration. After all, even if we stipulate that scapegoating occurs through an act of violence that justifies itself, it does not follow that every act of violence that justifies itself is therefore an act of scapegoating. In the language of simple set theory, to say that all X is Y is not to say that all Y is X. Thus we recognize the obvious fallacy in saying something like: "All automobiles are four-wheeled vehicles; therefore, all four-wheeled vehicles are automobiles." Similarly, to say that all scapegoating occurs through an act of violence that justifies itself is not to say that all violence that justifies itself is therefore an act of scapegoating. This is disproven by any act of violence in which the justification is obviously legitimate, meaning that the explanation for violence is not rationalization (i.e., the subconscious exploitation of a convenient victim-scapegoat) and not a flight from the truth about oneself.

Logically proponents of the scapegoating view must grant such a possibility. To refuse to grant it would be to deny that the assumption in question

---

the criteria identified by Girard—and not just LDS authors' versions of his theory—is another question, but one I leave aside. It is LDS authors' use of Girard that matters for my purposes.)

requires demonstration. But this would be equivalent to asserting that any instance of violence that justifies itself is scapegoating violence *by definition*, thus robbing the claim of any actual content. It would be no different than saying, "This skateboard is an automobile because, after all, all four-wheeled vehicles are automobiles"—a logical *ignis fatuus* that actually assumes what it is appearing to prove. It would seem that to avoid logical vacuity of this sort the scapegoating view must grant the possibility that *some* violence that justifies itself can be legitimate and thus not be an instance of scapegoating.

Such instances are not difficult to find. To choose just one example, this is seen in the Lord's own statement to the Nephites, reported by Mormon, that "ye shall defend your families even unto bloodshed" (Alma 43:47).[23] Here we have violence and also justification (the violence of defense is committed in order to "defend your families"). So this is an act of violence that justifies itself, but, because Jesus Christ himself is the one who is both framing the matter and promoting the violence (and actually helping the Nephites execute it, for that matter[24]), it is manifestly *not* an act of scapegoating. This is obvious since scapegoating is an act performed in order to conceal the violence in oneself rather than to confront and heal it; thus to consider this episode an act of scapegoating would be to see the Lord himself as both needing to confront and heal the violence in himself and failing to do so. Because this is ludicrous, the conclusion from this example, and from the many like it, is straightforward: *Not* all acts of violence that justify themselves are acts of scapegoating; the implicit assumption that they are is mistaken.[25]

---

23. Recall that I have already supplied one correction to the idea that we can dismiss prophets' reports of the Lord's communications to them (such as Mormon's report, here, that the Lord commanded the Nephites to defend themselves). See the section in Chapter 8, "Examining the Corollary of the Narrative Approach: The Example of the Lord's Own Conduct." In addition, recall that from the narrative point of view the general impulse to dismiss spiritual leaders' statements supporting violence rests on the conclusion that the Book of Mormon as a whole conveys a pacifist message—a conclusion that justifies dismissing elements of the text that are contrary to this theme. But what we are discovering in this chapter is that narrative arguments provide no support for seeing the Book of Mormon as a pacifist document, which means that they provide no support for dismissing non-pacifist elements of the text, including prophets' reports of the Lord's communications to them.

24. See Chapter 7.

25. Although this narrative argument relies on an unstated premise, in itself this presents no problem. Arguments of this kind ("enthymemes") are common because much of the time the hidden premise in a line of reasoning is so obvious that spelling it out would be both unnecessary and tedious. At other times, the unstated assumption may be far from true, even if the author does not see this. Then it is important to locate the underlying assumption and to demonstrate its mistakenness. That is the

There is no surprise, of course, in discovering that acts of violence are not necessarily acts of scapegoating. As shown repeatedly in previous chapters, if we read the Book of Mormon comprehensively we see that while the Lord abhors violence, and abhors the wickedness that occasions it, he does not reject violence itself in all conceivable circumstances. Not all violence is illegitimate and exploitative, and thus not all violence is an act of scapegoating.

What follows from all of this is that we have no reason to suppose that Nephi's slaying of Laban was anything like an act of scapegoating. If the Lord could justify violence in one instance, then he could justify it in another. There is no more reason to imagine that Nephi was lying about divine involvement in his slaying of Laban than there is to imagine that Mormon was lying about divine involvement in the case he reports about the Nephites in general. The narrative interpretation of Nephi's slaying of Laban can be rejected.[26]

Nephite wars as "sacrificial violence." It is worth recalling that the narrative approach refers to the wars waged by the Nephites as "sacrificial violence." The idea seems to be that such wars were all simply recapitulations (on a large scale) of Nephi's initial slaying of Laban: an act of killing that was justified in

---

case here. It may appear to be obvious that all violence that justifies itself is necessarily an act of scapegoating violence, but, appearances aside, the assumption is mistaken.

26. It is not the only claim about Nephi that is problematic. For example, in the course of discussing the narrative approach we are also told that Nephi was disingenuous in how he described Laman and Lemuel—in truth they were only "half-hearted assassins" who are turned into mere "caricatures" by Nephi's account (Madson, "A Non-Violent Reading of the Book of Mormon," 20, referring to Grant Hardy, *Understanding the Book of Mormon*). Nephi is therefore as inauthentic in how he describes his brothers as he is in how he describes the incident with Laban. But to treat the actions of Laman and Lemuel this way seems to disregard explicit episodes that appear in the record. These include the time Laman and Lemuel beat Nephi and Sam with a rod and had to be constrained by an angel (1 Ne. 3:28–30); the time they bound Nephi, seeking to leave him in the wilderness to be killed and eaten by predators—and were prevented from doing so only by the power of God (1 Ne. 7:16–18); the time they attempted to throw Nephi "into the depths of the sea" and failed only because they were constrained, again, by the power of God (1 Ne. 17:48); Lehi's own report that Laman and Lemuel actually "sought to take away [Nephi's] life" (2 Ne. 1:24); and Nephi's fleeing into the wilderness to escape his brothers' efforts to kill him (2 Ne. 5:1–5). Nephi's way of putting the matter is relevant here: "Now I do not write upon these plates all the words which they murmured against me. But it sufficeth me to say, that they did seek to take away my life" (2 Ne. 5:4). In short, in considering the attempts of Laman and Lemuel to harm Nephi, it is important not to overlook Nephi's stealth in avoiding their efforts, nor to overlook God's own interventions in saving his life. When we bear such elements of the text in mind, it is not obvious that "half-hearted" is the best description of Laman and Lemuel's aggression.

terms of sacrificing the one for the many. When Jesus denounced all sacrifice in his Third-Nephi teachings, then, he denounced justification of this kind and thus denounced justification for Nephite wars.

But all of this rests on the idea that Nephi's original act itself was an act of sacrifice, and this is a mistake. There is no reason to accept a scapegoating analysis of Nephi's slaying of Laban and actually every reason to reject it. There is thus no reason to think of Nephite wars as recapitulations of Nephi's act or as in any way sacrificial. And this means there is further reason to reject the narrative assertion that Jesus' remarks in Third Nephi were at all related to war.[27]

There is an additional reason why sacrifice is a poor analogy for what happened in Nephite wars. Inherent in the term "sacrifice" is the assumption that the sacrificed life is not itself a threat to those performing the sacrifice. This is what we see, for example, when we consider cases of animal sacrifice or of Abraham's incident with Isaac. There is no sense in which those performing the sacrifice in these cases were defending themselves from any actual threat posed by the animal or person they were sacrificing. That's why the sacrificial act is called sacrifice rather than defense.[28]

But this is far from the case in Nephite wars. Throughout the vast majority of their history the Nephites never initiated violence. When they went to war it was only because the Lamanites were *attacking* them. Sacrifice is not the best analogy for what people are doing when they are defending themselves against being murdered.

Thus, while the idea of scapegoating attempts to cast Nephite wars in terms of sacrificial violence the effort does not succeed. It is a mistake to see Nephi's slaying of Laban in this way, and it is a mistake to see subsequent Nephite wars in this way as well.[29]

---

27. See the section "Forbidding the Shedding of Blood" earlier in this chapter.

28. In Girard's work the threat presented by the scapegoat is not genuine, but simply part of the subsequent mythology that grows up around the sacrificial act.

29. Similarly, for two primary reasons it is a mistake to make a statement like this: "The mission of Ammon and his brothers to the Lamanites, specifically in defiance of Nephite cultural stereotypes, ultimately demonstrates that acts of love and service can break through false cultural narratives, unite kingdoms, and convert thousands to Christianity where violence could not" (Joshua Madson, "A Non-Violent Reading of the Book of Mormon," 24). One reason this statement is a mistake is that it presents a false dichotomy: it presupposes that violence was a method the Nephites used to try to "unite kingdoms" and "convert thousands to Christianity," contrasting it with "acts of love and service" directed toward the same end. But the Nephites never employed violence as a way to convert the Lamanites; they employed violence *only when the Lamanites were attacking them*. In this context, then, "violence" and "acts of love and service" are not competing alternatives for achieving the same end. A more accurate statement, therefore, would be: "Lamanites' happiness, following their conversion, ultimately demonstrates

Conclusion:
On the Narrative Approach and a Pacifist Book of Mormon

Identified in Chapter 8 were three intellectual questions the narrative approach must answer. First, what exactly is the evidence for the claim that Book of Mormon prophets are wrong part of the time (specifically regarding conflict)? What reason do we have to believe that such prophets are to be trusted at some times, but not at others, particularly when both are part of the scriptural canon? Second, even if there is a distinction between times when prophets can be trusted and times when they cannot, how valid is the narrative principle that tells us which times are which? And finally, how is it that all Book of Mormon prophets are wrong on exactly the same topic—i.e., the matter of violence and conflict?

The narrative answer to the first question is that we know that various prophets in the Book of Mormon are wrong because at various times their statements and/or actions contradict the overall pacifist moral of the book, and the answer to the second is that we know *where* such prophetic figures are wrong because it is simply wherever they are non-pacifist and thus generate this inconsistency.

Both answers depend on the claim that the Book of Mormon is in fact a pacifist document. Yet the narrative view fails to demonstrate this. Three of its central claims concern Mormon, the story of Nephite civilization, and the Lord's teachings in Third Nephi, and, as we have discovered in this chapter, every one of them is mistaken. None of them infuses the Book of Mormon with a pacifist message. The narrative reading thus cannot be used to claim that certain teachings and/or actions in the scriptures are wrong. It is this narrative reading that is wrong. And this means that we have no reason to wonder about where—and where not—to trust prophets, because, in the end, the narrative reading gives us no reason to mistrust prophets anywhere.

The narrative answer to the final question is found in the fourth central claim of the narrative approach: namely, that Nephi's slaying of Laban set Lehite society on a violent path, planting the concept of scapegoating/

---

that responding to acts of love and service from representatives of God could bring them happiness where attacking Nephites and killing them could not." *This* statement presents us with genuine alternatives that are true to the text. The second reason this statement is a mistake is that it overlooks Ammon's own violence at the very beginning of his ministry among the Lamanites—his killing a number of Lamanite marauders and his cutting off the arms of others (Alma 17:26–39; 18:16). And later, when Lamoni's father threatened Ammon, Ammon's response was to engage him in battle, defeat him, and then threaten to kill the king if he did not fulfill Ammon's righteous desires (Alma 20:1–24). It is a sizeable oversight to refer to the mission of Ammon and his brethren in terms of "acts of love and service" and to omit the way in which central elements of that very service were violent, both in threatening death and in causing it.

sacrificial violence at the very center of Nephite culture and establishing a conceptual momentum that subsequent generations could not escape. Book of Mormon leaders thus all erred in the same way because they were all captive to the same false founding narrative.

This answer, however, depends on the claim that Nephi's slaying of Laban was in fact an act of sacrificial violence, and yet it is evident that it was not. And because it was not such an act it could not have established a false founding narrative for subsequent generations of Nephite leaders. Succeeding prophets were not the captives this interpretation imagines. The natural conclusion to draw from the Book of Mormon, then, is not that its leaders were all wrong on the same issue; the natural conclusion to draw is that they were not wrong at all. Moreover, even if it were true (though it is not) that these prophets *were* all wrong on the same issue, the narrative view still could not account for this: its explanation based on scapegoating and sacrificial violence does not succeed. It would appear, therefore, that this narrative view provides an explanation that doesn't work to account for a circumstance that doesn't exist.[30]

We have seen a number of significant scriptural reinterpretations that follow from a pacifist reading of the Book of Mormon. These include: determining that a host of prophets have been routinely wrong in their teachings and/or conduct regarding conflict; deciding that multiple Book of Mormon

---

30. In other words, the *explanans* and the *explanandum* are both false. There is an additional reason for finding the idea of cultural constraints implausible. Mormon came very late in Nephite history and he, of all people, could be considered constrained by Nephite cultural norms regarding violence. But such a view encounters the same type of obstacle that we saw in the case of Joseph Smith earlier in this chapter and with Nephi in Chapter 8 (see the earlier section "The Prophet Joseph Smith" and the section "Examining the Corollary of the Narrative Approach: The Example of Nephi" in Chapter 8): such constraint seems implausible in light of Mormon's stature and in light of how the Lord treated him. Mormon saw the Lord at the age of fifteen (Morm. 1:15), he taught canonized doctrine by the power of the Spirit (e.g., Helaman 12; 3 Ne. 29, 30; Morm. 7; Moro. 7–9), he was visited by the Three Nephites (3 Ne. 28:24–26), he received multiple revelations from the Lord (e.g., 3 Ne. 30; Moro. 8:7–9; W of M: 1:6–7), and he was entrusted with the responsibility to craft the primary instrument for gathering Israel in the last days. Given all that the Lord was able to teach Mormon it seems implausible to suppose that he couldn't teach him the true standard regarding conflict and violence, whatever we might imagine the cultural norms to have been. And the same is true of numerous others, including Alma and Mormon's son Moroni. From the "captive" view it follows that the Lord was able to appear to these prophets and to teach them truths of a magnificent and eternal nature, but, because of Nephi's act centuries earlier, he couldn't teach them that it is wrong to fight. This is a possible view, but it would take a robust argument to make it seem compelling.

reports about the Lord are false; concluding that Nephi was a liar and a murderer; and discovering that we cannot take seriously Nephi's reports of his divine manifestations and of the authenticity of his teachings based on them. All of these face serious textual obstacles in their own right, but might nevertheless be defended in one way or another if the narrative approach were to succeed in framing the Book of Mormon as a pacifist document. As we have seen, however, it does not do this. The central claims of the narrative view fail and with them the intellectual consequences they yield. If the Book of Mormon contains a pacifist message it appears that it will take a different argument to show it.[31]

---

31. As a final comment it is worth noting how prominently Nephi figures in the narrative approach. Not only does he provide the scheme with a dramatic example of a spiritual figure doing wrong—committing murder and lying about it—but that wrong is then used to explain a thousand years of subsequent Nephite conflict, including the violent destruction of Nephite civilization at the end. But what we have discovered is an absence of any textual support for these claims. What the text shows is a devoted disciple and a prophet of immense spiritual capacity. We encounter a Nephi who was specifically raised up by the Lord to provide the means of salvation for a branch of the house of Israel and, so far as the last days are concerned, for the entire house of Israel. The record displays his suffering all manner of hardship and persecution to do so, risking death more than once, and fulfilling his charge faithfully and to the letter. We share in his seeing the Lord, entertaining angels, and viewing the visions of eternity, all while laboring through a desert wilderness, crossing the sea in a ship he constructed in accordance with visions from the Lord, establishing a new civilization, and defending himself from the assault of those who would kill him. And we see him penning a record of it all that brims with the Spirit and that bears a witness of the Lord and of his divinity that is unsurpassed in all scripture. It is hard to see how it is anything but sad beyond words that Nephi continues to this day to suffer the slings and arrows of critics.

Chapter 10

Three Arguments for Pacifism

In addition to a narrative approach, three other arguments offer a scriptural case for pacifism. It is important to treat them, at least briefly, since all of them pursue paths that might appear promising.

A Continuum of Acceptable Approaches to War

One way to read the Book of Mormon is to see it as a mix of both pacifism *and* just-war thinking.[1] While the book "generally condemns the terrible fruits of war, the Book of Mormon also explicitly suggest just warfare, rightly applied, is a divine strategy for resisting violence." Nevertheless, "the text never suggests just warfare is the *only* or even *most* divine resistance strategy."[2] Rather, the most divine and moral strategy is non-violent action. According to this view, the Book of Mormon does not present us with a stark dichotomy between an approach that is righteous and one that is not, but instead presents us with a continuum of acceptable approaches to war, with just-war thinking on one end of the spectrum and pacifism—the more moral, more divine approach—on the other.[3]

An argument of this sort seems appealing because it appears to capture a wider truth: rather than either explicitly or implicitly condemning Book of Mormon figures who went to war, this approach honors them, and it does so while simultaneously presenting us with a standard of conduct that is even higher. The soundness of this approach, however, depends on whether such a continuum actually appears in the text. Does the Book of Mormon, while countenancing just-war thinking, also present pacifism as a higher, more divine standard?

The Ammonites' Strategy of Self-Sacrifice

One way to argue for the greater divinity of the pacifist approach is to point to its effectiveness. For example, in praising the Ammonites' peaceful conduct in Alma 24 and 27 we are told that they did not flee or submit to their

---

1. J. David Pulsipher, "The Ammonite Conundrum," 1–12.
2. Ibid., 9; emphasis in original.
3. The author dislikes the term "pacifism" for capturing his sense of dynamic nonviolence, preferring the locution "weapons of love" instead. However, what he has in mind explicitly includes the standard pacifist view that rejects all violence, so the expression is accurate as far as it goes. For this reason, and for brevity's sake, I take the liberty of using the term "pacifism" to capture what the author has in mind in offering an alternative to just-war attitudes.

enemies' demands, but rather that "they went out and met their enemies—confronted them, even—armed only with love and prayer." Furthermore, "a careful reading of the text indicates their strategy of love and prayer prevented further aggression for at least four years, a remarkable stretch by Book of Mormon standards."[4] From all of this it seems natural to conclude that it was the Ammonites' self-sacrifice, love, and prayer that brought the aggression against them to an end, and that this is a persuasive case for the superiority of pacifist conduct over active defense.

The Ammonites' different behavior in subsequent circumstances. However, if this strategy of self-sacrifice is all there is to the story—and if following this path was so effective—then we are forced to ask why the Ammonites did not continue to sacrifice themselves in this way. To consider just one example, why did they emigrate to the land of Jershon for protection rather than simply approach their enemies, once again, armed only with love and prayer as they had done before?

This is an important question if we want to understand the Ammonites, and particularly if we want to follow their example.[5] Why didn't they continue to sacrifice themselves when faced with conflict? According to the record, the answer is that the Lord himself instructed the Ammonites to leave for their safety, observing that, because of Satan's hold on the hearts of their enemies, the Ammonites would "perish" if they remained (Alma 27:11–12). This makes it clear that the Lord himself did not believe the Ammonites would end the conflict in this circumstance by prostrating themselves in front of their enemies. Indeed, he instructed them not to do so precisely because he foresaw that the "strategy of love and prayer" would *not* end the aggression against them. The same issue arises in light of the Ammonites' behavior years later. When the Nephites were faced with destruction and the Ammonite sons went to war in order to help (Alma 53), it is noteworthy that the Ammonite elders did not prevent this by again rushing out to prostrate themselves before their enemies. According to the continuum theory, this kind of self-sacrifice had worked before and had brought an end to the violence, so why didn't the Ammonite elders act similarly this time?

---

4. Ibid., 10. Nibley too thinks this was an effective strategy. The Ammonites' course "was wisdom," he tells us, "for presently the Lamanites realized what they were doing and 'did forbear from slaying them,' and ended up joining their society in large numbers." Hugh Nibley, *Since Cumorah*, 342.

5. The idea that others should try to follow the Ammonites' example, as found in Alma 24 and Alma 27:2–3, is implicit in the claim that their conduct in those places constitutes the more moral, more divine approach. The same idea is implicit in all who emphasize the righteousness of the Ammonites' self-sacrifice. Nibley, of course, is explicit on the matter, saying that the Ammonites' conduct in these passages provides "the perfect example of what to do when faced with a conflict: refuse to take up arms." See Boyd Jay Petersen, *Hugh Nibley: A Consecrated Life*, 221.

The same question arises when we consider the Ammonites' behavior some years after they had relocated to the land of Jershon, and prior to the events of Alma 53. At this time the Nephites confronted the Lamanite armies in the borders of Jershon, and the record tells us that, upon confronting the Nephite military presence, the Lamanite armies "were exceedingly afraid of the armies of the Nephites," whereupon they departed in search of easier Nephite targets (Alma 43:19, 21–22). It is instructive that the Lamanite invaders were turned away from the land occupied by the Ammonites not because of any act of self-sacrifice on the part of the Ammonites themselves, but because of the diligent preparation and imposing presence of a well-equipped Nephite army. Indeed, we have no report that the Ammonites even considered a course of self-sacrifice at this time.

Such incidents tell us that the Ammonite elders did not follow a pattern of self-sacrifice throughout their lives. But this raises the obvious point: There seems little reason to suggest that everyone should follow the Ammonites' example in Alma 24 when the record is clear that even they didn't follow it. It says much about a strategy of self-sacrifice when its primary exemplars themselves failed to pursue it in subsequent circumstances and when the Lord himself—precisely in order to "preserve" the Ammonites—also instructed them not to follow that course.

Ammonite Elders vs. Ammonite Sons

Another way to argue for the continuum view is to indicate that the Ammonites themselves occupy both ends of the spectrum. The sons are heralded in the text for their righteousness and bravery in waging war (Alma 56–58), and the Ammonite elders are equally praised for burying their weapons, allowing themselves to be slaughtered, and entering a covenant eschewing war (Alma 24, 27). What could be clearer evidence of the existence of a divine spectrum and what could be more poetic than to find its poles represented by different generations of the same population?[6]

The non-pacifist character of the Ammonite elders. The problem is that the Ammonite elders were not in fact the pacifists this argument assumes them to be.[7] Read comprehensively, the record indicates that their attitude toward war was no different than the younger Ammonites' attitude. Indeed, at the very time these sons chose to go to war their elders desired to go to war as well.[8] The only difference was that the elder Ammonites had been guilty of

---

6. See J. David Pulsipher, "The Ammonite Conundrum," 9–10.

7. See Chapters 4–5 regarding Ammonite pacifism.

8. See Alma 53:10–22. See particularly the sections in Chapter 5 "How Did the Ammonites Behave After Entering Their Covenant?" and "Refutation of the Ammonites as Pacifist Examples."

murder and thus had entered a covenant of penance that prohibited their taking up the sword, whereas the Ammonite sons carried no such guilt and thus had made no such covenant. They were spiritually free to take up arms to defend themselves and their families, and they made their own covenant to do so. The two generations cannot be used to represent different ends of a continuum because they actually held the same attitude toward war.

Limhi and Alma vs. Other Nephite Leaders

A third way to argue for a continuum approach is to contrast the conflict strategies of two leaders in the Book of Mormon, Lehi and Alma the elder, with other leaders that appear in the text. Whereas most Nephite figures, such as Mormon and Gidgiddoni, typically took up arms when confronted with situations of conflict, Limhi and Alma both adopted a "stealth" strategy, meaning that they fled their situations and thus avoided conflict altogether.[9] The continuum is thus represented with leaders like Mormon and Gidgiddoni on one end, and Limhi and Alma on the other.

The inaptness of comparing Limhi and Alma to other Nephite leaders. However, drawing a contrast between the two sets of leaders is a mistake for three reasons. First, unlike other Nephite leaders, the experiences of both Limhi and Alma took place in the land of their enemies. Limhi's people found themselves situated among the Lamanites because a previous generation had explicitly sought occasion to settle there (Mosiah 9). Alma's people found themselves situated among their enemies because, by converting, they dramatically separated themselves, at least spiritually, from the surrounding society of which they had been a part (Mosiah 18), and later, because they were completely overwhelmed and subjugated by Lamanite occupiers (Mosiah 23–24). In all three cases, these people found themselves embedded within a much larger enemy population, and, for all practical purposes, escape was the only possible strategy.

But this was far from the case in other examples of war the Book of Mormon provides. In these numerous cases every conflict occurred on *Nephite* lands. The Nephites were settled in their homes, and on their own lands, and it was there that the Lamanites attacked them. Far from taking initiative to escape, the Nephites found themselves merely trying to prevent the Lamanites from coming in and killing them.

Second, the relative population sizes of the cases being compared are completely dissimilar. This makes a critical difference in the appropriateness of

---

9. This illustration is taken up in a single footnote, but it is worth treating because it is a highly revealing expression of the general thinking that occurs in this account. J. David Pulsipher, "The Ammonite Conundrum," 11. The story of Limhi's stealth strategy is recounted in Mosiah 21–22 and Alma's in Mosiah 23–24.

different strategies. The numbers associated with both Limhi and Alma were dramatically smaller than the numbers involved in other conflicts we read about,[10] and it was precisely their small populations that made escape a plausible avenue for them. But it was not so for other Nephite leaders, who led much larger populations. While it is easy to imagine a few hundred people escaping, it is much harder to imagine the same for populations numbering in the many thousands. Not only would it be impossible for them to escape unnoticed, but they would also travel at an extremely slow pace and against huge logistical obstacles. Neither Limhi nor Alma faced hardships anywhere near such size and scope, and that's why it is inapt to say that their strategy was in any way morally superior to the conflict strategies that other Nephite leaders followed.

Third, it is relevant that Limhi had little chance of winning any war he might have tried to wage against those who surrounded him. The record attests that "the Lamanites being so numerous, it was impossible for the people of Limhi to contend with them, thinking to deliver themselves out of bondage by the sword" (Mosiah 22:2). Alma was no different; his band of believers was small, and certainly included no army, which means that there was little, if any, possibility that they might have prevailed had they attempted armed conflict. Because of such minuscule chances of success, most would agree that Limhi and Alma would have been unwise—not to mention wrong—to thrust their people into war.

But this is completely different from other cases in the Book of Mormon. In those situations the Nephite population was far larger and their chances of prevailing in self-defense far greater—a reality borne out by the actual experience of Nephite armies ultimately repelling repeated Lamanite invasions. There is therefore no comparison in the chances of success between Alma and Limhi on one hand, and other Book of Mormon figures on the other, and further reason why these cases should not be compared.

Although the argument for a continuum approach to war in the Book of Mormon makes a number of additional claims, they are all less important to consider since they either derive from, or illustrate the matters we have just examined and found to be inaccurate. In the end the argument provides no support for the continuum hypothesis itself, and thus no support for pacifism in general.[11]

---

10. Alma's people, for example, numbered only about four hundred and fifty around the time they fled the people of Noah (Mosiah 18:35).

11. During the presentation of this continuum view we are also told that "a just war position" would disapprove of the behavior of Limhi and Alma since, according to that view, "it is better to fight evil than to appear to submit to or flee from it" ibid., p. 11. Though intuitively this might seem the case, this attitude toward evil is actually not a feature of just-war theory. The just-war framework specifically countenances war only when diplomatic means are not sufficient, and specifically prohibits fighting when the

Doctrine and Covenants Section 98

Another way to approach war from a scriptural perspective is to focus on Doctrine and Covenants Section 98 and to argue that that revelation establishes "an immutable covenant of peace."[12] The essence of this immutable covenant—a compact incumbent upon all the Saints—is the principle that war is permitted only when the Lord specifically commands it. Thus a state is to absorb trespasses or smiting from an enemy at least three times and then await a direct commandment from the Lord before engaging that enemy in war.[13] On this basis we are told that the United States was wrong to invade Vietnam, Afghanistan, and Iraq (presumably both times) and that it was wrong for Latter-day Saints to be involved in those conflicts as U.S. military personnel.[14] The upshot of the argument is that we are to adopt a position of pacifism in all circumstances except where it is specifically superseded by a direct and contrary command from the Lord.

While such an approach appears plausible at first glance, four elements embedded in the view render it unpersuasive.

Ambiguity

The argument begins with the assertion that Section 98 (building on Section 97) "unambiguously" sets out admonitions for guiding conduct in the face of conflict.[15] But it is difficult to see how this can be so. The great majority of the discussion in this section about conflict is framed in terms of suffering a "smiting," a "coming upon," or a "trespass" from an enemy,[16] but nowhere is any of these terms defined, illustrated, or even characterized. What is a "trespass," after all? Do enemies trespass against others only when they assault those persons directly, or does their menacing approach by itself constitute a trespass? Or is a trespass something in between? The revelation does not tell us, and the account we are considering does not provide any clarification of its own.

The matter of definition is especially important when we consider the trespass of one state against another, and particularly when we consider the requirement that victims suffer trespass at least three times. When the Japanese attacked Pearl Harbor in 1941, the assault occurred in two waves and involved

---

cost would be too great and/or the odds of prevailing too slim. See the section "Jus ad Bellum: The Justice of War" in Chapter 1.

12. See Ron Madson, "D&C 98: The 'Immutable' Rejected Covenant of Peace," 219–34.
13. Ibid., 225, 232.
14. Ibid., 233.
15. Ibid., 222.
16. References to "smiting" appear in verses 23, 25, and 26; to "coming upon" in verses 28, 29, and 39; and to "trespassing against" in verses 40, 41, 42, 43, 44, 47, and 48.

six aircraft carriers and more than three hundred-fifty planes. During the attack the Japanese damaged or sank sixteen U.S. ships, destroyed some one hundred-ninety planes, killed twenty-four hundred Americans, and wounded twelve hundred more. Now, which one of these numbers is most pertinent to the commandment that an aggressed party (the United States in this case) must suffer "trespass" three times before responding? Would this assault on Pearl Harbor fall short of that threshold altogether since it was only a single attack and occurred in only two waves? If we saw the matter this way, then it would seem that the United States was obligated to suffer two more attacks from the Japanese before being justified in declaring war in response. The language of Section 98 implies the necessity of three separate incidents, as does the account of it that we are examining, but most would not think that the United States was really required to endure two more Pearl Harbors, and suffer thousands of additional deaths, before it could respond to Japan's aggression. They would think the idea of three trespasses cannot mean *that*.

Another view, congenial to more, would see the Japanese attack as passing the threshold of "three trespasses" on the basis of the damage it inflicted, even though it all occurred in a single assault—damage that included the harming and sinking of numerous ships, the destruction of scores of aircraft, and the killing of thousands of soldiers. It is easy to think that the harm indicated by these numbers is a better measure of trespasses than the number of incidents involved, even though Section 98 does seem to be phrased in terms of incidents. Be that as it may, even on this view there still remains considerable ambiguity. We must still decide, for instance, exactly *which* damage constituted the required three trespasses. Was it the first three shots fired by Japanese aircraft? Was it the first three targets that suffered damage? Was it the first three injuries that occurred? Was it the first three deaths? Different readers would have different opinions on the matter and the revelation itself says nothing that would decide it.

Still a third view would see the Japanese as passing the threshold the moment their aircraft carriers began their threatening journey—when they first departed Japan, days earlier, to reach the area north of Hawaii from which the attack would be launched and during which they were planning to, and would, cause the damage identified above. According to this view, leaving Japan was itself the beginning of the assault since the very intention of the journey was to reach Hawaii and attack it. The intention to commit such serious harm, combined with specific action toward this end, constituted all the trespass that was required to justify response.[17]

---

17. This view is related to the matter of pre-emptive attacks, a topic that will be discussed in the section "Self-Defense? The Question of Pre-Emptive Action" in Chapter 12.

Since all of these views could be defended to one degree or another it is hard to see how an account of Section 98 can be sufficient if it fails to consider these kinds of matters with care. The difficulty is that the revelation itself does not do this. Section 98 is not a self-contained document, spelling out the meaning of all of its terms and exemplifying all of its principles—illustrating their application in a wide array of contexts so that we pick up their nuances as well as their outlines. We know neither what the revelation's key terms *mean* (i.e., "smiting," "trespass," "coming upon"), nor exactly what it means to suffer them three times. That is considerable ambiguity, and this account of Section 98 does not help us resolve it, even though it must do so if it is to make its conclusions persuasive.

Overlooked Distinction

The account we are considering also overlooks a distinction that is central to determining the conclusion we draw from Section 98. We are told, for example, that a people can defend themselves only after they have suffered three "smitings" or "trespasses" and further, that they can defend themselves only after receiving a specific command from the Lord to do so.[18]

Now as we consider this matter it is natural to have in mind the general gospel prohibition against any and all acts of personal retaliation, or vengeance.[19] Although we can support civil authorities in their legal punishment of criminal acts that might be committed against us, we are to bear our losses, unjust and devastating as they might be, without personal retaliation.

But this raises an obvious next question: does it follow from this prohibition against vengeance that we are also prohibited from performing acts of *defense*? Although it is true, for instance, that we cannot take revenge for an attack we might suffer, does it follow that we cannot defend ourselves against that attack in the first place, particularly if it poses serious harm? Is it impermissible to prevent the attack if we can, and, if we cannot prevent it, is it then impermissible to fight back in order to minimize the harm we suffer? And how *can* this be impermissible since elsewhere we learn that "all men are justified in defending themselves, their friends, and property, and the government, from the unlawful assaults and encroachments of all persons in times of exigency" (D&C 134:11)?

---

18. Ron Madson, "D&C 98: The 'Immutable' Rejected Covenant of Peace," 225, 232.

19. Consider, for example, the Lord's teachings regarding turning the other cheek, giving our cloak to one who takes away our coat, and doing good to those who hate us (3 Ne. 12:39–44; Matt. 5:39–44). And consider the Lord's command that we are not to revile "against revilers" (D&C 19:30), and Mormon's clear approval of such a stance in his report of one period in which "some were lifted up in pride, and others were exceedingly humble; some did return railing for railing, while others would receive railing and persecution and all manner of afflictions, and would not turn and revile again, but were humble and penitent before God" (3 Ne. 6:13).

The same question applies to relations between states. Even if states were never justified in vengeance-driven violence,[20] would that entail a restriction against defending themselves from assault in the first place and repelling it if they could? If, for instance, the United States had discovered the attacking Japanese planes before they reached Pearl Harbor, would they have been justified in attacking those planes and preventing their assault on that target? Or would the standard of suffering three trespasses require them to withhold any act of defense and permit the attack? A similar question arises regarding further assaults. If we suppose that the aggressed nation was caught by surprise and couldn't repel the first attack, would it be prohibited from defending itself against further attack by that aggressor nation until it had been attacked at least two more times? And what if those further attacks took a million lives and completely decimated the aggressed nation's defensive firepower, so that by the time the state was eligible to defend itself it was no longer able to do so?

It is difficult to see how defense could be prohibited in such circumstances, particularly in light of the explicit approval of self-defense found in D&C 134:11. Such acts are completely unlike acts that are motivated purely by vengeance, and we have already seen that contrast in motivation is central to the difference in moral status between aggressors and their victims.[21] This kind of contrast seems similarly central to the moral status of acts motivated by vengeance versus those motivated by defense. This is why it is insufficient to overlook the difference between vengeance and defense. That distinction is crucial if we want to draw concrete and firm conclusions from the language found in Doctrine and Covenants 98.

Inadequate Conception of Jesus' Personality

In developing its general pacifist conclusion from Section 98 the account also suggests an inadequate conception of the Lord and of his attitude toward violence. This appears in the approving report of signs displayed at a protest rally against a speech given by Condoleeza Rice at BYU that read "Who would Jesus waterboard?"[22] These signs, at the very least, pose the question of how Jesus would react to violence, and at the most imply an idea reminiscent of Eugene England's observation, speaking specifically of Christ, that "we

---

20. I put the matter this way because, although scriptural provision is made for nations to avenge themselves under certain circumstances (see D&C 98:34–37), those circumstances are irrelevant to the point being addressed here. In other circumstances vengeful reprisals are not countenanced by scriptural approval (see Morm. 3:10–16).

21. See the sections "Anti-Violence Based on Wrong Action" and "The Relational Foundation of Right and Wrong" in Chapter 2.

22. Ron Madson, "D&C 98: The 'Immutable' Rejected Covenant of Peace," 234.

are confronted, in scripture and experience, with a God who is completely without violence."[23]

But if we want to draw conclusions about how Jesus would act in a modern situation on the basis of what he is and is not like, we should bear in mind more of Jesus' conduct than just those scriptural descriptions that support a given position about him. Most famously, Jesus cleared the temple in Jerusalem aggressively, even violently (Matt. 21:12–13; Mark 11:15–17). And following his earthly ministry, he destroyed the inhabitants of fifteen Book of Mormon cities for their wickedness, causing those localities and their inhabitants either to be burned, sunk "in the depths of the sea," or sunk "in the depths of the earth" (3 Ne. 9:1–12).

Additionally, it is interesting and relevant that, according to Latter-day Saint scripture, everyone who goes to hell is sent there by Jesus. Those who suffer the "lake of fire and brimstone, whose flames are unquenchable" (Jacob 6:10; 2 Ne. 28:23) do so because they have been consigned to that fate by him.[24] It is no surprise, therefore, that Jesus is the one identified as saying: "Therefore I command you to repent—repent, lest I smite you by the rod of my mouth, and by my wrath, and by my anger, and your sufferings be sore—how sore you know not, how exquisite you know not, yea, how hard to bear you know not" (D&C 19:15). He is also the one who consigns the sons of perdition to their fate, of whose condition he says that "their worm dieth not, and the fire is not quenched, which is their torment—and the end thereof, neither the place thereof, nor their torment, no man knows . . . wherefore, the end, the width, the height, the depth, and the misery thereof, they understand not" (D&C 76:44–48).

In addition, it is this same Jesus who is identified as saying, regarding events of the last days, that "I the Lord God will send forth flies upon the face of the earth, which shall take hold of the inhabitants thereof, and shall eat their flesh, and shall cause maggots to come in upon them; and their tongues

---

23. Eugene England, "Thou Shalt Not Kill: An Ethics of Non-Violence," 171. Consider also Joshua Madson's statement that, "claims in support of violence [by Book of Mormon figures] are inherently suspect because they are not in harmony with the life, words, and death of Jesus of Nazareth." See Joshua Madson, "A Non-Violent Reading of the Book of Mormon," 16.

24. Contemplating this fact, one wag observed: "Over the course of your life you might be told once or twice to go to hell. But when it happens at the end of your life, and Jesus is the one saying it, you know you're in trouble." That Jesus is the one who judges us is made clear, among other places, by his own observation that "the Father judgeth no man, but hath committed all judgment unto the Son" (John 5:22), and by Mormon's teaching that "every soul who belongs to the whole human family of Adam" must all stand "before the judgment-seat of Christ" (Morm. 3:20).

shall be stayed . . . and their flesh shall fall from off their bones, and their eyes from their sockets; and it shall come to pass that the beasts of the forest and the fowls of the air shall devour them up" (D&C 29:18–20).

Indeed, the canon teaches that it is this same Jesus who will yet "take vengeance upon the wicked" (D&C 29:17) and cause "the proud, yea, and all that do wickedly [to be as] stubble" (Mal. 4:1). He will also be heard to say: "I have trodden the wine-press alone, and have brought judgment upon all people . . . and I have trampled them in my fury, and I did tread upon them in mine anger, and their blood have I sprinkled upon my garments, and stained all my raiment; for this was the day of vengeance which was in my heart" (D&C 133:50–51).[25]

Given these descriptions it does not seem sufficiently discriminating to characterize the Lord's attitude toward violence by means of a four-word rhetorical taunt: "Who would Jesus waterboard?" We must not be too quick in forming a conception of the Lord's personality. An accurate conception requires thoughtful consideration of the totality of his works, from beginning to end—including the actions he will perform at the end of the world.

Deficient Consideration of the Prophetic Role

The view we are examining also leads to an inadequate conception of the prophetic role. It claims that D&C 98 teaches that we are to eschew war in all cases except where the Lord specifically commands it, and therefore that President Hinckley's remarks on war[26]—against the backdrop of the hostilities current at the time—were faulty because they did not deliver this message. Instead, President Hinckley simply proclaimed that there are cases where waging war is just and right, and emphasized that those who are in the military are not morally culpable for engaging in war under the command of their sovereign.

The view we are examining finds all of this objectionable. It even considers President Hinckley's remarks regarding the non-culpability of U.S. soldiers to be equivalent to the papal issuance of indulgences during the Crusades.[27] In view of such objections, the account reasons that "the principles in section 98 seem to be currently marginalized, if not wholly ignored,"[28] and that "to the extent that we as a faith community have not renounced recent wars or applied the requirements set forth in section 98, we have . . . rejected this peace

---

25. Further references in which the Lord acts violently include: Gen. 7:13; Ex. 9:22–26; Moses 7:34; Isa. 11:4; 2 Ne. 23:11; 30:10; Alma 19:21–23; Hel 13:9–13; D&C 45:50; 76:30–34; among others.

26. See President Gordon B. Hinckley, "The Times in Which We Live," and "War and Peace."

27. Ron Madson, "D&C 98: The 'Immutable' Rejected Covenant of Peace," 231.

28. Ibid.

covenant"[29]—which is to say, we have rejected the word of the Lord regarding these matters. Essentially, President Hinckley led the Church astray in what he said regarding U.S. action.[30] This leads to the announcement: "Personally, I have no interest in citing any rationale or doctrine, only the words of Jesus when it comes to matters of life and death—accepting no other filter and no other person as my guide, no matter their authority."[31]

Two central problems. There are two central problems with this approach regarding the prophetic role, however. The first is that in propounding such views the argument seems to paint itself into an intellectual corner. On one hand, as we have seen, the account asserts that no war is justified unless God specifically commands it—a command which, presumably, would be communicated to the Saints by the prophet living at the time. (Who else?) On the other hand, the argument declares that listening to the prophet is not a reliable guide to keeping the "covenant of peace" revealed in the Doctrine and Covenants. But that raises this problem: If the prophet is not a reliable guide to keeping the covenant of peace revealed in the Doctrine and Covenants, then it is not clear why he would be a reliable guide to deciding whether or not God commands us to engage in war. If we can reject the prophet in one case, there is no reason we cannot reject him in the other. Practically speaking, one instruction this argument gives us ("obey only God's specific command") is cancelled by the other instruction it gives us ("do not trust prophets to tell you what God commands"). The result is an intellectual cul-de-sac.

The second problem is the account's failure to be thoughtful about the relationship between the scriptural canon and the teachings of living prophets. Based on a particular reading of Section 98, the account concludes that that scripture contradicts the teachings of President Gordon B. Hinckley and therefore that President Hinckley's teachings are wrong in important ways. However, while it is true that the scriptural canon takes precedence over the teachings of any individual, including a President of the Church,[32] it is obvious that any apparent discrepancy between them calls for the most careful

---

29. Ibid., 232.

30. Madson says of President Hinckley that "he did not specifically 'renounce' either war [Afghanistan or Iraq]" (ibid., 230), and that specifically "in light of . . . President Hinckley's talks the principles in section 98 seem to be currently marginalized, if not wholly ignored" (p. 231), and, as quoted in the text, "to the extent that we as a faith community have not renounced recent wars or applied the requirement set forth in section 98, we have once again rejected this peace covenant" (p. 232).

31. Ibid., 233.

32. This principle has been taught prominently. See Joseph Fielding Smith, *Doctrines of Salvation*, 3:203–4; and Bruce R. McConkie, *Doctrines of the Restoration*, 231.

scrutiny. In this particular case, for example, it is noteworthy that Section 98 itself is highly ambiguous. We have already seen that it gives us no definitions of some of its central terms—"smiting," "trespass," "coming upon"—and that it does not address the prima facie distinction between vengeance and defense. Nor does this account do anything of its own to address and resolve such questions. This is a slippery basis from which to pass judgment on the teachings of others, particularly prophets.[33]

It is also important to appreciate that the revelation seems to presuppose circumstances that are completely unlike the circumstances faced by President Hinckley. The Lord says (v. 32) that he taught the concepts in this revelation to Abraham, Isaac, Jacob, Joseph, and Nephi, for example, all of whom were prophet-leaders who presided over collections of God's people that were collocated geographically and that were recognizable as distinct public bodies. Each was a virtual *res publica*, capable of being assaulted as an independent unit, apart from all others. This is completely unlike the circumstances of President Hinckley, however, who, though a prophet, presided over nothing like an independent public body that was itself being assaulted. Instead he found himself presiding over Saints whose host society had suffered assault. Because his situation was different from that of these ancient prophets it is difficult to imagine that the concepts in this revelation (even if we understood them) would apply in precisely the same way to both. Thus, even if we supposed this reading of Section 98 to be sound, it does not follow that President Hinckley would be bound by it. In his case, departure from the revelation in one way or another would actually be expected.[34]

This observation underscores a general principle regarding the relationship between scriptural declarations and the teachings of individual prophets. The prudent way to approach any difference that seems to appear is to read the two sets of passages in light of each other. That is to say, we read a prophet's teachings in light of the scriptural passage and we read the scriptural passage in light of

---

33. Further discussion on this revelation appears in the section "Doctrine and Covenants 98" in Chapter 15, where I present additional difficulties in trying to understand the revelation's meaning.

34. This reality highlights another ambiguity in the revelation. After listing such prophets as Nephi and Abraham by name, the Lord also says that he taught these principles to his ancient apostles (v. 32). However, the apostles dwelling in the Holy Land were much like President Hinckley: rather than leaders of a public entity of their own (as Nephi and Abraham were) that could actually go to war, these apostles were simply members of a host society and had no public standing. The Twelve dwelling in the Americas could be considered leaders of such a body, but nowhere (unless it is here) are they referred to as "apostles." Like much in this revelation, it is not obvious what we are to make of the reference.

the prophet's teachings, seeking maximum illumination of both. We recognize that the prophet has the same access to the scriptural passage that we have and therefore can suppose that his own remarks are already informed by it. What we cannot do is reach a conclusion about a scriptural passage that does not even consider a prophet's teachings on the same topic and then dismiss that teaching because it is different from the conclusion we reached *without* considering it. Seeking maximum illumination is particularly required in this case since Section 98 is not only highly ambiguous, but also appears to presuppose circumstances that are different from those faced by President Hinckley in any event. This account fails to recognize and resolve such matters and thus fails to be persuasive.[35]

This approach to Doctrine and Covenants 98, then, does not achieve its aims. While it is unique, and while it presents a nuanced approach to the justifiability of war from a scriptural perspective, the account fails to provide a number of elements that an approach to war based on this section requires. These include careful delineation of the revelation's key terms, attention to an important distinction between vengeance and defense, a robust examination of the Lord's attitudes toward violence, and thoughtful consideration of the role of prophets and of their relationship to our personal scriptural conclusions. Deficient in these ways, the argument does not succeed.

A "Pacifist Manifesto"

A third approach analyzes the Book of Mormon and its attitude toward war by paying attention to how various peoples in the book are treated: do they, or do they not, receive divine approval?[36] By paying attention to such divine affirmations and disaffirmations, this approach concludes that the Book of Mormon is a "pacifist manifesto,"[37] a "comprehensive pacifist injunction,"[38] and that "pacifism is the code of conduct of full conversion."[39]

---

35. Incidentally, in light of all this it is interesting to note that President Hinckley himself spoke about safety in following the prophet—and specifically about himself. "You don't need to worry very much about Gordon Hinckley," he said. "The Lord is directing this work, and He won't let me or anyone else lead it astray." See "Excerpts from Recent Addresses of President Gordon B. Hinckley." It is also worth pointing out that it is simply a logical error to equate President Hinckley's remarks about soldiers' non-culpability with the papal decrees of the eleventh through thirteenth centuries. It is one thing to say that soldiers will not be held responsible for the normal acts of war they commit under the command of their legal sovereign, and another to say that, by engaging in war, soldiers will actually obtain remission from the temporal penalties that otherwise would attach to their sins. These are completely different claims.

36. See F.R. Rick Duran, "Pax Sanctorum," 57–79.

37. Ibid., 57.

38. Ibid.

39. Ibid., 74.

Everything in this argument depends on its conception of pacifism and on various claims it makes about the text. The argument does not succeed, however, because it turns out to be inaccurate on both counts.

Conception of Pacifism

Consider first the argument's version of what "pacifism" means, a conception that emerges in its description of various Book of Mormon figures. We are told, for example, that Lehi's departure from Jerusalem was a species of pacifist conduct since Lehi did not take up arms, but actually fled the environs peaceably—thus exemplifying a pacifist approach to conflict situations.[40] In addition to Lehi, all Book of Mormon figures who "prize peace over war, as a means of solving problems" are also identified as pacifist.[41] Since an attitude of this sort is obviously included in pacifism, the attitude is assumed to *constitute* pacifism. We are also told: "King Benjamin suggests that his people's pacifism and righteousness were their defense against their enemies"[42]—implying that pacifism was their sole defense—and that they "were protected in righteousness from their enemies for forty-three years."[43]

Upon examination each of these examples turns out to be mistaken. Lehi's conduct would count as an example of pacifism, for instance, only if violence had actually been an option for him. In that case we could imagine Lehi seriously considering taking up arms against the multitudes of Jerusalem, and then choosing to depart peaceably with his family as the moral alternative to pursuing such violence. The problem is that Lehi did neither. Nothing in the record suggests that he ever considered entering a violent struggle with the people of Jerusalem, and he actually left the land because the Lord commanded him to do so in order to plant the seeds of a new civilization elsewhere. Not having to take up arms was a natural concomitant of Lehi's departure, but it was not the purpose of his leaving.

Nor does it constitute pacifism merely to prize peace over war as a means of solving problems. As seen in Chapter 2, this is a view that excludes few.[44] If we were to accept this conception of pacifism we would have to consider Nephi, King Benjamin, Alma, Captain Moroni, Helaman, Lehi, Teancum, Gidgiddoni, Mormon, and Moroni to be pacifists because they all prized peace over war—even though every one of them led men into war.

Finally, we can sustain a view of King Benjamin as a pacifist only if we imagine him—as this approach seems to—as a Gandhian figure who practiced

---

40. Ibid., 76.
41. Ibid., 75.
42. Ibid., 68.
43. Ibid., 61.
44. See the section "Getting Clear about Pacifism."

only peaceful resistance whenever conflict arose.⁴⁵ But in truth this was far from the case. King Benjamin was an active warrior and we are told that, in defense of his people, he "gathered together his armies;" fought "with the strength of his own arm;" contended "in the strength of the Lord;" slew with his army "many thousands of the Lamanites;" and contended against the invading armies until they had "driven them out of all the lands of their inheritance" (W of M 1:13–14). The record is clear: King Benjamin was manifestly not the pacifist figure this argument assumes him to be, and he also receives "divine approval" in the record. Thus, far from supporting the claim that the Book of Mormon is a "pacifist injunction," King Benjamin actually disproves it.

These examples all illustrate a central problem in this effort to see the Book of Mormon as a pacifist document. The problem is: if Lehi's leaving Jerusalem can count as pacifism—and if merely favoring peace over war, and behaving as King Benjamin did, can count as pacifism—then there's not much that *can't* count as pacifism. To state that the Book of Mormon is a pacifist manifesto in this sense is thus to state a proposition devoid of content. We find ourselves able to call the Book of Mormon a pacifist document, but only because we have changed the meaning of the term.

Textual Claims

In addition to relying on an inadequate conception of pacifism, the account also makes assertions about the Book of Mormon that are not supported by the text.

Three related claims. Three such assertions are these: the book "groups [or holds] all combative factions in equal disregard";⁴⁶ as a people "we possess no holy texts or prophetic directives that would carry us to open conflict";⁴⁷ and, in the Book of Mormon, to "highly moral societies . . . violent conflict is both inconceivable . . . and unnecessary."⁴⁸

These are categorical and important claims. To reach these conclusions, however, we would have to overlook the way in which they all echo one or more of Nibley's claims and the fact that they are just as mistaken when they appear in this approach as when they appear in Nibley's. It is not necessary

---

45. I mention Gandhi only to capture the kind of figure the account seems to suppose King Benjamin to have been. In reality, of course, Gandhi never faced anything close to the level of conflict and aggression that confronted King Benjamin and his people. On matters of this sort, King Benjamin would gladly have traded places with Gandhi, and without a moment's thought.
46. Ibid., 69.
47. Ibid., 73.
48. Ibid., 72.

to rehearse all of the arguments and counterexamples here to see this,[49] but it is useful to be reminded of one case—namely, the instance in which the combined Nephites and Lamanites reached such a state of righteousness that the Lamanites' "curse was taken from them," that "their young men and their daughters became exceedingly fair," and that the people were so knit in unity that they became one people. Notwithstanding this peace and unity, they still had to fight to prevent the Gadianton robbers from destroying them (3 Ne. 2:11–17). In view of this single case, not to mention others, there seems to be no sense in which we can assert that the Lord held these combined Nephites/Lamanites and the Gadianton robbers "in equal disregard," that their story is not a "holy text" that exemplifies the righteous being involved in open conflict, that they were not a "highly moral" society, or that they found violent conflict both "inconceivable and unnecessary." This example, among others considered in earlier chapters, disproves these categorical assertions about the Book of Mormon and war.

War as the "work of death" and "murder." This view also finds it significant that Book of Mormon figures call war the "'work of death' and 'murder'" and concludes that statements of this sort are authoritative condemnations of war.[50] If war is the work of murder, it follows that war is wrong.

There are two central difficulties with this claim, however. First, there is nothing morally important, or surprising, about referring to war as the work of death. *Of course* war is the work of death. To describe war this way is not to indicate an attitude, but to state a fact.

Second, in making the further claim that Book of Mormon figures considered war to be murder, the account makes two mistakes. First, it cites verses that refer specifically to the Ammonites—and we have seen at length why the word "murder" actually does apply in their particular case, and why that usage of the term does not reflect their attitude toward normal acts of killing in conventional war.[51] Second, the account cites the episode of Moroni's refusal to kill drunken Lamanites—on the implication by Mormon that *that* would be murder (Alma 55:7–24)—failing to realize that this passage has no bearing on the matter of killing in war per se. To believe that killing these drunken Lamanites would be murder is to say nothing about the legitimacy of killing armed combatants on the field of battle. These two passages thus do nothing to support the idea that Book of Mormon figures considered killing in

---

49. See Chapters 4–7 for a treatment.
50. Ibid., 75.
51. See the sections "What Did the Ammonites Repent Of?" and "Refutation of the Ammonites as Pacifist Examples" in Chapter 5.

conventional, defensive war to be murder. Such an attitude actually appears nowhere in the record.

Righteousness and the absence of need for conflict. Elsewhere this view announces that Book of Mormon peoples provide a demonstration that "the righteous have no desire nor need for open conflict."[52] This is an important claim, and everyone will grant that the righteous have no *desire* for open conflict. But "need" is a different matter entirely. We have already seen multiple examples where the righteous needed to defend themselves in open conflict.[53] So what passages of the Book of Mormon does this view use to bolster its claim?

The first of two key passages reads: "Man shall not smite, neither shall he judge; for judgment is mine, saith the Lord, and vengeance is mine also, and I will repay" (Morm. 8:20). The interpretation seems to be that the Lord will exact justice himself and therefore that his people need never encounter conflict. But one problem with appealing to this verse is that it is speaking specifically of the persecution that would accompany the appearance of the Book of Mormon in the latter days. It is written regarding those who would issue threats at a future date and say, "Show unto me, or ye shall be smitten" (Morm. 8:12–18). Far from anything like a broad command against self-defense, the statement is a warning against those who would oppose and condemn the Book of Mormon itself. It is irrelevant to general claims about pacifism.

A second problem with appealing to this verse is that doing so relies on a key and problematic assumption. Based on the statement in the passage that vengeance is the Lord's and that he will repay, the argument seems to assume that the Lord's righteous followers need never be involved in conflict for *any* reason. But to assume this is to confuse one motive for conflict with another. After all, the righteous do not fight to gain vengeance, which is the subject of this verse, but only to defend themselves.[54] Because they are separate topics, claims about the Lord's prerogatives regarding vengeance say nothing about his followers' prerogatives regarding self-defense. That the righteous may not seek vengeance is clear in scripture, but that they may defend themselves is equally clear. Thus, to take this verse to be a condemnation of self-defense is to confuse what is forbidden as a motive for entering conflict with what is explicitly permitted as a motive for entering conflict. In this case, again, the verse is irrelevant to general claims about pacifism.

The second verse this view cites to deny that the righteous will ever face a need to enter conflict is the report that "God would make it known unto them [the Nephites] whither they should go to defend themselves against

---

52. Ibid., 76.
53. See Chapters 6 and 7.
54. See Chapter 7 for more on aggressed parties defending themselves.

their enemies, and by so doing, the Lord would deliver them" (Alma 48:16). The supposition appears to be that since the Lord delivers the righteous, they therefore do not "need" open conflict. But to suppose this appears to miss the point of the passage. The Lord revealed troop movements to the Nephites precisely in order to help them *engage* in open conflict. Indeed, they were sent where they needed to go to confront their enemies, not to evade them.[55] So here the account does more than appeal to a passage that is irrelevant to its claim. It appeals to a passage that straightforwardly disproves it.

Absence of divine support for violence. The account we are considering also asserts that all examples of violence in the Book of Mormon are "void of divine support,"[56] meaning that the Lord never approved of anyone taking up arms, even in order to defend themselves, and that he never actually helped them do so. But the text provides us with numerous examples of the Lord doing exactly that—commanding his people to defend themselves and explicitly helping one side in conflict against the other.[57] These include the Lord revealing troop movements of the enemy so that the Nephites could better wage war against them (Alma 16:5–8; 43:23–24), assisting Alma in defeating and killing Amlici in hand-to-hand combat (Alma 2:29–31), and preserving the Ammonite sons from being slain in battle (Alma 56:43–56; 57:25–27; 58:39). It is hard to see what conception of the absence of divine support could apply to such cases and explain these actions of the Lord.

Nephi's violence and lack of faith. Finally, we are told: "The personal tragedy of violence, and thus the warning against its allure, occupies the plates' opening narrative. Long before armies mass on armies, Nephi records his first violence, personally damaging and tragic; an omen to those who may ponder following spiritual promptings into acts of violence. Not trained in violence in his youth, never entertaining violence, he justifies his act on the grounds of providential urging." We then learn that one of Nephi's first acts "even before building a temple—was to 'make many swords,' thus accepting violence as inevitable and divine protection as improbable or insufficient."[58]

Thus Nephi's slaying of Laban was not only "personally damaging and tragic," but also an "omen" to us. And not only did Nephi act duplicitously—

---

55. As we saw in Chapter 7, when scriptural passages speak of God delivering his people, they routinely contemplate a circumstance in which God is helping his people *in* their conflicts, not exempting them from having to defend themselves. See the sections "God's Role in the Battles of the Righteous: The Importance of Context" and "How God Most Often Fights the Battles of the Righteous" in Chapter 7.

56. Ibid., 70.

57. See Chapter 7 in particular.

58. Ibid., 72, 73, citing 2 Nephi 5:14.

"justifying" his act by appealing to the Spirit—but he was also lacking in faith, relying on the sword rather than the Lord for self-defense.

While provocative, all of this is mistaken. We have already seen the fallacies inherent in the claim that Nephi lied. That assertion is groundless.[59] Moreover, as will be demonstrated in the next chapter, there is no evidence that the slaying of Laban was "personally damaging and tragic" for Nephi. This is an assertion without substantiation, and it can be set aside—along with any "omen" it might be thought to contain for us.[60] And finally, as to Nephi's lack of faith, the Book of Mormon is replete with accounts of his faith—so much so that his commitment to "go and do" (1 Ne. 3:7) has become a touchstone of faithfulness throughout Mormon culture. It is difficult to see how any reading of the Book of Mormon can disregard these features of the record when trying to reach a judgment about Nephi's degree of reliance on the Lord. Nevertheless, this reading does so and thus ends up in the improbable position of lecturing *Nephi* about faith.[61]

Although the pacifist reading we are considering here makes many additional claims, the examples already examined are interesting and give insight into the general approach the account takes toward the Book of Mormon. Overall, the assertions made in this argument are inadequate in one of two

---

59. See the section "Examining the Corollary of the Narrative Approach: The Example of Nephi" in Chapter 8. The section "The Narrative Approach and Nephi's Inauguration of Nephite Culture" in Chapter 9 also bears on the matter.

60. On this matter see the section "Nephi and Laban" in Chapter 11.

61. I have already rehearsed elements of the text that demonstrate Nephi's impressiveness (see note 40 in Chapter 8 and note 31 in Chapter 9). It is difficult to find faith anywhere in scripture that surpasses Nephi's. That is why it is hard to imagine complaining, in any measure, about Nephi's faith: to do so requires disregarding overwhelming evidence of his confidence in the Lord and of his intimacy with him. Nevertheless, pacifist arguments must ultimately account for Nephi somehow and naturally end up diminishing him in some manner. It is difficult to see how any effort of this sort is true to the text, however—Nephi's faithfulness and the Lord's esteem of him are on abundant display. The alternative is to overlook those dimensions of the text or, ultimately—if one wants to go so far—to claim that they are simply Nephi's fabrications: he did not really experience the divine manifestations and miracles that he reports (a matter addressed earlier, in the section "Examining the Corollary of the Narrative Approach: The Example of Nephi" in Chapter 8). It is logically possible to adopt this position, of course, but if we do, we must adopt it in the face of a complete absence of textual support. As we are discovering, when we read the Book of Mormon comprehensively and with care on the topic of violence, we find no reason whatever to diminish Nephi. His stature as an extraordinary disciple and prophet of God remains unchanged. Reading this way we come away from the text filled not with condescension toward Nephi, but awe.

ways: they are either based on misapplications of the text or they end up supporting a sense of pacifism that is not pacifism—resulting in a claim for the Book of Mormon as a "pacifist manifesto" that in the end is no claim at all.

Reproach without Evidence

In the last three chapters we have seen more than one argument adopt a reproachful and condescending tone toward Nephi (and in one case, toward the entire Nephite record as a "propaganda piece"), and another do the same toward President Gordon B. Hinckley. In two of the cases, the attitude logically extends to many other prophetic figures as well. We have also seen Nibley adopt a glib tone toward important Book of Mormon figures, as well as toward others. When examined, all of these treatments turn out to be based on arguments that do not succeed. The critical tone is completely unjustified.

These are not the only instances. A similar style of reproach-without-evidence is found in another treatment of war and pacifism, though this time toward the United States.[62] The discussion expresses bemusement at the way we depict ourselves in the Declaration of Independence and informs us that Americans have "a proclivity to violence," a tendency evident even in our movies. "We love to reduce our enemies to pure evil and thereby justify the exertion of unfettered force. We show our manhood and our humanity by fighting," all of which leads to the question: "How can world leadership be trusted to a people who love violence, who search for justification to unpack their pistols?"[63]

Unfortunately, the discussion gives no information that illustrates these claims (what is meant by terms like "unfettered force" and "searching for justification," for example?) or that does anything to substantiate them. The most specific thing we are told (and even this is extremely general) is that Europeans are unhappy with the United States—an appeal to authority which, it seems to be hoped, will obviate the need for evidence. But of course it does not obviate that need at all. The combination of a condescending tone with a total absence of analysis is conspicuous.

Another example of reproach-without-evidence occurs in a discussion of the Ammonites. The brief commentary is adamant that these Book of Mormon figures were pacifists, and calls "fatuous" an article that contests this understanding.[64] Nothing is offered in the way of evidence to support this claim, however; instead, the article is dismissed in one brief paragraph, and by simple assertion. Moreover, "fatuous" is a term of insult, which means

---

62. Richard Lyman Bushman, "Aftermath," 267–71.
63. Ibid., 269–70.
64. Gordon Conrad Thomasson, "'Renounce War and Proclaim Peace': Personal Reflections on Mormon Attempts at Peacemaking," 214. Thomasson does not identify the article he has in mind.

that this treatment not only fails to address the question of the Ammonites through evidence and reasoned discussion, but that it also substitutes invective for doing so.[65]

The same difficulty appears in Eugene England's review of a volume about the Book of Mormon in which he harshly criticizes the contributors for their failure to address the pacifist message he finds in the book, specifically in regard to the Ammonite episode.[66] Unfortunately, he marshals no evidence to substantiate his insistence. Of course, as we have seen in Chapters 4 and 5, it would be difficult to do so since the Ammonite episode does not have a pacifist message (a matter that was apparently perceived and appreciated by the authors England criticizes, but which was not evident to England himself.) Nevertheless, presenting evidence and argument still seems required to the extent that it is possible. But England does not do this, proceeding instead with criticisms that are both harsh and unsubstantiated. It is a further instance of reproach despite the absence of evidence.[67]

Conclusion

The arguments covered in this chapter all fail in their aims. There is no evidence for a continuum of divine approaches to conflict in the Book of

---

65. The resort to insult immediately follows the first-person declaration: "I personally have spent the last four-plus decades . . . trying to understand the principles of peace and follow my own pacifist commitments." See Thomasson, "'Renounce War and Proclaim Peace': Personal Reflections on Mormon Attempts at Peacemaking," 214. The juxtaposition stands out because insult does not seem like one of the properties of pacifist commitment. (Of course this could be wrong. The prominent book editor Kingsley Martin observed that the most pugnacious people he had come across were all pacifists. See Paul Johnson, *Intellectuals: From Marx and Tolstoy to Sartre and Chomsky*, 204.)

66. Eugene England, "Hugh Nibley as Cassandra," 104–16.

67. It is true, of course, that one can find non-pacifist statements that also combine a reproachful attitude with an absence of evidence or at least of strong argument. In these chapters, however, the focus is on pacifist views. When it exists, the combination of weakness and reproachful tone is conspicuous in such arguments partly because the scriptural consequences of pacifist interpretations are so significant. They lead us, for example, to the conclusion that Nephi was a liar and a murderer, that Nephi did not have sufficient faith, that a host of prophets from Nephi to Gordon B. Hinckley have behaved and/or taught wrongly in important ways, that multiple Book of Mormon reports about the Lord are false, and so forth. A reproachful tone attracts attention when the views being expressed are as large and counterintuitive as these are. That tone attracts additional attention if the arguments for these views then fade under scrutiny. From a scriptural perspective, non-pacifist arguments that are weak, that are stated in reproachful language, and that entail large scriptural consequences should receive identical attention.

Mormon, with pacifism as its most divine pole. The proffered reading of Doctrine and Covenants 98 falls far short of addressing all of the matters required to substantiate its claims. And, given any reasonable conception of pacifism, or any reasonable interpretation of the text, the Book of Mormon does not qualify as anything like a pacifist manifesto. Interesting and varied as these three approaches are, in the end they provide no support for the claim that pacifism is the message of Latter-day Saint scripture. Finally, it is useful to bear in mind the thread of reproach-without-evidence that has manifested itself in more than one pacifist approach. A judgmental tone is no substitute for argument, of course. And in the cases we have seen over multiple chapters, it also turns out to be completely unjustified.

Chapter 11

Eugene England's Anti-Violence Ethic

To this point we have examined a substantial number of claims that either flow from, or are thought to support, a pacifist reading of scripture and thus support a pacifist point of view. Although all of these claims have been found wanting, there is a final set of matters to address, namely those that Eugene England raises over the course of a number of his essays. It is valuable to consider them because they are the very issues that would likely occur to anyone who felt a deep disapproval and rejection of violence. Any consideration of the merits of pacifism requires attention to these remaining "England-esque" arguments.

As we proceed it is helpful to note that England himself presents a slightly fuzzy picture. On one hand he expresses support for World War II,[1] as well as telling us that "absolute non-violence may not be clearly required by the scriptures."[2] He also informs us that he would use violence to protect his family from attack.[3] On the other hand, however, England also: (1) informs us, in speaking specifically of Christ, that "we are confronted, in scripture and experience, with a God who is completely without violence;"[4] (2) tells us that "the ethic of Christ is pacifist;"[5] (3) refers to "the central role pacifism plays in Christ's mission;"[6] (4) tells us that Christ not only "utterly rejects violence" but that he also "demands that we do the same;"[7] (5) asserts that "Christ's atonement put an end to all claims for the legitimacy . . . of *any* kind of violence;"[8] (6) reports "Christ's demand that we reject all violence;"[9] and (7) argues that nothing can justify violating the basic right of humans to be

---

1. See Eugene England, "A Case for Mormon Christian Pacifism," 101; see also Eugene England, "'Thou Shalt Not Kill': An Ethics of Non-Violence," 172–73, and also Eugene England, "The Prince of Peace," 242–43.
2. England, "'Thou Shalt Not Kill,'" 171.
3. See England, "A Case for Mormon Christian Pacifism," 100–101. See also England, "'Thou Shalt Not Kill,'" 173.
4. England, "'Thou Shalt Not Kill,'" 171.
5. England, "The Prince of Peace," 243.
6. Eugene England, "Why Nephi Killed Laban: Reflections on the Truth of the Book of Mormon," 143.
7. Ibid., 142.
8. Ibid., 150 (emphasis in original).
9. Ibid., 146.

treated as persons (which violence does)—"not even a so-called just war."[10] Overall, these many assertions seem to insist that pacifism—the rejection of all violence—is the only proper Christian perspective, but here and there England does carve out an exception or two. At a minimum his thinking is vigorously anti-violence in character and that is why it is so useful. It helps us see how such a perspective plays out in thinking about various scriptural matters and thus allows us to evaluate the perspective itself. We will look at five such scriptural issues in this chapter.

Nephi and Laban

The first matter to consider is the confrontation in early Book of Mormon history in which Nephi killed Laban (1 Ne. 4:7–18).[11] While on the face of it this seems to be a straightforward case of justified violence—which is how Nephi presents the matter to his readers—we can see this as a lesson in *non-violence* if we believe, as England does, that Nephi later came to regret his action and to feel sorrow for it. According to this view, when Nephi years later posed to himself the self-reflective query, "Why am I angry because of mine enemy?" (2 Ne. 4:27), he was specifically looking back on the episode with Laban and expressing remorse for it.[12] Reading the matter this way, we may conclude that the event with Laban actually exacted "a toll of anguish" on Nephi—a toll demonstrated in Nephi's "psalm of repentance" and the "harrowing, complex memory of the event years later."[13] On this interpretation we can also see Nephi's experience as offering us something of a cautionary tale regarding violent action, and thus decry members who "use [the Laban episode] to justify troubling, violent rhetoric and even violent action" and who assume "that the Spirit indeed teaches that the end justifies the means."[14]

Four Problems with Seeing Nephi as Remorseful

At first glance it may seem persuasive to see Nephi as eventually coming to regret his slaying of Laban and to feel remorse for doing so. Nevertheless, four elements of the text cumulatively show this interpretation of Nephi's conduct and attitude to be untenable.

---

10. England, "'Thou Shalt Not Kill,'" 161.

11. I have previously addressed some of the other matters raised by this episode. See the section "Examining the Corollary of the Narrative Approach: The Example of Nephi" in Chapter 8 and the section "The Narrative Approach and Nephi's Inauguration of Nephite Culture" in Chapter 9.

12. This is England's approach in ibid., 144, 147. F.R. Rick Duran appears as if he might be drawing the same connection in his "Pax Sanctorum," 73.

13. This is the way the matter is presented in England, "Why Nephi Killed Laban," 147.

14. Ibid., 143.

First, it is significant that years had passed by the time Nephi wrote his account of slaying Laban and recorded his worry about experiencing anger toward his enemies. During that time he had faced multiple enemies. Jacob tells us that Nephi had been "a great protector" of the people and that he had "wielded the sword of Laban in their defence" (Jacob 1:10), and indeed, immediately prior to expressing regret for his anger, Nephi speaks specifically of having faced "enemies" (2 Ne. 4:22)—plural. Nephi's confrontation with multiple enemies over many years is the context displayed in this passage; it is not the context of the single episode with Laban.

Second, it is noteworthy that immediately prior to his query about anger Nephi wrote that the Lord had confounded his enemies "unto the causing of them to quake before me" (2 Ne. 4:22). The record tells us that Laman and Lemuel quaked before Nephi (1 Ne. 17:47–54), and it may have been true of others as well, but it was manifestly not true of Laban. On this basis alone there is no reason to think that Nephi was referring to Laban when writing in this passage about his enemy. Not only did Nephi have in mind multiple enemies, but he also had in mind those who had quaked before him. A focus on Laban is inconsistent with both features of the account.

Third, it is significant that Nephi wrote this passage in the present tense even though he was writing years after the incident with Laban. Nephi writes, "Why *am* I angry because of mine enemy?" Nephi's use of the present tense indicates that he was either referring to a contemporary enemy or using the term "enemy" in a general sense. Either way, Nephi could not have meant only Laban in this passage. Indeed, there is every reason to think Laban was *not* the enemy Nephi had in mind.

Finally, it is important to note that Nephi speaks in this verse specifically of his anger toward his enemy. But nowhere does Nephi indicate that he had anger toward Laban in killing him. Indeed, he tells us that he slew Laban only after being prompted by the Lord and only after resisting that prompting. There is thus no reason to connect this account of anger to Nephi's incident with Laban—indeed, the only way to claim this connection is to assert that Nephi *must* have been angry, even though there is no textual evidence for it. But then we are resorting to mere makeshift, ad hoc, theorizing and simply attributing to Nephi whatever conduct or attitude we must in order to sustain a conclusion about him that we have already reached.

In short there is nothing in the text to indicate that Nephi ultimately felt remorse for slaying Laban, and we can therefore discard the idea. Nevertheless, according to England there are two additional aspects of the story that suggest additional reasons to question this account.

The Effect of Nephi's Example

First, in seeing Nephi's action to slay Laban as wrong—and thus seeing Nephi as later coming to regret the action—it is natural to have concern about the example that such an incident sets for modern readers. England worries about members who have used the Laban episode to "justify troubling, violent rhetoric and even violent action," having in mind a set of unbalanced Utah fundamentalists who appealed to the verse to justify murder.[15] He imagines that these fundamentalists' behavior counts against the conventional reading of the episode (i.e., that Nephi was right in his action) because no interpretation can be right if it lends itself to such grotesque misapplication.

But a conclusion of this sort is obviously a non sequitur since the deranged among us can appropriate many passages, if not all of scripture. That is not a problem unique to this verse. Such misappropriation counts against the mental and moral capacity of the murderers who misappropriate it, not against the prima facie interpretation of the verse itself.

The End Justifying the Means

Second, England is troubled by the very idea that the Spirit could teach "that the end justifies the means."[16] Rejecting this moral formulation—and pointing out that it is identical to the approach Caiaphas used to condemn Christ himself before the Sanhedrin[17]—England questions Nephi's account. Assuming that since the Spirit could not teach something so obviously wrong as the principle that the end justifies the means, England is forced to reconsider Nephi's report of the episode and specifically of the Spirit's role in it: perhaps it was all due to Nephi's rationalization and/or self-delusion.[18]

Inherent in this reframing, however, is the conviction that the end *cannot* justify the means—that the rightness of a course of action is never a function of its consequences. But this is a simplistic view of ethical matters. This becomes evident when we consider England's own report that he would use violence to defend his family. This willingness suggests that he would justify

---

15. England, "Why Nephi Killed Laban," 143.
16. Ibid., 143.
17. Ibid., 142.
18. England does not consider Nephi's wrongness—and his subsequent rationalization and/or self-delusion—to be the best explanation of the incident, but it is a possibility he takes seriously (ibid., 143–45.) England's treatment of what he believes is the best explanation (see ibid., esp. 145–46) is also problematic, but in the interest of space I will leave that account aside. For more on the problems that inhere, in general, in failing to take Nephi at his word regarding his slaying of Laban, see the section "Examining the Corollary of the Narrative Approach: The Example of Nephi" in Chapter 8.

violence in that circumstance precisely because such violence *would protect his family*, and that otherwise he would not think it justified. But if this is England's reasoning it is a perfect example of an end (protecting one's family) justifying the means (employing violence). Such reasoning explicitly justifies violence by an appeal to the positive result such violence would produce.[19]

Seeing this feature as a likely element in England's thinking is not surprising, of course, since most people think this way on some level. They believe that whether a given end justifies a particular means depends on what the end and the means are specifically. It is important to recognize this apparent feature of *England's* thinking, however, because it is partly a repugnance toward the "end justifying the means" character of the Nephi/Laban episode that leads England to question it. He is suspicious of the idea that "the Lord slayeth the wicked to bring forth his righteous purposes" and that "it is better that one man should perish than that a nation should dwindle and perish in unbelief" (1 Ne. 4:13). Yet this is precisely the kind of "end justifying the means" thinking that England himself employs in justifying defense of his family—an approach that most would adopt in the same circumstance. But if we utilize a calculation of this sort in one domain of our moral experience we can hardly consider it a fatal flaw in another.

In short, if Nephi's narrative is morally problematic, it requires far more sophistication than a *tout court* rejection of the proposition "the end justifies the means" to demonstrate it.

---

19. It is true that one could justify defending one's family on the basis (for example) of the difference in moral status between aggressors and victims—a matter first discussed in Chapter 2—rather than on the basis of the interaction between ends and means. But it is unlikely that England himself would go this direction since nowhere does he draw the distinction between the moral status of aggressors and victims. See the next section, "Abortion and Capital Punishment," for the most obvious example of a case in which people normally rely on the difference in individuals' moral status in making ethical judgments, while England does not even consider the distinction. It is thus highly probable that England's willingness to defend his family rests, at least inchoately, on a calculation regarding ends and means. Of course, it would be far from *wrong* for England to consider both ends and means in thinking about his family: as mentioned in the text, most people's ethical views include consideration of both dimensions in determining the rightness of courses of action, whatever other moral distinctions they might also draw. The same is true even of most moral philosophers. However, while it would not be wrong for England to make calculations of this sort, it *would* be inconsistent for him to do so, since that is exactly the kind of thinking he condemns in discussing Nephi and Laban. For somewhat more on the relationship between ends and means in moral philosophy, see note 7 in Chapter 3.

Abortion and Capital Punishment

Another scriptural matter in regard to the issue of non-violence is the comparison England makes between abortion and capital punishment. England assumes that it is inconsistent to favor the second if one abhors the first. The idea is that if we oppose abortion on the basis of the sanctity of life, how can we simultaneously favor an act by the state which consists in taking life?[20]

But to see this view as inconsistent is to ignore certain assumptions held by those who espouse it, namely, that there is a moral difference between, say, a fetus and a serial killer—an asymmetry that makes a difference in determining the nature of their rights and the nature of our obligations toward them. To say that it is inconsistent to treat a fetus differently than we treat a murderer is either to disregard, or to deny, this moral distinction. It is as if we were also to say (to return to the example from Chapter 2) that it is inconsistent to believe that Cain is not permitted to kill Abel, but that Adam *is* permitted to kill Cain. After all, since both are acts of killing, to be consistent we must believe that both acts are wrong.

Most people, however, would reject this line of reasoning because, as discussed at length in Chapter 2, it disregards the distinction between aggressors and victims and thus fails to notice the moral difference between the two figures Cain and Adam. Though not identical, a similar distinction is at work in the case of abortion and capital punishment. Just as there is a difference in moral status between an aggressor and a victim in cases of attack, so also there is a difference in moral status between a fetus (a life that is obviously innocent of any wrongdoing) and a serial killer (a life that is guilty of monstrous wrongdoing) in the respective cases in which they are killed. This is why it is simplistic to merely assert, with no further argument, that reverence for life applies identically in the two cases. There is a difference in moral status between a fetus and a murderer and this difference must at least be relevant in determining what ought, and ought not, be done to them. Certainly we cannot disregard this prima facie difference between the two with no argument whatever.[21]

---

20. England expresses this view in his "'Thou Shalt Not Kill': An Ethics of Non-Violence," 167.

21. England argues that the Kantian right to be treated as a person is inalienable and that it cannot be lost; nor, he says, can we be excused from our responsibility to treat others as persons—as ends in themselves; see England, "'Thou Shalt Not Kill,'"170. This is a defensible position. I argued in Chapter 2 that persons who initiate violence toward others forfeit certain rights that would otherwise attach to them (for example, the right not to suffer violence and the right not to be lied to), but these are narrower than the broad right to be treated as an end. But this distinction between broad and narrower rights highlights the important questions that England fails to address: What exactly does treating others as ends *mean* in one circumstance or another, and

Of course such moral dissimilarity does not support capital punishment by itself; further argument would be required to complete justification for it. Nevertheless, it seems difficult to deny (a) that there exists a difference in moral status between a fetus and a murderer; (b) that this difference is relevant to any discussion of the comparison between abortion and capital punishment; and (c) that someone who relies on this distinction can be thoroughly consistent in both opposing abortion and favoring capital punishment.[22] Difference in moral status is both a common and a seemingly obvious dissimilarity, and thoughtful people draw the distinction and account for it in their thinking all the time, even if they are not able to articulate it as explicitly as a philosopher might.[23]

---

can it vary by circumstance? Does treating all people as ends entail treating them all identically? Why would persons who are so morally different as serial killers and fetuses draw from us the obligation to treat them as if they weren't morally different? In short, why is there only one conceivable instantiation of the Kantian imperative, regardless of difference in circumstances and regardless of difference in moral status? The prima facie answer to this question is that there isn't—something we will explore in the section "God's Violence and Treating People as Ends" later in this chapter.

22. Although he explicitly appeals to Kant in this essay as one of the foundations for his thinking about ethical matters, England fails to mention that Kant himself explicitly argues for capital punishment in the case of murder. See, for example, the selection of Kant's *The Philosophy of Law* (1887). At a minimum England should note this fact and suggest why his view can still be maintained on Kantian grounds, or at least explain why (and how, logically) he departs from Kant on this particular issue. Unfortunately, he does neither. For one who tries something in these directions, see Nelson T. Potter, Jr., "Kant and Capital Punishment Today."

23. Illustrating the importance of thinking carefully about these issues—rather than jumping too quickly to conclusions—Kamm observes: "Some argue against capital punishment on the ground that it violates a human right not to be killed. They favor incarceration instead. But in the same sense . . . in which there is a right not to be killed, there is a right not to be deprived of liberty. If one can forfeit a right to liberty by bad acts, and so can be permissibly incarcerated as punishment, then it is not clear why one could not forfeit the right not to be killed (even when one is not presently a threat). Some argue that there is a human right not to be tortured. Others argue that it would take the need to stop a ticking bomb that threatens an enormous number of people to justify torturing even those who set the bomb. But suppose that a villain is about to set a bomb that will shortly kill one child. Presumably, the villain has no right that we not kill him, if only this would stop his setting the bomb. Furthermore, torturing someone for a short period seems less bad for him than death. Then why does the villain also have no right not to be tortured, if torturing him rather than killing him would also stop his setting the bomb? And if we are unable to kill him, but only able to torture him in order to stop his setting the bomb, might he not also have no right not to be tortured?" See F.M. Kamm, *Intricate Ethics: Rights, Responsibilities, and Permissible Harm*, 238.

Old Testament Violence and the Prince of Peace

A third scriptural matter in regard to the issue of non-violence is the way England thinks about pacifism in light of the Savior's status as the God of the Old Testament. England reports that some Latter-day Saints resist pacifism on the grounds that the God of the Old Testament was Jesus Christ, and that he therefore committed acts of violence. It follows that he is not really the Prince of Peace that the New Testament presents him to be and that pacifism therefore cannot genuinely be incumbent on the Saints (or on Christians generally).[24]

The first thing to recognize about this conclusion, however, is the mistaken assumption it makes. It imagines Latter-day Saints to resist the idea that Jesus was a pacifist on the basis that he was the God of the Old Testament and therefore committed acts of violence—implying that the Saints *would* accept Jesus as a pacifist if only he had not been the God of the Old Testament. But this assumption is obviously mistaken. If Jesus had not been the God of the Old Testament then (presumably) the Father would have been, and since the Father would then have been committing acts of violence it would still be impossible to see Jesus as a pacifist. Since Latter-day Saints understand that the Father and the Son are completely one in character and purpose, it follows for them that if the God of the Old Testament was not a pacifist, then neither was the God of the New, whether they were the same divine personage or not. Thus, there is no special problem in seeing Jesus as a pacifist based on his Godhood of the Old Testament, because, due to the essential unity of the Godhead, that problem exists regardless of who happens to be the God of the Old Testament.

Of course, even if we fail to see the false assumption at play here we might nevertheless think, as England does, that there is a problem with the divine acts of violence that appear in that record. We might be eager to discount them or explain them in a way that sustains our pacifist point of view and that demonstrates such violence to be illusory. Thus, England reports that "if we look carefully at the Old Testament that idea, that God himself is violent, can be rejected,"[25] and then offers a study of the Old Testament to support this thesis.

Unfortunately, England's analysis of the Old Testament is exiguous, consisting of three Old Testament passages, comprising a total of eleven verses,

---

24. He sets forth this characterization in England, "The Prince of Peace," 231–32. It is true of course that the Lord could require his people to be pacifists even if he is not, in the same way that he proscribes vengeance for his people and yet permits it for himself (see for example Morm. 3:14–15; 8:20). But this is not a matter we need to pursue since England makes no argument of this kind.

25. England, "The Prince of Peace," 232.

and requiring fewer than three pages of commentary.[26] Such brief treatment would be sufficient if the passages England chose were fundamental and served to reorient our thinking about all other relevant passages in scripture. Unfortunately, they are not pivotal in this way. And that is why, if we want to explain scriptural events in a way that sustains a view of the Lord as thoroughly non-violent—whether in the Old Testament or elsewhere—there are multiple episodes we need to consider. These include:

1. The Lord's destruction of the wicked through the flood at the time of Noah (Gen. 7:13; Moses 7:34).[27]
2. The Lord's extinction of countless Egyptians through the various plagues he sent to convince Pharaoh to release the children of Israel (see particularly Ex. 9 and 12).
3. The Lord's slaying of Pharaoh and "the host of the Egyptians" as they pursued the children of Israel at the Red Sea (Ex. 14).
4. The Lord's casting down "great stones from heaven" upon the enemies of Israel in one battle, killing them (Josh. 10:11).
5. The Lord's slaying of one who was attempting to kill Ammon in Ammon's vulnerable state at the time of Lamoni's conversion (Alma 19:21–23).
6. Jesus's aggressive, even violent, clearing of the temple in Jerusalem (Matt. 21:12–13; Mark 11:15–17).
7. The Lord's destruction of fifteen cities and their inhabitants, by flood, fire, and swallowing them up "in the depths of the earth" following his resurrection (3 Ne. 9:3–12).
8. Finally, the vengeance the Lord will visit upon the wicked incident to his second coming (for example, Isa. 11:4; D&C 45:50; and D&C 29:17).[28]

It is not obvious what arguments might render a pacifist interpretation of these and other events in scripture, but it is obviously inadequate to reach conclusions about the Lord's nature in the absence of such arguments, not

---

26. England's analysis is found in ibid., 232–34. Along the way England also quotes the experience in the Book of Moses in which Enoch queries God about his weeping over the wickedness of the inhabitants of the earth. But nothing in this passage, or in England's fifty-word commentary on it, reveals anything about God's violence, and thus—at least so far as I can see—it is extraneous to the point he is trying to make.

27. Note the Lord's language: "And the fire of mine indignation is kindled against them; and in my hot displeasure will I send in the floods upon them, for my fierce anger is kindled against them" (Moses 7:34).

28. Again, note the Lord's language in one instance: "I have trodden the wine-press alone, and have brought judgment upon all people; and none were with me; and I have trampled them in my fury, and I did tread upon them in mine anger, and their blood have I sprinkled upon my garments, and stained all my raiment; for this was the day of vengeance which was in my heart" (D&C 133:50–51).

to mention in the absence of any consideration at all of these episodes and others like them.

God's Violence and Treating People as Ends

Another effort England makes in interpreting scripture from a pacifist perspective is to employ Kant's principle of treating people as ends and not merely as means. This is an important and enduring moral concept and is central to thinking about the rights we possess.[29] Thus, in considering violence specifically from a scriptural perspective, England observes, "we are confronted, in scripture and experience, with a God who is completely without violence precisely because he treats all humans as infinitely precious, as persons, ends in themselves."[30]

While a formulation of this sort might seem appealing on the surface, it is actually problematic when we tease out the argument that the statement contains: The argument is that since God treats all persons as ends in themselves, and since it is not possible to treat persons as ends in themselves *and* to treat them with violence, it follows that God does not treat people with violence. The problem with an argument of this sort, however, is evident: it fails to give us reason to accept the second premise. Even if the first premise is granted—that God treats all persons as ends in themselves—what evidence or logic compels the idea that it is not possible to do this *and* to treat persons with violence?

This is a serious question for two reasons. First, over the course of this volume we have considered multiple examples of violence that, on a reasonable reading of the text, reflect either God's own actions or his support of human actions, and we have encountered no argument that succeeds in repudiating such a reading of these incidents.[31] The presence of divine violence seems evident both on a prima facie reading of the scriptures and on a careful reading of them. Without serious and comprehensive analysis, therefore, it just does not seem plausible to conclude something as categorical as "we are confronted, in scripture and experience, with a God who is completely without violence."

The second reason for questioning the idea that it is not possible to treat persons as ends in themselves and simultaneously to treat those persons with violence follows from the Kantian principle itself—a principle which England, for example, references frequently. To see why the question follows from the principle itself, note that according to Kant we human beings in-

---

29. See particularly the section "The Relational Foundation of Right and Wrong" in Chapter 2.

30. England, "Thou Shalt Not Kill,'" 171.

31. The narrative approach that we examined in Chapters 8 and 9 tries to repudiate these reports, but the effort fails. See particularly the section "Examining the Corollary of the Narrative Approach: The Example of the Lord's Own Conduct" in Chapter 8.

habit an intelligible world (a world independent of the laws of nature) and that because of this we are free and rational beings who are capable of giving the moral law to ourselves. Moreover, because reason does the choosing of whatever moral law we give ourselves, and because we all have the same reason, we all give the same moral law to ourselves. This law is Kant's categorical imperative, which, in his second formulation, means respecting persons, or treating others as ends, never merely as means.[32] But it is important to note what this entails. It entails that to be treated as "human, as a person" includes being treated *as free and rational* as well, or in other words, to be treated as beings who are capable of giving ourselves the moral law and conforming to it. Being a person, and being free and rational, are thus inseparable features of a single reality. Both are ingredient in being an end in ourselves.

Now all of this explains (at least in light of this Kantian context) how God can treat us as "infinitely precious, as ends in ourselves," and simultaneously consign us to conditions that entail anguish and suffering beyond the capacity of words to convey.[33] On England's own terms, if God treats all of us as ends in ourselves, then he also treats all of us as free and rational beings. Therefore, if we are evil he treats us as beings who have freely chosen to become evil. If darkness is what we have chosen, then receiving darkness seems to be the perfect expression of treating us as ends in ourselves. It is hard to see what would better honor our status as the free and rational persons that we are. Arguably, from England's Kantian perspective, it is the only way we *can* be treated if our status as free and rational persons is to be fully acknowledged and respected. To treat us differently than this would be to indulge us; it would be to treat us as less free and rational than we are, and this would not be treating us as ends.[34]

---

32. See Immanuel Kant, *Groundwork of the Metaphysics of Morals*.

33. Although I choose the matter of judgment here because it is the most harrowing and enduring of what we would consider the Lord's violent acts, any example of God's destruction of the wicked would serve equally well. As for the inadequacy of words to capture the torment that some will suffer, consider the Lord's description of sons of perdition as those whose "worm dieth not, and the fire is not quenched, which is their torment—and the end thereof, neither the place thereof, nor their torment, no man knows . . . wherefore, the end, the width, the height, the depth, and the misery thereof, they understand not" (D&C 76:33, 44–48). And of hell more generally, the Lord says that "surely every man must repent or suffer," and that "woes shall go forth, weeping, wailing and gnashing of teeth, yea, to those who are found on my left hand" (D&C 19:4–5). He adds: "Therefore I command you to repent—repent, lest I smite you by the rod of my mouth, and by my wrath, and by my anger, and your sufferings be sore—how sore you know not, how exquisite you know not, yea, how hard to bear you know not" (D&C 19:15).

34. If we were to put the same point in Martin Buber's terms, another of England's influences, we would say that the Lord is always in an I-Thou relationship with us,

Moreover, since England says that we have the *right* to be treated as ends, it follows that others have the *obligation* to treat us in this way. For the sake of argument, if we make certain assumptions about God being the perfect follower of the rules of the universe, then even God is obligated to treat us as ends. But if so, then God also has the moral obligation to treat us as free and rational—which means not only that it is fitting that God consign us to darkness if darkness is what we have chosen, but that he also has the *duty* to do so. In consigning us to misery and torment, then, God, according to England's Kantian perspective, is simply doing what he morally must do. He is not *permitted* to treat us as less free and rational than we are. Unfortunately, in the circumstances we have created, it seems that the only way he can avoid treating us as less free and rational than we are is to deliver us to the state that befits the person we have become and that we sustain of our own volition. This God is obligated to do in order to truly treat us as ends in ourselves.[35]

---

and this includes when we suffer for our wickedness: he refuses to treat us as less fully human and free than we are. For his influential discussion of I-Thou and I-It relationships, see Martin Buber, *I and Thou*. England identifies Buber as an influence in England, "'Thou Shalt Not Kill.'" In one way or another, all of this is reminiscent of Alma's teachings to his son Corianton in Alma 41.

35. I cast all of the points in this section in Kantian terms because England specifically references Kant as an influence and because he consistently employs Kantian language—and it seems best to examine the logical conclusion of England's reasoning in terms of his own choosing. However, it was only in what is called his pre-critical period that Kant considered the matter of God's punishment per se, entertaining the possibility that natural disasters are God's punishment for the sins of the world. See Immanuel Kant, *The One Possible Basis for a Demonstration of the Existence of God*. Other than that, while Kant has an argument in his *Critique of Practical Reason* that—broadly speaking, at any rate—regards rewards in the next life, he does not cast this in terms of punishment. There, after reasoning that we must postulate the immortality of the soul, Kant argues that: (1) the moral law commands us to seek the highest good; (2) it ought to be the case that we enjoy happiness to the degree that we seek the highest good—happiness should be "proportioned to that morality"; (3) but in this world there is actually little correlation between morality and happiness; (4) furthermore, no person in this world can assure that our happiness will "thoroughly harmonize" with our morality; therefore, (5) we must postulate the existence of a supreme cause, God, who *can* assure in the next life "exact harmony of happiness with morality." In short, because *we* cannot arrange life so that we enjoy happiness to the degree that we deserve it in this world (whether it is little happiness or much), the moral law that we give ourselves, with all of its logical implications, requires that we suppose there exists a being who *can* harmonize life in this way. This being is God, and creating the exact correlation between persons' morality and their happiness is something God will achieve in the continuation of life after this one. (Kant was explicit in denying that this argument constitutes a proof of the existence of God, saying instead that the idea is

Any claim, therefore, that "God is completely without violence because he treats each person as an end in himself" seems in the final analysis to be both false and ironic. The assertion is false because of the significant evidence that God is not, in fact, completely without violence; and it is ironic because—far from prohibiting God from committing any acts of violence—an insistence that God treats us as ends implies that he is actually *obligated* to commit acts of violence against us when he does so. Thus, the second clause in England's formulation seems to require God to be precisely what England's first clause says he isn't.

Ending Conflict

Another way a pacifist perspective can manifest itself scripturally is in a claim such as this from England: "[In cases of conflict,] when either side is willing to obey Christ's commands, to lay down their weapons or angry words and stop fighting or competing, even if they thus sacrifice their lives, as Christ did, they stop the violence."[36] In other words, we might hold the view that one side in a conflict can bring the conflict to an end by abandoning all "fighting or competing" against the other. Pacifist response to conflict is sufficient to end conflict.

On one hand, this assertion is true by definition because the moment one side in a conflict capitulates, the conflict *as* a conflict is ended: there is no fighting because there is no fighting *back*. But it is hard to see how light is shed on important matters by making assertions that are true by definition. The claim actually has substance only if we mean by it that aggressors will *abandon* their endeavors in the face of such pacifist response, not merely that conflict has ceased in the sense that the other side is now letting the aggressors have their way. But once we recognize what the statement must be understood to claim, is the claim true? Is pacifist response sufficient to avoid and/or end others' aggression? Three scriptural cases help address this question.

The Ammonites

On one hand, it might appear that the Ammonites' experience supports the claim that a pacifist response to aggression will prevail and bring an aggressor's malevolent designs to an end. This is what happened the first time the Anti-Nephi-Lehies were attacked (Alma 24), and it is a case that England

---

a matter of "pure *rational faith*" [emphasis his]. "It is *morally* necessary to assume the existence of God," he adds, meaning that the logic of the moral law requires it.) See Immanuel Kant, *Critique of Practical Reason (and Other Works on the Theory of Ethics)*, 106–110: all quotations are from these pages.

36. England puts the matter this way in his "Healing and Making Peace, in the Church and the World," 8–9.

clearly has in mind as an illustration of the claim.[37] On the other hand, however, this is far from all that occurred the second time the Ammonites suffered assault, which is why God instructed the Ammonites to flee to the land of Jershon (Alma 27)—an action which indicates that *the Lord* did not believe pacifist response from the Ammonites would end others' violence against them. Nor, apparently, did the Ammonites themselves believe this. Though they had further opportunity to do so, the Ammonites never again followed the practice of self-sacrifice that they practiced in the beginning.[38] Apparently, they believed that if they prostrated themselves once again, their enemies—far from abandoning their wicked and violent purposes—would simply pursue those designs without the inconvenience of opposition.

Christ's Death

Consider also the matter of the Savior's death. If pacifist response to conflict is sufficient to end others' aggression, it seems to follow that Christ's sacrifice of his own life should also have brought an end to violence. This is a natural implication of the claim, and it is a conclusion that England makes explicit when he says, "as an innocent victim, [Christ] would end the violence by refusing to participate in it, thus stopping the cycles of retaliation."[39]

There are at least two significant problems with a claim of this sort, however. First, in making the assertion that Christ's death brought an end to violence, we might be saying either of two things, and each of them is intellectually problematic. On one hand we might be saying that violence came to an end toward Christ himself once Christ allowed himself to be killed. But if this is the point we want to make, the argument is conceptually hollow. After all, while it is true that Christ's persecutors ceased exercising violence toward him once their violence had brought about his death, it is hard to see the virtue in an end to violence that occurs only because the target is now *dead*.

The other claim that might be made is that violence came to an end in general with the death of Christ. But it is hard to imagine what evidence there might be for this claim. For what people did violence come to an end, in what period of time, and for what duration, as a result of the Savior's death? England himself does not say anything about this, much less anything specific, and it is difficult to see what anyone might say. The conclusion seems implausible on any reading of events in the Holy Land in the aftermath of the Savior's life, ministry, and death—events of violence which he himself had foretold (Matt. 24; JS–Matthew).

A second problem arises if, in emphasizing that Christ refused to participate in the violence that was visited upon him and that led to his death, we

---

37. See ibid., 9, where he explicitly mentions the Ammonites in this context.
38. See the section "The Ammonites' Strategy of Self-Sacrifice" in Chapter 10.
39. England, "The Prince of Peace," 229.

further imagine that his conduct in these circumstances sets the proper example for others to emulate—i.e., that we are to accept brutality and murder without defense as he did. Imagining this is problematic because it overlooks the reality that Christ was ordained to die, and that for eternal and divine purposes his death was necessary and intended. As the Lord said at the beginning of the end as Peter raised a sword in his defense: "The cup which my Father hath given me, shall I not drink it?" (John 18:10–11). Appreciating this crucial aspect of the Lord's suffering and death is essential to understanding his conduct during the events leading up to and including his crucifixion: because he was *born* to be crucified and die for us, it was only natural that he capitulate to his captors and refuse to defend his life. That feature of his circumstances is obvious and explains why he behaved as he did.

That feature of his circumstances also explains why his behavior during these events does not establish the pattern for all people to follow in all circumstances. Not everyone is ordained to suffer an early and violent death as the Lord was. Indeed, if we overlooked this fact, and thought that the Lord's conduct *did* establish a pattern that all should follow, then by the same logic we would be forced to conclude that since Christ destroyed fifteen Book of Mormon cities for their wickedness following his death (3 Ne. 9:1–12), we too ought to destroy people for their wickedness. Since we are supposed to follow his example that can only mean that we should behave as he behaved.

We obviously don't say this, however, because the folly of such an argument is evident: our roles and circumstances are similar to the Lord's in some very general respects, but radically different in others. This is obvious, and we must account for such distinctions in any effort to explain how the Lord's behavior in his role and circumstances applies to us in our roles and circumstances. Unfortunately, accounting for such prodigious asymmetries is precisely what we fail to do if we simplistically assert that everyone should respond to aggression in the same way that Christ responded to the aggression that ended his life. There is no basis for such a conclusion.

The War in Heaven

Finally, if we believe that by ceasing their "fighting or competing" one side will bring both conflict and the other side's malevolence to an end, we must give some thought to the war in heaven (Rev. 12:7–9). While we do not know much about this conflict, and while it is difficult to imagine how physical violence could have been involved, we do know that it was a contest of wills sufficiently vigorous to be called war. We also know that Lucifer "rebelled" against Christ (D&C 76:25, 28), that he actually "sought to take the kingdom of our God and his Christ" (D&C 76:28), that he and Michael (and their cohorts) "fought" one another (Rev. 12:7), and that he was finally "thrust down" (D&C 76:25). Such actions are certainly subsumed in England's reference to "conflict," "competing," "fighting," and "angry words." So if we assert that cessation of "fighting" or "competing" with the other will bring both conflict and the aggressor's evil designs to an end, we are forced to say that the war in heaven itself could have been avoided if only God had responded to Lucifer in this manner.

But it seems safe to presume that if that could have prevented Lucifer's malevolence it is exactly what God would have done. Indeed, it would seem that God's failure to do this itself demonstrates that such a course would not have ended Lucifer's threatening conduct. Nevertheless, because God did not respond in this way, England's view would force us to see Michael, the Savior, and the Father all to be wrong in "fighting" and "competing" with Lucifer. In the universe of absurdities, most would find it difficult to imagine one to exceed this.

Such an example demonstrates once again that there is no reason to suppose that aggressors will uniformly abandon their destructive aims just because we ourselves "stop fighting or competing" with them. If it were as simple as that, members of the Godhead would obviously have behaved differently in the pre-earth existence than they actually did.[40]

Conclusion

In the end, there is no reason to accept any of the following views: (1) years after slaying Laban, Nephi regretted his action and felt remorse for it; (2) Latter-day Saints are morally inconsistent if they oppose abortion while favoring capital punishment; (3) we can reject as illusory the appearance of divine violence in the Old Testament (not to mention in other scripture); (4) because God acts according to the principle of treating people as ends, it follows that he is "completely without violence;" and (5) pacifist response to aggression brings an end to aggressors' designs. On their face such views might seem persuasive, but all of them suffer when scrutinized more deeply. Given their inadequacy, none of them can be thought to support a pacifist view toward violence.

---

40. We might think that since the plan of salvation required a Satan, God and others ensured this result precisely *by* contending with Lucifer, thereby guaranteeing a war in heaven, the subsequent expulsion of Lucifer and his hosts, and the necessary opposition between good and evil on earth. But this would mean that God acted in a way that he knew would eventually result in the torment of Satan and of his angels in eternity (D&C 76:30–49), even though Lucifer would not have become the kind of being who would merit such a fate had God only acted differently. On such a view we end up with the absurdity of God pouring out his wrath on Satan in eternity even though it was God's unnecessary provocation that was responsible for Lucifer becoming Satan in the first place.

Chapter 12

Self-Defense, Pre-Emptive Action, and Holocaust

In considering the perspective Eugene England offers, we must also consider a statement made by President David O. McKay in 1942 while he served as second counselor in the First Presidency. England emphasizes President McKay's explicit support in this statement for Allied nations' entrance into the Second World War—an action President McKay viewed as properly defensive in nature and therefore legitimate. But England also accents President McKay's rejection in the same statement of any war that is "an attempt to enforce a new order of government . . . however better the government . . . may be."[1] On the basis of such a statement, we might well conclude, as England does, that this standard would condemn each of the military actions of the United States since World War II. According to England, these include "in Korea (at least after we crossed the 39th parallel), in Vietnam, in Grenada, in Angola, and in Iraq."[2]

But if we want to take President McKay's statement as a guide it is important to consider his statement in full. For instance, in the course of these same remarks in 1942 President McKay also declared that there are "two conditions which may justify a truly Christian man to enter—mind you, I say *enter, not begin*—a war: (1) An attempt to dominate and to deprive another of his free agency, and, (2) Loyalty to his country. Possibly there is a third, viz., Defense of a weak nation that is being unjustly crushed by a strong, ruthless one."[3] So according to President McKay, while war is unjustified to "enforce a new order of government" it is not, as we have already seen, unjustified in self-defense, and it can even be justified in assisting another government in defending itself from hostilities. These are important elements of President McKay's message and, in attempting to apply the teachings of President McKay as England desires to do, it is a mistake to overlook them.

Furthermore, if we want to use President McKay's remarks as a guide for making judgments about the involvement of the United States in various

---

1. This is England's statement in "The Prince of Peace," 242–43.
2. Ibid., 243. Unfortunately, England gives us no insight into his thinking about such matters, but condemns the actions in Vietnam, Grenada, Angola, and Iraq all in a single sentence.
3. David O. McKay, "The Church and the Present War"; emphasis in the original.

wars since World War II, it is important to think about such instances with a reasonable degree of care. Should some of those conflicts be categorized differently than England categorizes them, for example? Do some of them only appear on the surface to be cases of "enforcing a new order of government" (an action condemned by President McKay), when in reality they are better understood as cases of "assisting a government in defending itself" (the kind of action provisionally approved by him)? And do any of them actually qualify as instances of *self*-defense? These seem to be important questions to have in mind if we want to draw moral conclusions about one conflict or another, particularly if we want to take guidance from the full scope of President McKay's remarks. Certainly it seems inadequate to disregard such questions altogether.

A Historical Example

In pursuing our own thinking about these matters it is useful to consider one of England's examples: Grenada.[4] This is probably the simplest case of his to describe, and taking up this historical incident will permit us to explore a number of issues regarding war, including the question of pre-emptive action.

Background of the Grenada Invasion

Grenada is a small Caribbean island state, located a hundred miles north of Venezuela. The country first established a constitutional regime upon gaining independence from the United Kingdom in 1974. Political strife riddled the nation in the years following, and in 1979 a military coup overthrew the government and established the People's Revolutionary Government (PRG), led by Maurice Bishop, as the new leadership of the nation. Over time the PRG established close relations with Cuba and began construction of an unusually large airstrip with Cuban military help. The airstrip was thought by the U.S. government to be large enough to accommodate military transport aircraft and thus feared that it could, and would, be used to facilitate Cuban and Soviet Union attempts to arm Communist insurgents in the hemisphere. At the same time the PRG also began planning the development of a large military presence in the region.

---

4. Although it is important to say more than England does about the cases he mentions, the specific facts about these historical incidents are actually less important than the questions they help us consider. I take a brief look at Grenada—and later, even more briefly, at Cambodia—simply to illustrate the kinds of considerations that are raised in any serious thinking about international conflict. Readers who dislike these examples, or who think I summarize them inaccurately, are welcome to pick other historical incidents that call for consideration of similar matters.

Although cooperative with Cuba and the Soviet Union, Bishop also sought to maintain relations with the West, an attitude not shared by the hardline Marxist members of his government, including Deputy Prime Minister Bernard Coard. In October 1983 Coard led a coup against Bishop, placing him under house arrest and establishing a strongly pro-Communist government. Mass public demonstrations led to the freeing of Bishop, but as he attempted to regain authority over the government the military quickly captured and executed him and several members of his cabinet. They also established martial law in the country—including a shoot-on-sight order for citizens (or others) caught leaving their homes without approval at any time of day, and for any reason. On October 25, 1983, the United States invaded Grenada and defeated the military government, moving so quickly that all U.S. troops were removed before the end of December. Grenada then returned to the constitutional order that had existed prior to Bishop's coup in 1979 and in 1984 held its first elections in eight years.

Enforcing a New Order of Government?

Now we might choose to classify this conflict as a case of "enforcing a new order of government," as England does, and thus see it as an action expressly prohibited by President McKay's statement. However, this may not be the most apt characterization of the event. It seems that it could just as easily be seen as a case of the United States assisting a government in defending itself against overthrow—a situation considered justifiable in President McKay's comments. Indeed, the United States acted within days of the attacks on Bishop and his cabinet when there was no settled government in place of the Bishop regime other than the Coard coalition. It is not obvious why this coalition obtained legitimacy simply because it had assassinated Bishop and members of his cabinet, and thus it is not obvious why it would be immune to attack under President McKay's criteria. England assumes all this, but it is not apparent why he should.

Self-Defense? The Question of Pre-Emptive Action

Though the matter of classification is important in its own right, of primary concern regarding this military action is the degree to which the United States was acting to defend itself. In justifying its invasion of Grenada, the United States relied partly on two claims of self-defense. On one hand, it asserted the need to protect nearly one thousand Americans in Grenada, and on the other, the United States resisted the spread of Communism in the Western hemisphere generally and considered the encroachment of Soviet military influence in Western nations not only harmful to the nations themselves, but a nascent threat to the United States as well. The Monroe Doctrine had long prohibited international interference in the hemisphere in the interest of self-defense, and the Cuban missile crisis of 1962 had materially demonstrated the heightened threat to U.S. security posed by Communist nations in close proximity to U.S. borders. Thus, the Reagan administration was fearful of growing Soviet influence and resisted it as a matter of both regional and national security.[5]

Threat of violence. The legitimacy of that fear was reinforced when, once on Grenada, U.S. military personnel discovered a cache of Soviet and Cuban weapons much larger than had been expected. Furthermore, it was more than reasonable for the United States to dread the incursion of Communist influence in the region. Recent estimates of the deaths due to twentieth-century Communist regimes range from 85–100 million—numbers that fully quadruple the deaths attributable to the Nazis.[6] And these are not estimates reached by those with a distrust or hatred of Communism in the first place, but by French scholars—some of them Communists themselves—who ten years before their research "would have refused to believe"[7] their own findings. The examples they share of atrocities committed in the name of Communism are voluminous.[8] Long before Mao established China as a Communist state, for instance, his ideological predecessors fomented terror among Chinese villages. We are told that:

> The whole people were invited to public trials of "counterrevolutionaries," who almost invariably were condemned to death. Everyone participated in the executions, shouting out "kill, kill" to the Red Guards whose task it was to cut victims into pieces. Sometimes the pieces were cooked and eaten, or force-fed to members of the victim's family who were still alive and looking on. Everyone was then invited to a banquet, where the liver and heart of the former landowner were shared out, and to meetings where a speaker would address rows of severed heads freshly skewered on stakes.[9]

---

5. For Reagan's views on Grenada, as found in his personal letters, see Kiron K. Skinner, Annelise Anderson, and Martin Anderson, eds. *Reagan: A Life in Letters*, 496–503.

6. Stéphane Courtois, "Introduction: The Crimes of Communism," in Stéphane Courtois, et al., eds., *The Black Book of Communism: Crimes, Terror, Repression*, 15. It is interesting, and, I think, indisputable, that Nazi atrocities are more prominent in historical memory than Communist atrocities, despite the disparity in numbers and despite the greater nearness in time, overall, of the Communist experience. Alain Besançon takes up this matter and the reasons for it in his *A Century of Horrors: Communism, Nazism, and the Uniqueness of the Shoah*.

7. Martin Malia, "Foreword: The Uses of Atrocity," in *The Black Book of Communism: Crimes, Terror, Repression*, ed. Stéphane Courtois, et al., xx.

8. Stéphane Courtois, et al., eds., *The Black Book of Communism: Crimes, Terror, Repression*.

9. Jean-Louis Margolin, "China: A Long March into Night," in Stéphane Courtois, et al., eds., *The Black Book of Communism: Crimes, Terror, Repression*, 470–71. Although

Additionally, one author speaks of "the central place of terror in the political and social history of the U.S.S.R."[10] And although one of these academics calls Communism's influence "the most colossal case of political carnage in history,"[11] this is evident not only in hindsight,[12] but had become generally known long before the U.S. invasion of Grenada.[13] At least by the "1940s and 1950s, many facts about [Communist] atrocities had become public knowledge and undeniable," even though many remained ignorant due to "ideologically motivated self-deception."[14]

The inherent character of the violence: "the brotherhood of the pure." It was also evident that the threat of such violence from Communist insurgency was not merely contingent—something that might, but also might not, occur. Alain Besançon identifies the root cause of Communist (as well as of Nazi) violence in the fundamental character of the goal each sought—namely, "to achieve a perfect society by uprooting the evil that hindered its creation." He adds: "They claimed to be philanthropic because they sought the good . . . but what they have most in common is that they arrogated to themselves the right—and even the duty—to kill." This both regimes did "with similar methods" and "on a scale unknown in history."[15] Violence was thus inherent in the very

---

China was not established as a Communist state until 1949, the odyssey that led to this result began in 1922, under the direction of P'eng P'ai, who created a regime of terror by instigating polarization and enmity between peasants and landowners. This was the basis of the kind of atrocities described in the text. P'eng P'ai was the first to create militarized Communism in rural China and was a key influence in Mao's thinking on peasant movements. Although Mao did not ascend to authority over all of China until 1949, he first proclaimed a Chinese Republic of Soviets in one Chinese province in 1931, in which he presided over the Council of People's Commissars.

10. Nicholas Werth, "A State against Its People: Violence, Repression, and Terror in the Soviet Union," in Stéphane Courtois, et al., eds., *The Black Book of Communism: Crimes, Terror, Repression*, 267.

11. Martin Malia, "Foreword: The Uses of Atrocity," in Stéphane Courtois, et al., eds., *The Black Book of Communism: Crimes, Terror, Repression*, x.

12. Khrushchev, for example, spoke openly of one class of Stalin's atrocities in a speech in 1956. For the full text, see Nathaniel Weyl, *Anatomy of Terror*.

13. See, for just two examples from the '70s, Robert Conquest, *The Nation Killers: The Soviet Deportation of Nationalities* and John Barron and Anthony Paul, *Murder of a Gentle Land: The Untold Story of Communist Genocide in Cambodia*. Newspapers of the time also reported the genocide in Cambodia.

14. Stéphane Courtois, "Introduction: The Crimes of Communism," in Stéphane Courtois, et al., eds., *The Black Book of Communism: Crimes, Terror, Repression*, 11.

15. Alain Besançon, *A Century of Horrors: Communism, Nazism, and the Uniqueness of the Shoah*, trans. Ralph C. Hancock and Nathaniel H. Hancock, xiii.

logic of Communist influence: whatever impeded the creation of the perfect society was evil, and whatever was evil must be eradicated.

This pursuit of a "perfect society" is what Paul Johnson calls the twentieth century's "most radical vice"[16] and "the fatal temptation of modern times":[17] namely, "social engineering—the notion that human beings can be shoveled around like concrete."[18] Johnson adds that for mass-murderers who led Communist (as well as Nazi) movements politics was "the cure for human ills"[19] and indeed *meant* "the engineering of society for lofty purposes" since political action was "the only sure means of improving humanity."[20] On such a basis, these leaders thought, states could be transformed into Utopias, however variously they might define that notion.[21]

What the results of such cataclysmic movements show, however, is that human beings cannot actually be shoveled around like concrete. People have a hard time satisfying whatever criteria one ruling class or another deems necessary for inclusion in their particular Utopia. As a consequence of this, such humans become dispensable objects—nothing but impediments to the Utopian ideal and thus candidates for easy, and justified extermination. Thus one observer of the Communist genocide in Cambodia between 1975 and 1979 described the purge as "the translation into action of a particular vision of man [*sic*]: A person who has been spoiled by a corrupt regime cannot be reformed, he must be physically eliminated from the brotherhood of the pure."[22] Motivated in this way, the leaders of such regimes "saw themselves as the moral guardians of society and were proud of their right to send anyone they chose to his death."[23] In the words of one such leader, speaking specifically of the bourgeoisie and of the literal nature of class warfare, "if the enemies do not surrender, it is up to us to exterminate them."[24]

An early appearance of this calamitous phenomenon was the French Revolution. One leader of this revolution, Jean-Paul Marat, when told that to reach the revolution's ideal "you will have to cut off many heads," replied: "So

---

16. See Paul Johnson, *Modern Times: The World from the Twenties to the Nineties*, 130.
17. Ibid., 710.
18. Ibid., 130.
19. Ibid., 784.
20. Ibid.
21. Ibid., 587.
22. François Ponchaud, cited in James A. Tyner, *Genocide and the Geographical Imagination: Life and Death in Germany, China, and Cambodia*, 145. For Ponchaud's early volume on Cambodia, see François Ponchaud, *Cambodia: Year Zero*.
23. Stéphane Courtois, "Conclusion: Why?" in Stéphane Courtois, et al., eds., *The Black Book of Communism: Crimes, Terror, Repression*, 748.
24. Ibid., 749.

be it. Where gangrene has set in, you have to slice off the limb to save the body. We sow in blood and tears so that those after us can reap joy."[25] Marat himself was later killed as part of the revolutionary violence, as were Robespierre and other leading figures of the revolution, along with at least 30,000 others who also lost their lives in the eleven-month Reign of Terror.[26] But even this number pales in comparison to the deaths suffered in the Vendean region of France in the following year. Though specific numbers are controversial, no one doubts that deaths were immense in number, with one range of estimates starting at nearly 120,000 and going much higher from there.[27] And, as we have seen, Nazi and Communist movements added another 110 million or so deaths to that number in the twentieth century.

Johnson and Besançon see such outcomes as inherent in the Utopian logic that motivates such movements: namely, the willingness to uproot whatever evil (notably, whatever class of people) hinders the creation of a perfect society—what Marat earlier called the sowing of blood and tears in order to reap a later joy.[28]

Immediate and proximate threats. Based on appreciation of such matters, the United States thought it prudent to defend against Communism's presence in the region. The history of such regimes had demonstrated a record of violence, and from this contingent fact alone one could predict violent activity.

---

25. Cited in Erik Durschmied, *Blood of Revolution: From the Reign of Terror to the Arab Spring*, 39.

26. See William Doyle, *The Oxford History of the French Revolution*, 258–59.

27. See Peter McPhee, "Review of Reynald Secher, *A French Genocide: The Vendée.*"

28. Tragically, what history has shown is that movements of this sort sow an ocean of blood and tears—visiting upon humanity a scale of suffering and grief that is beyond imagination—while reaping no later joy whatever. Such is the price to achieve the "brotherhood of the pure." In this connection, one of the great political quarrels of the twentieth century occurred between the two French intellectuals, and friends, Albert Camus and Jean-Paul Sartre in regard to Communist violence. As the Cold War began to unfold and the violence of the Soviet Union—the premier beacon of Communism—became evident, Sartre came to embrace such violence as necessary to accomplish Communism's ends. Camus, on the other hand, repudiated that view, seeing the hypocrisy in "slave camps under the flag of freedom, massacres justified by philanthropy or [thinking of Nazism] by a taste for the superhuman"(see Albert Camus, *The Rebel*, 4), and took aim at Communism in particular. He saw the "central tool" of the Communist revolution to be "murder" and considered intellectuals friendly to such violence to be in complicity "with murder" and their victory to be "the victory of the slaughterhouse" (see Ronald Aronson, *Camus and Sartre: The Story of a Friendship and the Quarrel that Ended It*, 119, 107). Camus famously said of such revolutions: "Those who pretend to know everything and settle everything finish by killing everything" (ibid., 107).

In addition to this, however, the central logic of Communist aims actually made violence not just predictable, but inevitable. In light of all this, one could argue that the mission in Grenada qualified as a defensive action both of other nations and of the United States itself, which is how the Reagan administration viewed the matter.

One line of argument against such a claim, however, is that there was no proximate threat, much less an immediate one, either to the region or to the United States, and therefore that no military action was justified in this situation. Wasn't this a case of the United States striking first, and initiating hostilities, rather than merely defending itself against others' hostilities? And isn't such pre-emptive military action wrong?

Such questions raise the issue of exactly when, in the absence of any direct attack, a threat becomes proximate enough to justify action, and what principle determines this if not the kind of principle embodied in the Monroe Doctrine. However that may be decided, it seems difficult to rule out, as a matter of principle, the very possibility of legitimate response to a proximate threat and to claim that no such action is ever permissible. Suppose, for example, that there existed a legitimate threat in the region near the southern border of the United States, and that the United States followed a policy of inaction until the threat became immediate. And suppose further that the United States miscalculated in a circumstance that posed danger and that it was unable to prevent an actual attack on its southern border. Would we then say that it would have been wiser to prevent the threat when it was small and easy to thwart, even though only proximate, rather than wait until it had resulted in actual violence and in the deaths of some of our citizens?[29]

---

29. To make the question more personal, imagine that children of yours lived in that region and that they were killed in the conflict that ensued and that was fought on U.S. soil. Would it seem to you that it would have been wiser to anticipate the threat once it became evident and to deal with it before it materialized into an actual attack? Or would it seem to you that the death of your children was simply the price that had to be paid in a world where conflict occurs? Although such questions can be difficult for U.S. citizens to take seriously since they have never faced this kind of threat on their borders, it is important to try to think about conflict in such concrete and personal terms. Otherwise it is easy to think only in generalities and to fail to appreciate the concrete suffering that would be entailed by enemy attack. The matter is all too real for citizens of some other countries, of course, who need no imagination to think concretely about such issues. For many of them, the loss of loved ones due to enemy assault is both a memory and a perpetual risk. The possibility of terrorist attack, of course, can help U.S. citizens appreciate the concrete reality of aggression's harm. It also helps show why considering the matter of border assault is only illustrative: since terrorists operate in small numbers and by stealth, they are not limited by geography in their attacks.

Or suppose the United States followed a policy of taking no action until a threat was highly proximate—but at least before it became immediate. And suppose, because it was unimpeded, the threat then grew significantly in size and capability so that when it eventually had to be confronted the military action required to do so was much greater than it would have been in the beginning and the loss of life significantly higher. In such circumstances would we say that it would have been better to arrest the development of such a threat in the first place, when it was small? The actual Grenada invasion resulted in fewer than a hundred Cuban, Grenadian, and American deaths. Certainly this is regrettable, but how does it compare to a more bloody alternative?[30]

Calculating odds. Now we might reject this kind of thinking altogether and claim that we cannot calculate the odds of the latter scenario precisely enough to permit a comparison between it and the immediate prospects of pre-emptive action. But a claim of this sort seems unpersuasive, since some calculation of odds regarding future events is an unavoidable feature of life generally and certainly of matters between states. Such calculations will be flawed, in part because all intelligence is imprecise and incomplete, and because shifting currents of power and interest always exist within and between states. But if we are in a position of authority, it is difficult to see how the flawed nature of such calculations can justify us in refusing to compute the odds the best that we can. It would seem that we still must apply our best and wisest judgment to the historical patterns, stated objectives, and current behavior of the state in question, and if we decide not to take action against what appears to be a serious proximate threat we must explain why. We must demonstrate either that the apparent threat is not genuine and there is little risk that current events will escalate and present a serious danger in the future, or that, even if there *is* a reasonable risk of this threat, it is nevertheless best to take that risk rather than defend against it. In no case does it seem acceptable to ignore or minimize the risk or to refuse to address it thoughtfully.

Of course such judgments about risks and about how best to confront them are among the most serious matters that states face, since a central feature of any national government's duty is to ensure the security of its citizens,

---

30. Again, to make the question more personal, imagine that you have children serving in the military and, because the threat has grown large and menacing, they have to be involved in the sizeable military campaign now necessary to thwart it. If they are killed or injured in such large military action, would it seem to you that it would have been wiser to act earlier, when the threat could have been averted with a much smaller response that risked far fewer lives?

both now and in the future.³¹ While it is wrong to be cavalier in sending citizens into battle, it would seem no less wrong to be cavalier in overlooking developments that portend a genuine threat to those same citizens down the road. Given the nature of such a choice, and given the central role that some calculation of the odds must play in deciding it, it would seem morally indefensible to eschew such calculations altogether. It is hard to see how the difficulty of making such a judgment is sufficient to justify the refusal to make it.

Moral responsibility in pre-emptive action. This may not settle the matter, however. We still must confront the question of moral responsibility in pre-emptive action. After all, it is clear that an aggressor who attacks us is responsible for all the deaths that result from the military action we take to defend ourselves. But where does moral responsibility lie in the case of pre-emptive action? If we attack another state in anticipation of its attack on us, then it obviously has not yet attacked us. In this case are we the aggressor and are we responsible for the deaths caused by such military response? If we suppose this, it is natural to conclude that pre-emptive action is never justified, even if such intercession would result in the loss of fewer lives. This is because we may see ourselves as the cause of such loss of life and therefore feel morally culpable for that outcome. On the other hand, if we wait until we are under direct attack to respond militarily we may feel that whatever deaths occur are not our responsibility, even though following this course will almost certainly entail greater loss of life. It is regrettable that so many deaths occur, but now the moral blame rests entirely on the opposing state because they are the aggressors, not us. We are morally blameless.

To think about this argument it is useful to take England's example of defending his family against an attack.³² Doing so helps us focus on principles rather than on controversial historical details about actual international conflicts. We can focus simply on whether it is ever possible to take pre-emptive action in defense of oneself and others and not be morally culpable for the loss that occurs as a result of our doing so.

---

31. President McKay also had something to say on this topic: "The greatest responsibility of the state is to guard the lives, and to protect the property and rights of its citizens: and if the state is obligated to protect its citizens from lawlessness within its boundaries, it is equally obligated to protect them from lawless encroachments from without—whether the attacking criminals be individuals or nations." David O. McKay, "The Church and the Present War."

32. As mentioned in Chapter 11, see "A Case for Mormon Christian Pacifism," in Valerie M. Hudson and Kerry M. Kartchner, *Moral Perspectives on U.S. Security Policy: Views from the LDS Community*, 100–101. See also his "'Thou Shalt Not Kill': An Ethics of Non-Violence," in Eugene England, *Making Peace: Personal Essays*, 173.

To consider this question in terms of England's family, recall his report that he would be willing to mount violence in defending his family against an attack. Given this, would he refrain from a pre-emptive attack in order to thwart the planned aggression simply because he believes moral culpability would then shift to him? And would he feel this way even if a pre-emptive attack would actually save the lives of his family, whereas *failing* to make such an attack would result in some of them being killed when the aggressor later assaulted them? It is difficult to imagine any parent thinking about moral culpability in this way, and for good reason: it does not seem thoughtful enough on at least four counts.

The view fails to be sufficiently thoughtful, first, because it disregards the moral distinction that clearly seems to exist between aggressors and victims.[33] If your family has no intention of attacking and killing me, but I both have the intention of attacking and killing your family *and* take steps in that direction, we are not morally similar. You and your family are victims, and, all else being equal, you possess the right that all persons possess—the right not to suffer violence. However, I am an aggressor, and thus my moral status is different from yours. The violence I commit in my capacity as an aggressor is morally different from the violence you commit, in defending yourself, in your capacity as my victim, and this means that while you have the right not to suffer violence from me, I do not have the right not to suffer violence from you. Because our motivations are different, our moral status is different, and the actions we are justified in performing are therefore different as well. I have forfeited the right not to suffer violence, while you have forfeited nothing.

This does not mean that I forfeit the totality of my right not to suffer violence all at once. It seems that, all else being equal, my right not to suffer violence decreases at the rate that my threat to you increases. The violence acceptable to use against me, to stop me, must be proportional to the threat I pose and the degree of difficulty involved in thwarting me at that time. Nevertheless, to the degree I do pose a threat it seems that I clearly forfeit the right I would otherwise enjoy.[34]

---

33. See the sections "Anti-Violence Pacifism" and "The Relational Foundation of Right and Wrong" in Chapter 2.

34. For somewhat more on the idea of forfeiture see again the sections "Anti-Violence Pacifism" and "The Relational Foundation of Right and Wrong" in Chapter 2. Also, although what I briefly present here makes intuitive sense in this case, the question of killing in self-defense has many permutations, and reaching a comprehensive view requires consideration of far more cases than the simple one imagined here. To get a taste of the variations and issues it is possible to pursue, see Jeff McMahan, "The Basis of Moral Liability to Defensive Killing," 386–405; David R. Mapel, "Moral Liability to Defensive Killing and Symmetrical Self-defense"; and Jonathan Quong, "Killing in Self-Defense," 507–37.

Second, the view that physical attack must occur before any physical defense can be mounted also overlooks the roles played by intention and sequence in the nature of action. Consider again the case of the would-be murderer seen earlier.[35] We are permitted to lie to the person at our door, not because he is already physically attacking someone, but because he intends to attack and kill someone, and asking the whereabouts of the person he seeks to kill is part of the action of killing him: it is a deliberate act in the sequence of intentional acts that contributes to and culminates in the actual killing. We lie to him, of course, because he has no right to the truth in these circumstances.

Now imagine that I have prepared to attack and kill your family and that you see me, and others, striding in your direction with automatic rapid-fire assault weapons in hand.[36] At what point can we say that aggression has begun and that you are permitted to defend your family against me? Different people might have different answers to this question, but it is hard to imagine anyone saying that my action begins only as my cohorts and I fire the first volley, or even adopt a firing stance—any more than we would say that the action of the would-be murderer begins only when he has actually found his target and begun a physical assault. Just as we can impede the would-be murderer's action long before it culminates, so too, it would seem, you can take proportional measures to physically defend your family against my action long before *it* culminates.[37]

---

35. See the section "Wrong Acts" in Chapter 2.

36. Since this fanciful case (suggested by England's reference to defense of his family) is no more than an analogy for instances of international conflict, assume that there exists no civil body, endowed with political authority over our two families, that is responsible for enforcing peaceful conduct and thwarting violence of the sort I intend against you.

37. Our general willingness to interrupt threats before they result in actual harm is evident even in domains where intent is absent—in an area of life as ordinary as common traffic laws, for instance. Various rules of the road exist to minimize risk, and drivers who violate those rules suffer civil penalties whether they actually cause harm or not. More severe penalties exist for driving under the influence of alcohol (again, irrespective of whether a driver so impaired actually causes harm) simply because the risks of an accident and the harm it would entail are intolerably high in those circumstances. We see intoxicated driving itself as the proximate threat, and thus see it as grounds for arrest even in the absence of any actual damage or injury and even in the absence of any intent to cause damage or injury; we act to prevent the harm before it occurs. Our attitude toward threat in these situations is informative because such circumstances are insignificant in comparison to my threat against your family. Not only is the actual harm likely to be much greater, but it is a harm I am deliberately intending. I am conspiring and *preparing* to inflict injury and death. (It is worth mentioning that we obviously don't act to prevent all conceivable risk as a society. If that were the standard, automobiles themselves would be prohibited—not

Third, the difference in moral status between aggressors and victims affects how we should think about the nature of causation in a conflict. To see this, consider again the case of the rapist seen earlier.[38] If the victim can defend herself in this situation only by fatally shooting her attacker, in an important sense she is nevertheless not the cause of his death. He—not she—created the circumstances that made defense against him necessary, and thus he is the actual cause of his demise. And this makes him alone responsible for it. She is morally blameless.

The same analysis holds in the case of my attack against your family. If I mount an obvious and menacing threat toward your loved ones, and if I have the stated intent of attacking and killing them, then at any point in the process of arming myself, issuing threats, gathering others to join me, striding in your direction, preparing to fire, and firing, you have the right to prevent me from succeeding in my intent. Following the principle of proportionality mentioned earlier, the action you can take against me early in the process is different from the action you can take against me later, but most will agree that if the action you take is proportional to my threat at the time, and if you end up (justifiably) killing me (for example, because I escalate my aggression), in an important sense you are not the cause of my death, and that is one reason you are not morally responsible for it. I created the immoral threat in the first place and (again, other things equal) I alone am responsible for what I suffer as a consequence.

Finally, the view that we are morally responsible for the deaths we cause if we act before actually being attacked (no matter how small that number is), but that we are not responsible for the deaths that occur once the attack has begun and we are merely fighting back (no matter how large that number is), seems to overlook the moral responsibility we have for what we allow as well as for what we actually do. In the case of family defense that we are imagining, suppose that because of your inaction I get near enough to your family to begin my attack and that two of your children are killed in the ensuing battle. Most would not find it persuasive if you justified your inaction by claiming that even though you could have intercepted the aggression earlier and farther from your home (thus sparing the lives of your two children), at least you are not morally responsible for their deaths, whereas you *would* have been responsible for any deaths that occurred if you had taken initiative to thwart my aggression earlier. Most would not find this persuasive because, as we first

---

to mention countless other instruments and activities of daily life. Laws that penalize activities of one sort or another simply reflect legislative bodies' decisions about what exceeds the threshold of *acceptable* risk. Obviously, similar calculations about risk are required regarding intentional threats.)

38. See the sections "Anti-Violence Based on Wrong Action" and "The Difference between Aggressors and Victims" in Chapter 2.

saw earlier,[39] we recognize that we bear responsibility for more than what we do. We also bear responsibility for what we allow to happen—for wrong acts that we should have prevented if we could have prevented them. If you could have prevented me from taking the lives of your children by confronting my aggression earlier, and in line with the principle of proportionality, it is hard to see what the moral justification would be for refusing to do so. Failing to do what we could have done is to bear moral responsibility for what happens as a consequence of our inaction. This does not lessen the responsibility of the attacker himself, of course, but acknowledges that we have moral responsibility in the situation as well.[40]

In summary, while considering where moral responsibility lies for the loss of life that occurs in pre-emptive military action it is important to keep in mind the following: (1) aggressors and victims do not share the same moral status and thus their acts do not share the same moral status: the violent conduct aggressors use in assaulting their victims is morally different from the violent conduct victims might be forced to use in defending themselves; (2) aggression is not a one-time event, but a sequence of deliberate acts, over time, expressing aggressive intention; (3) when aggressors create circumstances that require defense, they are responsible for the loss of life incident to that defense; and (4) we bear moral responsibility for what we allow as well as for what we do.

Taken together, these moral notions make it hard to accept the idea that pre-emptive military action (even when otherwise acceptable) still locates moral responsibility in those taking such action. Indeed, it turns out that we do not automatically maintain moral blamelessness by waiting to defend

---

39. See the section "Innocence vs. Threat" in Chapter 3.

40. The difference between what we do, and what we allow to happen, is a time-honored topic in the philosophical literature, with many complex cases and many twists and turns in writers' arguments. It is impossible to bring all that literature to bear here, but three early and classic treatments are Jonathan Bennett, "Whatever the Consequences," 83–102; Philippa Foot, "The Problem of Abortion and the Doctrine of the Double Effect," in James Rachels, ed., *Moral Problems: A Collection of Philosophical Essays*, 59–70; and Judith Jarvis Thomson, "Killing, Letting Die, and the Trolley Problem," 204–17. The famous "trolley problem" was first presented in the essay by Foot, then made famous by Thomson, and since then discussed by many. Indeed, Kwame Anthony Appiah remarks that the literature on the trolley problem has grown so large that it "makes the Talmud look like *Cliffs Notes*." (See his *Experiments in Ethics*, 91.) Frances Kamm's approach is found in her *Intricate Ethics: Rights, Responsibilities, and Permissible Harm*, an approach criticized by Alistair Norcross in his "Off Her Trolley? Frances Kamm and the Metaphysics of Morality," 65–80; and by James O'Connor, "The Trolley Method of Moral Philosophy."

ourselves until we are under actual physical attack from an aggressor. We can imagine cases where we actually lose our moral blamelessness by doing so.

Pre-emptive Action: Conclusion. In thinking about the U.S. action in Grenada, or in any conflict like it, we must first reach a general point of view regarding pre-emptive action. Consideration of the matter thus far suggests that, whatever initial appeal it might have for us, an outright repudiation of such military activity is a mistake. This still leaves open for discussion the details that surround pre-emptive action, of course. Such matters include how to gauge immediate and proximate threats in the first place, the decision-making process for calculating (at least to the degree we can) the probability that one threat or another merits military response, the level of confidence we must have in that calculation to justify a military solution rather than a diplomatic one, and how to apply the principle of proportionality in all instances of action—deciding as precisely as we can when it is morally acceptable to act preventively, and with what force we may do so at the various stages of the development of aggression.

These are all matters of judgment, and the correct course ultimately depends on a multitude of facts and circumstances that vary in any given situation. And the difficulty of grasping and weighing so many variables is only compounded by the impossibility of actually possessing accurate information regarding many of them. And furthermore, in the end, it may be only a rare situation that justifies pre-emptive action in any case. Various forms of pressure, over time, might generally give sufficient odds of diminishing whatever threats loom on the international horizon. And it goes without saying that, all else being equal, it is always better to follow a course that does not jeopardize lives.

Nevertheless, the matters we have examined make it difficult to defend a view that would prohibit a state, in principle, from consideration of proportional pre-emptive action in any and all instances of threat against it. Such a state, it would seem, must do its best to reach the most accurate and thoughtful conclusions about such threats that it can, based on the widest and wisest consideration of the evidence available to it. But, given the obligations it has toward its citizens' safety, it would seem a dereliction to rule out such considerations in advance. One may question whether Grenada itself is an instance of proportional and justified pre-emptive military response, but it seems difficult to reject the moral possibility of pre-emptive action tout court.[41]

---

41. I will have somewhat more to say on the topic of pre-emptive defensive action, from a scriptural standpoint, in the section "Offensive vs. Defensive War" in Chapter 15. For more on the conditions that justify such conduct from a secular point of view, see Walzer's chapter on "Anticipations" in his *Just and Unjust Wars*, 74–85.

The Question of Holocaust

President McKay's remarks condemn any war that is undertaken simply to "enforce a new order of government"—a point that England emphasizes—but are there any circumstances in which President McKay would consider qualifications to this?

Cambodia's Khmer Rouge

Consider the case of Cambodia under the Communist Khmer Rouge regime from 1975–1979, a ruthless dictatorship that required more than 20,000 mass graves to bury those it tortured and executed (in addition to hundreds of thousands of deaths caused by other means).[42] In flawless expression of Communism's central logic—i.e., uprooting whatever evil impedes creation of the perfect society—the "crimes" for which people suffered this fate fell into six major categories: "having been a soldier, a student, a civil servant, a petty bourgeois vendor, an admirer of the monarchy, or having been related to someone with such characteristics."[43] Including the executions conducted for such "crimes," the total deaths due to Khmer Rouge policies, by the most careful estimates, range anywhere from one million to three million men, women, and children.[44] Speaking specifically of the cannibalism that occurred during the savage conditions imposed by the Khmer Rouge, we read of how "in one prison the fetus, liver, and breasts of a pregnant woman who had been executed were treated; the child was simply thrown away (others had already been hung from the ceiling to dry), and the rest was carried away with cries [from the guards to those who had been imprisoned] of 'That's enough meat for tonight!'"[45]

---

42. The research on mass graves is reported by Craig Etcheson in "'The Number'—Quantifying Crimes against Humanity in Cambodia."

43. Ibid.

44. See, for example, Bruce Sharp, "Counting Hell." See also Jean-Louis Margolin, "Cambodia: The Country of Disconcerting Crimes," in Stéphane Courtois, et al., eds., *The Black Book of Communism: Crimes, Terror, Repression*, 577–635.

45. Jean-Louis Margolin, "Cambodia: The Country of Disconcerting Crimes," in Stéphane Courtois, et al., eds., *The Black Book of Communism: Crimes, Terror, Repression*, 603. Two early reports of brutality under the Khmer Rouge are John Barron and Anthony Paul, *Murder of a Gentle Land: The Untold Story of Communist Genocide in Cambodia*, and François Ponchaud, *Cambodia: Year Zero*. Though dismissed by some at the time, research conducted in Cambodia after the reign of the Khmer Rouge ended (including data reported by Etcheson, Sharp, and Margolin who are cited above), has substantiated the themes found in these volumes. A gripping personal recounting of life under the regime is Haing Ngor with Roger Warner, *Survival in the Killing Fields*.

Moral Response to Genocide

The Khmer Rouge was in power and thus constituted the "government" of Cambodia (which it renamed Democratic Kampuchea); therefore, in such a case would it have been justified for a nation to wage war on the Khmer Rouge, if it could realistically have done so, in order to rescue Cambodia's people from their own government? Imagine television images of men, women, and children by the tens of thousands pleading for help and being butchered. Would President McKay have said it would be wrong for another nation to help because it is wrong to "enforce a new form of government"? It is hard to imagine that his answer would be anything but no; it is not likely that he was envisioning anything like this kind of circumstance when expressing his views. And in any case, was the Khmer Rouge the legitimate government of Cambodia in the first place? Did it become legitimate simply by virtue of its attack on the Lon Nol government that had previously held power? And even if the Khmer Rouge actually did enjoy legitimacy at the time of its formation, what became of that legitimacy once it not only failed to protect its people from enemies, but actually became the enemy from which the citizenry required protection? The answer seems obvious, and it seems certain that President McKay would see a nation that intervened in such circumstances as helping the weak defend themselves against the murderous activities of the ruthless and strong. This motivation, at least regarding states, he is willing to consider appropriate justification for entering war.

This is not the only possible view, however. Scenes of Communist terror in Cambodia were visible in 1975, and yet many objected to providing military aid such as weaponry and advisory support in that situation. Congressman Chris Dodd said at the time that "the greatest gift our country can give to the Cambodian people is peace, not guns,"[46] and, from the ground, Sydney Schanberg reported in the *New York Times* both that Cambodian lives could only be better with the Americans gone and that "it would be tendentious to forecast such abnormal behavior [i.e., the then-occurring Communist brutality toward citizens] as national policy under a Communist government once the war is over."[47] As a result of widespread views of this sort Congress refused to

---

46. Cited in Bret Stephens, "From WikiLeaks to the Killing Fields."
47. Cited in Jeff Jacoby, "American Leftists were Pol Pot's Cheerleaders." Jacoby references similar comments made at the time by Senator George McGovern, the historian Stanley Karnow, the *New Republic*, Ben Kiernan, *New York Times* columnist Anthony Lewis, and others. Schanberg later became famous for his reporting of Khmer Rouge barbarities following the group's capture of power in 1975, including winning a Pulitzer Prize in 1976. Ironically, Schanberg's career in observing Khmer Rouge cruelty began a mere four days after claiming that it would be "tendentious" to expect it. As cited by Jacoby, Stephens, and others, his remark appeared in the *New York Times* on April 13,

fund such assistance, and the United States never provided it. The involvement of the United States in the ensuing genocide was to observe it from a distance.

But let's take the United States out of the equation. The moral question is whether, if it was capable, *any* country should have committed resources to aid Cambodian citizens' resistance to the Khmer Rouge. If it realistically could have, should any country have engaged in war in order to protect the citizens of Cambodia? If the answer is no, is this because they would be attempting to "enforce a new order of government," or because of some other reason?

The question about assistance is particularly interesting in retrospect. This is true of Cambodia, as well as of Vietnam, where hundreds of thousands of deaths were caused by relocations, re-education prisons, and the need for massive flight from the country by boat once the Hanoi regime assumed control.[48] Whereas Dodd and Schanberg wrote in anticipation of events, England wrote in their aftermath, at a time when the human devastation in Cambodia and Vietnam had been chronicled in significant volume and grisly detail. Nowhere does England take up these matters, however, although it is difficult to see how one can reach thoughtful conclusions about war—not to mention about particular wars—without doing so.

1975 ("Indochina Without Americans: For Most, a Better Life") and the Khmer Rouge took over the capital of Cambodia on April 17. Even then Schanberg was not the quickest to appreciate what was happening, wondering if, seen from the revolutionaries' eyes, the forced evacuation of the capital city that began immediately, including hospitals, was "a harsh necessity" in order for the society to start "from the beginning;" see "Cambodia Reds Are Uprooting Millions As They Impose a 'Peasant Revolution.'" And of course the atrocities increased from there. Although Schanberg became famous for his reporting of these cruelties, others criticize him for a pattern of biased reporting from 1973 to 1975 that undermined support for the Cambodian government that was resisting the Communist insurgency at the time; see Reed Irvine, "Lost in the Killing Fields." William Shawcross has said that he focused too easily, in his own reporting, on the faults of the United States and its Southeast Asia allies during this period, and overlooked the reality of Communist inhumanity and the overwhelming threat it presented to the region; see William Shawcross, *Cambodia's New Deal: A Report*. Schanberg has not expressed any view like this regarding his own attitudes during that time, though it seems plain that they were not different from Shawcross's. For his writing on this and other wars see Sydney Schanberg, *Beyond the Killing Fields: War Writings*. In contrast to the journalistic tide of the time, President Gerald Ford accurately warned of a bloodbath in the absence of U.S. assistance in Cambodia. See Gerald R. Ford, "Transcript of President's News Conference on Foreign and Domestic Matters."

48. For a sampling of the reports regarding Vietnam, see R. J. Rummel, "Statistics of Democide," in his *Death by Government*; Ginetta Sagan, "Vietnam's Postwar Hell"; Le Thi Anh, "The New Vietnam"; Jacqueline Desbarats, "Repression in the Socialist Republic of Vietnam: Executions and Population Relocation."

The Question of Holocaust: Conclusion

Consideration of such episodes—where deaths number in the millions and the hundreds of thousands—is helpful, if not necessary, in testing one's thinking about elements of war related to President McKay's statement. In light of such acts of genocide, what exactly does it mean to say that it is wrong to "enforce a new order of government"? What are the boundaries of such a principle's application, if any, and how does the principle intersect in specific cases with principles that legitimize war—such as the propriety of defending the weak from a ruthless enemy? Whatever might be said about the merits of intervention in one specific case or another, if we follow England in valuing the declarations of President McKay on the topic, we will be far from eliminating the possibility out of hand, as England himself seems to do.

Part 3

Toward an LDS Theory of War

Chapter 13

Getting Past Pacifism

The first step in developing a moral approach to war is to determine if pacifism is a persuasive point of view. The only way to do this is to examine a reasonable range of arguments—both secular and spiritual—that purport to demonstrate this. That examination has been a major part of our task thus far and has shown that the prospects are not promising. No argument we have considered through the first two Parts of this book, whether secular or spiritual, seems sufficient to prohibit the justifiability of war in all circumstances.

Intellectual Explanation and Plausibility

In considering the various arguments for pacifism it is useful to bear in mind that each intellectual belief we hold is entangled in a larger conceptual framework that subsumes it—a complex, intricate, and largely unarticulated web of other beliefs, assumptions, predispositions, and preconceptions that we also hold. One consequence of this reality of intellectual life is that when we encounter compelling evidence against any of our beliefs—evidence suggesting that it is false, or at a minimum unlikely—we can continue to maintain that belief (despite such counterevidence) by simply altering some other dimension of this complex conceptual web. The modified positions that result are simply corollaries of our commitment to the original belief.

Thus, if we think that pacifism is the message of the scriptures, and if we then see (as we would have to) reports of the Lord's own non-pacifist conduct to be a problem for this claim, we must modify something else to maintain it—for example, the very way we view those reports. If this is the conceptual alteration we make, then we simply come to see reports of this sort in the Book of Mormon and other scripture to be false rather than true, and we come to see prophets as unreliable rather than reliable. These, or others like them, are corollaries of the pacifist point of view—the conceptual trade-offs we need to make if we are to maintain that position. Over the course of Parts One and Two we have considered numerous arguments and claims related to pacifism, and we have also seen numerous corollaries that follow from them. Summaries 1 and 2 at the back of this chapter review both.

Intellectual Revisions and Scientific Explanation

Speaking in the most general sense, and not just of pacifism, in principle we can continue to maintain any belief at all, in the face of practically any evidence at all, if we are willing to alter other dimensions of our conceptual web significantly enough.¹ To an appreciable degree, making conceptual trade-offs of this sort is the very nature of intellectual explanation. For example, when the great twentieth-century physicist John Bell encountered experimental results (based on his own revolutionary theorem) indicating that something other than Einstein's view of the quantum world must be correct, he did not respond by simply rejecting Einstein's view. Instead, he held onto that view by entertaining two possibilities that were universally anathematized in the thinking of other physicists: the idea of an ether and the idea that elementary particles can travel faster than light.² Similarly, when scientists discovered in the nineteenth century that Newton's theory of planetary motion failed to account for the orbit of Uranus and (later) of Mercury, they did not respond by rejecting Newton. Rather, they preserved his theory by instead revising their view of the solar system: they added planets to it, assuming that these additional planets existed, even though they had not been observed, and that their presence contributed to the orbital patterns of Uranus and Mercury.³

These examples illustrate the same intellectual reality that, because theoretical views are an elaborate web of interconnected concepts, information affecting one of these dimensions can be accommodated by making appropriate adjustments elsewhere.⁴ We can add planets that have never been observed and we can accept the idea of an ether even though no one else accepts it. Indeed, one great American scholar argued that the scientific community could revise even the laws of mathematics in the wake of experimental results that it deemed sufficiently unwelcome. At least in principle, anything can be revised; nothing is sacrosanct.⁵

---

1. Of course the capacity to maintain a belief is multiplied if we simply refuse to consider all of the evidence in the first place. We need not alter dimensions of our conceptual world in response to counterevidence if we resist even acknowledging such counterinstances. To the degree that is the case, however, the resulting holes in our scholarship will be due less to oversight than to willful blindness.

2. For more on this incident, and on the scientific controversies surrounding it, see my "The Spirit and the Intellect: Lessons in Humility," 88–107.

3. For more on this, see my "Of Science, Scripture, and Surprise," 191–93. Incidentally, the strategy turned out to be successful regarding Uranus, but unsuccessful regarding Mercury.

4. In Nozick's memorable and time-honored image, theoretical explanation in general is "like pushing and shoving things to fit into some fixed perimeter of specified shape.... You push and shove the material into the rigid area getting it into the boundary on one side, and it bulges out on another. You run around and press in the protruding bulge, producing yet another in another place. So you push and shove and clip off corners from the things so they'll fit"—i.e., fit into an overall view that can then be presented as "exactly how things are." Robert Nozick, *Anarchy, State, and Utopia*, xiii.

5. See generally W.V. Quine, *The Pursuit of Truth*, where he provides a more moderate version of his views than he held earlier in his career. This general view

Intellectual Revisions and Scriptural Claims for Pacifism

As mentioned, similar intellectual revisions occur in scriptural arguments for pacifism. If we want to maintain a pacifist view, but don't see how that is possible in light of Nephi's conduct and of his prophetic stature, we can simply adjust our view of Nephi to see him as a liar and a murderer, if that is what is required. We can also modify our view of Mormon or Captain Moroni, or many other spiritual leaders: rather than seeing them as historical figures who were reliable in expressing the Lord's will, we can see all of them as routinely, and seriously, mistaken. Similarly, we can view President Gordon B. Hinckley as a prophet who led the Latter-day Saints to reject an immutable covenant found in the Doctrine and Covenants, and we can see Joseph Smith as a prophet who apparently could neither discern the pacifist message of the Book of Mormon nor be taught it. And so forth. All of these revisions can be made if our desire to maintain pacifism is strong enough.

The most extreme example of the kind of revision some are willing to consider arises from the evidence of divine violence in the pre-Christian era. One way to claim that such scriptures are accurate in their portrayals of divine violence, but also to claim that pacifism is the correct and true standard, is to argue that God changed his mind about violence once he himself became the victim of it in the crucifixion and the events leading up to it.[6]

Although this is an interesting claim, and although much could be said in response to it,[7] it is sufficient to note the trade-off this argument makes: it maintains a commitment to pacifism by coming to see God as a being who is morally imperfect and who changes—which is to say, it comes to see God as a being who is not *God*.

---

toward the interconnectedness of concepts derives from Pierre Duhem (1861–1916) and, in its sophisticated form, is variously referred to as either "holism" or as the "Duhem-Quine thesis."

6. This view was brought to my attention by a reader of the manuscript who is well situated in the publishing world of LDS scholarly works and who reports that "many" have argued in this way.

7. The most obvious counterevidence to this claim is the Lord's own subsequent behavior: it wasn't long after suffering death that, the record tells us, he violently destroyed fifteen Book of Mormon cities and their inhabitants (3 Ne. 9:1–12). Thus, if the Lord changed his mind about violence following his crucifixion, it clearly didn't take him long to change it back. Such a view also contradicts the view of Christ as pacifist during his earthly ministry. After all, to say that he changed his mind after suffering the violence that led to his death is to say that he hadn't changed it yet—which entails that he was not actually pacifist during his personal ministry on earth. As to God's unchanging nature, see Morm. 9:19, Moro. 8:18, and D&C 76:4. As to his perfection, see Alma 7:20, 3 Ne. 12:48; and 1 John 1:5.

To take this path is to make a radical theological revision. Presumably the journey began with the aim of proving that God's standard is pacifism. But while that is indeed the outcome of the argument, it is reached only at the cost of concluding that God isn't actually God. It is hard, to say the least, to see this as a satisfactory exchange. And of course all of this raises a further question: If we possess a willingness to see God as a being who is not actually God, then how deeply did we ever really care what his standard was?

What an argument of this sort seems to reveal is that an a priori commitment to pacifism always came first. If the only way we can sustain pacifism is to deny God, and if that is in fact the intellectual trade-off we make, then it is hard to think that the question we started with was really whether pacifism meets God's standard. It would seem that the question we actually started with, however inchoate, was whether God meets pacifism's standard. Pacifism, it turns out, is God.

A conclusion of this sort merely illustrates that we can continue to maintain any belief if we are willing to alter enough other dimensions of our conceptual system significantly enough. That is why, from an intellectual standpoint, none of the revisions we have considered is illegitimate in principle. Again, trade-offs occur in the very nature of intellectual explanation, and, as mentioned, in principle even the laws of mathematics could be revised if the case to do so were strong enough. But under what conceivable circumstances would the case be strong enough? The question is the same for a pacifist view of scripture. In principle it is intellectually possible to maintain this view because it is always possible to make whatever adjustments are required anywhere in the canon to accommodate it.[8] But what reason is there to adopt the pacifist position in the first place and to embrace all of the interpretive

---

8. Incidentally, this is a deep reason why it is impossible either to prove, or to disprove, claims about the historicity of the Book of Mormon intellectually (to take just one claim of the Restoration). Any evidence, no matter how compelling in itself, can be accommodated by simply adjusting other assumptions or beliefs. Thus, if we say that Joseph's production of the Book of Mormon in approximately seventy working days is evidence of divine assistance, someone else can say, "Well, the 'vision' of the three degrees of glory is evidence of Joseph's abnormal imaginative powers. People assume that that was an actual vision because that's how Joseph (abetted by Sidney Rigdon) presented it, but if we abandon this assumption, we see that it is simply more evidence of Joseph's capacity for imagination—and that explains the pace of production of the Book of Mormon text." The possibilities for such back-and-forth argumentation are limitless because the possibilities for conceptual adjustment are limitless, and that's one reason why intellectual argument can never be sufficient. Ultimately, as Paul declared, one knows matters pertaining to God only by the Spirit of God (1 Cor. 2:10–14). Although intellectual arguments in defense of the Restoration are important, partly because they expose the weaknesses of intellectual arguments against it (and they are many), a conclusive answer is found in the realm of the Spirit, or not at all.

revisions that we must make in order to maintain it? Where is the case strong enough to justify all of this? From everything we have seen there isn't one.[9]

Plausibility

The upshot of all this is that it is not enough to make intellectual claims about the scriptures that in principle *could* be true. In principle, we could conclude that the moon is made of green cheese, and, intellectually speaking, that God is not actually God. If we make enough conceptual adjustments to our intellectual world we can find justification to believe anything—particularly if we submit those adjustments to no scrutiny whatever and if we ignore enough counterevidence. That is why, from an intellectual standpoint, the question is not whether one claim or another could conceivably be true, but whether such claims are compelling, or at least plausible. Many things that are possible are also preposterous. Mere possibility is the lowest of standards, and under no circumstances can we content ourselves to rest there.[10] Thus, all things considered, should a Latter-day Saint find it plausible to suppose that God is not God or to conclude that pacifism is the message of Latter-day Saint scripture? The answer to both questions is no.[11]

---

9. This is particularly obvious in the willingness to see God as a morally imperfect being who changes. While it is true, intellectually speaking, that we can maintain any belief whatever if we are willing to alter other dimensions of our conceptual system significantly enough, it would seem that a scriptural argument willing to sacrifice God in order to maintain pacifism has long since ceased to be an intellectual argument at all and has descended into mere fetishism.

10. John Bell argued explicitly for the plausibility and coherence of an ether and of elementary particles traveling faster than light, and scientists who posited the existence of planets that hadn't been observed also argued from the standpoint of plausibility and coherence. In neither case did they grasp at straws, resting their case on mere possibility in principle. (Neither, by the way, did they ignore the counterevidence to their conclusions; they reached their solutions in reasoned *response* to that evidence.)

11. Work in recent years on Book of Mormon geography illustrates what is required to examine all of the evidence and, all things considered, to reach the most plausible conclusions. Studies of this sort do not rest on mere possibility, but seek to address apparent counterexamples and to provide plausible answers to them. Plausibility is a matter of judgment, of course, and this guarantees disagreement about any number of conclusions. Nevertheless, there is a large difference between seeking to be comprehensive (which entails both acknowledging and addressing apparent counterexamples) and seeking to cherry pick the evidence, ignoring large swaths of apparent counterinstances that require attention. Works that illustrate the effort required to be comprehensive include: John L. Sorensen, *Mormon's Codex: An Ancient American Book*; John E. Clark, "Revisiting 'A Key for Evaluating Book of Mormon Geographies'"; Matthew Roper, "Joseph Smith, Revelation, and Book of Mormon Geography"; and Neal Rappleye, "War of Words and Tumult of Opinions:

Summary 1:
Direct Claims Related to Pacifism

This summary identifies the direct claims regarding pacifism that have been examined and found wanting in Parts One and Two, listed here roughly in the sequence in which they have appeared.

- Violence of any kind is morally prohibited because of the harm it causes
- Violence of any kind is morally prohibited because, in itself, violence is a wrong kind of act
- War is morally prohibited because it is not factually possible, in the modern era, to minimize noncombatant deaths sufficiently
- War is morally prohibited because of the moral innocence of even the aggressor soldiers in a situation of conflict
- The Ammonites thought that conventional killing in conventional war was murder
- The Ammonites repented of having performed such conventional killings
- The Ammonites repudiated war per se, and were pacifists
- Book of Mormon wars were always between bad guys and other bad guys, and thus no comfort regarding "righteous conflict" can be derived from the Nephites' engagement in war
- The Lord's early promise to Nephi meant that the Nephites would be protected from any attack whatever if they were righteous
- War can always be avoided by discussion
- Mormon and Moroni believed that war is unnecessary
- It is perverse, from a scriptural standpoint, to justify war in terms of the need to defend oneself
- People who are righteous do not need to defend themselves because God will fight their battles for them
- Ammon is an example of renouncing military solutions and of using missionary work as *the* way to deal with bad guys
- Mormon had a pacifist intent and theme in creating the Book of Mormon
- The story of Nephite civilization presents us with a pacifist moral
- Jesus teaches pacifism in Third Nephi, placing a prohibition on all shedding of blood, including engagement in war for any reason
- The example of the Ammonites and other Lamanites demonstrates that pacifism is the standard of true conversion

---

The Battle for Joseph Smith's Words in Book of Mormon Geography." Even the well-known authority Michael Coe has shown a willingness to reach conclusions without coming close to addressing all of the evidence, much less to providing plausible reinterpretations of it; see John L. Sorensen, "An Open Letter to Dr. Michael Coe."

Getting Past Pacifism   219

- A narrative interpretation demonstrates where prophets and other spiritual leaders are in error
- Nephi's act of slaying Laban was an act of scapegoating in accordance with René Girard's model of scapegoating violence
- Nephites' violence is contrastive to the "acts of love and service" performed by Ammon and his brethren among the Lamanites
- The Book of Mormon presents a continuum of moral responses to conflict, with pacifism as the more divine of the acceptable options
- One end of this continuum can be represented by the Ammonite elders and the other, more divine end by the Ammonite sons
- The Ammonites' strategy of self-sacrifice in Alma 24 and 27 presents a universal example for others to follow
- The stealth approach of some Nephite leaders was superior to the armed-conflict approach of other Nephite leaders
- Doctrine and Covenants 98 details a nuanced pacifist approach to conflict that can be straightforwardly applied to modern situations
- It is enlightening to ask, without explanation, "Who would Jesus waterboard?"
- Lehi's leaving Jerusalem was an act of pacifism
- Those who "prize peace over war" in the Book of Mormon are examples of pacifism
- The Lord holds all combative parties in the Book of Mormon in equal disregard
- We possess no holy texts that would carry us to open conflict
- The highly moral societies in the Book of Mormon found conflict both inconceivable and unnecessary
- King Benjamin believed that his people's defense against their enemies consisted in righteousness and pacifist response
- Book of Mormon figures considered the conventional killing that occurs in conventional war to be murder
- The righteous have no need for open conflict
- All examples of violence in the Book of Mormon are void of divine support
- Long after slaying Laban Nephi felt remorse of conscience for the act
- Nephi's slaying of Laban was personally damaging and tragic for Nephi
- A consistent non-violence ethic must condemn both abortion and capital punishment
- Acts of violence by God in the Old Testament can be dismissed by a consideration of eleven Old Testament verses
- God is a being completely without violence because he treats all persons as ends in themselves
- Righteous nations do not suffer assault from enemies
- Pacifist response brings an end to others' malevolence

- Various U.S. conflicts are ruled out by President McKay's observations regarding war
- Pre-emptive military action can never be justified
- God changed his mind about violence once he became the victim of it

Summary 2
Corollaries of The Direct Claims

The claims in Summary 1 are all mistaken. But if we failed to scrutinize these assertions and accepted them as true, we would then be saddled both with such mistaken claims *and* with the conceptual consequences that follow from them. Thus, depending on exactly which pacifist claim(s) we accepted, we would also be led to embrace some combination of the following implausible corollaries, all of which we examined in Parts One and Two.

- Rejecting violence on the basis of harm requires us both to prohibit violence and to commit it
- Morally there is no difference between an aggressive act of violence committed by Cain and a defensive act of violence committed by Abel (nor is there a moral difference between a rapist's attack and a victim's act of self-defense)
- It is not morally permissible to use violence to defend against the attacking soldiers of an aggressor nation
- The intrepid and faithful Teancum is, at some level, analogous to the evil, war-mongering Amalickiah
- Alma fails to qualify as a "good guy" in his combat with Amlici
- The Book of Mormon is Orwellian in describing various warriors as being motivated by peace
- Captain Moroni was wrong, not right, to act as he did
- Jacob, Alma, Mormon, President Gordon B. Hinckley, and other prophetic figures, were wrong in admiring and/or behaving like Captain Moroni
- Characterizations in the Book of Alma are wrong to paint Captain Moroni's behavior in a positive light
- A host of prophetic utterances and reports regarding war in the Book of Mormon (from such figures as King Benjamin, Alma, Helaman, the two thousand Ammonite sons, and Mormon) are the result of human bias and error: all of the teachings and/or episodes that seem to countenance conflict in one circumstance or another are inaccurate and thus are not normative for us
- By his teachings in Third Nephi, Jesus corrected actions of his own
- Book of Mormon prophets like Mormon, Jacob, Alma, and more—and modern prophets like President Gordon B. Hinckley—are trustworthy on a whole range of significant spiritual issues, but uniformly untrustworthy on one spiritual issue in particular

Getting Past Pacifism 221

- Prophets and other men of God—such as Alma, King Benjamin, Helaman, and Mormon—were mistaken in believing that God helped them in their battles
- Prophets and other men of God—such as Lehi, Nephi, King Benjamin, Alma, Captain Moroni, and Mormon—were all wrong in presupposing, based on the Lord's early promise to Nephi, that the Lord would help repentant/righteous Nephites in their battles
- Prophets and other men of God—such as Alma, Mosiah, Mormon, and Joseph Smith—were mistaken in quoting the Lord regarding his help in battle and/or his approval of it
- Multiple Book of Mormon reports about the Lord are false
- Prophets are good at following the Spirit on some matters, but not on others
- Nephi was a murderer who lied about it
- Mormon, the compiler of the Book of Mormon, was either weak or hypocritical with regard to pacifism in his own life
- Mormon was inconsistent as an author—more than once delivering a message in the Book of Mormon that contradicted the message he wanted to deliver *with* the Book of Mormon
- Mormon was self-contradictory in his actions—preaching condemnation of war as the message *of* the Book of Mormon, while praising and approving of Nephite warriors *in* the Book of Mormon
- Joseph Smith, the translator of the record, either did not discern, or at least did not heed, the pacifist message of the book in his own life
- The Lord could teach eternal truths to Nephi, Alma, Mormon, Moroni, and Joseph Smith—indeed, he could show them visions, send angels to visit and teach them, and personally appear to them—but he could not, or would not, teach them not to fight
- On one hand, Nephi was of such spiritual stature that he could receive revelations, see visions, entertain angels, and see the Lord, and on the other, he was a liar and a murderer
- Since he was a liar and a murderer, Nephi did not really have the divine manifestations that he reports
- Since Nephi did not really have the divine manifestations that he reports, the teachings he gives us based on them are inauthentic
- Various Book of Mormon prophets were all wrong on the subject of war, and Nephi's slaying of Laban explains the generational persistence of this error
- President Gordon B. Hinckley failed to appreciate the actual message of the Book of Mormon, and thus taught incorrectly about war and peace, leading the Church astray
- Nephi had insufficient faith, and thus relied on the sword, rather than the Lord, to defend himself and his people

- There would have been no war in heaven if only Michael, the Savior, and the Father had stopped "fighting or competing" with Lucifer, because Lucifer then would have abandoned his aggressive and malevolent aims
- God changed his mind about violence after his death and soon thereafter changed it back
- God is a morally imperfect being
- God is a being who changes

Chapter 14

The Sermon on the Mount

Fundamental Texts for Fashioning an LDS View of War

Once arguments for pacifism have been considered and set aside, it is not difficult to identify the core features of a positive framework for war. Since both secular and spiritual arguments for pacifism seem to fail, it is reasonable to conclude that any sound view of war must include in some measure its primary rival, just-war theory. However, since the modern just-war framework (even though it originated with the significant Christian figures Augustine and Aquinas) makes no explicit use of scripture, particularly of the Restoration canon, it seems obvious that it cannot be sufficient to address the concerns of Latter-day Saints. Specifically, five key texts require consideration to create a reasonable structure for thinking about war from a Latter-day Saint perspective. These are:

- The Sermon on the Mount in Matthew 5–7 and 3 Nephi 12–14
- Alma 48
- "The Times in Which We Live," by President Gordon B. Hinckley
- "War and Peace," by President Gordon B. Hinckley
- "The False Gods We Worship," by President Spencer W. Kimball

When we have a reasonable understanding of the standard works in their entirety, it seems apparent that these five texts express and distill all the major teachings the Latter-day Saint scriptures contain about war.[1] This chapter will treat the Sermon on the Mount, while the next will discuss Alma 48 and, additionally, explain why Doctrine and Covenants 98 is not a fundamental text for creating an LDS perspective on war. Chapter 16 will treat the messages of Presidents Gordon B. Hinckley and Spencer W. Kimball, and then the final chapter will bring everything together into a general perspective on war—a single gospel framework with multiple interweaving dimensions.

It is worth remarking that although the First Presidency issued a statement about war in 1942, all of its principles are found in the texts we will be

---

1. In Chapters 4–13 I have not conducted the kind of systematic study that would be required to prove the sufficiency of these texts, but we have seen enough scriptural passages in those chapters to make the claim a plausible one. Naturally, I would be happy to be shown a passage, or any number of passages, that would improve materially upon the scriptural view these five texts give us.

considering.² Also, although President David O. McKay delivered a full address on war against the backdrop of World War II, he delivered his remarks while a counselor in the First Presidency, rather than as president, and thus they are less authoritative than the texts we will examine.³ The same is true regarding President J. Reuben Clark Jr., who spoke about war as well, but who also did so as a counselor in the First Presidency.⁴ The same reduced level of authority applies to other counselors in the First Presidency as well, not to mention other general authorities who have spoken about war. Remarks by such Church leaders are thus not included here.⁵

The Sermon on the Mount: Introduction

Crucial to any consideration of war for Latter-day Saints is the ethic taught in the Sermon on the Mount, since the teachings found there are foundational for all aspects of living the gospel, including how we are to answer provocation. The discourse appears in both Matthew 5–7 and 3 Nephi 12–14 and the presentations are effectively identical in the passage most relevant to matters of violence. I have chosen to focus on the Book of Mormon version.⁶ Here is the relevant passage:

> But I say unto you, that ye shall not resist evil,
> but whosoever shall smite thee on thy right cheek,
> turn to him the other also.
> And if any man will sue thee at the law and take away thy coat,
> let him have thy cloak also.
> And whosoever shall compel thee to go a mile,
> go with him twain.

---

2. "First Presidency Message," *Conference Report*, April 1942, 88–97. A similar message was given in the October general conference of the same year; "First Presidency Message," *Messages of the First Presidency*, 6:175–80. In both cases, the statement on war is embedded in a much longer message from the First Presidency that addresses other topics as well.

3. See David O. McKay, "The Church and the Present War," *Conference Report*, April 1942, 70–74. We considered this address in Chapter 12, as part of discussing Eugene England's anti-violence ideas.

4. For a treatment of President Clark's views and public remarks, see D. Michael Quinn, "Pacifist Counselor in the First Presidency: J. Reuben Clark Jr., 1933–1961" and *J. Reuben Clark: The Church Years*, 197–219.

5. For a treatment of a wide variety of statements by Church authorities in the first half of the twentieth century, see Brian Q. Cannon, "Chastisement of the Nations," 427–46. Not every characterization of views found in this summary seems accurate, but the compilation is a valuable guide to a broad assortment of statements by Church leaders.

6. For a scholarly treatment that compares, in some detail, the two sermons in their totality, see John W. Welch, *Illuminating the Sermon at the Temple and Sermon on the Mount*.

> Give to him that asketh thee,
> and from him that would borrow of thee turn thou not away.
> And behold it is written also
> that thou shalt love thy neighbor and hate thine enemy.
> But behold I say unto you:
> Love your enemies!
> Bless them that curse you!
> Do good to them that hate you,
> and pray for them which despitefully use you and persecute you
> (3 Ne. 12:39–44).[7]

Here, we are told that we are not to "resist evil," but "turn the other cheek," give more than is required of us, and "love our enemies," "pray for them which despitefully use [us]," and "do good to them that hate [us]." However, although these expressions are familiar, and inspiring, their interpretation is not transparent. It is thus worthwhile to evaluate some possible directions to go in understanding the passage and to see how we might best interpret it.

Anti-Violence Readings of the Sermon on the Mount

There are two fundamental ways to read this passage from the Sermon on the Mount as an anti-violence text. One of these is to see it as prohibiting any form of violence, under any circumstances, while the other is to see it as forbidding violence up to a point, but permitting it thereafter. Although there can be variations on these themes—and different accounts can differ on any number of details—it is the core of such approaches that interests us. If the central logic of an approach is deficient, the details that surround it make little difference.

Forbidding Violence Altogether

One way to interpret this passage is to see it as forbidding resistance to evil on any scale, or in any circumstance, and to insist instead that we are to bear evil treatment patiently, forever. We are permitted to mount some form of non-violent resistance to mistreatment (e.g., fleeing, hiding, building fortifications, and so forth), but any form of self-defense that is violent in nature is impermissible. Maxims like turning the other cheek, not resisting evil, and loving our enemies all mean that we are never to exercise violence, no matter the threat or even the degree of destruction visited upon us. This seems to be Eugene England's view when he says that this discourse is the Book of Mormon's most powerful teaching of "the nonviolent ethic,"[8] that it entails a

---

7. Since having one sense per line is so valuable in aiding understanding, I follow here Royal Skousen's formatting and punctuation of the earliest Book of Mormon text. See Royal Skousen, ed., *The Book of Mormon: The Earliest Text*, 600.

8. Eugene England, "Hugh Nibley as Cassandra," 112.

complete rejection of all violence,[9] that such pacifism plays a "central role" in Christ's mission,[10] and that Nephi's slaying of Laban is in direct contradiction to Christ's rejection of violence and of his demand that we do the same.[11]

To test this way of reading the text, however, let's imagine the hypothetical situation of an aggressor assaulting me and cutting off one of my arms. In the spirit of turning my cheek, not resisting evil, and loving my enemy, do I offer him my second arm? Or suppose I have daughters, and someone rapes and kills one of them. Does turning the other cheek and giving my cloak mean that I now offer the aggressor my second daughter?[12] Further, imagine someone in the act of killing our neighbor and imagine that we can stop this venal act only by shooting the aggressor and killing him. Is that forbidden? Would it be forbidden if we could stop the murderer by shooting and merely wounding him, or by simply hurling a rock and knocking him unconscious?

In pondering whether the Sermon prohibits such acts of defense, it is helpful to think about civil authorities. Do they act wrongly when they exercise coercion in order to protect the public from imminent danger? It seems likely that few, if any, would answer no to this question, and this is instructive for those of us who do not possess civil authority. After all, since the officials we are considering act only as our agents, if it is not wrong for them to exercise coercion and even violence in performance of their duties, how can it be wrong, at least in principle, for us to do the same? If we believe that coercion is permissible when practiced by civil authorities, it seems that we are committed to believing that it would be permissible if practiced by anyone, at least under suitably defined circumstances (for example, if no authorities were available and we faced lethal force or bodily harm).[13] Certainly this principle

---

9. Eugene England, "Why Nephi Killed Laban: Reflections on the Truth of the Book of Mormon," 142.

10. Ibid., 143.

11. Ibid., 142. As first noted in Chapter 11, England here expresses a different stance than he takes in two other places (at least) where he asserts that he would use violence to defend his family. See his "A Case for Mormon Christian Pacifism," 100–101. See also his "Thou Shalt Not Kill: An Ethics of Non-Violence," 173. I leave aside here the problems inherent in England's reading of the Nephi/Laban episode. For a brief treatment of these see the section "Nephi and Laban" in Chapter 11.

12. And what if I have still other daughters? Assuming that we have pursued every possible means of non-violent defense (obstructing the aggressor's way and hiding from him, for example), and assuming that he locates us anyway, must I refuse to defend my other daughters from his assault? Is *no* defense that entails violence permissible?

13. This is true, at least regarding lethal threat, even in Kant's moral framework. Although he indicates in his *Critique of Practical Reason* that personal security is a matter of law enforcement and that legitimate coercive power resides only in civil authorities, this assumes an ideal state of affairs. Since civil authorities are not always

is found in the proclamation that "all men" are justified not only in defending themselves, but also in defending their friends and their property "in times of exigency" (D&C 134:11).

As a result of these considerations it seems unpersuasive to say that we should read the Sermon as prohibiting all violence under all circumstances. Certainly it is a rare person who would think it forbids violence in the cases we have considered above.[14]

---

able to protect individuals from aggression—a circumstance that is *non*ideal in character—Kant recognizes in his *Metaphysics of Morals* the right to use lethal force toward an assailant against one's life under what he calls the right of necessity. It is important to recognize that Kant generally writes from the standpoint of ideal theory (see for example his *Groundwork of the Metaphysics of Morals* and *Critique of Practical Reason*), while touching on matters of nonideal theory occasionally and in a much less-developed way (for example, in his *Lectures on Ethics* and *Metaphysics of Morals*). For more on the distinction between ideal and nonideal theory in Kant, see Christine Korsgaard, "The Right to Lie: Kant on Dealing with Evil" and Thomas E. Doyle II, "Kantian Nonideal Theory and Nuclear Proliferation." Sussman argues that in Kant's framework individuals in certain kinds of emergencies are best seen as implicitly deputized to enforce the law and thus that they act as extensions of the state rather than as violators of what rightly belongs to the state. See David Sussman, "On the Supposed Duty of Truthfulness: Kant on Lying in Self-Defense."

14. This means, as I have discussed previously, that I think England misreads the Lord on this score. As seen in the section "Old Testament Violence and the Prince of Peace" in Chapter 11, England does not even acknowledge, much less explain, all of the incidents in which the Lord has exercised violence in the past, and in which he will exercise it in the future. Among the more well-known of such incidents are: (1) his destruction of the wicked through the flood at the time of Noah (Gen. 7:13; Moses 7:34), a time at which he said that "the fire of mine indignation is kindled against them; and in my hot displeasure will I send in the floods upon them, for my fierce anger is kindled against them" (Moses 7:34); (2) the Lord's destruction of Pharaoh and his warriors at the Red Sea (Ex. 14); (3) Jesus's aggressive clearing of the temple in Jerusalem (Matt. 21:12–13; Mark 11:15–17); (4) his destruction of numerous Nephite cities and their inhabitants, by flood, fire, and (apparently) earthquake following his resurrection (3 Ne. 9:3–12); (5) the vengeance he will visit upon the wicked incident to his second coming (D&C 29:17; 45:50; 133:50–51); and so forth. Additional discussion of pacifist claims related to Christ are found in the sections "Examining the Corollary of the Narrative Approach: The Example of the Lord's Own Conduct" in Chapter 8, "The Narrative Approach and the Savior's Teachings in Third Nephi" in Chapter 9, "Inadequate Conception of Jesus' Personality" in Chapter 10, and "Christ's Death" in Chapter 11. Of course, every account of the Lord's involvement in conflict is a counterexample to claims about Christ's pacifism and thus a comment on them. Multiple examples and discussions of such involvement appear in Chapters 6–11. Thus, while England insists here on seeing the Lord as a pacifist, and on seeing

Permitting Violence after a Point

Another way to read the Sermon is to see it as permitting violence beyond a certain point. We must absorb mistreatment to some degree, but after that are permitted to respond with violence of our own. The most literal, and simplistic take on this approach would be to say that violence is prohibited only the first two times we suffer aggression. We are told to turn the other cheek, go the second mile, give up our cloak as well as our coat, and so forth, but since we only have two cheeks, and since the Sermon speaks only about a second mile (and not a third) and only of two articles of clothing (and not a third), it follows that we are not expected to absorb aggression forever. We must absorb it at least two times, but then we are permitted to exercise the necessary amount of violence to defend ourselves.

The more literal we are in this approach, however, the more difficulties we face. Considering our previous example, suppose again that an aggressor assaults me and cuts off one of my arms; do I still offer him my second arm, but now with the expectation that I will begin defending myself once I have satisfied the requirement that I submit two times? If this seems to be the requirement, then, if I have three daughters, I seem permitted to protect my third daughter from a rapist, but not the first two. Or if I have only one daughter, then I am permitted to protect her the third time she is attacked, but not the first two times. And if all of this is so, does it mean that Cain or some other murderer would be permitted to kill twice, but not a third time?[15] Further, imagine that I preside over a nation and another regime bombs and destroys one of my cities. Does the Sermon commit me to offering a second city for bombing before I can use force to defend the citizens of my state?

It is unlikely that anyone who had any belief in the justifiability of defense would suppose that such action is legitimate only after first bearing two attacks *without* defense. It would seem obvious that it is not number, but degree, that matters in these cases. We would defend others, and ourselves, long before the actual act of rape occurred, and long before someone cut off one of our arms, much less both of them. We would also not fail to defend Abel against Cain, and certainly would not allow Cain to assault another before we acted. And we would take defensive measures long before an enemy state bombed a second city. Thus, while the idea that we can defend ourselves

---

the relevant passage in the Sermon on the Mount as a collection of pacifist dicta, consideration of the entire scriptural record seems clearly to tell a different story.

15. Recall that the cases of Cain and the would-be murderer are considered in Chapter 2. See the sections "Anti-Violence Based on Wrong Action" and "The Relational Foundation of Right and Wrong."

at some point seems right, any attempt to be literal and to reduce this to a formula about numbers seems doomed.[16]

Other Scripture, Scale, Audience, and Paradox

These readings of the Sermon, then, both yield conclusions that are unconvincing. Such conclusions are taught nowhere else in scripture,[17] and they are conclusions that we reject partly *based* on our familiarity with other passages of scripture. As we have seen in our discussions over multiple chapters, the idea of self-defense is perfectly at home in the gospel, and nowhere is such defense couched in the framework of absorbing even massive violence a minimum of two times before self-defense is permitted.

And regarding the Sermon's applicability to matters of war and peace in particular, it is noteworthy that Jesus speaks specifically in this setting of cheeks and smiting, and not of killing and military devastation. The scale of life Jesus chooses to speak of is the scale of everyday living, not the scale of war between states. This is clear not only in the examples he selects, but also in the audience he is addressing. These are normal, everyday citizens faced with the decisions of ordinary life. They are not heads of state confronted with the complexities of international relations, including that of securing the lives and rights of their citizens.

It is also important to recognize that these imperatives regarding turning the other cheek and so forth, when applied literally, are paradoxical in any event. It has become common to point out that I cannot carry two people's burdens, let alone carry them for a second mile, if the two people are going in different directions. Nor can I give away my coat and my cloak to one person if I have already given them to another.[18] These observations, added to the

---

16. Similar matters arise in consideration of D&C 98. See the sections "Ambiguity" and "Overlooked Distinction" in Chapter 10.

17. Alma 43:46 reports the Lord's instruction that the Nephites could defend themselves "inasmuch as [they were] not guilty of the first offense, neither the second," but it is hard to know exactly what constitutes an "offense" in this instruction. If we were to apply it to individual cases of aggression, we would face the same questions as above regarding cutting off arms, rape, and murder. And of course, as mentioned in note 16, the same difficulty arises in considering D&C 98. There is ambiguity in that revelation about what to regard as an offense, whether it is called a "trespass," a "coming upon," or a "smiting," and to what extent matters of degree, rather than simple numbers of incidents, figure into the calculation. In addition to the discussion in Chapter 10, see also the matters raised in the section "Doctrine and Covenants 98" in Chapter 15.

18. Yoder attributes these observations to Reinhold Niebuhr. See John Howard Yoder, *Christian Attitudes to War, Peace, and Revolution*, 294. Eugene England approvingly refers to Walter Wink's commentary on this passage, who explains these features of Jesus' Sermon in terms of the Jews' subjugation to the Romans, and of

implausibility of the two interpretations we have considered above, make the Sermon a puzzle. What do the injunctions mean if an anti-violence reading of them does not conform to the weight of the other scriptural evidence, and if they are paradoxical in their application in any case?

Such considerations lead to a third reading of the Sermon on the Mount—one that permits using violence to defend oneself but that rests on two central distinctions.

A Third Reading of the Sermon on the Mount

The key to appreciating injunctions about turning the other cheek, going the second mile, giving our cloak, and the like, is that they seem not meant as edicts having to do with numbers any more than the command that we are to forgive until seventy times seven is about a number.[19] All such teachings

---

these practices as clever ways to frustrate Roman rules and customs. In doing so, England does not address how Wink's observations apply to the Nephites, who received the same instructions and yet who were not in bondage to the Romans, or to anyone else for that matter. More than one explanation seems possible for this, but England does not take up the question. See Eugene England, "The Prince of Peace."

19. Scriptural commentators have long viewed the expression "seventy times seven" in Matthew 18:21–22 as metaphorical rather than literal. In one argument for the view, Augustine refers to Colossians 3:13, which speaks of "forgiving one another, if any man have a quarrel against any: *even as Christ forgave you, so also do ye*" (for obvious reasons Augustine does not use this King James translation of the verse, but the sense is the same). "Here you have the rule," Augustine says: if Christ has forgiven us seventy times seven, but no more, then fair enough: the number is literal, and we ourselves should forgive others no more than seventy times seven. But if Christ has forgiven us for "thousands of sins upon sins," as indeed he has, then to forgive others *as* Christ has forgiven us (as Paul in this passage says we must) requires that we do the same: there is no limit to how much we should forgive, and this is therefore the actual meaning of the expression "seventy times seven": we are to forgive without end. In understanding Augustine it helps to know that he and the Church fathers, generally, interpret Jesus' remark "seventy times seven," when read literally, to refer to the number 77 ("70 times, plus 7 times") and not to 490 (70 times multiplied by 7), as modern readers typically interpret the text. Thus, Augustine also argues for the metaphorical interpretation of the expression by noting (1) that the number '11' denotes the concept of sin because it passes the number of commandments in the Decalogue, and (2) that the number '7' "is usually put for a whole; because in seven days the revolution of time is completed." Augustine then observes that if we multiply the number that denotes sin (11) by the number that denotes wholeness (7), we get the number 77, which thus denotes *sin in its wholeness, or totality*. And this means that in saying we are to forgive 77 times (again, the classical understanding of Jesus' expression) we are saying that we are to forgive the *whole* of sin, not some particular number: we are to forgive without limit. See Augustine, "Sermon 33 on the New Testament." Although this second argument of

by the Savior seem to be about something deeper than our external conduct and deeper than what can be counted. They are about a condition of soul—a general stance toward life. References to cheeks, cloaks, and miles are only illustrations, much like the metaphorical figures and allusions that appear in poetry or that populate the Lord's parables. They engage our souls and awaken our sensibilities to themes and feelings that go beyond what straightforward exposition typically conveys. Illustrations regarding turned cheeks and second miles simply evoke in us, in a poetic and picturesque way, a sense of the kind of people we are to be. We are to be people who are consumed not with our egos, our possessions, or our resentments, but with seeking and embracing the Lord: loving what he loves, seeking what he seeks, and bearing what he bears. It is to lose concern with ourselves and with the things of the world and to become people who, far from nursing our resentments, live without resentment. We are to love others as he loves them and to live with compassion toward them just as he lives with compassion toward them—and toward us. The images painted in the Sermon on the Mount thus illustrate what we are to care about—what is to matter to us. They point to a condition of bearing patiently the mistreatment of others, doing good to them despite their unkindness, and having the largeness of soul that allows us to pray for them and their welfare.

A Peaceable Heart and War

In regard to matters of violence, a most apt description of this state of heart is Mormon's characterization of disciples as the "peaceable followers of Christ" and his description of disciples' mortal journey as a "peaceable walk" with the children of men (Moro. 7:3–4). This is why the Sermon on the Mount is relevant to war, even though it is not about war. It is relevant, even critical, because it clearly identifies the approach we are to have toward all of life. Disciples of Christ are peaceable, and they go through life with what can only be described as a peaceable heart. This is a way of life perfectly captured in Mormon's report of one period in Book of Mormon history in which "some were lifted up in pride, and others were exceedingly humble; some did return railing for railing, while others would receive railing and persecution and all manner of afflictions, and would not turn and revile again, but were

---

Augustine's is tortured, his first (from Colossians 3:13) is credible, and supports the idea that we are to forgive without limit rather than up to a particular number. My point in the text, then—regarding forgiveness in particular—is that the Lord's command that we are to forgive completely and endlessly is tantamount to the command that we are to have a certain kind of *heart*; it identifies the condition of soul we are to possess. (The linguistic reasons for why the Church fathers were correct to understand "seventy times seven" to mean 77 are identified in a number of places; one of the most trenchant is Royal Skousen's "Through a Glass Darkly: Trying to Understand the Scriptures.")

humble and penitent before God" (3 Ne. 6:13). This is the peaceful way; it is reminiscent of the Lord's command in our day that we are to teach the gospel "with all humility," "reviling not against revilers" (D&C 19:30), and of King Benjamin's observation that the humble followers of God "will not have a mind to injure one another, but to live peaceably" (Mosiah 4:13).[20]

But none of this entails a wholesale prohibition of defense. The verdict of the canon on that score has been seen repeatedly. What the Sermon tells us is the condition of heart we are to have even if we must answer provocation and even if we must defend ourselves. The First Presidency has made it explicit that, "if Latter-day Saints must go to war, they should go in a spirit of truth and righteousness, with a desire to do good. They should go with love in their hearts for all God's children, including those on the opposing side."[21] Interestingly, this is the same point made by Hugh Nibley in a 1971 *Ensign* article.[22] In this paper Nibley emphasizes that we must vigorously renounce war and proclaim peace. We must seek it, strive for it, and hunger for it, but he also observes that though we may earnestly strive for peace, there are times we may have to fight for it, even noting the distinction between the general prohibition against war and the Lord's commandment of it in specific instances. He also observes that a crucial variable in war is the "spirit" in which it is conducted. He says: "We have Moroni both sparing his enemies every time he gets a chance and putting down a coalition by force of arms with some bloodshed. But there is no doubt in the world which course he would prefer. Though they fought a duel, David and Goliath were not animated by the same spirit."[23] Nibley closes the article with this emphasis: "In the end the most desperate military situation imaginable is still to be met with the spirit of peace and love."[24]

---

20. All of this is exemplified in the Church's official response to the mockery directed toward Latter-day Saints in the Broadway play *The Book of Mormon*: "The production may attempt to entertain audiences for an evening, but the Book of Mormon as a volume of scripture will change people's lives forever by bringing them closer to Christ." See The Church of Jesus Christ of Latter-day Saints, "*Book of Mormon* Musical: Church's Official Statement." It would be difficult to find a better example of "reviling not against revilers" than this.

21. First Presidency, "War," in *True to the Faith*, 184.

22. Hugh Nibley, "If There Must Needs Be Offense."

23. Ibid., 274. Nibley's text says "Mormon" but this is surely a mistake; the context makes it clear that he means Captain Moroni. Also, this article shows that Nibley's pacifist impulse was not as strong early on as it became later. Here he clearly sets out a view in support of defensive war. (For somewhat more on Nibley's publishing history on this score, see note 17 in Chapter 7.)

24. Ibid., 276. Incidentally, I believe Boyd Petersen, Nibley's biographer, misappropriates this statement of Nibley's. Petersen seems to take it to be an anti-war statement, but in the context of this article—in which Nibley explicitly supports

It seems surprising, if not completely counterintuitive, to say that those who must go to war should go "with love in their hearts" for those on the opposing side and that we are to engage even military situations "with a spirit of peace and love." What does it mean to say things like this? And how would it even be possible to do what such remarks tell us to do? To answer these questions, it helps to have in mind two conceptual distinctions.

Distinction One: The "Natural Man" and the "Spiritual Man"

The first distinction is between two general "types" that are presented to us in scripture: the "natural man"[25] on one hand, and the "man of Christ" or "spiritual man" on the other.[26] Whereas the term *natural man* connotes such characteristics as rebellion against God, selfishness, greed, pride, self-indulgence, and various forms of aggressiveness,[27] the term *spiritual man* connotes the opposite, namely, devotion to God, concern for others, benevolence, hu-

---

defensive war—this reading is counterintuitive. Instead, the statement seems simply to be re-emphasizing Nibley's point about the importance of the spirit in which things are done, even in self-defense. Nibley is thus not saying that defense is impermissible, but only that even in the most desperate circumstances we must still be motivated by the same spirit that motivated Moroni and David—which is an entirely different claim. For Petersen's take on the statement, see Boyd Jay Petersen, *Hugh Nibley: A Consecrated Life*, 221, and "The Work of Death: Hugh Nibley as Scholar, Soldier, Peace Activist," 167.

25. Relevant passages include Alma 41:11; Mosiah 3:19; Romans 8:7; Alma 42:10.

26. Mormon uses the expression "man of Christ" in Helaman 3:29. Of the numerous verses that identify the characteristics of such discipleship, some of the fundamental passages include: Matt. 22:36–40 (regarding love of God and of our neighbor); Omni 1:26 (which speaks of offering "our whole souls" to the Lord); Mosiah 3:19 (which lists characteristics of those who "putteth off the natural man"); and Gal. 5:21–23 (regarding the fruits of the Spirit).

27. The expression "natural man" refers to a certain set of characteristics that are natural to the world and that are at enmity with God, but the term suggests nothing about whether people are basically good or evil. Although all are in need of regeneration by Christ, it does not follow that all are essentially evil. Indeed, based on the primitive element from which all people ultimately derive ("the light of truth"—D&C 93:29), and based on the divine parentage from which all people issue as sons and daughters of God, it is obvious that, at the most fundamental level, people are basically good. Among statements to this effect are these remarks from President Boyd K. Packer: "There is a doctrine taught through much of traditional Christianity that men are conceived in wickedness and that men by nature are depraved and wicked and evil. . . . The doctrine that men are basically evil is false. It is wrong. It is a tremendous perversion of the truth. . . . We basically are good. . . . Now men can be led from a pattern of virtue into almost unspeakable depths of wickedness, but that is against their nature, because we are the sons and daughters of God." See Boyd K. Packer, *Mine Errand from the Lord: Selections from the Sermons and Writings of Boyd K. Packer*, 22. The term *natural man* is a scriptural designation that identifies the general

mility, self-discipline, and peacefulness. It is the state of heart described in the Sermon on the Mount.[28]

Distinction Two: Inner State and Outward Behavior

The second distinction is between the condition of our hearts and our outward behavior. This distinction arises when we consider whether the natural man and the spiritual man can ever exhibit the same outward behavior. In other words, can we ever be unrighteous and outwardly *look* righteous, and can we ever be righteous and outwardly *look* unrighteous?

Abstract descriptions of outward behavior. When we think of outward behavior in an abstract sense, the answer is clearly yes. It is not difficult, for instance, to live externally in conformity with the gospel while being motivated internally by selfishness to do so. The Pharisees of the New Testament are the quintessential example of exactly this phenomenon. Their interest in keeping every jot and tittle of the law was not, strictly speaking, an interest in being righteous; it was the opposite concern of *displaying* themselves as righteous. Although they kept the law outwardly and thus appeared to be devoted to God, that appearance was misleading because inwardly they were devoted only to themselves.[29] Their behavior was thus an imitation of righteousness, not a manifestation of it.

This relationship between our inner state and our outward behavior reaches in the other direction as well. Outward behavior that seems wrong on the surface can actually flow from the purest of spiritual motivations and thus from the condition of the spiritual man. It is easy to see a "natural man" becoming violent—for example, by knocking over tables, threatening people, and cracking a whip—and conclude that all such behavior reflects the natural-man condition and that it is therefore necessarily wrong. But since Jesus himself performed exactly these outward behaviors, and in the temple no less (Matt. 21:12–13; Mark 11:15–17; John 2:13–16), this is obviously a mistake. Whereas a "natural man" who pushes over tables and threatens

---

characteristics of fallen and unregenerated beings; it is not coextensive with the term *basic man* or *essential man*.

28. My earliest influence in thinking about this distinction is found in C. Terry Warner, "Commitment and Life's Meaning," 33–62.

29. Thus Jesus said to them: "Ye are like unto whited sepulchers, which indeed appear beautiful outward, but are within full of dead men's bones, and of all uncleanness. Even so ye also outwardly appear righteous unto men, but within ye are full of hypocrisy and iniquity" (Matt. 23:27–28; see generally verses 23–39). Similar denunciations appear in Matt. 6:1–8; Luke 7:37–50; 18:9–14. All of this is related to Mormon's general statement (apparently quoting the Lord) that "a man being evil cannot do that which is good; for if he offereth a gift, or prayeth unto God, except he shall do it with real intent it profiteth him nothing. For behold, it is not counted unto him for righteousness" (Moro. 7:6–7).

people is typically operating from the most selfish of motives, Jesus acted out of pure devotion to his Father by confronting, and thereby accentuating, the irreverent and profane conduct of people who had allowed themselves to become irreverent and profane. To some his outward behavior may have suggested that he was exercising violence in a fit of selfish temper, but if so, that interpretation was a mistake, because a description of this sort could not be further from the truth. The Lord's violence flowed not from a selfish concern with himself, but from an inner state of complete devotion to his Father and to all of God's children (including those whose obscene conduct he terminated) and the eternal and holy design the temple represented for them. Furthermore, as Creator and Redeemer, and thus as the God of this earth, Jesus had the spiritual authority to behave as he did. He did not act from false beliefs as some mortals might and he did not seek honor or glory for himself. He acted from a position of both spiritual authority and moral selflessness.

Outward behavior, then, can be misleading when described abstractly. What appears to be "right" behavior can flow from the natural-man state and what appears to be "wrong" behavior can flow from the spiritual-man state. This means that abstract descriptions of external conduct are inherently insufficient: From the fact that two people are performing the same general outward behavior, it does not remotely follow that they are doing the same thing or that their conduct has the same moral character.

Deeper descriptions of outward behavior. The reason abstract descriptions are inadequate is that behavior is more than a set of visible movements and audible sounds: it is the expression of inner intention. When the Lord described the prayer of the Pharisee ("God, I thank thee, that I am not as other men are," etc.) and of the publican ("God be merciful to me a sinner") in Luke 18:9–14, it was only in a highly abstract sense that both acts could be called "prayer" in the first place. Though both spoke toward God, what the Pharisee and publican were actually doing could hardly have been less alike because their intent in doing so could hardly have been less alike. Indeed, their acts, while superficially similar, were exact opposites when seen at the deepest and most accurate level.[30]

---

30. The relationship between who we are and what we do, along with the complexities involved in how others understand who we are and what we do, is a subtle dimension of the academic work of C. Terry Warner on self-deception. His rigorous conceptual exploration demonstrates how we can create a psychological state in which we systematically foreclose ourselves from seeing both that we are in that state *and* that we are the ones who created it—and, if that weren't enough, that we are also the ones who sustain it with relentless tenacity. Self-deception is a perverse form of self-constitution. Warner's conceptual exploration of these matters has found expression in academic papers and in a popular book. The papers include: "Anger and Similar Delusions;"

Mormon expressed this reality when he observed that "a bitter fountain cannot bring forth good water; neither can a good fountain bring forth bitter water" (Moro. 7:11), as did Jesus when he taught that "a good tree cannot bring forth evil fruit, neither a corrupt tree bring forth good fruit" (3 Ne. 14:18). They each taught, in metaphorical terms, that a corrupt heart cannot yield spiritually right behavior and a pure heart cannot yield spiritually wrong behavior.[31] Martin Luther summarized this idea in his remark that "it is not right to judge a man merely by the kind of works he does; one should judge him on the basis of why he does them . . . on the spring and fountain whence they flow."[32] It is only in this way that it is possible to know the genuine character of any external conduct and to characterize it accurately.

The Almas and Amlicis of the World

With these distinctions in mind it is easy to appreciate how radically different Alma, Captain Moroni, and Teancum were from Amlici, Amalickiah, and Gadianton. It is true that all of these men fought in war, but it is also true that the similarity ends there. Alma and those like him had one kind of heart, fighting only in defense of sacred human values and in conformity to God's commandments. Amlici and those similar to him had another kind of heart entirely, fighting only in pursuit of power and greed, and in explicit disobedience to God's commandments. In these two sets of figures we see the distinction between the two general types (the spiritual man and the natural man) as well as the distinction between condition of heart and outward behavior. We thus see the abstract sense in which their violence was the same, but also the deep sense in which their violent conduct could not have been more different.

"What We Are;" "The Social Construction of Basic Misconceptions of Behaviour;" "Irony, Self-deception, and Understanding;" "Self-deception as Vacuous Experience;" and "Locating Agency." The book is *Bonds that Make Us Free*.

31. That Mormon means this as a necessary relationship, and not a contingent one, is seen in his further statement (a chiastic one, incidentally) that "wherefore, a man being a servant of the devil cannot follow Christ; and if he follow Christ he cannot be a servant of the devil" (Moro. 7:11). Here Mormon is equating the "good water" he has already mentioned with *following* Christ, and he is equating the "bitter water" he has already mentioned with *serving* the devil. In other words, it is not just that the behavior (the "water") happens to be, or even is likely to be, right or wrong ("good" or "bitter"). It is that the behavior is inherently "good" or "bitter" because it is inherently an act of *following*—the following of either Christ or Satan. The action is more than a set of visible movements and audible sounds. While that is how we might describe conduct at the most general level, the deeper truth, as mentioned earlier, is that outward behavior is a set of visible movements and audible sounds that are the expression of an inner intention.

32. Martin Luther, in Edwald M. Plass, ed., *What Luther Says: An Anthology*.

The two sets of figures had completely different hearts and their respective acts were completely different forms of violence.[33]

This difference bears some relation to the fundamental distinction between aggressors and victims first explored in Chapter 2.[34] Morally speaking, the violent conduct of a victim who is defending herself against rape is nothing like the violent conduct of her assailant. No one would think to compare them. Nor is the violent conduct of a victim who is merely defending himself against murder anything like the conduct of his would-be murderer. Because aggressors and victims do not share the same moral status, their violent *acts* do not share the same moral status. Thus, despite the accuracy (in the abstract) of a label like "violence" to describe both, in reality such acts are morally antithetical.[35]

---

33. In the secular literature, the Arbinger Institute makes this same set of points by drawing a distinction between "way of being" and outward behavior. Building on the work of Martin Buber, the idea is that there are two fundamental ways of being—two core ways in which we can regard others. We can see them either as people whom we are alive to and whom we see to be just as real as we are, or we can see them as mere objects in our world whom we see to be *less* real than we are. Importantly, almost any behavior can be done from either way. For example, I can give a compliment to someone I see as a person, and I can give a compliment to someone I see as a mere object (e.g., as someone to curry favor from). At an abstract level it may seem that I am doing the same thing in both situations—"giving a compliment"—but this is actually not the case. Because my way of being is different in the two circumstances—because *I* am different in the two circumstances—my compliments are not the same. Coming from different ways of being, they are different actions, and they will feel different. The same is true of war. I can engage in war with those I see as mere objects and thus as less real than I am, and I can engage in war with those I see as people and thus just as real as I am. Although in both cases I am involved in war, my way of being is different in the two circumstances—*I* am different in them—and thus my involvements are not the same: my motives are different, my concerns are different, my aims are different, my hopes are different, my decisions are different. Coming from different ways of being, they are different involvements in war, and they will *feel* different. For detailed discussion of these concepts, see The Arbinger Institute, *Leadership and Self-Deception*, and, specifically regarding conflict, *The Anatomy of Peace*. Regarding Martin Buber, see his *I and Thou*. The work of the Arbinger Institute is formally based on the academic work of C. Terry Warner, its founder. For more, see note 30 earlier in this chapter.

34. See the sections "Anti-Violence Based on Wrong Action" and "The Relational Foundation of Right and Wrong." Additional discussions appear in the sections "Self-Defense and the Unrighteous" in Chapter 7 and "Moral Responsibility in Preemptive Action" in Chapter 12.

35. All of this would be different if victims of assault ended up pursuing aggressive and vicious acts of their own. At that point they would no longer be victims and they would thus lose that moral status. But none of the cases we have considered takes

All of the matters we have considered demonstrate why, though it is easy to do, it is nevertheless a mistake to generalize about war from the Amlicis of the world. The wickedness of such men is transparent and it is reflected both in their hubristic ambition and in their eagerness to engage in bloodshed. People of this sort are no analogy whatever to the Almas of the world. The righteousness of such leaders is as transparent as Amlici's evil and it is reflected both in their repudiation of power and in their willingness to enter, however reluctantly, only wars that they *have* to win—wars thrust upon them by the murderous actions of the Amlicis that surround them.

Such attitudes are conspicuous in prominent Book of Mormon leaders. Over the long history of their conflict with the Lamanites, not only were leaders such as Alma invariably the aggressed parties, but they also managed to maintain their defensive status and to eschew hatred and lust for vengeance against their tormentors. Enos, Mormon, and Moroni, for example, all experienced repeated aggression from the Lamanites and yet all were motivated to make and preserve sacred records specifically in order to bless them.[36] Moroni's situation is particularly poignant. The text reports that following the final destruction at Cumorah the surviving Nephites were hunted by the Lamanites until they were all destroyed (Morm. 8:2) and that Moroni wandered where he could in order to preserve his life (Moro. 1:1–3). And yet, despite the Lamanites' destruction of his whole people, their killing of his father, and their ongoing threat to kill Moroni if they found him, Moroni's last words were written to "*my brethren*, the Lamanites," imploring them to "come unto Christ" and to be "sanctified in Christ by the grace of God" (Moro. 10:1, 32–33).

The righteousness of such leaders is further reflected in their complete devotion to the Lord and in their relentless efforts to help their people repent and develop the same spiritual devotion. The early promise to Nephi, which explicitly required remembrance of God, was highly familiar to later Nephite leaders, and creating this remembrance was their first and central concern in preparing the Nephites to thwart Lamanite assault.[37]

All of these matters are significant and it would seem that one type of commitment to pacifism is due to little more than a failure to appreciate them. Conceptual distinctions between aggressors and victims, between the natural man and the spiritual man, and between the condition of our hearts and our outward behavior all make important contributions to our moral evaluations of

---

this form. In examples of genuine aggression and genuine defense, the moral contrast between the parties could hardly be more pronounced.

36. See Enos 1:11–17; W of M 1:6–8; Morm. 7; Moro. 1:4; 10:1; Title Page.

37. For more on this see: "The Ancient Promise to Nephi" in Chapter 6; "A Genuine Theme Regarding Book of Mormon Violence: The Ancient Promise to Nephi" in Chapter 9; "Faithfulness to God" in Chapter 15; and Appendix 2.

violent conduct. It turns out that the spiritual man—the man of Christ—can indeed engage in war and the scriptural canon is full of those who have.

Condition of Heart and War: A Modern Example

The Sermon on the Mount teaches us the state of heart we are to have. We are to embody the "spiritual man" that is presented to us in scripture. We are to be devoted to God, loving toward others, benevolent, humble, self-disciplined, and peaceable. This is the state we are to have even when faced with aggression. We are to love our enemies even when recognizing that they are our enemies and even when recognizing that we must thwart them.

Elder George F. Richards' famous dream regarding Hitler is a moving experience that demonstrates the love it is possible to have, even for our enemies, and even when in conflict. In the dream, Elder Richards saw Hitler and his soldiers preparing weapons to kill Elder Richards and those who were with him. At a certain point in the dream he faces Hitler, and says to him: "I am your brother. You are my brother. In our heavenly home we lived together in love and peace. Why can we not so live here on the earth?" Elder Richards then records: "And it seemed to me that I felt in myself, welling up in my soul, a love for that man, and I could feel that he was having the same experience, and presently he arose, and we embraced each other and kissed each other, a kiss of affection." Subsequently, he faced Hitler again, and Hitler "embraced me again, with a kiss of affection." Elder Richards then says:

> I think the Lord gave me that dream. Why should I dream of this man, one of the greatest enemies of mankind, and one of the wickedest, but that the Lord should teach me that I must love my enemies, and I must love the wicked as well as the good? Now, who is there in this wide world that I could not love under those conditions, if I could only continue to feel as I felt then?[38]

Elder Richards' dream teaches us, in a startling way, the quality of heart we are to have, or at least the quality of heart we are to seek. Ridding ourselves of personal animosity to the degree that we can, and relying on the Lord's help to do so, we are to engage in the world with a disposition of peace and charity toward all, including toward those we must fight. In sum, even in war we must go "with love in [our] hearts for all God's children, including those on the opposing side," and it will show.

The Standard and How We Meet It

The Sermon on the Mount sets for us a high standard. And the standard is not just a hope or a wish, but a command. The Lord states explicitly toward the beginning of the discourse that, "except ye shall keep my commandments,

---

38. George F. Richards, "Love for Mankind."

which I have commanded you at this time, ye shall in no case enter into the kingdom of heaven" (3 Ne. 12:20). Later, after completing the discourse, he says: "Behold, I have given unto you the commandments; therefore keep my commandments" (3 Ne. 15:10). Therefore, for Latter-day Saints, this is more than a sermon: it is a set of requirements.

Again, this standard is high, but it is the way of discipleship and it is a challenge we do not—and indeed, cannot—meet alone. As always, the Lord provides the means for living in the way he commands. This is found in the opening promise of the Sermon on the Mount itself—in the Book of Mormon—where the Lord explains that "after that ye are baptized with water, behold, I will baptize you with fire and with the Holy Ghost" (3 Ne. 12:1). This places the core of the gospel plan at the very heart of the Sermon. This core consists in giving ourselves to the Lord wholeheartedly and then his extending to us the regenerating and sanctifying powers of the Spirit. This divine process enlivens us spiritually; it changes our hearts by degrees from that of the natural man to that of the spiritual man, transforming us into a "child of Christ" and quickening us "in the inner man" (Titus 3:5; Mosiah 5:7; Eph. 3:16–17; Moses 6:65). Possessing this Spirit, we increasingly enjoy the fruits of the Spirit: "love, joy, peace, longsuffering, gentleness, goodness, faith, meekness, temperance" (Gal. 5:22–23). Having given our hearts to Christ, our hearts are changed by him, and thus, insofar as we sustain and grow in this changed state, we can live the higher level he demands of us—or at least come ever closer to living that standard. What the Lord makes mandatory he also makes possible.

Even in times of conflict, then, we can possess the heart the Lord requires of us. But it is not possible without him. These twin truths are both embedded in the Sermon on the Mount.

Conclusion

The most plausible interpretation of the Sermon on the Mount, it would appear, rests on two central distinctions: between the natural man and the spiritual man, and between the condition of our hearts and our outward behavior. The message of the Sermon is that we are to have a certain state of heart in all the circumstances of life. We are to be the spiritual man regardless of whatever outward behavior might be required of us. If circumstances demand that we answer provocation or even enter conflict, even then we must seek the spiritual state of a peaceable heart—entering with love in our hearts for all of God's children, even for those who are on the opposing side. Though unattainable in the natural-man state, this condition of heart is nevertheless available, and we will enjoy it to the degree that we yield our hearts to the Lord and allow ourselves to be changed by him. In this, multiple Book of Mormon leaders show the way.

Chapter 15

Alma 48 and Doctrine and Covenants 98

Eight Features about War in Alma Chapter 48

Also helpful in developing a sound scriptural view of war is Alma 48. Eight specific features regarding war stand out in this chapter. Although all of these elements appear in multiple scriptural locations and thus receive elucidation in those passages, their presence here, in a single chapter, makes Alma 48 a key text for understanding war from a Latter-day Saint perspective.

The Reality of Evil Men

The first feature that Alma 48 displays is the existence of genuinely evil men with genuinely evil motives, including a lust for power. We are told of Amalickiah, the Nephite deserter, who: "inspired the hearts of the Lamanites against the people of Nephi"; sought to "reign over all the land, yea, and all the people who were in the land, the Nephites as well as the Lamanites"; and desired to "bring [the Nephites] into bondage" (Alma 48:1–4). Additionally, Amalickiah: "hardened the hearts of the Lamanites and blinded their minds, and stirred them up to anger" against the Nephites; gathered together "a numerous host" in preparation for war against the Nephites; and accomplished all this "by fraud and deceit" (Alma 48:3–7). Later, after a defeat in battle, Amalickiah "was extremely wroth," cursing both God and Moroni, and "swearing with an oath that he would drink [Moroni's] blood" (Alma 49:27). For those who doubt the existence of truly evil men, Amalickiah stands as a paradigmatic case.

Gadianton and Giddianhi are obvious additional examples. We are told not only that Gadianton was "exceedingly expert in many words" and that he was able to "flatter" other evil men in a conspiracy to gain power, but that his very craft was to execute "the secret work of murder and of robbery" (Hel. 2:4–5). It was on this basis that he joined the band of Kishkumen, which would become known as "Gadianton's robbers and murderers" (Hel. 6:18), whose secret oaths permitted its members to "murder, and plunder, and steal, and commit whoredoms and all manner of wickedness" (Hel. 6:23).

Later, when Giddianhi was the governor of this secret society, the group had become so numerous that they slew "many of the people," laid waste to "many cities," and spread "death and carnage throughout the land" (3 Ne. 2:11). So dependent were they on aggression and plunder in order to sustain themselves that we are told "there was no way that they could subsist save it were to plunder and rob and murder" (3 Ne. 4:5). Yet Giddianhi was as expert with words and propaganda as Gadianton had been. Absurdly, he informed Lachoneus that he knew the works of his society to be "good" and that its members were only trying to recover the "rights of government" that the Nephites had denied them (3 Ne. 3:9–10). All of this evil, we are told, stems ultimately from Satan, who is "the author of all sin" and who carries on "his works of darkness and secret murder, and doth hand down their plots, and their oaths, and their covenants, and their plans of awful wickedness, from generation to generation according as he can get hold upon the hearts of the children of men" (Hel. 6:23–30).

Amalickiah, Gadianton, and Giddianhi all illustrate the same reality: there are evil men, with evil motives, who are inspired by Satan and who will stop at nothing in their thirst for power.

Faithfulness to God

The second feature to appear in Alma 48 is Moroni's preparation for war through strengthening the Nephites' faith in God. We learn that while Amalickiah had been obtaining power through deceit and murder, Moroni "had been preparing the minds of the people to be faithful unto the Lord their God" (Alma 48:7). While Moroni also pursued military preparations, the first element of Moroni's defense was his effort to improve the spirituality of the people. In this, Helaman and the other sons of Alma played an essential role by preaching the word of God and baptizing "unto repentance all men whosoever would hearken to their words." The efforts paid off; the record reports that "the people did humble themselves because of their words, insomuch that they were highly favored of the Lord" (Alma 48:18–20).

Lachoneus, governor of the Nephites decades later, pursued the same course at the time his people were under threat from the robbers of Gadianton. His first action was to "cause that his people should cry unto the Lord for strength" and even while making defensive preparations he taught them that, "except ye repent of all your iniquities, and cry unto the Lord, ye will in nowise be delivered out of the hands of those Gadianton robbers" (3 Ne. 3:12–15). Some two or three years later, when the Nephites had finally prevailed against those robbers, "their hearts were swollen with joy . . . [for] they knew it was because of their repentance and their humility that they had been delivered from an everlasting destruction" (3 Ne. 4:33).

The role of righteousness in Nephites' safety was evident at the very beginning of the society. Both Nephi and Lehi received the promise that those who kept the commandments would prosper in the land, and this included freedom from rule by external parties. Thus, not only do we see leaders over the course of Nephite history preaching the gospel and encouraging their people to repent as part of their defense against threat, but we see this same emphasis in the Lord's communications at the very beginning of the record. Regarding conflict, the central feature of Nephite culture was the Lord's ancient promise to Nephi and the emphasis it placed on remembering the Lord and keeping his commandments.[1] The preaching efforts of Moroni and the sons of Alma in Alma 48 reflect what was situated at the core of Nephite culture at its inception.

Quality of Heart

The next feature appearing in the chapter is the condition of soul found in Moroni, especially in contrast to Amalickiah. Mormon tells us that Moroni was a man "of a perfect understanding . . . [who] did not delight in bloodshed . . . [but who joyed] in the liberty and the freedom of his country, and his brethren from bondage and slavery" (Alma 48:11). These characteristics were earlier displayed dramatically when Moroni repeatedly gave Zerahemnah every chance to end the fighting during one battle, saying: "Behold, Zerahemnah, that we do not desire to be men of blood. Ye know that ye are in our hands, yet we do not desire to slay you" (Alma 44:1). Moroni displayed this same disposition later when he refused to attack Lamanite soldiers who were asleep, and drunk, and who could easily have been slain (Alma 55:18–19). Mormon further tells us that Moroni's heart "did swell with thanksgiving to his God," that he was "firm in the faith of Christ," and that he gloried in "doing good, in preserving his people, yea, in keeping the commandments of God, yea, and resisting iniquity" (Alma 48:12–16). Further, Mormon tells us that "if all men had been, and were, and ever would be, like unto Moroni, behold, the very powers of hell would have been shaken forever; yea, the devil would never have power over the hearts of the children of men" (Alma 48:17).

We also learn from the record that Moroni was a man "like unto Ammon," that he was like "the other sons of Mosiah," and that he was even like Alma (Alma 48:18)—high priest at the time, and someone who had seen angels and beheld the Lord (Alma 36:5–22). Moreover, Moroni, in his exemplary righteousness, was not alone in his aversion to conflict. Mormon tells us that the Nephites at this time contended with the Lamanites "reluctantly," indeed with "much reluctance," and that they "were sorry to take up arms against the Lamanites, because they did not delight in the shedding of blood . . . [and that] they were sorry to be the means of sending so many of their brethren out of this world into an eternal world, unprepared to meet their God" (Alma

---

1. For more on the promises to Nephi and Lehi, see the section "The Ancient Promise to Nephi" in Chapter 6, as well as Appendix 2. For a discussion of what occurred when the people did not repent when faced with threat, see the section "A Genuine Theme Regarding Book of Mormon Violence: The Ancient Promise to Nephi" in Chapter 9.

48:21–23). Manifesting the quality of heart enjoined by the Sermon on the Mount, both Moroni and the people at this time demonstrated the possibility of engaging in war reluctantly, even sorrowfully, saddened by the fate that they believed those who were attacking them would suffer.

Military Defense

Moroni's active effort to defend his people militarily is the next element to appear in Alma 48. The record informs us that during a period of peace, but with threat mounting, Moroni "had been strengthening the armies of the Nephites, and erecting small forts, or places of resort; throwing up banks of earth round about to enclose his armies, and also building walls of stone to encircle them about, round about their cities and the borders of their lands; yea, all round about the land." He put the largest number of men in the weakest areas "and thus he did fortify and strengthen the land" (Alma 48:8–9). These actions by Moroni instantiated the command from the Lord, recorded in Alma 43, that "ye shall not suffer yourselves to be slain by the hands of your enemies" and also that "ye shall defend your families even unto bloodshed" (Alma 43:46–47). Indeed, later we are told that Moroni "had kept the commandments," specifically in "preparing for the safety of his people" in equipping them to defend themselves (Alma 49:18–27).

We see the same pattern in the efforts of Lachoneus, whom we saw above, and "whose words and prophecies" were "great and marvelous" and whom Mormon considered "a great prophet" (3 Ne. 3:16, 19). Even while Lachoneus was admonishing his people to cry unto the Lord and to repent, still he "caused that fortifications should be built round about them, and the strength thereof should be exceedingly great. And he caused that armies, both of the Nephites and of the Lamanites, or of all them who were numbered among the Nephites, should be placed as guards round about to watch them, and to guard them from the robbers day and night" (3 Ne. 3:14).

As in other cases in the Book of Mormon, Moroni and Lachoneus instructed their people not only to be faithful to God but also to be vigilant in defense. This, of course, was true generally over the course of Nephite history. Significant spiritual figures in the Book of Mormon repeatedly took up arms to defend themselves or others.[2] Moreover, as we will be reminded shortly, the record reports the Lord himself helping these leaders in their defensive efforts, which reinforces the message that defense is both approved and expected in cases where it is needed.

---

2. These leaders included Nephi, King Benjamin, Ammon, Alma, Captain Moroni, Helaman, Gidgiddoni, Lachoneus, Mormon, and Moroni. See Chapter 7 in particular for more detail on this subject.

Righteousness of Motive

The Nephites' set of motives for engaging in war is the fifth element to appear in the chapter. We are told that their desire was "to support their liberty, their lands, their wives, and their children, and their peace, and that they might live unto the Lord their God, and that they might maintain that which was called by their enemies the cause of Christians" (Alma 48:10). Mormon tells us that Moroni was motivated by the "welfare and safety of his people" and that he had sworn with an oath "to defend his people, his rights, and his country, and his religion." We also learn that the Nephites defended themselves against their enemies in order "to preserve their lives" (Alma 48:12–14) and to prevent their wives and their children from being "massacred by the barbarous cruelty" of those who would destroy them (Alma 48:24). This is consistent with the earlier report that "the Nephites were inspired by a better cause, for they were not fighting for monarchy nor power," but for "their homes and their liberties, their wives and their children, and their all, yea for their rites of worship and their church," and again, for "their families, and their lands, their country and their rights, and their religion" (Alma 43:45, 47).[3]

We see the same pattern in Mormon near the end of the Book of Mormon. As the Nephites faced dire circumstances, Mormon urged them "with great energy . . . [to fight for] their wives, and their children, and their houses, and their homes" (Morm. 2:23). Whereas their enemies sought for power and subjugation, the Nephites were urged to defend sacred matters of family and freedom.

It is also interesting to consider Ammon. Although he embarked on his mission to the Lamanites in peace, that didn't stop him from wielding a sword and killing enemies when circumstances became threatening and defense was required. However, Ammon never harmed, or even threatened, anyone for reasons of power or gain or self-aggrandizement. He took up the sword only when defense required it (Alma 17:19–39; 20:1–27).

We see the same pattern with Shule, an important figure in the history of the Jaredites, recorded in Ether 7. Shule's father, king of the Jaredites, was betrayed by one of his sons who had rebelled, grown an army, and then taken the king into captivity. While in confinement the king fathered Shule who "waxed strong, and became mighty as to the strength of a man; and he was also mighty in judgment" (Ether 7:7–8). Eventually Shule raised an army of his own, gave battle to his traitorous older brother, defeated him, and, rather than claiming the kingdom for himself, restored dominion to his father. His

---

3. Skousen's work indicates that the reference here to "rites" of worship should actually be to "rights" of worship. See Royal Skousen, ed., *The Book of Mormon: The Earliest Text*, 432.

father, greatly aged by this time, bestowed the kingdom upon Shule, and the record informs us that Shule "did execute judgment in righteousness" (Ether 7:11). Most remarkably, when Shule's older brother repented of all that he had done Shule forgave him and gave him authority in the kingdom. In the course of additional family drama over a period of years, which included wars and multiple shifts of Jaredite power, Shule again showed remarkable expansiveness of soul in the wake of the treachery and threat that had been imposed upon him. Toward the end of his days, Shule provided protection to prophets who had been sent to declare repentance to the people, "and by this cause the people were brought unto repentance" (Ether 7:25).

Though he engaged in numerous wars, Shule was never motivated by greed or the desire for power. A perfect expression of the principles found in Alma 48, he fought only in defense of right and was impressive in his generosity toward others. It is no surprise that the record concludes that Shule "remembered the great things that the Lord had done for his fathers in bringing them across the great deep into the promised land; wherefore he did execute judgment in righteousness all his days" (Ether 7:27).

Offensive vs. Defensive War

Appearing next in Alma 48 is the report that the Nephites were taught "never to give an offense" (Alma 48:14). This seems a reiteration of what is given in more detail in Alma 43, in which the Lord said: "Inasmuch as ye are not guilty of the first offense, neither the second, ye shall not suffer yourselves to be slain by the hands of your enemies" (Alma 43:46)—a clear prohibition against instigating hostilities. Disciples of Christ may have to defend themselves against aggressors, but they are never to be the aggressors themselves.

Such a prohibition does not forbid the range of aggressive and pre-emptive tactics that are part of an overall defensive posture, however. In Captain Moroni's battle with Zerahemnah in Alma 43–44, for example, Moroni first adopted offensive measures in sending spies and establishing a favorable geographical location in which to attack Zarahemnah's approaching army (Alma 43:30–42). Then, once Moroni clearly gained the advantage in battle, he stopped the fighting in order to offer Zerahemnah conditions under which the conflict could be ceased permanently—namely, the surrender of all their weapons and the taking of an oath that they would never again come to war against the Nephites. But when Zerahemnah refused these conditions, Moroni unilaterally resumed the battle and "commanded his people that they should fall upon [the Lamanites] and slay them" (Alma 44:18).

A similar example is found in the case of Gidgiddoni, whom Mormon praises and who was himself a prophet (3 Ne. 3:19). We are told that, at the end of one battle, as the Gadianton robbers were retreating, "Gidgiddoni commanded that his armies should pursue them as far as the borders of the wilderness, and that they should not spare any that should fall into their hands by the way" (3 Ne. 4:11–13). Later, when those robbers were laying siege against the Nephites, their plan backfired and they found themselves suffering for want of food "insomuch that the robbers were about to perish with hunger" while "the Nephites were continually marching out by day and by night, and falling upon their armies and cutting them off by thousands and by tens of thousands" (3 Ne. 4:20–21). As their situation worsened, the Gadianton robbers determined not only to withdraw from their siege but to withdraw more fully—to "march into the furthermost parts of the land northward" (3 Ne. 4:23). But knowing that this was not the end of the matter, Gidgiddoni "did send out his armies in the night-time, and did cut off the way of their retreat, and did place his armies in the way of their retreat" so that "when the robbers began their march, they were met by the armies of the Nephites both in their front and in their rear." Surrounded, the Gadianton robbers could not retreat from battle. As a result many were taken prisoner "and the remainder of them were slain" (3 Ne. 4:25–27).

Alma behaved similarly in his encounter with Lamanite invaders. In one battle he led, as the Nephites finally gained the upper hand and as the Lamanites began to flee, "the Nephites did pursue them with their might, and did slay them. Yea, they were met on every hand, and slain and driven" (Alma 2:35–37).

This is reminiscent of the occasion, during the long war between the Nephites and Lamanites recorded in Alma, that Moroni and Pahoran marched with an army toward the land of Nephihah "being determined to overthrow the Lamanites in that city" (Alma 62:14). On their way they came upon a large army of Lamanites, whereupon the Nephite army "slew many of them" and took their weapons and provisions (Alma 62:15). Then, proceeding on its march, Moroni's army reached Nephihah and managed to enter the city by night. As the Lamanite soldiers fled the city the next morning upon seeing the Nephite army, Moroni "did cause that his men should march forth against them," and they "slew many" (Alma 62:25). Moroni then proceeded to the land of Lehi to free that land of its Lamanite captors. The record tells us that, although the Lamanites were frightened and "fled before the army of Moroni" (Alma 62:31), he "did pursue them from city to city" until finally overtaking them in the land of Moroni where "they did slay them with a great slaughter" (Alma 62:38).

Although all of these are examples of offensive action in war, they all occur strictly in the context of waging wars of defense. Indeed, prior to the incident with Gidgiddoni's army Gidgiddoni had forbidden the Nephites to start war themselves. They had desired "to go up upon the mountains and into the wilderness, that we may fall upon the robbers, and destroy them in their own lands," but were forbidden (3 Ne. 3:20). Similarly, centuries later Mormon refused to lead the Nephites in battle once they became hostile in outlook and were motivated by the desire for vengeance. Indeed, "they had sworn by all that had been forbidden them by our Lord and Savior Jesus Christ, that they would go up unto their enemies to battle, and avenge themselves of the blood of their brethren" (Morm. 3:14). In these examples, the Nephites' actions were forbidden because they were not purely defensive. In contrast, in the cases we have considered, the Nephites were always engaged in defense against the assaults of others and were themselves never the instigators of hostilities. In such cases offensive tactics are both permissible and important.[4]

God's Help

The next dimension to appear in Alma 48 is the report that God would "prosper" the Nephites if they were "faithful in keeping the commandments of God," a promise that included prompting them to flee, warning them to prepare for war, and instructing them "whither they should go" to engage their enemies (Alma 48:15–16). All of these were ways in which the Lord would deliver the Nephites and prosper them in the land.

The same principle is exemplified in many other places. We are told in Moses 7, for example, that enemies went to battle against the people of Enoch, and that as Enoch "spake the word of the Lord . . . the earth trembled, and the mountains fled . . . and the rivers of water were turned out of their course . . . so powerful was the word of Enoch . . . and so great was the fear of the enemies of the people of God, that they fled and stood afar off" (Moses 7:13–14). The record then tells us that a "curse" was placed upon all those who "fought against God" and that "the fear of the Lord was upon all nations, so great was the glory of the Lord, which was upon his people" (Moses 7:16–17).

---

4. For some remarks on the suitability of pre-emptive action from a secular standpoint, see the section "Self-Defense? The Question of Pre-Emptive Action" in Chapter 12. As mentioned there, Michael Walzer takes up the topic of "anticipations" in his *Just and Unjust Wars*, 74–85. He argues, rightly I believe, that pre-emptive strikes cannot be merely preventive in character, but must also be in response to actual willful actions by an adversary. This, of course, is the case (and more) in every Book of Mormon example of offensive-action-in-a-defensive-war that I have included above. Morgan Deane covers the topic of offensive tactics in warfare more fully than I do here, and with a focus on different examples, in his "Offensive Warfare in the Book of Mormon and a Defense of the Bush Doctrine," 29–39. It is also worth noting that Captain Moroni once threatened to follow the Lamanites into their own land and to wage war until the Lamanite invaders were "destroyed from off the face of the earth." But since the Lamanite leader Ammoron agreed to Moroni's conditions for prisoner exchange—the demand that preceded the warning—Moroni did not pursue this threat. (See Alma 54:12–13.)

According to Exodus 14, the children of Israel witnessed the same power of God at the Red Sea. Experiencing the protection of the "angel of God, which went before the camp of Israel," the "pillar of the cloud" stood between the Egyptians and the children of Israel, protecting them, at the same time that Moses "stretched out his hand over the sea" and the Lord, by means of strong winds through the night, divided the waters (vs. 19–21). The children of Israel thereupon crossed over upon dry ground, the waters "a wall unto them on their right hand, and on their left" (vs. 22, 29). When the Egyptians later pursued over the same ground, the Lord commanded Moses to stretch forth his hand, whereupon "the waters returned, and covered the chariots, and the horsemen, and all the host of Pharaoh that came into the sea" (vs. 23, 26–28). The record concludes: "Thus the Lord saved Israel that day out of the hand of the Egyptians" and "Israel saw that great work which the Lord did upon the Egyptians; and the people feared the Lord, and believed the Lord, and his servant Moses" (vs. 30, 31).

Examples of such help from God could be multiplied. The Lord's willingness to help his people in their battles is a common feature of the Book of Mormon;[5] indeed, it is a theme we have seen across the scriptural canon.[6] And not only do we observe this principle in action in multiple places, but the prospect of the Lord's help is actually presupposed in the very promise to Nephi with which the Book of Mormon begins.[7] All of this supports what we learn about God's help in Alma 48.

Minimizing Bloodshed

Finally, Alma 48 demonstrates that bloodshed, if necessary, should be minimal. The chapter teaches us of Captain Moroni's character and tells us more than once that he had no desire to shed blood (Alma 48:11, 16)—an attitude demonstrated in his earlier conflict with Zerahemnah. In that confrontation Moroni attempted to end the fighting the moment the Nephites gained the upper hand against their attackers (Alma 43:17–44:7), and he later ended the fighting altogether when the Lamanites finally accepted his conditions (Alma 44:16–20). On a later occasion Moroni refused to attack defenseless Lamanite soldiers when he easily could have attacked them be-

---

5. Recall that there is no validity to the argument that we cannot rely on reports of God's help in his people's battles. This matter is addressed in the section "Examining the Corollary of the Narrative Approach: The Example of the Lord's Own Conduct" in Chapter 8.

6. See Chapter 7 in particular.

7. For more on this, see "The Ancient Promise to Nephi" in Chapter 6, "A Genuine Theme Regarding Book of Mormon Violence: The Ancient Promise to Nephi" in Chapter 9, and Appendix 2.

cause "this was not the desire of Moroni; he did not delight in murder or bloodshed, but he delighted in the saving of his people from destruction" and therefore he "would not fall upon the Lamanites and destroy them" (Alma 55:18–19). Moroni demonstrated his hatred of bloodshed by the determined way in which he minimized and avoided it whenever possible.

Summary

Rich in elements that relate to war, Alma 48 teaches both that evil men exist and that defense against them begins with faithfulness to God. We learn that it is possible for people to have the peaceable, righteous hearts described in the Sermon on the Mount and yet to engage in war to defend themselves. We also see that, in the face of threat, righteous disciples actively prepare defense against the danger and maintain righteous motives in waging war if war is thrust upon them. Moreover, although disciples can engage in pre-emptive and aggressive actions in the course of defending themselves from hostilities, they never instigate hostilities themselves. And finally, Alma 48 teaches that God helps his people wage war in defending themselves and that such people always seek to minimize bloodshed.

Doctrine and Covenants 98

Since a large portion of Doctrine and Covenants 98 is devoted specifically to the topic of violence, it seems only natural to consider it in any discussion of war. However, because this revelation is a complex document with multiple layers and ambiguities, applying its statements turns out to be far from simple.[8]

Different Scales of Conflict

To begin, the section seems to identify three different scales of conflict. The first is described in terms of "smiting you or your families" and, equivalently, as "coming upon you or your family." The Lord says that "if men will smite you, or your families, once and ye bear it patiently and revile not against them, neither seek revenge, ye shall be rewarded" (D&C 98:23). The Lord uses the expression "come upon you or your children" in later verses, apparently with the same meaning (D&C 98:26–29). The relevant concepts in these verses are "family" and "men"—expressions that seem to presuppose conflict on a localized and small scale.

The topic then shifts to war between nations. The Lord begins with the commandment that "if any nation, tongue, or people should proclaim war against them, they should first lift a standard of peace unto that people, nation, or tongue" (D&C 98:34), and then continues in this international con-

---

8. I identified a partial list of the questions that must be asked regarding the revelation in the sections "Ambiguity" and "Overlooked Distinction" in Chapter 10.

text through verse 38. Here the relevant terms are "nation," "people," and "war"—expressions that, far from suggesting matters located at the level of individuals or families, presuppose conflict on a grand scale.

The section then shifts back to the all-inclusive language of "thine enemy" who "comes upon thee" or "trespasses against thee" (D&C 98:39). Here it is difficult to tell if the section is shifting away from the context of war between nations and focusing again on smaller-scale conflict, or if it is just continuing the thread of the previous five verses and expanding on the conditions that pertain to war between states. Different people could reach different judgments on this matter.

Over the course of twenty-five verses, then, Section 98 speaks of adversaries in three different ways: as "men," as "nations," and simply as "thine enemy." These do not seem to be identical in meaning, and they thus suggest different classes and sizes of adversary as well as widely differing circumstances. But what is meant precisely in using all three terms—and what exactly is the relationship among them—seems impossible to say.

Different Types of Aggression and the Definition of "Repentance"

Over the same set of verses the section also speaks of aggressive conduct by an adversary in terms of "smiting," "coming upon," "seeking thy life," "proclaiming war," and "trespassing against." Not only do these suggest different scales of conflict, but also different levels of aggressiveness, since (for example) "trespassing against" others does not seem identical to actually "seeking" their lives.

But differences of this sort do not mean that the expressions are precise. What exactly counts as a "coming upon" or a "trespass"? What degree of agreement could we achieve in applying such terms? And if we want to apply every declaration in this section to every scale of conflict, the importance of clarity about these terms becomes even greater. In an age of devastating—not to mention nuclear, weapons—what exactly counts as a "trespass," a "smiting," and so on—particularly when such weapons can be launched from great distances? At a time when a single brief assault can result in thousands of deaths, it is natural to wonder whether "seeking one's life" requires an actual attack or whether that condition is satisfied by the combination of aggressive intent and initial steps undertaken to fulfill it. In general, it is unclear how matters of proximity, intention, and degree of harm relate to these scriptural terms since none of these issues is addressed in the revelation.[9] And yet if we are to understand this section—particularly as it applies to the possibilities of the current age—these are questions that need to be addressed.

---

9. This topic receives more attention in the section "Self-Defense? The Question of Pre-Emptive Action" in Chapter 12.

It is also important to understand the nature of the repentance that would be required for the sort of attacks described in Section 98. This is required by the Lord's declaration that "if after thine enemy has come upon thee the first time, he repent and come unto thee praying thy forgiveness, thou shalt forgive him . . . and so on unto the second and third time; and as oft as thine enemy repenteth of the trespass wherewith he has trespassed against thee, thou shalt forgive him, until seventy times seven" (D&C 98 39–40). But if an enemy can repent of these actions—and if the aggressed party is to forgive such wrongs "until seventy times seven"—it is important not only to know what these terms actually signify, but also to know what would be required to repent of them. After all, it would certainly qualify as a "coming upon" or a "trespass" if one state's attack on another caused, say, five thousand deaths, but it is less clear what would qualify as repentance for such an act. Suppose, for example, that the aggressing state expressed remorse for its attack and prayed for forgiveness, but then attacked again. What is the meaning of forgiving an enemy "until seventy times seven" in a circumstance of this sort?[10] If we are careless in how we think about such matters we would eventually reach a point at which no one would be left to grant forgiveness because everyone who could do so would be dead.

For this reason it is important to note the statement in this revelation that an enemy must restore "four-fold" for its trespasses against the aggressed party (D&C 98:44, 47). The Lord identifies this condition specifically in the context of an enemy that has already trespassed four times, but surely some application of this principle must apply in any act of repentance performed by an aggressing state, even after a single attack. Restitution for harm is a longstanding principle of genuine repentance, and it is natural to suppose that it would apply in cases of this sort as well.[11]

---

10. Regardless of whether we take the literal meaning of forgiving "seventy times seven" to refer to the number 77 (as the Church fathers did) or to the number 490 (as modern readers typically do), or whether we interpret the expression metaphorically to mean "without limit" (as Augustine did), the consequences in terms of military assault are monumental. On the expression "seventy times seven" see the section "A Third Reading of the Sermon on the Mount" in Chapter 14, particularly note 19.

11. The importance of restitution appears prominently in Exodus 22:1–15, where various transgressions are identified, along with the required restoration for what was lost (ranging from simple restitution to restitution equal to five times the loss). Other Old Testament mentions of restitution include Lev. 5:16; 6:4; 24:18–21. An interesting mention of four-fold restoration, in particular, is found in the judgment David pronounced on the mythical malefactor presented to him by Nathan—a scale of restitution that David pronounced on this fictional figure in addition to the death penalty (2 Sam. 12:1–6). Four-fold restoration is also the standard to which one New

But this doesn't mean that it is easy to identify exactly what form restitution must take in cases of military attack. It is easy to imagine what kind of restoration would be required for lost and damaged property (although we would still have to decide what multiplier—two-fold? four-fold?—would be appropriate), but what is the restitution for causing thousands of deaths? The section does not say, and, short of direct revelation on the subject, the opinions on such a matter would be many.

Different Responses to Aggression

Finally, the section speaks in various ways of the proper responses that aggrieved victims must demonstrate toward the provocations of their adversaries. For example, after explaining that we are to forgive three times any "smiting" or "coming upon" us, the Lord then says that upon the fourth time, if we do not forgive, "thine enemy is in thine hands; and if thou rewardest him according to his works thou art justified; if he has sought thy life, and thy life is endangered by him, thine enemy is in thine hands and thou art justified" (D&C 98:31). Exactly what we are justified in doing in such circumstances is not identified, however, and it is certain that people would have different opinions on this.

The message regarding the proper response is at least somewhat clearer in the case of war between nations. The Lord says that if a nation sues for peace three times and its adversary persists in proclaiming war against it, "then I, the Lord, would give unto them a commandment, and justify them in going out to battle against that nation, tongue, or people" (D&C 98:36). However, while this is a clear statement regarding an adversary's proclamation of war, it assumes a case—a minority case, it would appear—in which the enemy nation is announcing its intention to wage war rather than starting the war by simply attacking without warning.

The ambiguity regarding response to provocation returns when the Lord commands that we forgive each of three trespasses against us whether or not our adversary repents, but that, upon the fourth unrepentant trespass: "Thou shalt not forgive him, but shall bring these testimonies before the Lord" (D&C 98:44). This command is conspicuous because it is a departure from what this section stated earlier (i.e., that we are permitted to forgive the fourth "coming upon us" if we desire). This alone suggests that the "smiting" and "coming upon" of the early verses in this passage (D&C 98:23–33) are different from the "coming upon" and "trespass" of later verses (D&C 98:39–48), even though we are not told exactly how they are different.

Testament figure held himself in his treatment of others (Luke 19:1–8). The Lord also speaks of a four-fold restitution requirement in the case of individuals mismanaging stocks regarding the Nauvoo House (D&C 124:56–71).

Moreover, it is difficult to know what it means to "bring these testimonies before the Lord." Earlier we are told that we are "justified" in our treatment of our adversary (D&C 98:23–31),[12] and that we are justified in going to battle to defend ourselves (D&C 98:34–38), but here we are told only that if our adversary fails to repent four times we are to "bring these testimonies before the Lord" and that "they shall not be blotted out" until the adversary repents and recompenses us four-fold (D&C 98:39–44). There is nothing in this that suggests any action on our part toward this adversary, however—which is a significant departure from the first two mentions of proper response to an adversary's aggressive conduct.

For all of these reasons it is difficult to see how Section 98 can be considered a document that identifies (with any degree of specificity at least) how we are to behave in situations of conflict. Any attempt to derive concrete applications must supply assumptions that are not themselves part of the revelation. What seems evident is that Joseph Smith understood far more by the Spirit than appears in the words of this text. It is reasonable to suppose that for him there lay deep meaning in expressions such as "smiting," "trespass," "in thine hands," "justified," "bring these testimonies before the Lord," and so forth, even though they are unclear to us.[13] This is why the Book of Mormon is so helpful on the issue of war. In its pages we observe the actions of God, his

---

12. Again, we are told that we are justified in our treatment, but we are not told what that treatment is.

13. Scripture makes clear that it is possible to understand and to know more than one actually says—indeed, more than one is able to say. One example is seen in the report of the Lord's praying at the time of his visit to the Nephites. We are told that "the things which he prayed cannot be written" and that "no tongue can speak, neither can there be written by any man, neither can the hearts of men conceive so great and marvelous things as we both saw and heard Jesus speak" (3 Ne. 17:15, 17). And the record tells us of a later prayer by the Lord that "tongue cannot speak the words which he prayed, neither can be written by man the words which he prayed" and "so great and marvelous were the words which he prayed that they cannot be written, neither can they be uttered by man" (3 Ne. 19:32, 34). Speaking of the role of words in revelation generally, Elder Packer once remarked that "we cannot express spiritual knowledge in words alone" and even explained that "should an angel appear and converse with you, neither you, nor he would be confined to corporeal sight or sound in order to communicate." Instead, the communication could be by "pure intelligence" flowing into our minds. See Boyd K. Packer, *That All May Be Edified*, 335–36. And of one spiritual manifestation Elder Packer said, "I could not describe to you what happened if I were determined to do so." See Lucile C. Tate, *Boyd K. Packer: A Watchman on the Tower*, 60. All of this suggests that one who receives revelation often comprehends more than words alone convey, and the text of D&C 98 seems a quintessential instance of exactly this phenomenon.

prophets, and other men of God in concrete circumstances, and this removes much of the uncertainty that is unavoidable in more abstract declarations. In general, it seems safer to draw inferences from specific actions and teachings in concrete situations than to generate conclusions from broad statements that employ terms ambiguous or opaque to us in the twenty-first century.

In the end, Section 98 gives us a theme—namely, that we should be slow to enter conflict and that we should be quick to forgive. However, because the ambiguities in the revelation are many, the revelation does not lay out for us details of application. Because the theme of the section is found elsewhere in scripture, and because we cannot confidently apply the section's declarations across a wide range of conflict situations, it is not a central text in working toward an LDS framework about war.

Chapter 16

Two Modern Prophets

President Gordon B. Hinckley's
General Conference Addresses

In addition to the Sermon on the Mount and Alma 48, significant sources regarding war for Latter-day Saints are found in two general conference addresses by President Gordon B. Hinckley. These are noteworthy both because they are recent statements and because they are couched in concrete contexts. Far from mere abstract declarations, each address was delivered against the background of specific hostilities occurring at the time: one given at the time of the initial U.S. attacks in Afghanistan,[1] and the second at the time of the invasion of Iraq.[2]

In the first address, President Hinckley refers to the terrorist attacks against the United States on September 11, 2001 as "vicious and ugly," "cruel and cunning," and as "an act of consummate evil." He compares the terrorists to the Gadianton robbers, calling them "a vicious, oath-bound, and secret organization bent on evil and destruction." According to President Hinckley, "in their day [the Gadianton robbers] did all in their power, by whatever means available, to bring down the Church, to woo the people with sophistry, and to take control of the society. We see the same thing in the present situation." But such did not begin with the robbers of Gadianton, President Hinckley tells us: "From the day of Cain to the present, the adversary has been the great mastermind of the terrible conflicts that have brought so much suffering. Treachery and terrorism began with him."[3]

President Hinckley adds, speaking for members of the Church in the United States, that we should "stand solidly with the president of our nation. The terrible forces of evil must be confronted and held accountable for their actions." Then, speaking of the requirement to be a peace-loving people, he says: "We are people of peace. We are followers of the Christ who was and is the Prince of Peace. But there are times when we must stand up for right and decency, for freedom and civilization, just as Moroni rallied his people in his day to the defense of their wives, their children, and the cause of liberty (see Alma 48:10) . . . Let us pray for the forces of good [in this conflict]." President Hinckley ends his remarks with this observation and plea: "Our

---

1. Gordon B. Hinckley, "The Times in Which We Live."
2. Gordon B. Hinckley, "War and Peace."
3. Hinckley, "The Times in Which We Live."

safety lies in repentance. Our strength comes of obedience to the commandments of God. Let us be prayerful. Let us pray for righteousness. Let us live worthy of the blessings of heaven, reforming our lives where necessary and looking to Him, the Father of us all."[4]

In his second address, President Hinckley recounts the conditions extant at the time, and says: "The question arises, 'Where does the Church stand in all of this?'" He then answers by referring to general principles regarding peace and war as drawn from the scriptures. He says, for example, that we are to "renounce war and proclaim peace" (D&C 98:16), that we are a people "who long for peace, who teach peace, who work for peace." Yet, he points out, "it is clear from these and other writings that there are times and circumstances when nations are justified, in fact have an obligation, to fight for family, for liberty, and against tyranny, threat, and oppression."[5] Emphasizing the necessity of combating evil, he observes that: "We are a freedom-loving people, committed to the defense of liberty wherever it is in jeopardy. I believe that God will not hold men and women in uniform responsible as agents of their government in carrying forward that which they are legally obligated to do. It may even be that [God] will hold us responsible if we try to impede or hedge up the way of those who are involved in a contest with forces of evil and repression."[6]

In these two conference addresses President Hinckley emphasizes that there are evil people who commit evil acts and that Satan is behind them. While we are people of peace, there are valid justifications, and even obligatory reasons, for going to war, including defense of family and liberty, fighting against tyranny and threat and oppression, and confronting the forces of evil. We should pray for the forces of good against evil and recognize that ultimately our safety lies in repentance and keeping the commandments of God.

President Spencer W. Kimball's 1976 *Ensign* Message

A fifth important text in developing an LDS framework about war is a 1976 First Presidency message by President Spencer W. Kimball entitled "The False Gods We Worship."[7] President Kimball begins by remarking on the wickedness of the world:

> The Lord gave us a choice world and expects righteousness and obedience to his commandments in return. But when I review the performance of this people in

---

4. Ibid.
5. This is reminiscent of President David O. McKay's statement that "we love peace, but not peace at any price. There is a peace more destructive of the manhood of living man than war is destructive of the body. 'Chains are worse than bayonets.'" See David O. McKay, "Righteousness Key to World Peace."
6. Hinckley, "War and Peace."
7. Spencer W. Kimball, "The False Gods We Worship."

comparison with what is expected, I am appalled and frightened. Iniquity seems to abound. The Destroyer seems to be taking full advantage of the time remaining to him in this, the great day of his power. Evil seems about to engulf us like a great wave, and we feel that truly we are living in conditions similar to those in the days of Noah before the Flood.

He adds:

I have traveled much in various assignments over the years, and when I pass through the lovely countryside or fly over the vast and beautiful expanses of our globe, I compare these beauties with many of the dark and miserable practices of men, and I have the feeling that the good earth can hardly bear our presence upon it.

Then, in the most relevant passage for our purposes, President Kimball condemns mortals' reliance upon themselves rather than upon God:[8]

In spite of our delight in defining ourselves as modern, and our tendency to think we possess a sophistication that no people in the past ever had—in spite of these things, we are, on the whole, an idolatrous people—a condition most repugnant to the Lord. We are a warlike people, easily distracted from our assignment of preparing for the coming of the Lord. When enemies rise up, we commit vast resources to the fabrication of gods of stone and steel—ships, planes, missiles, fortifications—and depend on them for protection and deliverance. When threatened, we become antienemy instead of pro-kingdom of God; we train a man in the art of war and call him a patriot, thus, in the manner of Satan's counterfeit of true patriotism, perverting the Savior's teaching: "Love your enemies, bless them that curse you, do good to them that hate you, and pray for them which despitefully use you, and persecute you; that ye may be the children of your Father which is in heaven." (Matt. 5:44–45)

We forget that if we are righteous the Lord will either not suffer our enemies to come upon us—and this is the special promise to the inhabitants of the land of the Americas (see 2 Ne. 1:7)—or he will fight our battles for us (Exodus

---

8. At this point in his address, because he speaks of delighting in modernism and sophistication, President Kimball seems to be speaking particularly of the United States. It is difficult to be certain, however, since, throughout his message, President Kimball employs the first-person plural pronouns "we," "our," and "us" without identifying their antecedents (at least not with any degree of specificity). The most general category such pronouns might refer to is the class of all mortals (he speaks, for example, of flying "over the vast and beautiful expanses of our globe"), while a less general category would be the class of U.S. citizens. Still less general would be the class of Church members. President Kimball seems to refer to all three at different times but there are multiple places where readers might disagree about exactly whom he has in mind. It *is* apparent, however, that for the most part he is addressing people outside the Church, since, as we will see shortly, he explicitly invites his readers to join the Church. Moreover, in bewailing the wickedness he has in mind, he finds it "scarcely believable" that such things should be found "*even* among the Saints to some degree." Here, members of the Church are obviously a mere subset of the much larger population he is actually addressing.

14:14; D&C 98:37, to name only two references of many). This he is able to do, for as he said at the time of his betrayal, "Thinkest thou that I cannot now pray to my Father, and he shall presently give me more than twelve legions of angels?" (Matt. 26:53). We can imagine what fearsome soldiers they would be. King Jehoshaphat and his people were delivered by such a troop (see 2 Chr. 20), and when Elisha's life was threatened, he comforted his servant by saying, "Fear not: for they that be with us are more than they that be with them" (2 Kgs. 6:16). The Lord then opened the eyes of the servant, "And he saw: and, behold, the mountain was full of horses and chariots of fire round about Elisha" (2 Kgs. 6:17).

What are we to fear when the Lord is with us? Can we not take the Lord at his word and exercise a particle of faith in him? Our assignment is affirmative: to forsake the things of the world as ends in themselves; to leave off idolatry and press forward in faith; to carry the gospel to our enemies, that they might no longer be our enemies.

President Kimball then makes it clear that his message is an admonition to the world. He says that "we must leave off the worship of modern-day idols and a reliance on the 'arm of flesh,' for the Lord has said to all the world in our day, 'I will not spare any that remain in Babylon'" (D&C 64:24). He adds, "our message is the same as that which Peter gave," and "we believe that the way for each person and each family to prepare as the Lord has directed is to begin to exercise greater faith, to repent, and to enter into the work of his kingdom on earth, which is The Church of Jesus Christ of Latter-day Saints," adding, "we invite and welcome all men, everywhere, to join in this work."

Six Teachings about War from President Spencer W. Kimball

Although the entirety of President Kimball's message is important to consider, for our purposes we can distill the essentials for thinking about war down to six elements:

1. We should not be warlike, depending upon our own devices rather than upon God.
2. We should become pro-kingdom of God rather than anti-enemy when under threat.
3. We should not confuse studying the art of war with patriotism.
4. We should embrace the teachings of the Sermon on the Mount.
5. If we are righteous the Lord will either not permit our enemies to come upon us, or he will fight our battles for us.
6. Our assignment is affirmative: to forsake the things of the world as ends in themselves; to leave off idolatry and press forward in faith; to be baptized and join in the work of the Lord; and to carry the gospel to our enemies, that they might no longer be our enemies.

First four elements. Elements one and two remind us of Moroni. While under threat from the Lamanites, the first action Moroni undertook was to encourage his people's faithfulness to God. Although he also undertook military preparations, he, like President Kimball, recognized that defense begins with righteousness. The third element indicates that patriotism is much larger, and much more, than preparing to fight. Moroni was a patriot *par excellence* and yet he hated war. He was willing to fight to the end but he was also eager to cease the bloodshed at the earliest possible moment that he could secure peace.[9] The fourth element points toward the Sermon on the Mount, which teaches that we must maintain a peaceable walk, even with those who mistreat us, and that if circumstances require conflict it must be entered into with a peaceable heart. We must go with love in our hearts for all of God's children, even toward those who are on the opposing side.[10]

Fifth element: God's role in his people's battles. The fifth element of President Kimball's message takes the form of a conditional: if we are righteous God will either protect us from suffering attack or he will fight our battles for us. President Kimball offers no further commentary on this statement, but, since we have already examined all of the scriptures he cites, along with many more,[11] it is not difficult to determine what he intends. In one passage cited by President Kimball (D&C 98:37), for example, the Lord speaks of fighting battles for his people, but he says this only after he speaks of giving them "a command" and justifying them in going to battle themselves. It is one instance of what we have found to be the case generally: it is not unusual to find God saying that he will fight for his people, but he most often (and by far) means by this that he will help them *in* their battles, not that he will substitute for them in conflict.[12]

President Kimball also cites Exodus 14:14, which reports the Lord's promise to the children of Israel that he would fight for them, which he did when he destroyed Pharaoh and his warriors at the Red Sea. In this case, of course, the children of Israel did not have to enter battle at all, as the Lord destroyed the Egyptians on his own. This is a good example of the difference that circumstances seem to make in how the Lord helps people at different times.[13] Later in their history, for instance, the record tells us that the Lord commanded

---

9. For a brief summary of these aspects of Moroni, see the sections "Faithfulness to God," "Offensive vs. Defensive War," and "Minimizing Bloodshed" in Chapter 15.

10. See the full discussion in Chapter 14.

11. See particularly Chapters 6 and 7.

12. See the sections "God's Role in the Battles of the Righteous: The Importance of Context" and "How God Most Often Fights the Battles of the Righteous" in Chapter 7.

13. See the section "What Accounts for the Difference?" in Chapter 7.

the Israelites to go to war and, although he certainly helped them, they were explicitly expected to arm and wage battle themselves. The difference seems to be that in the first instance the Israelites had no chance whatever of prevailing in conflict, while later their capability had greatly increased.

That the promise of God's help (rather than his wholesale substitution for us) is President Kimball's central theme is highlighted by his citing of 2 Nephi 1:7:

> Wherefore, this land is consecrated unto him whom he shall bring. And if it so be that they shall serve him according to the commandments which he hath given, it shall be a land of liberty unto them; wherefore, they shall never be brought down into captivity; if so, it shall be because of iniquity; for if iniquity shall abound cursed shall be the land for their sakes, but unto the righteous it shall be blessed forever.

Here the claim is not that the people in the promised land will never suffer attack if they serve the Lord, nor is it that God will unilaterally fight for them so that they have no need to fight for themselves. The claim is only that, if such people serve the Lord, they "shall never be brought down into captivity." This does not preclude the possibility of assault from enemies (indeed, it almost seems to assume such assault), nor the possibility of people of the land having to fight in order to defend themselves. The passage promises only that if the inhabitants of the promised land are righteous, no enemy force will ever *subjugate* them. This promise is consistent with the dominant theme that appears in scripture: even though God will help the righteous prevail in conflict, he does not typically prevent conflict from occurring in the first place and he does not typically exempt his people from having to expend their own efforts to defend themselves.[14] Again, cases of prevention and exemption are infrequent. Since it seems safe to presume that President Kimball would be aware of the context of these passages and other instances of this sort in scripture, it seems clear that in citing these passages he intends to convey precisely what they convey: since God will help the righteous when they are under threat, it is foolish to ignore the call to repentance and, persisting in an *un*righteous state, to rely on our own devices instead. This is a clear message, and it is consistent with the theme we find in the scriptural canon.[15]

Sixth element: affirmative assignments. Finally, President Kimball teaches that we are to forsake wickedness and the things of the world, build up the Church,

---

14. In addition to Chapters 6 and 7 generally, see particularly the section "The Ancient Promise to Nephi" in Chapter 6.

15. This is especially evident in the Book of Mormon. See, for example, the section "A Genuine Theme Regarding Book of Mormon Violence: The Ancient Promise to Nephi" in Chapter 9.

live the gospel, and, in an approach reminiscent of Ammon (who entered enemy lands to do nothing other than share the gospel with the Lamanites) take the gospel to our enemies so that they are no longer our enemies. The fruits of Ammon's efforts were momentous; indeed, he and his brethren succeeded in converting thousands of Lamanites to the gospel, making them fellow-citizens with the Saints. And, according to President Kimball, this is the model for what should always be first in our minds regarding those we consider to be our adversaries.

A Pacifist Statement?

It should be noted that Eugene England approaches President Kimball's remarks differently than how they are presented above. In England's words, President Kimball's message "states about as clearly as I can imagine it being stated that the ethic of Christ is pacifist."[16]

But for two primary reasons this interpretation seems to be a plain misreading. First, to say that President Kimball's message is pacifist overlooks the context and circumstances of the various passages that President Kimball cites. This is an oversight by England that certainly cannot be attributed to President Kimball himself: what are the odds that *he* is reading the passages out of context or without consideration of the total weight of scripture on the topic of war?

Second, if England thinks President Kimball is genuinely teaching pacifism, he is committed to thinking that President Kimball is teaching what no other latter-day prophet, including Joseph Smith, has taught, and also that he is teaching the opposite of what Gordon B. Hinckley later taught. Indeed, it would be the opposite of how the actions of prophetic figures, and even the Lord himself, are consistently depicted in the Book of Mormon.[17] It seems improbable, to say the least, that any of these contradictions between President Kimball and other prophetic leaders, not to mention the Lord, could be the case. Much less does it seem that all of them could obtain. Nevertheless, this is what England's reading entails, and it does so without a bare acknowledgment of the contradictions, much less any attempt to reconcile them.

---

16. Eugene England, "The Prince of Peace," 243.

17. This is true regarding Nephi, King Benjamin, Alma, Lachoneus, Gidgiddoni, Mormon, and Moroni, for example, as well as of the Lord himself who, the record tells us, actually helped such leaders in their conflicts and instructed them to defend themselves in the first place. All of this has been covered at length, particularly in Chapters 6 through 11, and recall that we have encountered no argument that succeeds in invalidating these reports about the Lord's involvement (see particularly the section "Examining the Corollary of the Narrative Approach: The Example of the Lord's Own Conduct" in Chapter 8).

Necessary and Sufficient Conditions

In understanding President Kimball's message it helps to keep in mind that his broad audience is the world at large, and that the overall context of the message is his worry about the wickedness in which the world is engulfed. It "appalls and frightens" him, he tells us. Given this state of things it is no wonder that President Kimball would emphasize forsaking evil and turning to God, particularly regarding matters of defense. This is precisely the path that Captain Moroni pursued.

But it is reasonable to conclude from this only that in this message President Kimball considers righteousness to be a *necessary* element of national defense, not that he considers it to be sufficient. The process of repenting and growing in faithfulness is a central feature of what must be done when confronted with danger, but that does not mean it is all that must be done. This is easily understood from the context of the passages President Kimball cites, as well as from a host of other scriptural episodes and teachings regarding war that we have seen.[18] England fails to appreciate this, and reads President Kimball's message as pacifist in character because he thinks President Kimball is identifying turning to God as sufficient rather than necessary for national defense. This fundamental error of confusing necessary and sufficient conditions is, it seems, a central reason for England's misinterpretation of President Kimball's statement.

A Mistaken Assumption

However, beneath this mistake of imagining righteousness to be sufficient for defense lies a deeper error. This is the assumption that righteousness is sufficient for defense precisely because *God* will do all of the fighting on behalf of those who are righteous. After all, if we are to avoid destruction, and if we need to do nothing more than maintain righteousness in order to assure this, then the Lord must make up the difference. Thus, England tells us that according to President Kimball the "alternative to violence" is the "nonviolent direct action" of teaching the gospel and of "acting mercifully, constructively . . . in all we do to others" and emphasizes President Kimball's questions: "What are we to fear when the Lord is with us? Can we not take the Lord at his word and exercise a particle of faith in him?"[19] The idea seems to be that people who are righteous have done enough already and that, if they have "a particle of faith," they will not need to defend themselves but can simply wait upon the Lord to protect them.

We have already seen, however, that this assumption about merely waiting on the Lord is mistaken: the passages President Kimball cites indicate that

---

18. See Chapters 6 and 7 and the section "Military Defense" in Chapter 15.
19. Eugene England, "The Prince of Peace," 244.

this was not his meaning. The idea that the righteous can simply rely on God for defense is false and thus, contrary to England's apparent line of thinking, it provides no basis either for embracing a pacifist approach to conflict or for applying a pacifist reading to President Kimball.

A Self-Contradiction and Its By-Products

Nevertheless, it is important to notice England's evident assumption because it raises a significant question about this kind of view regarding violence in general.[20] Again, in emphasizing certain parts of President Kimball's message, England seems to think that we can be pacifists because God will destroy our enemies *for* us. But that raises the question of why we should think God's involvement makes a difference. If we are serious about rejecting violence, what moral difference does it make *who* performs it?[21]

To see the force of this question, recall the well-known example of Enoch. It is apparent from the record that God unilaterally protected Enoch and his people from enemies who came against them (Moses 7:13). Nevertheless, even though Enoch and his people did not physically, and personally, attack their assailants, their resort to God's miraculous interventions through faith had exactly the same effect. Enemies no doubt perished as Enoch "spake the word of the Lord" and caused the earth to tremble, mountains to move, and rivers to turn out of their course. Those adversaries thus ended up just as dead and terrorized as if an army of a hundred thousand warriors had descended upon them.[22] The only difference was that Enoch's people did not visit this destruction on their assailants personally. But it is difficult to see how this made much difference to those enemies. Could they have cared?

It is not obvious, then, why we should find satisfaction in the notion that if we possess sufficient righteousness God will destroy our enemies for us. That does not create any actual difference for those enemies. Moreover, their

---

20. As we saw in Chapter 7, Nibley also emphasizes the matter of God fighting the battles of the righteous, so the difficulties identified in this section apply equally to him. (To all appearances he also reads President Kimball's message regarding military matters in the same way England reads it. See his "We Will Still Weep for Zion," 366–67.)

21. It is important to see that this is a question of moral difference. After all, the pacifist view being examined here is not that God will fight battles for the righteous simply to spare their lives or, for that matter, to spare them the messiness of battle. Pacifism is the view that such violence is morally wrong, and thus God's fighting battles for the righteous is valuable precisely because it spares the righteous from performing such action. If we valued God's protection solely (for example) because it would preserve our lives and spare us the adversity of conflict, then our motivation would not be a *moral* rejection of conflict and thus would not be pacifist in character.

22. For those who imagine that lives were not lost due to these events, simply substitute a report such as God's destruction of Pharaoh and his armies at the Red Sea (Ex. 14).

deaths are still a result of *our* action even in that case: we actively exercised faith and prayed for such an intervention. Thus, regardless of whether we destroy our enemies personally, or God destroys them for us, the effect is the same and so is our intention. This makes it difficult to see any meaningful distinction between the two cases. What is the moral difference between attacking someone with a sword and attacking them with a *mountain*?

An argument for pacifism that relies on God's defense seems, therefore, to amount to a self-contradiction. If it is wrong to destroy enemies by the power of the sword, then, to be consistent, it should also be wrong to exercise faith so that those same enemies are destroyed by the power of God. And if it is right to exercise faith so that enemies are destroyed by the power of God, then, to be consistent, it should also be right to destroy those same enemies by the power of the sword. The cases seem to rise or fall together. The idea that God will fight battles for his people (specifically so that they won't have to exercise violence themselves) appears to end in contradiction. It is vacuous as a moral argument for pacifism.

By-products. Moreover, this view further appears to entail that God himself must do wrong. After all, if, as one part of the argument maintains, it is wrong to destroy our enemies with the sword, and if, as seems to follow from this, it is also wrong to destroy those enemies even through faith, then it would seem that God himself must do wrong if he responds to our faith and destroys our enemies for us. That is what this type of view wants him to do, and it is what he did in Enoch's case. But if it is wrong to exercise faith in order to bring about the destruction of our enemies, then it appears that God must be wrong if he answers that faith by carrying out our wishes.[23]

Thus, although we might not see it, in the world created by the pacifist assumption about God's defense, one upshot is that we seem to avoid unrighteous conduct of our own by calling upon *God* to perform unrighteous conduct. We want him to do exactly what part of the argument entails would be wrong for him to do. Furthermore, in an even greater irony, it is precisely

---

23. One way to try to get around this difficulty would be to argue that while it is wrong for humans to perform violent action, it is not wrong for God to do so, and that is the moral difference between the two cases. The most obvious problem with this type of reply, however, is that it fails to account for the reports of God's active support of his people's defense of themselves, not to mention of his explicit command that they do so (see Chapters 6 and 7 in particular). If it is wrong for humans to commit violent action, then it must be wrong for God to command them to do it. And it must also be wrong for him to then actively *help* them do so. Far from getting around the difficulty in this way of thinking, such an approach simply reintroduces it. (Again, recall that efforts to discredit reports of the Lord's involvement in conflict do not succeed. See note 17 above.)

because we are righteous that we expect him to be unrighteous for us (recall that righteousness is what qualifies us for God's help in the first place). In such a conceptual world, it seems, our righteousness requires God to be unrighteous, and his unrighteousness is morally valuable because it allows us to maintain our righteousness.

In addition to vacuity, contradictions also yield absurdities. To all appearances that is the case here.

As a final matter, it is useful to notice an inconsistency in England's thinking about God's nature. In his pacifist reading of President Kimball, for instance, England depends on God to be a being of violence: he assumes that we need not exercise violence ourselves because God will do that for us. In another argument, however (and in the same essay), he specifically repudiates the idea that God is ever violent.[24] Thus, in his reading of President Kimball England relies on God to be exactly what he elsewhere expressly denies him to be.[25] England's efforts to reject violence seem to force him, unwittingly, to hold different views of God at different times for different arguments.

In the end, all of these considerations indicate that there is no reason to accept a pacifist reading of President Kimball's message. There is actually every reason to reject it.

Unity of the Key Texts

The last three chapters have taken us through an examination of five key texts that, together, seem to capture all the major scriptural teachings regarding war. In addition to providing a comprehensive perspective, these texts are also consistent with one another. They are unified.

Part of this unity is a function of straightforward logical relationships. The Sermon on the Mount, for example, presupposes circumstances of life in which it is possible to live as the Sermon directs, such as expressing devotion to God, observing religious practices, and demonstrating concern for one's brothers and sisters. In presupposing such circumstances of life the Sermon implies that it is permissible to resist regimes that would make the realization of such circumstances impossible. Similarly, Captain Moroni's diligence in defending not only the lives, but also the religious rights of his people, doc-

---

24. Eugene England, "The Prince of Peace," particularly pages 231–35 and 243–44.

25. This discrepancy would not be a problem if it reflected a simple change of mind, of course; it is perfectly legitimate for authors to modify their thinking. But that is not the case here, since, as mentioned, England includes these inconsistent views in the same essay. That makes it difficult to see this as a case of altered judgment rather than of simply failing to notice the contradiction. Regarding England's general repudiation of God's violence, see the sections "Old Testament Violence and the Prince of Peace" and "God's Violence and Treating People as Ends" in Chapter 11.

trinally presupposes the existence and importance of those rights and simultaneously implies the necessity of living at the standard those rights represent. And so forth. All of the texts share similar logical connections.

More important is the spiritual harmony displayed by these various teachings. This is evident, for example, when we notice that Alma 48 and the Sermon on the Mount invite us to see Captain Moroni in identical ways. Read casually, of course, the Sermon on the Mount (unlike Alma 48) might seem to suggest that Moroni was actually similar to Amalickiah. Since both men resorted to violence they seem to be importantly alike; indeed, on such a reading Captain Moroni seems to resemble Amalickiah far more than he resembles Christ. But when we recognize the key distinctions discussed in Chapter 14, we appreciate that the Sermon on the Mount does not suggest Moroni and Amalickiah to be importantly alike at all. That view misconceives Moroni, Amalickiah, *and* Christ. It also misconceives the Sermon on the Mount. As seen in Chapter 15, the record depicts Moroni helping defend his people from being murdered with the very quality of heart required by that discourse, whereas it depicts Amalickiah as one of the murderers against whom the Nephites required defense and who had nothing like the heart taught by the Lord on that occasion.

Thus, although they have different emphases, Alma 48 and the Sermon on the Mount do not compete. The principles of one do not acclaim Moroni while the principles of the other condemn him. Far from it. The depiction of Moroni actually manifests both sets of teachings because those sets of teachings manifest each other. Indeed, Alma 48 *exhibits* part of what we learn in the Sermon on the Mount. Moroni was a man of Christ in every essential respect, Amalickiah in none, and both texts reveal this.

The same is true about these teachings in regard to Nephi. Despite what some accounts might suppose, the Sermon on the Mount invites us to see Nephi in every respect the same way that Alma 48 invites us to see him. The principles of both texts acclaim him to be exactly the consummate disciple and prophet of God that the record depicts him to be. Whether regarding Captain Moroni, Nephi, or anyone else, the Sermon on the Mount does not yield verdicts that conflict with Alma 48 because it does not teach principles that conflict with Alma 48. This is apparent when we keep in mind the distinctions introduced in Chapter 14.

The same deep harmony is evident when we compare President Hinckley's discourses with President Kimball's. When President Kimball cites the particular scriptural passages he chooses regarding war, it is obvious that he acknowledges and assumes exactly what President Hinckley acknowledges and assumes—namely, that righteousness is a necessary condition for national defense, but not a sufficient one. Just as in the case of Alma 48 and the Sermon on the Mount, the emphases in these leaders' statements might be different, but the points of view are the same.

The same connectedness seems apparent in every direction. While the Sermon on the Mount, Alma 48, the messages of President Hinckley, and the message of President Kimball all emphasize different elements of the gospel, they also all complement and exemplify one another. President Kimball's teachings do not yield different consequences than the principles found in Alma 48, and neither of President Hinckley's messages conflicts with the Sermon on the Mount. And so forth. All of the texts cohere both logically and spiritually in a single gospel point of view; they presuppose, illuminate, and even instantiate one another.[26] Such harmony might not be obvious when these texts are considered only in broad outline, but when we look a bit more deeply, as attempted in the last three chapters, their symmetry actually seems conspicuous.[27] As a result of this, and of their comprehensiveness, these teachings help provide the basis for constructing an LDS framework regarding war.

---

26. The same is true regarding the books of scripture generally. As I said earlier, I emphasize these five main texts because they appear to capture what the canon as a whole teaches regarding war. Also, while it would be possible to examine every connection among these texts, the examples I raise seem sufficient to illustrate the point.

27. Since each set of teachings was examined independently of the others, this symmetry is not circular. For example, pacifist readings of President Kimball and the Sermon on the Mount have been abandoned not because of a prior commitment to make them conform to the other texts, but because of their own factual and logical deficiencies. These pacifist interpretations fail on their own merits. Read free of such mistakes, the teachings of the Sermon on the Mount and President Kimball synchronize naturally with the other texts, and participate equally with them in their collective illumination of this gospel topic.

Chapter 17

An LDS Framework Regarding War

If we distill the themes seen in the five LDS texts from the previous chapters, if we keep in mind the lessons learned in examining the many arguments for pacifism, and if we combine all of this with important elements of the formal just-war theory with which we began, then it seems possible to create a workable framework for an LDS view of war. Here are the elements:

THE REQUIREMENT OF RIGHTEOUSNESS

1. The most important requirement for any society is to be righteous—to be devoted to following God
2. A society that is not righteous must repent and begin seeking righteousness[1]
3. As part of this righteousness such a society (a) must seek to bring its enemies to Christ, and (b) must never provoke or seek conflict, but endeavor vigorously to achieve peace and avoid war

CONDITIONS THAT JUSTIFY WAR AND QUALIFY FOR GOD'S HELP

4. If such a society:
    (a) is ultimately compelled, as a final resort, to fight in defense of important human values against the aggression of evil leaders;[2]
    (b) fights only to defend those important human values and not to achieve any unworthy purpose;
    (c) stands a reasonable chance of success in defending itself; and
    (d) can reach a reasonable judgment that the benefits of waging a war of defense are proportional to the costs of doing so;[3] then,

---

1. Recall that, except at the very end, when the Nephites were unrighteous and found themselves under threat, they repented and remembered the Lord. See, for instance, the section "A Genuine Theme Regarding Book of Mormon Violence: The Ancient Promise to Nephi" in Chapter 9.

2. These values include life, family, liberty, freedom from tyranny and oppression, and exercise of devotion to God.

3. Although 3(c) and 3(d) are most explicitly evident in just-war theory, they are also apparent in the general history of Book of Mormon conflict. Regarding 3(c) recall that Limhi and Alma the elder both followed stealth strategies to avoid conflict, and that this was preferable in their cases partly because they stood no real chance of prevailing militarily; see the section "Limhi and Alma vs. Other Nephite Leaders" in Chapter 10. Regarding 3(d), note that implicit in every justification of war in the Book of Mormon, including the Lord's, is the judgment that going to war in that situation was worth it. The justifications assume proportionality. (Some of these justifications are treated

(e) that society may use military means in its defense, and it will qualify to enjoy God's help in doing so (in rare cases, he may even fight the necessary battles unilaterally)[4]

CONDITIONS THAT GOVERN THE CONDUCT OF WAR AND QUALIFY FOR GOD'S HELP

5. Engaged in such defensive conflict, the society must:
    (a) foremost, continue to repent and to recognize and embrace its dependence on God and the necessity of faithfulness to him;
    (b) maintain a peaceable heart, after the manner of the Sermon on the Mount;
    (c) spill as little blood as necessary;
    (d) aim only at legitimate military targets, minimizing civilian suffering and risk—including assuming greater personal risk in order to do so;
    (e) not use weapons that are intrinsically heinous—that cause mutilation and suffering beyond the need simply to *stop* the aggressors;

---

explicitly in Chapter 7, but they also appear in Chapters 6 through 12 *passim*.) Recall, from Chapter 1, that there is no formula in just-war theory that determines the exact threshold at which the chance of success in resisting aggression ceases to be "reasonable" (3c); nor is there a universal formula for determining what is and is not proportional in weighing the benefits of war against its costs (3d); see the section "Jus ad Bellum: The Justice of War" in Chapter 1. Reasonable people can and will disagree on such matters. The key idea is that these issues require consideration; they cannot be ignored. Absent revelation that would override these principles, there is at least some point at which the prospects of succeeding in resisting aggression are so slim that it would be wrong to impose the ravages of war on one's populace to do so. Similarly, there are at least some circumstances in which the benefits of waging a war of defense are not sufficient to outweigh the costs of engaging in such war. In addition to their explicit codification in just-war theory, the examples of Limhi and Alma also at least suggest both of these principles. Since not all defense is necessarily justified defense, considerations of risk and proportionality cannot be disregarded a priori.

4. As seen particularly in Chapters 6 and 7, and as reviewed in Chapter 16, qualifying for the Lord's help does not remotely entail exemption from conflict. For reasons of his own the Lord chooses how and to what degree he will supply assistance. The Ammonites, for example, obviously qualified for the Lord's help, and yet he permitted them to be slaughtered on two separate occasions before directing that they flee for their safety (Alma 27:11–12). This exemplifies the Lord's general pattern of providing help to his people while simultaneously requiring them to make substantial sacrifices of their own. While those who are righteous, or who are repenting, qualify for the Lord's help, that help comes in his way and at his time and might not be evident at all to many people. Zerahemnah, for example, could not detect the Lord's hand in the Nephites' success against his aggression even though it was obvious to Captain Moroni (Alma 44:3–10).

(f) engage only in military tactics whose benefits are proportional to their costs;

(g) maintain its righteousness of intent in fighting; and

(h) end the fighting the minute peace and freedom can be secured without fighting.

This framework is obviously non-pacifist. It acknowledges the necessity of war in particular circumstances, but it outlines the parameters of righteousness, repentance, motive, quality of heart, and conduct that govern both the entrance into war and the execution of it. Although we have focused on five major texts, this brief outline combines all of the scriptural teachings considered over the course of this volume, as well as the formal just-war framework treated in Chapter 1. The outcome is a model for thinking about war that expresses what appears to be a genuine LDS outlook. No doubt others can and will supply improvements, but it does not seem likely that a thoroughly satisfactory model will differ too significantly from this approach, at least in fundamental structure.

Zion and Non-Zion Societies

This framework assumes a more-or-less-Zion society. This is a society in which the citizens are devoted to God, keep the commandments in their fullness, are united, live with purity of heart, and, through the law of consecration, have no poor among them.[5] Only a society that approaches these characteristics can fully satisfy the spiritual requirements of this framework regarding war.[6]

---

5. Familiar passages about Zion include Moses 7:16–21 and D&C 97:21, and, although the Book of Mormon does not so designate it, it is also reasonable to attach the label *Zion* to the society described in 4 Nephi 1:1–18. Although it is doubtful that any community in this last dispensation has fully qualified as a Zion society, these scriptural examples paint a picture of the ideal we seek, at least in broad outline. The most in-depth doctrinal analysis of a Zion society, including the role of the law of consecration in Zion's operations, is Hyrum L. Andrus, *Doctrines of the Kingdom*. In regard to the role of the law of consecration, in particular, it is important to avoid a simplistic understanding. That law has multiple dimensions, and only one of them is the end state of economic equality. It is a mistake, therefore, to reduce the whole law to this single aspect and to conclude that, in the world at large, various economic policies that seek equality are themselves approximations of the law of consecration. Nibley, for one, assumes they are, but this is clearly mistaken. For more on this see my "Do Liberal Economic Policies Approximate the Law of Consecration?"

6. It is difficult to see how a different type of society could meet the criteria of faithfulness to God, overt repentance, dependence upon God, the effort to bring enemies to Christ, maintaining peaceable hearts even in the midst of war, and sustaining righteousness of intent throughout the duration of conflict—all of which are elements of this framework.

It thus seems that (all else being equal) only a Zion society will qualify to enjoy the fullness of God's favor and help in defending itself from hostile forces. Nevertheless, even societies that fall short of Zion can still satisfy the spiritual conditions to some extent, particularly as they repent and begin to seek righteousness, and they can actually meet the criteria of the standard just-war framework fully. As a result, even clearly non-Zion societies are justified in waging war if (1) they are doing so only in defense of important human values and (2) they are abiding by the other (i.e., the non-spiritual) principles of the framework. As the Book of Mormon attests, and as we have seen in earlier chapters, the Lord justifies societies in defending themselves from destruction even when they live below the level of righteousness that he desires. And as they repent, such societies then qualify for the Lord's help in their efforts to defend themselves from such destruction.

The United States

So how should we think about the United States in particular? We are far from a Zion society, so how should a Latter-day Saint think about the national security of the United States from a gospel perspective? Here is Valerie Hudson's approach:

> Accept with me the premise that the state of America's gospel-defined security is not great: there are many good people in America, but the amount of societal evil in which they have to live increases almost daily . . . Given this assumption, what should American national security objectives be? A two-pronged strategy is called for: (1) domestic reformation and (2) a foreign policy strategy based on the parable of the unjust steward (Luke 16), that preserves the nation while we pursue objective number one.[7]

In Hudson's telling of the parable from Luke 16, the unjust steward has lost the trust of his lord, but he at least manages to act wisely "according to the wisdom of the world," and is actually commended by his lord for doing so. All of this leads to the moral Hudson draws: "If you cannot be just, better to be unjust and worldly wise than unjust and stupid."[8] Hudson then tells us that the United States is in the same position:

> I believe the Lord's trust is not with our nation because of our society's present state. Yet we are still very powerful, and we should parlay that power into temporal security for our nation in the hopes that domestic reform efforts will prove fruitful and reestablish the Lord's support. God may currently perceive us

---

7. Valerie M. Hudson, "What Should America's National Security Objectives Be?: The Problems and Possibilities of an LDS Perspective," 31–32.

8. Ibid., 33.

as unjust, but that is no reason for us to be stupid. If we are left to rely on our own strength, then let us do so with all prudence and wisdom.[9]

This seems exactly right. In Nephite society, men of God implored the people both to repent and to defend themselves. The highest priority was spiritual, but they worked on that while they simultaneously created a defense. In our time the requirement is the same: to maintain a stout defense at the same time we try to bring about a spiritual change in the national character, which is the change that matters most. Such an interest in defense, though a longstanding common-sense notion, is reinforced by careful research regarding war and its causes. In a lengthy examination of the conditions that most often lead to conflict, one scholar concludes that the risk is highest when a state believes that conquest of another state would be easy. Though other variables influence the likelihood of war as well, the single greatest cause is the belief by a state that it possesses superior power and resolve in comparison to its adversaries, and that its prospects in waging war are therefore highly promising. When a state views its adversary as formidable, on the other hand, it is far less likely to seek conflict, or even to risk it.[10]

A Multi-Faceted, but Single, Gospel Outlook

The framework outlined above appears to establish a sound way of looking at war. No nation satisfies all of these principles, but, as mentioned, to the degree that states at least fulfill the criteria of the standard just-war framework, they are justified in defending themselves militarily. And of course, the closer a state approaches a Zion condition and satisfies the criteria of the full gospel framework outlined above, the more fully it qualifies for God's help in doing so.

A structure like this also helps us see, again, how different expressions of the gospel coalesce into a single comprehensive view. Just as we should expect, and as discussed in Chapter 16, we see that the teachings and examples of the Sermon on the Mount, Alma 48, President Hinckley, and President Kimball all mesh perfectly with one another at a deep level. While each emphasizes different aspects of the gospel, these elements are mutually illuminating rather than contradictory, and cohere in a single, but multi-faceted, gospel outlook. These, along with appropriate elements of just-war theory, comprise a general perspective on war that would seem to address the concerns of Latter-day Saints.[11]

---

9. Ibid.
10. See Stephen Van Evera, *Causes of War: Power and the Roots of Conflict*.
11. Although I have not attempted to demonstrate this, even the classical elements of just-war theory (e.g., that we are to minimize civilian suffering and risk, use methods of defense that are not inherently heinous, and so forth) are derivable from scriptural teachings. It seems intuitive how rules of this sort follow naturally from pronouncements

President David O. McKay

All of this also helps us appreciate why there is no actual inconsistency when President David O. McKay, by his own admission, seems to be contradicting himself in an address when he insists at length that war is completely incompatible with Christ's teachings, but also emphasizes his support for the United State's engagement in World War II.[12] He says, in making the transition from the first point to the second, that "in the face of all this, I shall seem inconsistent."[13]

But President McKay is obviously correct to say that this only "seems" inconsistent. This is made obvious by his statement in the same address that there are "two conditions which may justify a truly Christian man to enter—mind you, I say *enter, not begin*—a war," which he then goes on to identify.[14] This statement tells us that President McKay condemns both starting war and entering it too easily when provoked. But he does not condemn waging war to protect life and other paramount human values. Thus President McKay is not contradicting himself in the slightest. He is simply drawing attention to two different aspects of a single, but comprehensive gospel view. We are forbidden to be aggressors (as well to enter war casually), but we are nevertheless permitted, as genuinely threatened and defensive-only victims, to protect ourselves from the ruthless assaults of others. To see the two parts of his message accurately is to see that they are actually part of the same message; they are just different features of a single, but multi-faceted, gospel outlook that recognizes and assumes important moral distinctions. It is also worth noting that President McKay strongly emphasizes the necessity of righteousness in his attitudes on war, identifying it as the "key" to reaching and maintaining world peace.[15]

---

such as "thou shalt love thy neighbor as thyself" and "all things whatsoever ye would that men should do to you, do ye even so to them" (Matt. 22:39; 7:12) when they must be applied in extreme circumstances involving evil designs, aggression, brutality, and murder. Although it does not seem necessary to bring additional passages to bear on this topic, and to provide a tight step-by-step argument to track the connections between scripture and such rules of war, it would be possible to do so.

12. See David O. McKay, "The Church and the Present War." This discourse, delivered by President McKay when he was second counselor in the First Presidency, was discussed in Chapter 12 in examining Eugene England's views on international conflict.

13. Loyd Ericson remarks on this matter in his "Eugene England's Theology of Peace," 178. Robert Hellebrand does the same in his paper, "General Conference Addresses during Times of War," 133.

14. These are: "(1) An attempt to dominate and to deprive another of his free agency, and, (2) Loyalty to his country. Possibly there is a third, viz., Defense of a weak nation that is being unjustly crushed by a strong, ruthless one." The emphasis in the text is his.

15. David O. McKay, "Righteousness Key to World Peace."

In all these various dimensions President McKay simply reflects the mutually reinforcing teachings of the texts we have considered, including those of both President Hinckley and President Kimball. President McKay's discourse is consistent with the larger LDS framework outlined above, and indeed is a partial expression of it.

Conclusion

The ultimate purpose of creating a model for thinking about war is to help us evaluate future incidents. It is valuable to have readily available a conceptual framework that indicates the questions to ask and the matters to weigh in judging whether we want to support conflict in one circumstance or another, or whether we want to resist it. But a model of this sort is also beneficial in evaluating the past, since we naturally want to identify which wars have been justified and which have not been over the course of time. However, the task of examining particular wars in this way is best left to another occasion, since this kind of factual examination requires considerable care and space of its own.[16] Still, an overall gospel framework for evaluating war, once we know the facts, is an important part of the equation, and that, so it seems, we are able to identify.

It is only in appreciating the full scope of scriptural teachings and episodes that we can begin to approach what Latter-day Saints most desire on this topic: an understanding of the Lord's attitude toward war. Of course, it is unlikely that anyone writing on the topic of violence can boast of complete comprehension of the Lord's disposition; nevertheless, having examined numerous pacifist arguments and searched the scriptural canon in some degree of detail, of one thing, at least, we can be certain: It was nothing close to an aberration when the Lord instructed the Nephites to defend their families "even unto bloodshed." That command, when understood in all of its dimensions, expresses a genuine, profound, and conceptually rich scriptural principle.

The framework sketched above is one attempt to capture this principle. To the degree it does so it resolves a tension that seems inherent in Christian discipleship: Since the Lord abhors violence, how, even in self-defense, can we consider employing it? The tension feels genuine because, while the scrip-

---

16. This is because so much of our judgment in any individual case depends on a huge number of facts, and discerning those facts is an exacting and slippery undertaking at best, regarding both the circumstances leading up to any given war and the actual execution of it. Short of such analysis, the most we can do is to construct hypothetical conditionals: "*If* a . . . z are the facts, *then* this war was (was not) justified." The framework outlined here helps us determine the consequent of this conditional, but not the antecedent: determining "a . . . z" requires study of its own.

tural abhorrence of violence is real, so are the scriptural cases of God's people righteously defending themselves.

What we can see at this point, however, is that this question actually presents us with a false dichotomy and that the tension is a mirage. Various answers to this question are wrong because the question itself is wrong. It harbors the assumption that all violence is morally equivalent and that all of it is abhorrent for that reason. But we have seen repeatedly that this is mistaken. The violence of aggressors is an obvious mistreatment of those they assault; it is a violation of their rights. But victims do not mistreat their attackers; they cannot violate their assailants' rights because those assailants have already forfeited their rights. Preventing them from committing murder does not mistreat them.

Thus not all violence is immoral. It is all abhorrent, of course, but not for that reason. And this means that we are actually faced with a different question: Given that we may defend ourselves from violent mistreatment, how can we do so without our own violence being a mistreatment? How do we keep it from being *morally* abhorrent?

Latter-day Saints find the answer in the gospel of Jesus Christ. In this plan the Lord transforms our souls as we yield our hearts to him. Living and growing in this newness of life, we do not hate our enemies even when we must thwart them. We do not seek vengeance, but only to secure peace and, in every way we can, to share with them what we have found. This is the way of the Lord. It is the way followed by Nephi and Mormon and Moroni, all of whom cherished the Savior, and all of whom maintained their devotion to him and to their Lamanite brethren even while forced to fight. The framework presented above simply attempts to capture such dimensions and circumstances of genuine discipleship. It is one more step toward an LDS theory of war.

Appendices

Appendix 1

Considering the Size of the Ammonite Population

Chapter 4 explores the Ammonites' place in Lamanite society, and learning what we can about their population size helps in some measure to do this. Although we do not know much about their size or how large a fraction they were of the total Lamanite society, it is possible to draw some broad conclusions based on clues in the text.

To begin, it appears that Lamanite society was organized into various lands and cities with each land presided over by a territorial king, who in turn was superintended by the king of the entire Lamanite population. For example, we know that Lamoni and Antiomno were kings of separate Lamanite lands (Alma 17:21 and 20:4), while king Lamoni's father was king "over all the land" (Alma 20:8; 22:1) and had power to restrict or expand, at least to some degree, the rights of the other kings (Alma 20:24, 26; 21:21). Indeed, Lamoni's father had sufficient authority that he was able, following his conversion, to grant the sons of Mosiah protection from Lamanite persecution "in whatsoever place they should be, in any part of their land" (Alma 23:1) so that the word of God "might go forth throughout *all* the land" (Alma 23:3).

In this context we are told that "thousands" of Lamanites were converted to the Lord in the lands of Ishmael, Middoni, Shilom, and Shemlon, as well as in the cities of Nephi, Lemuel, and Shimnilom (Alma 23:5, 8–13).[1] The king of the whole land, Lamoni's father, was among these converts (Alma 22). Those who were not converted included the Amalekites[2] and the Amulonites

---

1. After referring to some of these entities as "lands" and to some of them as "cities," the record summarizes by saying that "these are the names of the *cities* of the Lamanites which were converted unto the Lord" (Alma 23:13). The listing itself suggests that "city" and "land" were different geographical categories, but the summary suggests that they were either identical or closely related. The relationship appears to be similar to the land/city designation that Nibley first identified fifty years ago. See Hugh Nibley, *An Approach to the Book of Mormon*, 100–102.

2. These were arguably the Amlicites, the Nephite dissenters who waged war against the Nephites in the fifth year of the reign of the judges (circa 87 BC), were defeated by Alma's army, and then, while retreating, joined forces with an attacking Lamanite army (see Alma 2). They appear in the record again, beginning in Alma 21, in Mormon's recounting of Aaron's missionary labors among the Lamanites and where the record refers to them as "Amalekites." Christopher Conkling draws attention to

(both of whom were Nephite dissenters), as well as all of the Lamanites "in that part of the land wheresoever [the Amalekites and Amulonites] dwelt . . . in all their villages and all their cities" (Alma 23:14); these included the lands of Amulon, Helam, and Jerusalem (Alma 24:1).

A quick count tells us that four "lands" and three "cities" of the Lamanites were converted to the Lord while three "lands" (including all the villages and cities associated with them) remained unconverted. Although Mormon does not say that this is an exhaustive list of all the Lamanite groups, this comparison might suggest that the converts were at least a significant portion of the overall Lamanite populace, and perhaps even a majority. But we should not be too quick to conclude this. After all, Mormon does no more here than list those who were converted and then simply report that all of the Nephite dissenters (and all of the Lamanites who lived near them) remained *un*converted. But this says nothing of any Lamanites who did not live in proximity to the Nephite dissenters and who also remained unconverted. For all we know that number could have been large; the record simply does not tell us. It is also worth noting that a comparison of "lands" and "cities" is not by itself a sound measure of population numbers in any event, since lands and cities can vary widely in population. So we must be careful not to conclude too much from Mormon's comparison. The most we can say is that the converts appear to have been at least a significant portion of the total Lamanite population.

Could they have been as large as half the Lamanite total—or at least something close to that? On the face of it the answer would seem to be no. After all, if we suppose that the Ammonites comprised half of the total Lamanite population, then their abandonment of enmity toward the Nephites (beginning in Alma 23) would have reduced the Lamanite threat to the Nephites by that same half. But if the size of the Lamanite threat was reduced by that much and only a few years later they still came close to capturing all the Nephite lands in the ensuing wars (Alma 43–62), then it is difficult to explain why the Lamanites did not have more success in attacking the Nephites previously (i.e., while the Ammonites were still united with them and thus

---

Royal Skousen's work, which shows how the change in spelling likely occurred during the transcribing and printing of the Book of Mormon. See J. Christopher Conkling, "Alma's Enemies: The Case of the Lamanites, Amlicites, and Mysterious Amalekites." In his Yale edition, Skousen places 'Amlicites' wherever the term 'Amalekites' appears in other editions of the Book of Mormon, including the 1981 imprint. (See Skousen, *The Book of Mormon*, 356 ff.) For the sake of convenience, I will use 'Amalekites,' since that is the expression most familiar to readers.

while their numbers were twice as large).³ Why would the Lamanites be more successful with smaller numbers than they had been with larger?

The answer is found in Nephite dissensions. The Book of Mormon tells us that at least by the time of Alma 43 Nephite dissenters who had joined the Lamanites and swollen their ranks were nearly as numerous as the *whole* remaining Nephite population.⁴ So by the time the war began in Alma 43 it was the Nephite population that, over time and through attrition, had been practically halved in size. This obviously made the Nephites more vulnerable than they had been in previous years and naturally explains the pattern we see of Lamanite success against them. Furthermore, because the infusion of Nephite dissenters was so significant, that infusion would have offset the loss of the Lamanite converts even if that loss was large. Therefore, there is no reason (based on the Lamanites' success in war, at any rate) to suppose that the Lamanite converts must have been a small fraction of the total Lamanite population.

Other clues we have regarding the Ammonite numbers are the "thousand and five" who were slain the first time the Ammonites refused to defend themselves from attack (Alma 24:22) and the "two thousand and sixty" sons of the Ammonites who were of military age some years later (Alma 57:19). Though we are not told how many were not slain, we could still try to extrapolate population sizes based on such figures. Such calculations are complex, however, and

---

3. I am indebted to Kimberly White for drawing this question to my attention. Regarding the Lamanites' repeated attempts to destroy the Nephites, see the section "What Were the Lamanites Like Before Their Conversion?" in Chapter 4.

4. Royal Skousen's work on the earliest Book of Mormon manuscripts provides clarification here. The current edition of the Book of Mormon tells us that the Lamanites at this time "were a compound of Laman and Lemuel and the sons of Ishmael and all those which had dissented from the Nephites, which were Amlicites and Zoramites and the descendants of the priests of Noah," and adds that "those *descendants* were as numerous nearly as were the Nephites" (Alma 43:13–14). This appears to tell us that the descendants of the priests of Noah, by themselves, were nearly equal in number to the total Nephite population. But if this were the case the Nephites would have been astronomically outnumbered by the Lamanites—a population which included the Lamanites proper, *plus* all of the Nephite dissenters, *plus* all of the descendants of the priests of Noah (which, again, by themselves nearly equaled the total Nephite population, according to this reading). This of course makes the Nephite number implausibly small—even absurdly so. The earliest manuscripts, however, reveal that the text should say that "those *dissenters* were as numerous nearly as were the Nephites": in the transmission process the word 'descendants' was mistakenly used instead of 'dissenters.' This of course changes the scale and meaning of the text significantly: it was *all* of those who had dissented from the Nephites—a number which included, but was certainly not limited to, the descendants of the priests of Noah—that was comparable in size to the Nephites. (See Skousen, *The Book of Mormon*, 428–29.) I am indebted to Skousen for this point.

rest on several assumptions, and, as a result, any conclusions reached in this way would be inexact and highly tentative. In any case they would not give us much in the way of comparison to total Lamanite figures since we have even less information about the overall population. For all of these reasons we can generate no more than hunches based on the number of Ammonites slain and the number of their sons who appear in the record some years later. Do the numbers strike us as large or as small? Obviously, that is not much to go on, and this argues for tentativeness in any conclusion we might draw.

It is also relevant, perhaps, that the converted Ammonites proved a sufficient offense to the Lamanites that the Lamanites sent an army to destroy them and the king, so that they could "place another in his stead" (Alma 24:20). So whatever their size, the converted Ammonites certainly held a certain status. Furthermore, it seems likely that there was at least some relationship between the size of the king's following and the desire of the Lamanites to confront him in war. After all, if the converts had been only five percent of the Lamanite total, would the Lamanites have found it easier simply to ignore the old king and to establish a new ruler on their own? What about twenty percent, or forty? At what point would it seem necessary to conquer the king (because he represented a military threat, if for no other reason) rather than to ignore him and simply move on? The answer is not obvious, but it seems likely that there was at least some relationship between the size of the king's following and the motivation to dethrone him militarily. The Lamanites' attack suggests a population size that was larger rather than smaller. But of course this is just a hunch and could easily be mistaken.[5]

In the end we can make no more than plausible guesses about the relative sizes of the Ammonite and Lamanite populations.[6] All things considered, it seems safe to say that the Ammonites were at least a significant fraction of

---

5. It would also be helpful to know more about the land of Jershon. Were the Ammonites granted this land because their numbers required it? If so, just how large was the land? Did the Nephites have to relocate a large group of people in order to accommodate the Ammonites? A small group? Was relocation necessary at all? Information of this sort would provide helpful clues in estimating population sizes, but the record tells us none of it.

6. See James E. Smith, "Nephi's Descendants? Historical Demography and the Book of Mormon." Smith reminds us of the difficulty of calculating ancient populations in general, not to mention the various subgroups within those populations, and he says of the Book of Mormon in particular that "the historical demographer's requirement for data . . . presents a daunting challenge. The book presents no demographic description of any of its populations—not even a total population size" (280). He discusses the complexity of extrapolating population figures from wartime casualties on pages 289–90.

Lamanite society. They numbered in the "thousands," and though it is only suggestive, it is at least relevant that Mormon lists a greater number of "lands" and "cities" that were converted to the Lord than he lists of those who were not. We also learn that Nephite dissensions were of such a size that they could have offset even a large fraction of converts leaving Lamanite society. We further know that the Lamanites found the Ammonites significant enough to attack, which may suggest something about the significance of their size as well. None of this is dispositive, but as a collection these features of the record suggest that the Ammonites were at least a significant element of Lamanite society, and that this was true both of their size and of their status.

Appendix 2

The Promises to Nephi and Lehi

As discussed in Chapter 6, writers in the Book of Mormon frequently refer to promises made by the Lord early in Nephite history. The first of these (and the one that Hugh Nibley cites) is given to Nephi in 1 Nephi 2:20–24. Two elements of this promise relate specifically to Nephi: if he kept the commandments he would "prosper" by being led to a choice land of promise (v. 20), and he would be made a ruler and a teacher over his brethren (v. 22). The remaining elements of the promise relate to the Nephites and Lamanites in general: if Nephi's brethren rebelled they would be "cut off from the presence of the Lord" and be cursed "with a sore curse" (vv. 21–22), and the Lamanites would have "no power" over the seed of Nephi unless Nephi's seed rebelled against the Lord also (vv. 23–24).

Another promise is later mentioned by Lehi when he quotes the Lord: "Inasmuch as ye shall keep my commandments ye shall prosper in the land; but inasmuch as ye will not keep my commandments ye shall be cut off from my presence" (2 Ne. 1:20). Here the idea of "prospering" is applied to all of Lehi's posterity, and it involves the same condition: keeping the commandments of the Lord. Furthermore, since Lehi is speaking following their arrival in the promised land, "prospering" in this promise does not refer to *reaching* the choice land (as it does in the Nephi promise), but refers to flourishing *in* the land now that they have reached it. Part of such "prospering in the land" is related to freedom: Lehi explains that if they keep the commandments "they shall never be brought down into captivity" and "there shall be none to molest them, nor to take away the land of their inheritance; and they shall dwell safely forever" (2 Ne. 1:7, 9). Here the subject is not the Nephites' freedom from Lamanite rule, but the freedom of *all* of Lehi's family from external rule.

Therefore the promises to Nephi and Lehi are not identical, either in scope or in meaning, but do overlap on one general dimension, namely, the assurance that those who would keep the commandments would be free from rule by external parties. It is unsurprising, then, that King Benjamin combines the language of both of these promises when he tells his people that "if ye shall keep the commandments . . . *ye shall prosper in the land*, and *your enemies shall have no power over you*" (Mosiah 2:31). Using the language of both, it is clear that to Benjamin they were effectively a single promise where "prospering in the land" is at least roughly equivalent to the Lamanites' lack of "power over" the Nephites.

Furthermore, once the Nephite and Lamanite division occurred—and there was no longer any sense in speaking of the Lehites as a whole—it became the norm for Book of Mormon figures, in war situations at least, to apply the language of the promise given to Lehi to relations between the Nephites and Lamanites. As already discussed, in one passage Mormon tells us that the Nephites could not permit the Lamanites to massacre them, "for the promise of the Lord was, if they should keep his commandments they should prosper in the land" (Alma 48:25). Here Mormon equates Lehi's language of "prospering in the land" with the ability to avoid defeat by the Lamanites. In another passage he first explicitly refers to the prosperity promise given "unto Lehi," saying that "inasmuch as they [the children of men] shall keep my commandments they shall prosper in the land" (Alma 50:20), and then, one verse later, explains that it was precisely the Nephites' failure to keep the commandments that "brought upon them their wars and destructions" at the hands of the Lamanites (Alma 50:21). Throughout this passage Mormon, like Benjamin, understands the promises given to Lehi and Nephi as being equivalent. He does the same later when he explains that the Nephites "did not prosper" because of their wickedness, but instead "were afflicted and smitten, and driven before the Lamanites" (Hel. 4:13). Then, when the Nephites later repented, Mormon again reports that "they did begin to prosper," specifically in regaining many of the lands they had earlier lost to the Lamanites (Hel. 4:15–16).

Additionally, Jarom tells us that the Nephites during his time became rich because of their righteousness and, among other things, made "weapons of war" that permitted them to repel Lamanite attacks—an outcome that Jarom specifically ties to the Lehi promise that "inasmuch as ye will keep my commandments ye shall prosper in the land" (Jarom 1:8–9). Amaron does the same. He reports that in his time the wicked among the Nephites were destroyed in direct fulfillment of the promise made to Lehi about "prospering in the land" (Omni 1:6–7). Both record keepers correlate the condition of prospering in the land with prevailing in war against the Lamanites.

Early in the Book of Mormon, then, these Nephite record keepers treat the language of the promise given to Lehi as effectively equivalent to that given to Nephi, at least in wartime situations. For them, prospering in the land at a minimum *includes* being kept from destruction by the Lamanites. At a general level at least, in their minds the two promises are one.[1]

---

1. It is different outside of war situations, however. In those cases, the Lehi promise is used to evoke the idea of prospering in the more general sense. (See for example Mosiah 1:7; 2:22; Alma 9:13–14; 36:1, 30; 37:13; 38:1; and 3 Nephi 5:22.) For a wide discussion on prospering in general, see Steven L. Olsen, "Prospering in the Land of Promise," 229–45.

Appendix 3

A Sketch of Joseph Smith's Divine Manifestations

Although many reports of the Prophet's spiritual manifestations are familiar, unless one catalogues them it is easy to lose sight of just how impressive the list is. This matter is underscored when we appreciate that the Prophet is reported to have enjoyed far more visitations than those recorded in standard documents. For example, in addition to seeing the Father and the Son in the First Vision and enjoying numerous visits from the angel Moroni, familiar sources record visits from Peter, James, John, John the Baptist, Moses, Elias, and Elijah, in addition to references regarding Adam, Gabriel, and "Raphael."[1] John Taylor expands the list, however, reporting that

> the principles which he had, placed him in communication with the Lord, and not only with the Lord, but with the ancient apostles and prophets; such men, for instance, as Abraham, Isaac, Jacob, Noah, Adam, Seth, Enoch, and Jesus and the Father, and the apostles that lived on this continent as well as those who lived on the Asiatic continent.[2]

On another occasion, after speaking specifically of Abraham and Noah—in conjunction with other past prophets who had visited Joseph Smith—John Taylor reported that "they all combined together to impart to him the keys of their several missions," a reality that explained the Prophet's "familiarity with all these various dispensations and the men who administered in them." He added that "if you were to ask Joseph what sort of a looking man Adam was, he would tell you at once; he would tell you his size and appearance and all about him."[3] Indeed, on one occasion the Prophet said of his brother Alvin that he "was a very handsome man, surpassed by none other but Adam and Seth."[4]

Joseph's visions were numerous. In addition to the First Vision, he saw the Father and Son at the time of receiving Doctrine and Covenants Sections

---

1. See the well-known accounts in JS–H, D&C 2, 13, 110, 128, and 137.
2. John Taylor, "Discourse by President John Taylor." Sources for many firsthand reports of spiritual manifestations at the beginning of this dispensation include: Mark L. McConkie, *Remembering Joseph: Personal Recollections of Those Who Knew the Prophet Joseph Smith*; Hyrum L. Andrus and Helen Mae Andrus, *They Knew the Prophet: Personal Accounts from Over 100 People Who Knew Joseph Smith*; and John W. Welch, ed., *Opening the Heavens: Accounts of Divine Manifestations, 1820–1844*.
3. John Taylor, "A Funeral Sermon."
4. In B.H. Roberts, ed., *History of the Church*.

76 and 137,[5] as well as on other occasions.[6] He also saw in vision Adam, the Lord, and Adam's children gathered in the valley of Adam-ondi-Ahman at the end of Adam's life.[7] In addition, the Prophet reported that he learned "a hundred fold more" from the vision on the degrees of glory than he ever reported[8] and that in general he experienced visions that "roll like an overflowing surge before my mind."[9] He also received detailed revelations on significant events yet future;[10] received all the authority of the apostleship, including the sealing power;[11] received power to arrange and perform the ordinances of the

---

5. The recording of the vision in Section 137 states that Joseph saw "the blazing throne of God, whereon was seated the Father and the Son." Perhaps the Prophet saw the Father and the Son as separate divine Personages on this occasion, in which case his use of the singular verb form "*was* seated"—rather than the plural "*were* seated"—is a simple grammatical error. On the other hand, it might have been Christ alone, in his capacity as *both* Father and Son, whom he saw on this occasion and that is why he uses the singular verb form "*was* seated" and why there is mention of only one throne. The revelation is typically understood in the first way, but because of the important sense in which Christ is both Father and Son there seems to be no reason to reject the second interpretation out of hand, especially since that reading has the virtue of honoring the singular noun and verb usage and since an appearance of this sort is not without precedent in any event (as, for example, in the Lord's appearance and description of himself to the brother of Jared in Ether 3:14).

6. Zebedee Coltrin, an original member of the School of the Prophets, spoke more than once of a visitation from both the Father and the Son in that school. Of a "personage" passing through the rooms, the Prophet told the brethren: "That is Jesus, our elder brother, the Son of God." Of a being in the house "clothed in fire" and "wrapped in flames," Joseph said that it was "God the Father." (Zebedee Coltrin, "Zebedee Coltrin Papers.") As far as official published accounts go, it is important not to overlook the Savior's appearance to Joseph Smith and Oliver Cowdery recorded in D&C 6:37.

7. In 1839 Joseph Smith reported that "I saw Adam in the valley of Adam-ondi-Ahman" and then supplied details basically as we have them in D&C 107:53–56, a section received in 1835. See Joseph Fielding Smith, comp., *Teachings of the Prophet Joseph Smith*, 158.

8. Ibid., 305.

9. Ibid., 296. The comment was recorded by Willard Richards for the Prophet's diary; see Andrew F. Ehat and Lyndon W. Cook, *The Words of Joseph Smith: The Contemporary Accounts of the Nauvoo Discourses of the Prophet Joseph*, 196.

10. See, for example, D&C 29:8–20; 45:15–59, 87; 88:84–116; 101:10–35; 133:17–56, JS–M.

11. Mention of receiving the Melchizedek priesthood is implicit in mention of receiving the apostleship. Such mention is made in D&C 20:2–3 and 27:12. It is notable too that inherent in the authority Joseph Smith had received was the power to seal worthy individuals to eternal life, as they were made known by revelation. (See D&C 68:12.)

Temple, including the power to seal families;[12] was given power to make significant emendations to the Bible and to deliver the Book of Abraham to the world;[13] and, among all the spirit children available to choose from in the premortal world, was commissioned to preside over the dispensation of the fulness of times (D&C 27:13).

In addition to all this—and more—the Prophet was also privileged to see in vision events from the Book of Mormon itself, and to do so even before receiving the plates. Oliver Cowdery reported that as Moroni spoke to Joseph Smith "the vision was opened, so that our brother was permitted to see and understand"[14] and Joseph himself reported being shown "a brief sketch of [Book of Mormon peoples'] origin, progress, civilization, laws, governments, of their righteousness and iniquity, and the blessings of God being finally withdrawn from them."[15]

Reports thus display Joseph Smith as a man who walked with God, saw the visions of eternity, interacted with multiple prophets who had lived over the earth's history, viewed in vision Book of Mormon peoples and events, translated the book by the gift and power of God, and saw in vision the demise of the Nephite civilization. Indeed, so evident was the Prophet's spiritual power to his associates that Wilford Woodruff (whose own accounts of divine manifestations are both significant and many) could say of him that "his mind, like Enoch's, expands as eternity, and God alone can comprehend

---

12. In published revelations the Lord began speaking of temples in this dispensation as early as 1830 (D&C 36:8), and frequently thereafter (e.g., D&C 42:36; 57:2–3; 88:119–120; 97:15–17), leading up to the sacred events surrounding the Kirtland temple in 1836 (D&C 110). Here Joseph Smith and Oliver Cowdery received all the authority and/or knowledge necessary to complete the building of the kingdom of God on earth, including the performance of family sealing ordinances.

13. Since so little is known about Joseph Smith's revelatory process, including his work on products commonly referred to as "translations," there exists a variety of opinions on how best to characterize such works, as well as the process by which they were produced. For starters on the topic, see Royal Skousen, "How Joseph Smith Translated the Book of Mormon: Evidence from the Original Manuscript"; Stephen E. Robinson, "The 'Expanded' Book of Mormon?"; Brant A. Gardner, *The Gift and Power: Translating the Book of Mormon*; and Jeffrey M. Bradshaw, "Sorting Out the Sources in Scripture." A recent study that introduces a new angle into the study of Book of Mormon language is Stanford Carmack, "What Command Syntax Tells Us about Book of Mormon Authorship."

14. Oliver Cowdery, *Messenger and Advocate 1*.

15. Joseph Smith, Jr., "The Wentworth Letter." The Prophet shared details about Book of Mormon peoples with his family long before beginning the translation of the record. See Lucy Mack Smith's report in Scot F. and Maurine Jensen Proctor, eds., *The Revised and Enhanced History of Joseph Smith by His Mother*, 112.

his soul."[16] It is against this background that, as mentioned in Chapter 9,[17] it seems implausible to imagine the Book of Mormon to contain a message that Joseph Smith did not discern, or to imagine that if the Prophet did fail to discern the message, the Lord would not have explained it to him.

---

16. In Matthias F. Cowley, *Wilford Woodruff: History of His Life and Labors*, 68. Wilford Woodruff is a credible witness of others' spiritual capacity because he was the recipient of so many significant manifestations of his own. One example of many is his report of a time in which he "became wrapped in vision" and records: "I was like Paul; I did not know whether I was in the body or out of the body. A personage appeared to me and showed me the great scenes that should take place in the last days. One scene after another passed before me. I saw the sun darkened; I saw the moon become as blood; I saw the stars fall from heaven; I saw seven golden lamps set in the heavens, representing the various dispensations of God to man—a sign that would appear before the coming of Christ. I saw the resurrection of the dead. In the first resurrection those that came forth from their graves seemed to be all dressed alike, but in the second resurrection they were as diverse in their dress as this congregation is before me today, and if I had been an artist I could have painted the whole scene as it was impressed upon my mind, more indelibly fixed than anything I had ever seen with the natural eye." (G. Homer Durham, ed., *The Discourses of Wilford Woodruff*, 285.) His life was filled with many such manifestations; indeed, long before he became president of the Church, one of his visions—regarding the nation, the inhabitants of Zion, the "destruction that awaited" the nation, and "the great responsibility which rested upon the Quorum of the Apostles"—was submitted to the Quorum of the Twelve just prior to the April conference of 1880 and "accepted by that body as the word of the Lord." (In Matthias F. Cowley, *Wilford Woodruff: History of His Life and Labors*, 530–31.)

17. See the section "The Prophet Joseph Smith."

Bibliography

Andrus, Hyrum L. *Doctrines of the Kingdom*. Salt Lake City: Bookcraft, 1973.

———. *Joseph Smith: The Man and the Seer*. Salt Lake City: Deseret Book, 1960.

Andrus, Hyrum L. and Helen Mae. *They Knew the Prophet: Personal Accounts from Over 100 People Who Knew Joseph Smith*. American Fork, Utah: Covenant, 2004.

Arbinger Institute. *Leadership and Self-Deception*. 2nd ed. San Francisco, Calif.: Berrett-Koehler, 2010.

———. *The Anatomy of Peace*. San Francisco, Calif.: Berrett-Koehler, 2008.

Anh, Le Thi. "The New Vietnam." *National Review*, April 29, 1977, http://jim.com/ChomskyLiesCites/When_we_knew_what_happened_in_Vietnam.htm.

Anscombe, Elizabeth (G.E.M.). "War and Murder." In Richard A. Wasserstrom, ed., *War and Morality*. Belmont, Calif.: Wadsworth, 1970.

———. "Mr. Truman's Degree." 1958 http://www.pitt.edu/~mthompso/readings/truman.pdf.

Appiah, Kwame Anthony. *Experiments in Ethics*. Cambridge, Mass.: Harvard University Press, 2008.

Aquinas, Thomas. *Summa Theologica*, Part II http://ethics.sandiego.edu/Books/Texts/Aquinas/JustWar.html.

Augustine. *The City of God*. Book XIX, chapter 7 http://www.newadvent.org/fathers/120119.htm.

———. Sermon 33 on the New Testament. http://www.newadvent.org/fathers/160333.htm.

Barron, John and Anthony Paul. *Murder of a Gentle Land: The Untold Story of Communist Genocide in Cambodia*. New York: Reader's Digest and Crowell, 1977.

Bennett, Jonathan. "Whatever the Consequences." *Analysis*, 26 (1966): 83–102.

Bentham, Jeremy. *An Introduction to the Principles of Morals and Legislation* (1879). In J. Bowring, ed., *The Works of Jeremy Bentham*. Vol.1. New York: Russell & Russell, 1962.

Bourke, Joana. *An Intimate History of Killing: Face-to-Face Killing in Twentieth-Century Warfare*. New York: Basic Books, 1999.

Boyce, Duane. "A Betrayal of Trust." *FARMS Review of Books*, 9/2 (1997): 147–63.

———. "Do Liberal Economic Policies Approximate the Law of Consecration?" *The FARMS Review*, 21/1 (2009): 197–213.

———. "Faith as a Holy Embrace." *Religious Educator*, 13/2 (2012): 107–27.

———. "Of Science, Scripture, and Surprise." *The FARMS Review*, 20/2 (2008): 163–214.

———. "The Spirit and the Intellect: Lessons in Humility." *BYU Studies*, 50/4 (2011): 75–107.

———. "Were the Ammonites Pacifists?" *Journal of the Book of Mormon and Other Restoration Scripture*, 18/1 (2009): 33–47.

Bradshaw, Jeffrey M. "Sorting Out the Sources in Scripture." *Interpreter: A Journal of Mormon Scripture* 9 (2014): 215–72, available online at http://www.mormoninterpreter.com/sorting-out-the-sources-in-scripture/#sdfootnote76sym.

Buber, Martin. *I and Thou*. Trans. Ronald Gregor Smith. New York: Charles Scribner's Sons, 1958.

Bushman, Richard Lyman. "Aftermath." In Patrick Q. Mason, J. David Pulsipher, and Richard L. Bushman, eds., *War and Peace in Our Time: Mormon Perspectives*. Salt Lake City: Greg Kofford Books, 2012.

Callender, Lenval A. "In Defence of Kant's 'Infamous' Reply to Constant: 'On a Supposed Right to Lie from Benevolent Motives.'" 2008, http://lenvalcallender.co.uk/.

Cannon, Brian Q. "Chastisement of the Nations, 1914–15." In Roy A. Prete, ed., *Window of Faith: Latter-day Saint Perspectives on World History*. Provo, Utah: Religious Studies Center, Brigham Young University, 2005.

Carmack, Stanford. "What Command Syntax Tells Us about Book of Mormon Authorship." *Interpreter: A Journal of Mormon Scripture*, http://www.mormoninterpreter.com/what-command-syntax-tells-us-about-book-of-mormon-authorship/

Ceadel, Martin. *Thinking about Peace and War*. Oxford: Oxford University Press, 1989.

Ceulemans, Carl. "The Military Response of the U.S.-Led Coalition to the September 11 Attacks." In Bruno Coppieters and Nick Fotion, eds., *Moral Constraints on War*. Lanham, Md.: Lexington, 2002.

Chang, Iris. *The Rape of Nanking: The Forgotten Holocaust of World War II*. New York: Basic Books, 1997.

Church of Jesus Christ of Latter-day Saints, The. "Book of Mormon Musical: Church's Official Statement." The Newsroom Blog, http://www.mormonnewsroom.org/article/church-statement-regarding-the-book-of-mormon-broadway-musical.

Clark, John E. "Revisiting 'A Key for Evaluating Book of Mormon Geographies.'" *Mormon Studies Review* 23/1 (2011): 13–43.

_____. "Searching for Book of Mormon Lands in Middle America." *FARMS Review* 16/2 (2004): 1–54.

Coltrin, Zebedee. "Zebedee Coltrin Papers," Church History Library, Salt Lake City, Utah, and "Minutes of School of the Prophets," October 3, 1883, Church History Library, Salt Lake City, Utah.

Conger, George. "Leading Philosopher says Christian Pacifism is the Only Road to Peace: CEN 11.02.07 p 8," Conger: The Religious, Political and Cultural Journalism of George Conger, https://geoconger.wordpress.com/2007/11/01/leading-philosopher-says-christian-pacifism-is-the-only-road-to-peace-cen-110207-p-8/.

Conkling, J. Christopher. "Alma's Enemies: The Case of the Lamanites, Amlicites, and Mysterious Amalekites." *Journal of Book of Mormon Studies*, 14/1 (2005): 108–17.

Conquest, Robert. *The Nation Killers: The Soviet Deportation of Nationalities*. London: Macmillan, 1970.

Coppieters, Bruno and Nick Fotion, eds. *Moral Constraints on War*. Lanham, Md.: Lexington, 2002.

Courtois, Stéphane, et al., eds. *The Black Book of Communism: Crimes, Terror, Repression*. Cambridge, Mass.: Harvard, 1999.

_____. "Conclusion: Why?" In Stéphane Courtois, et al., eds., *The Black Book of Communism: Crimes, Terror, Repression*. Cambridge, Mass.: Harvard, 1999.

_____. "Introduction: The Crimes of Communism." In Stéphane Courtois, et al., eds., *The Black Book of Communism: Crimes, Terror, Repression*. Cambridge, Mass.: Harvard, 1999.

Cowdery, Oliver. *Messenger and Advocate* 1 [April 1835] available online at http://contentdm.lib.byu.edu/cdm/ref/collection/NCMP1820-1846/id/7160.

Cowley, Matthias F. *Wilford Woodruff: History of His Life and Labors*. Salt Lake City, Utah: Bookcraft, 1964.

Crawford, Paul. "The Crusades." Catholic Education Resource Center, http://catholiceducation.org/articles/history/world/wh0018.html.

D'Souza, Dinesh. *What's So Great about America*. Washington, D.C.: Regnery, 2002.

Deane, Morgan. "Offensive Warfare in the Book of Mormon and a Defense of the Bush Doctrine." In Patrick Q. Mason, J. David Pulsipher, and Richard L. Bushman, eds., *War and Peace in Our Time: Mormon Perspectives*. Salt Lake City: Greg Kofford Books, 2012.

Desbarats, Jacqueline. "Repression in the Socialist Republic of Vietnam: Executions and Population Relocation." 1990, http://jim.com/repression.htm#ref1.

Doyle, Thomas E. II. "Kantian Nonideal Theory and Nuclear Proliferation." *International Theory*, 2/1 (2010): 87–112, https://portfolio.du.edu/portfolio/getportfoliofile?uid=170635.

Duran, F.R. Rick. "Pax Sanctorum." In Patrick Q. Mason, J. David Pulsipher, and Richard L. Bushman, eds., *War and Peace in Our Time: Mormon Perspectives*. Salt Lake City: Greg Kofford Books, 2012.

Durham, G. Homer, ed. *The Discourses of Wilford Woodruff*. Salt Lake City, Utah: Bookcraft, 1990.

Dworkin, Ronald. *Taking Rights Seriously*. Cambridge, Mass.: Harvard University Press, 1978.

Eaton, Robert I. and Henry J. Eyring. *I Will Lead You Along: The Life of Henry B. Eyring*. Salt Lake City, Utah: Deseret Book, 2013.

Ehat, Andrew F. and Lyndon W. Cook. *The Words of Joseph Smith: The Contemporary Accounts of the Nauvoo Discourses of the Prophet Joseph*. Provo, Utah: Religious Studies Center Brigham Young University, 1980.

England, Eugene. "A Case for Mormon Christian Pacifism." In Valerie M. Hudson and Kerry M. Kartchner, *Moral Perspectives on U.S. Security Policy: Views from the LDS Community*. Provo, Utah: David M. Kennedy Center for International Studies, Brigham Young University, 1995.

_____. "Healing and Making Peace, in the Church and the World." In Eugene England, *Making Peace: Personal Essays*. Salt Lake City: Signature Books, 1995.

_____. "Hugh Nibley as Cassandra." *BYU Studies*, 30/4 (1990): 104–16.

_____. "The Prince of Peace." *Making Peace: Personal Essays*. Salt Lake City: Signature Books, 1995.

_____. "'Thou Shalt Not Kill': An Ethics of Non-Violence." In Eugene England, *Making Peace: Personal Essays*. Salt Lake City: Signature Books, 1995.

———. "Why Nephi Killed Laban: Reflections on the Truth of the Book of Mormon." In Eugene England, *Making Peace: Personal Essays*. Salt Lake City: Signature Books, 1995.

Ericson, Loyd. "Eugene England's Theology of Peace." In Patrick Q. Mason, J. David Pulsipher, and Richard L. Bushman, eds., *War and Peace in Our Time: Mormon Perspectives*. Salt Lake City: Greg Kofford Books, 2012.

Etcheson, Craig. "'The Number'—Quantifying Crimes against Humanity in Cambodia." Documentation Center of Cambodia, 1999, http://www.mekong.net/cambodia/toll.htm.

Evera, Stephen Van. *Causes of War: Power and the Roots of Conflict*. Ithaca and London: Cornell University Press, 1999.

Ferzan, Kimberly Kessler. "Self-Defense, Permissions, and the Means Principle: A Reply to Quong." *Ohio State Journal of Criminal Law*, vol. 8 (2011): 503–13, http://moritzlaw.osu.edu/osjcl/Articles/Volume8_2/Ferzan.pdf.

First Presidency. General Conference April 1942, http://moralagency.blogspot.com/2010/09/first-presidency-message-in-conference.html.

———. General Conference October 1942, http://emp.byui.edu/marrottr/FirstPresOct1942.htm.

———. "War." In *True to the Faith*. Salt Lake City: Church of Jesus Christ of Latter-day Saints, 2004.

Fisher, John Martin and Mark Ravizza. "Quinn on Doing and Allowing." *Philosophical Review*, 101/2 (1992): 343–52.

Foot, Philippa. "The Problem of Abortion and the Doctrine of the Double Effect." In James Rachels, ed., *Moral Problems: A Collection of Philosophical Essays*. 2nd ed. New York: Harper, 1975.

Ford, Gerald R. "Transcript of President's News Conference on Foreign and Domestic Matters." *New York Times*, March 7, 1975, http://www.paulbogdanor.com/left/cambodia/bloodbath1.pdf.

Ford, John C., S.J. "The Morality of Obliteration Bombing." In Richard B. Miller, ed., *War in the Twentieth Century: Sources in Theological Ethics*. Louisville, Ky.: Westminster/John Knox, 1992.

Freedman, Lawrence, ed. *War*. Oxford: Oxford University Press, 1994.

Fried, Charles. *Right and Wrong*. Cambridge, Mass.: Harvard University Press, 1978.

Gardner, Brant A. *The Gift and Power: Translating the Book of Mormon*. Salt Lake City, Utah: Greg Kofford Books, 2011.

Gessel, Van C. "Coming to Terms: The Challenge of Creating Christian Vocabulary in a Non-Christian Land." *BYU Studies*, 50/4 (2011): 33–59.

Girard, René. *Things Hidden since the Foundation of the World*. Stanford, Calif.: Stanford University Press, 1987.

———. *Violence and the Sacred*. Baltimore: Johns Hopkins University Press, 1977.

Grabczynska, Arlette and Kimberly Kessler Ferzan. "Justifying Killing in Self-Defence." *The Journal of Criminal Law and Criminology*, 99/1 (2009): 235–53.

Grotius, Hugo (1583–1645). *On the Law of War and Peace*, http://www.constitution.org/gro/djbp.htm.

Hafen, Bruce C. *A Disciple's Life: The Biography of Neal A. Maxwell.* Salt Lake City, Utah: Deseret Book, 2002.
Hamblin, William J. "Basic Methodological Problems with the Anti-Mormon Approach to the Geography and Archaeology of the Book of Mormon." *Journal of Book of Mormon Studies* 2/1 (1993), at http://publications.maxwellinstitute.byu.edu/fullscreen/?pub=1382&index=11.
———. "That Old Black Magic." *FARMS Review of Books*, 12/2 (2000): 225–394.
Hardy, Grant. *Understanding the Book of Mormon.* New York: Oxford University Press, 2010.
Hellebrand, Robert. "General Conference Addresses during Times of War." In Patrick Q. Mason, J. David Pulsipher, and Richard L. Bushman, eds., *War and Peace in Our Time: Mormon Perspectives.* Salt Lake City: Greg Kofford Books, 2012.
Hempel, Carl G. *Philosophy of Natural Science.* Englewood Cliffs, NJ: Prentice-Hall, 1966.
Henshaw, Mark, Valerie M. Hudson, Eric Jensen, Kerry M. Kartchner, and John Mark Mattox. "War and the Gospel: Perspectives from Latter-day Saint National Security Practitioners." In Patrick Q. Mason, J. David Pulsipher, and Richard L. Bushman, eds., *War and Peace in Our Time: Mormon Perspectives.* Salt Lake City: Greg Kofford Books, 2012.
Hinckley, Gordon B. "Excerpts from Recent Addresses of President Gordon B. Hinckley." *Ensign*, July 1996, https://www.lds.org/ensign/1996/07/excerpts-from-recent-addresses-of-president-gordon-b-hinckley.
———. "In . . . Counsellors There is Safety." *Ensign*, November 1990, https://www.lds.org/general-conference/1990/10/in-counsellors-there-is-safety.
———. "The Times in Which We Live." General Conference October 2001, http://www.lds.org/general-conference/2001/10/the-times-in-which-we-live.
———. "War and Peace." General Conference April 2003, http://www.lds.org/general-conference/2003/04/war-and-peace.
Holmes, Robert. *On War and Morality.* Princeton, N.J.: Princeton University Press, 1989.
Holzapfel, Richard N. and Kent P. Jackson. *To Save the Lost: An Easter Celebration.* Provo, Utah: Religious Studies Center, Brigham Young University.
Hudson, Valerie M. "What Should America's National Security Objectives Be?: The Problems and Possibilities of an LDS Perspective." In Valerie M. Hudson and Kerry M. Kartchner, eds., *Moral Perspectives on U.S. Security Policy: Views from the LDS Community.* Provo, Utah: David M. Kennedy Center for International Studies, Brigham Young University, 1995.
Irvine, Reed. "Lost in the Killing Fields." *AIM Report*, March 13, 1985, http://www.aim.org/publications/aim_report/1985/03b.html.
Jacoby, Jeff. "American Leftists were Pol Pot's Cheerleaders." *Boston Globe*, April 30, 1998, http://www.boston.com/news/globe/editorial_opinion/oped/articles/1998/04/30/american_leftists_were_pol_pots_cheerleaders/?page=full.
Johnson, Chalmers. "The Looting of Asia." *London Review of Books*, vol. 25 no. 22, 20 November 2003, http://www.lrb.co.uk/v25/n22/chalmers-johnson/the-looting-of-asia.

Johnson, Paul. *Intellectuals: From Marx and Tolstoy to Sartre and Chomsky.* New York: Harper Perennial, 2007.

Jolley, JoAnn. "Blessed Are the Peacemakers: LDS in the Military." *This People*, June/July, 1984, 66–73.

Kamm, F. M. "Failures of Just War Theory: Terror, Harm, and Justice." *Ethics*, 114/4 (2004): 650–92.

———. *Intricate Ethics: Rights, Responsibilities, and Permissible Harm.* Oxford: Oxford University Press, 2007.

Kant, Immanuel. "Concerning a Pretended Right to Lie from Motives of Humanity" (1797) http://www.jstor.org/stable/25665827?seq=1.

———. *Critique of Practical Reason (and Other Works on the Theory of Ethics).* Trans. Thomas Kingsmill Abbott. New York: Barnes and Noble, 2004. (The *Critique* was first published in 1788.)

———. *Groundwork of the Metaphysics of Morals* (1785). Rev. ed. Ed. Mary Gregor and Jens Timmerman. Cambridge: Cambridge University Press, 2012.

———. *Lectures on Ethics.* Ed. Peter Heath and J.B. Schneewind. Cambridge: Cambridge University Press, 1997.

———. *The Metaphysics of Morals* (1797). Trans. Mary J. Gregor. Cambridge: Cambridge University Press, 1991.

———. *The One Possible Basis for a Demonstration of the Existence of God* (1763). Trans. Gordon Treash. Lincoln, Neb.: University of Nebraska Press, 1994.

———. *The Philosophy of Law* (1796). http://faculty.msmary.edu/Conway/PHIL%20 400x/Kant%20Retributive%20Theory.pdf.

Kimball, Spencer W. "The False Gods We Worship." *Ensign*, June 1976 http://www.lds.org/ensign/1976/06/the-false-gods-we-worship.

Korsgaard, Christine. "The Right to Lie: Kant on Dealing with Evil." *Philosophy and Public Affairs*, 15/4 (1986): 325–49.

Lazar, Seth. "The Responsibility Dilemma for *Killing in War*: A Review Essay." *Philosophy and Public Affairs*, 38/2 (2010): 180–213.

Leverick, Fiona. *Killing in Self-Defence.* Oxford: Oxford University Press, 2006.

Levinas, Emmanuel. *Totality and Infinity: An Essay on Exteriority.* Trans. Alphonso Lingis. Pittsburgh: Duquesne University Press, 1969.

Lippmann, Walter. "The Futility of Pacifism." In Martin T. Woods and Robert Buckenmeyer, eds., *The Morality of Peace and War.* Santa Barbara, Calif.: Intelman, 1974.

McConkie, Mark L. *Remembering Joseph: Personal Recollections of Those Who Knew the Prophet Joseph Smith.* Salt Lake City, Utah: Deseret Book, 2003.

McKay, David O. "The Church and the Present War." General Conference April 1942, http://www.keepapitchinin.org/library/david-o-mckay-the-church-and-the-present-war/.

———. "Righteousness Key to World Peace." Conference Report, April 1955, pp. 24–28, http://scriptures.byu.edu/gettalk.php?ID=753.

McMahan, Jeff. "The Basis of Moral Liability to Defensive Killing." *Philosophical Issues*, 15 (2005): 386–405, http://philosophy.rutgers.edu/dmdocuments/Basis_of_Moral_Liability_to_Defensive_Killing.pdf.

———. "Debate: Justification and Liability in War." *The Journal of Political Philosophy*, 2008 http://philosophy.rutgers.edu/dmdocuments/Justification_Liability_in_War.pdf.

———. *Killing in War*. Oxford: Clarendon, 2009.

———. "Pacifism and Moral Theory." *Diametros*, 23 (2010): 44–68, http://www.diametros.iphils.uj.edu.pl/pdf/diam23mcmahan.PDF.

———. "Self-Defense Against Morally Innocent Threats." In Paul H. Robinson, Stephen P. Garvey, and Kimberly K. Ferzan, eds., *Criminal law Conversations*. New York: Oxford University Press, 2009.

Madson, Joshua. "A Non-Violent Reading of the Book of Mormon." In Patrick Q. Mason, J. David Pulsipher, and Richard L. Bushman, eds., *War and Peace in Our Time: Mormon Perspectives*. Salt Lake City: Greg Kofford Books, 2012.

Madson, Ron. "D&C 98: The 'Immutable' Rejected Covenant of Peace." In Patrick Q. Mason, J. David Pulsipher, and Richard L. Bushman, eds., *War and Peace in Our Time: Mormon Perspectives*. Salt Lake City: Greg Kofford Books, 2012.

Mahon, James Edwin. "The Truth about Kant on Lies." 2009, http://wlu.academia.edu/JamesMahon/Papers/152941/The_Truth_About_Kant_On_Lies.

Malia, Martin. "Foreword: The Uses of Atrocity." In *The Black Book of Communism: Crimes, Terror, Repression*, ed. Stéphane Courtois, et al. Cambridge, Mass.: Harvard, 1999.

Mapel, David R. "Moral Liability to Defensive Killing and Symmetrical Self-defense." *The Journal of Political Philosophy*. 2009, http://sobek.colorado.edu/~mapel/Publications/JOPPSelf-Defense.pdf.

Margolin, Jean-Louis. "Cambodia: The Country of Disconcerting Crimes." In Stéphane Courtois, et al., eds., *The Black Book of Communism: Crimes, Terror, Repression*. Cambridge, Mass.: Harvard, 1999.

———. "China: A Long March into Night." In Stéphane Courtois, et al., eds., *The Black Book of Communism: Crimes, Terror, Repression*. Cambridge, Mass.: Harvard, 1999.

Masek, Lawrence. "All's Not Fair in War: How Kant's Just War Theory Refutes War Realism." *Public Affairs Quarterly*, 16/2 (2002): 143–54.

Mason, Patrick Q. "Introduction." In Patrick Q. Mason, J. David Pulsipher, and Richard L. Bushman, eds., *War and Peace in Our Time: Mormon Perspectives*. Salt Lake City: Greg Kofford Books, 2012.

Mason, Patrick Q., J. David Pulsipher, and Richard L Bushman., eds. *War and Peace in Our Time: Mormon Perspectives*. Salt Lake City: Greg Kofford Books, 2012.

Mill, John Stuart. *Utilitarianism, Liberty, and Representative Government*. New York: E.P. Dutton, 1951.

Mitton, George L. and Rhett S. James. "A Response to D. Michael Quinn's Homosexual Distortion of Latter-day Saint History." *FARMS Review of Books*, 10/1 (1998): 141–263.

Nagel, Thomas. *Mortal Questions*. Canto Edition, Cambridge: Cambridge University Press, 1991.

Narveson, Jan. "Pacifism: A Philosophical Analysis." In Richard A. Wasserstrom, ed., *War and Morality*. Belmont, Calif.: Wadsworth, 1970.

Neu, Michael. "Why McMahan's *Just* Wars Are Only *Justified* and Why That Matters." *Ethical Perspectives*, 19/2 (2012): 235–55.

Ngor, Haing, with Roger Warner. *Survival in the Killing Fields*. New York: Carroll and Graf, 2003.

Nibley, Hugh. *An Approach to the Book of Mormon*. 3rd ed. Salt Lake City: Deseret Book and FARMS, 1988.

———. "Brigham Young and the Enemy." In Hugh Nibley, *Brother Brigham Challenges the Saints*, ed. Don E. Norton and Shirley S. Ricks. Salt Lake City: Deseret Book and FARMS, 1994.

———. "'Exemplary Manhood.'" In Hugh Nibley, *Brother Brigham Challenges the Saints*, ed. Don E. Norton and Shirley S. Ricks. Salt Lake City: Deseret Book and FARMS, 1994.

———. "Freemen and King-men in the Book of Mormon." In Hugh Nibley, *The Prophetic Book of Mormon*, ed. John W. Welch. Salt Lake City: Deseret Book and FARMS, 1989.

———. "If There Must Needs Be Offense." In Hugh Nibley, *Brother Brigham Challenges the Saints*, ed. Don E Norton and Shirley S. Ricks. Salt Lake City: Deseret Book and FARMS, 1994.

———. "In the Party but Not of the Party." In Hugh Nibley, *Brother Brigham Challenges the Saints*, ed. Don E. Norton and Shirley S. Ricks. Salt Lake City: Deseret Book and FARMS, 1994.

———. "Last Call: An Apocalyptic Warning from the Book of Mormon." In Hugh Nibley, *The Prophetic Book of Mormon*, ed. John W. Welch. Salt Lake City: Deseret Book and FARMS, 1989.

———. "Leaders to Managers: The Fatal Shift." In *Brother Brigham Challenges the Saints*, ed. Don E. Norton and Shirley S. Ricks. Salt Lake City: Deseret Book and FARMS, 1994.

———. "The Prophetic Book of Mormon." In Hugh Nibley, *The Prophetic Book of Mormon*, ed. John W. Welch. Salt Lake City: Deseret Book and FARMS, 1989.

———. "Renounce War, or a Substitute for Victory." In Hugh Nibley, *Brother Brigham Challenges the Saints*, ed. Don E. Norton and Shirley S. Ricks. Salt Lake City: Deseret Book and FARMS, 1994.

———. "Scriptural Perspectives on How to Survive the Calamities of the Last Days." In Hugh Nibley, *The Prophetic Book of Mormon*, ed. John W. Welch. Salt Lake City: Deseret Book and FARMS, 1989.

———. *Since Cumorah*. 2nd ed. Ed. John W. Welch. Salt Lake City: Deseret Book and FARMS, 1988.

———. "Warfare and the Book of Mormon." In Hugh Nibley, *Brother Brigham Challenges the Saints*, ed. Don E. Norton and Shirley S. Ricks. Salt Lake City: Deseret Book and FARMS, 1994.

———. "We Will Still Weep for Zion." In Don E. Norton, ed., *Approaching Zion*. Salt Lake City and Provo, Utah: Deseret Book and FARMS, 1989.

———. "What is Zion? A Distant View." In Hugh Nibley, *Approaching Zion*, ed. Don E. Norton. Salt Lake City: Deseret Book and FARMS, 1989.

Norcross, Alistair. "Off Her Trolley? Frances Kamm and the Metaphysics of Morality." *Utilitas*, 20/1 (2008): 65–80, https://journals.cambridge.org/action/displayFulltext?type=1&fid=1729508&jid=UTI&volumeId=20&issueId=01&aid=1729500.
Nozick, Robert. *Anarchy, State, and Utopia*. New York: Basic, 1974.
Oaks, Dallin H. *Life's Lessons Learned: Personal Reflections*. Salt Lake City, Utah: Deseret Book Co., 2011.
O'Connor, James. "The Trolley Method of Moral Philosophy." *Essays in Philosophy*, 13/1 (2012), http://commons.pacificu.edu/cgi/viewcontent.cgi?article=1413&context=eip.
O'Dea, Thomas F. *The Mormons*. Chicago: University of Chicago Press, 1957.
Olsen, Steven L. "The Covenant of the Chosen People: The Spiritual Foundations of Ethnic Identity in the Book of Mormon." *Journal of the Book of Mormon and Other Restoration Scripture*, 21/2 (2012): 14–29, http://maxwellinstitute.byu.edu/publications/jbms/?vol=21&num=2&id=643.
———. "Prospering in the Land of Promise." In *FARMS Review*, 22/1 (2010): 229–45, http://maxwellinstitute.byu.edu/publications/review/?vol=22&num=1&id=797.
Orend, Brian. "A Just-War Critique of Realism and Pacifism." *Journal of Philosophical Research*, vol. 26 (2001): 435–77.
Otsuka, Michael. "Killing the Innocent in Self-Defense." *Philosophy and Public Affairs*, 23/1 (1994): 74–94.
Pace, George W. *Our Search to Know the Lord*. Salt Lake City, Utah: Deseret Book, 1988.
Packer, Boyd K. *That All May Be Edified*. Salt Lake City, Utah: Bookcraft, 1982.
———. "I Say Unto You, Be One." *BYU Speeches of the Year*, February 12, 1991, http://speeches.byu.edu/?act=viewitem&id=373.
———. "Jesus is the Christ." *Church News*, December 25, 2010, 3.
Petersen, Boyd J. "The Work of Death: Hugh Nibley as Scholar, Soldier, Peace Activist." In Patrick Q. Mason, J. David Pulsipher, and Richard L. Bushman, eds., *War and Peace in Our Time: Mormon Perspectives*. Salt Lake City: Greg Kofford Books, 2012.
———. *Hugh Nibley: A Consecrated Life*. Salt Lake City: Greg Kofford Books, 2002.
Peterson, Daniel C. "The Gadianton Robbers as Guerilla Warriors." In *Warfare in the Book of Mormon*, ed. Stephen D. Ricks and William J. Hamblin. Salt Lake City: Deseret Book and FARMS, 1990.
Ponchaud, Francois. *Cambodia: Year Zero*. New York: Henry Holt, 1978.
Potter, Nelson T. Jr. "Kant and Capital Punishment Today." *The Journal of Value Inquiry*, 36 (2002): 267–282, http://digitalcommons.unl.edu/cgi/viewcontent.cgi?article=1004&context=philosfacpub.
Proctor, Scot F. and Maurine Jensen, eds., *The Revised and Enhanced History of Joseph Smith by His Mother*. Salt Lake City, Utah: Bookcraft, 1996.
Pulsipher, J. David. "The Ammonite Conundrum." In Patrick Q. Mason, J. David Pulsipher, and Richard L. Bushman, eds., *War and Peace in Our Time: Mormon Perspectives*. Salt Lake City: Greg Kofford Books, 2012.
Putnam, Hilary. "The 'Corroboration' of Theories." In *Mathematics, Matter and Method: Philosophical Papers*. 2nd ed. Cambridge: Cambridge University Press, 1979: 1:250–69.

Quine, W.V. *The Pursuit of Truth*. Cambridge, Mass.: Harvard University Press, 1990.

Quinn, D. Michael. "Pacifist Counselor in the First Presidency: J. Reuben Clark Jr., 1933–1961." In Patrick Q. Mason, J. David Pulsipher, and Richard L. Bushman, eds., *War and Peace in Our Time: Mormon Perspectives*. Salt Lake City: Greg Kofford Books, 2012.

———. *J. Reuben Clark: The Church Years*. Provo, Utah: Brigham Young University Press, 1983.

Quinn, Warren S. "Actions, Intentions, and Consequences: The Doctrine of Doing and Allowing." *Philosophical Review*, 98/3 (1989): 287–312.

———. "Actions, Intentions, and Consequences: The Doctrine of Double Effect." *Philosophy and Public Affairs*, 18/4 (1989): 334–51.

Quong, Jonathan. "Killing in Self-Defense." *Ethics*, 119/2 (2009): 507–37.

Rappleye, Neal. "'War of Words and Tumult of Opinions': The Battle for Joseph Smith's Words in Book of Mormon Geography." *Interpreter: A Journal of Mormon Scripture* 11 (2014): 37–95, at http://www.mormoninterpreter.com/war-of-words-and-tumult-of-opinions-the-battle-for-joseph-smiths-words-in-book-of-mormon-geography/.

Rawls, John. *A Theory of Justice*. Cambridge, Mass.: Harvard, 1971.

Richards, George F. "Love for Mankind." General Conference October 1946 http://scriptures.byu.edu/gettalk.php?ID=268.

Ricks, Stephen D. "'Holy War:' The Sacral Ideology of War in the Book of Mormon and in the Ancient Near East." In *Warfare in the Book of Mormon*, ed. Stephen D. Ricks and William J. Hamblin. Salt Lake City: Deseret Book and FARMS, 1990, http://maxwellinstitute.byu.edu/publications/books/?bookid=66&chapid=725.

Ricks, Stephen D. and William J. Hamblin. *Warfare in the Book of Mormon*. Salt Lake City: Deseret Book and FARMS, 1990.

Robinson, Stephen E. "The 'Expanded' Book of Mormon?" In *The Book of Mormon: Second Nephi, the Doctrinal Structure*, ed. Monte S. Nyman and Charles D. Tate Jr. Provo, Utah: Religious Studies Center, Brigham Young University, 1989.

Roper, Matthew. "Joseph Smith, Revelation, and Book of Mormon Geography." *FARMS Review* 22/2 (2010): 15–85.

———. "Limited Geography and the Book of Mormon: Historical Antecedents and Early Interpretations." *FARMS Review* 16/2 (2004): 225–76.

———. "Swimming in the Gene Pool: Israelite Kinship Relations, Genes, and Genealogy." In *The Book of Mormon and DNA Research*, ed. Daniel C. Peterson. Provo, Utah: Maxwell Institute, 2008.

Ross, W.D. *The Right and the Good*. Oxford: Clarendon, 1930.

Rummel, R. J. "Statistics of Democide." In his *Death by Government*, http://www.hawaii.edu/powerkills/SOD.CHAP6.HTM.

———. "Statistics of Japanese Democide: Estimates, Calculations, and Sources." http://www.hawaii.edu/powerkills/SOD.CHAP3.HTM.

Russell, Lord of Liverpool. *The Knights of Bushido: A History of Japanese War Crimes During World War II*. New York: Skyhorse Publishing, 2008.

Sagan, Ginetta. "Vietnam's Postwar Hell." *Newsweek*, May 3, 1982, http://www.paulbogdanor.com/left/vietnam/sagan.pdf.

Schanberg, Sydney H. "Cambodia Reds Are Uprooting Millions As They Impose a 'PeasantRevolution.'" *New York Times*, May 9, 1975, http://www.columbia.edu/itc/hs/pubhealth/boothby/forced_migration/files/Schanberg-5-9-1975.pdf.

———. "Indochina Without Americans: For Most, a Better Life." *New York Times*, April 13, 1975.

———. *The Killing Fields: War Writings*. Washington, D.C.: Potomac, 2010.

Scott, Richard G. "Personal Strength through the Atonement of Jesus Christ." General Conference October 2013, available at http://www.lds.org/general-conference/2013/10/personal-strength-through-the-atonement-of-jesus-christ.

Sharp, Bruce. "Counting Hell." http://www.mekong.net/cambodia/deaths.htm#fn33.

Shawcross, William. *Cambodia's New Deal: A Report*. Washington, D.C.: Carnegie Endowment for International Peace, 1994.

Skinner, Kiron K., Annelise Anderson, and Martin Anderson, eds. *Reagan: A Life in Letters*. New York: Free Press, 2003.

Skousen, Royal, ed. *The Book of Mormon: The Earliest Text*. New Haven and London: Yale University Press, 2009.

———. "Changes in the Book of Mormon." *Interpreter: A Journal of Mormon Scripture*, 11 (2014), 161–76, available at http://www.mormoninterpreter.com/changes-in-the-book-of-mormon/.

———. "How Joseph Smith Translated the Book of Mormon: Evidence from the Original Manuscript." *Journal of Book of Mormon Studies*, 7/1 (1998): 22–31, available online at http://publications.maxwellinstitute.byu.edu/publications/jbms/7/1/S00005-50be28d378b0e4Skousen.pdf.

———. "Through a Glass Darkly: Trying to Understand the Scriptures." *BYU Studies*, 26/4 (1986): 2–20, https://byustudies.byu.edu/PDFLibrary/26.4SkousenThrough-9190171e-49a0-4c0b-a887-6427fbd8fce1.pdf.

Smith, James E. "Nephi's Descendants? Historical Demography and the Book of Mormon." *FARMS Review of Books*, 6/1 (1994): 255–96.

Smith, Joseph, Jr. "The Wentworth Letter." March 1, 1842, available online at http://www.moroni10.com/wentworth_letter.html.

———, comp. *Teachings of the Prophet Joseph Smith*. Salt Lake City: Deseret Book, 1972.

Solis, Gary. *The Law of Armed Conflict: International Humanitarian Law in War*. Cambridge and New York: Cambridge University Press, 2010.

Sorenson, John L. *An Ancient American Setting for the Book of Mormon*. Salt Lake City: Deseret Book, 1985.

———. "An Open Letter to Dr. Michael Coe." *Interpreter: A Journal of Mormon Scripture* 1 (2012): 91–109, at http://www.mormoninterpreter.com/?s=Coe&submit.

———. "Ancient Voyages Across the Ocean to America: From 'Impossible' to 'Certain.'" *Journal of Book of Mormon Studies* 14, no, 1 (2005), http://publications.maxwellinstitute.byu.edu/fullscreen/?pub=1399.

———. *Mormon's Codex: An Ancient American Book*. Salt Lake City, Utah: Deseret Book and the Neal A. Maxwell Institute for Religious Scholarship, 2013.

———. *Mormon's Map*. Provo, Utah: FARMS, 2000.

———. "Viva Zapato! Hurray for the Shoe!" *Review of Books on the Book of Mormon* 6/1 (1994): 297–361.

———. "When Lehi's Party Arrived in the Land, Did They Find Others There?" *Journal of Book of Mormon Studies*, 1/1 (1992): 1–34.

Steinhoff, Uwe. "Debate: Jeff McMahan on the Moral Inequality of Combatants." *The Journal of Political Philosophy*, 16/2 (2008): 220–26.

Stephens, Bret. "From WikiLeaks to the Killing Fields." *The Wall Street Journal*, July 27, 2010, http://online.wsj.com/article/SB10001424052748703700904575390951264307766.html.

Stern, Robert. "Does 'Ought' Imply 'Can'? And Did Kant Think It Does?" *Utilitas*, 16/1 (2004): 42–61, http://eprints.whiterose.ac.uk/298/1/sternr1.pdf.

Stubbs, Brian D. "Elusive Israel and the Numerical Dynamics of Population Mixing." In *The Book of Mormon and DNA Research*, ed. Daniel C. Peterson. Provo, Utah: Maxwell Institute, 2008.

Sussman, David. "On the Supposed Duty of Truthfulness: Kant on Lying in Self-Defense." In Clancy Martin, ed., *The Philosophy of Deception*. New York: Oxford University Press, 2008.

Tate, Lucile C. *Boyd K. Packer: A Watchman on the Tower*. Salt Lake City, Utah: Bookcraft, 1995.

Taylor, John. Discourse by President John Taylor, delivered at Ephraim, Sanpete County, on Sunday Morning, April 13, 1879, reported by Geo. F. Gibbs on pages 91–101 of volume 21 of the *Journal of Discourses*; available online at http://journalofdiscourses.com/21/12.

———. A Funeral Sermon, Preached by Elder John Taylor, delivered at the 7th Ward Meetinghouse, Salt Lake City, on Sunday Afternoon, Dec. 31, 1876, reported by Geo. F. Gibbs on pages 324–35 of volume 18 of the *Journal of Discourses*; available online at http://journalofdiscourses.com/18/41.

Teichman, Jenny. *Pacifism and the Just War*. Oxford: Basil Blackwell, 1986.

———. *The Philosophy of War and Peace*. Charlottesville, Va.: Imprint Academic, 2006.

Thomasson, Gordon Conrad. "'Renounce War and Proclaim Peace": Personal Reflections on Mormon Attempts at Peacemaking." In Patrick Q. Mason, J. David Pulsipher, and Richard L. Bushman, eds., *War and Peace in Our Time: Mormon Perspectives*. Salt Lake City: Greg Kofford Books, 2012.

Thomson, Judith Jarvis. "Killing, Letting die, and the Trolley Problem." *Monist*, 59 (1976): 204–17.

———. "Self-Defense and Rights." In Judith Jarvis Thomson, *Rights, Restitution, and Risk: Essays in Moral Theory*, ed. William Parent. Cambridge, Mass.: Harvard University press, 1986.

———. "Self-Defense." *Philosophy and Public Affairs*, 20/4 (1991): 283–310.

Tolstoy, Leo. "Law of God vs. Law of the State." In Martin T. Woods and Robert Buckenmeyer, eds., *The Morality of Peace and War*. Santa Barbara, Calif.: Intelman, 1974.

Toulmin, Stephen and J. Goodfield. *The Fabric of the Heavens*. New York: Harper and Row, 1961.

Tyner, James A. *Genocide and the Geographical Imagination: Life and Death in Germany, China, and Cambodia.* Lanham, Maryland: Rowman & Littlefield, 2012.
Walzer, Michael. *Arguing about War.* New Haven: Yale University Press, 2004.
_____. *Just and Unjust Wars: A Moral Argument with Historical Illustrations.* 4th ed. New York: Basic, 2006.
Warner, C. Terry. "Anger and Similar Delusions." In Rom Harré, ed., *The Social Construction of Emotion.* Oxford: Basil Blackwell, 1986.
_____. *Bonds that Make Us Free.* Salt Lake City, Utah: Shadow Mountain, 2001.
_____. "Commitment and Life's Meaning." In Truman G. Madsen and Charles D. Tate Jr., eds., *To the Glory of God: Mormon Essays on Great Issues.* Salt Lake City, Utah: Deseret Book, 1972.
_____. "Irony, Self-deception, and Understanding." Linacre Philosophical Society, Linacre College, University of Oxford, 1986.
_____. "Locating Agency." In Daniel N. Robinson and Leendert P. Mos, eds., *Annals of Theoretical Psychology.* Vol. 6. New York: Plenum, 1990.
_____. "Self-deception as Vacuous Experience." University of Manchester and University of Warwick, 1987.
_____."The Social Construction of Basic Misconceptions of Behaviour." Published as "La construcción de los errores basicos en la conceptuación de las conductas." In Tomas Ibáñez Gracia, ed., *El Conocimiento de la Realidad Social.* Barcelona: Sendai Ediciones, 1988.
_____. "What We Are." *BYU Studies,* 26/1, 1986, 39–63.
Welch, John W. *Illuminating the Sermon at the Temple and Sermon on the Mount.* Provo, Utah: FARMS, 1999.
_____. "Law and War in the Book of Mormon." In *Warfare in the Book of Mormon,* ed. Stephen D. Ricks and William J. Hamblin. Salt Lake City: Deseret Book and FARMS, 1990.
_____, ed. *Opening the Heavens: Accounts of Divine Manifestations, 1820–1844.* Salt Lake City, Utah: Deseret Book and Provo, Utah: BYU Press, 2005.
Werth, Nicholas. "A State against Its People: Violence, Repression, and Terror in the Soviet Union." In Stéphane Courtois, et al., eds., *The Black Book of Communism: Crimes, Terror, Repression.* Cambridge, Mass.: Harvard, 1999.
Weyl, Nathaniel. *Anatomy of Terror.* Washington, D.C.: Public Affairs Press, 1956.
Wink, Walter. *Jesus and Nonviolence: A Third Way.* Minneapolis: Augsburg Fortress, 2003.
Yoder, John Howard. *Christian Attitudes to War, Peace, and Revolution.* Grand Rapids, Mich.: Brazos, 2009.
Zinn, Howard. *The Power of Nonviolence: Writings by Advocates of Peace.* Boston: Beacon Press, 2002.

Index

A

abortion, 180–81
Abraham, 28, 90n6, 31n24
Abraham, Book of, 291
Adam, 90n6, 289–90
Adam-ondi-Ahman, 290
Afghanistan, 41–42, 114
aggression
  and exploitation, 30
  prohibited in LDS framework, 271
  responses, 253–54
  types of, 251
aggressors
  Lamanites as, 53–57, 59–63, 76–77, 92
  defense against, even if morally innocent, 34–38
  and victims, 22–31, 36n6, 180, 92–93, 237, 278
Alma (elder), 98, 99–100, 154–55, 155n11
Alma (son)
  and Amlici, 103–5, 236–38
  example of non-pacifism, 19, 91, 96, 98, 165
  and narrative approach, 113–15
  and revelation in war, 97, 121–23, 119, 125, 168–69
Amalickiah
  example of evil, 241–42
  and Teancum, 103
Amaron, 82, 119, 288
Amlici, 103–5, 236–38
Ammon, 56–57, 183, 245
  Hugh Nibley on,, 105–6
  and self defense, 105, 147n29
Ammonites
  burial of weapons by, 63–64, 65
  converts, 51–52, 281–82
  covenant of, 63–68, 70, 453–54
  Eugene England on, 50, 172, 187–88
  Hugh Nibley on, 45, 49–50, 102
  and murder, 62–66, 69n10, 153–54, 167–68, 218
  name, 53
  and narrative approach, 113–15, 141, 142
  and pacificism, 65–71, 109, 172
  population, 53–53, 59, 281–85
  repentance of, 63, 65
  righteousness of, 64, 71
  self–sacrifice of, 64, 65, 151–53
  sons of , 65, 69, 154
  and sons of Mosiah, 51
  support of Nephite armies, 64, 67–68
Anscombe, G.E.M., 12n10, 20, 23n14
Anti-Nephi-Lehi, 59–63
Anti-Nephi-Lehies. *See* Ammonites.
Aquinas, Thomas, 7, 42, 223
Arbinger Institute, 237n33
Augustine, 230n19, 252n10

B

battles of the righteous, 95–102, 108
Benjamin (King), 19, 90–91, 96, 107, 165–66
Bentham, Jeremy, 36n7
Bell, John, 214, 217n10
Besançon, Alain, 194–97
Bishop, Maurice, 192–193
bloodshed, minimizing, 48, 249–50, 272
Book of Mormon
  divine promise of, 138
  importance in war, 254–55
  and mistakes by prophets, 113–15, 117–18, 129, 148, 149, 213
  and pacifism, 109
  as pacifist manifesto, 164–73
Buber, Martin, 24n16, 185n34, 237n33
Bushman, Richard Lyman, 171

C

Cain, 22–23, 29–31, 189, 228
Cambodia, genocide in, 196, 206
Camus, Albert, 197n28
capital punishment, 180–81
Captain Moroni. *See* Moroni (Captain).
China, 194
Christian discipleship, 277–78
civilians. *See* noncombatants.
Clark, J. Reuben Jr., 43, 224
Coard, Benjamin, 193. *See also* Grenada
Communism
   atrocities of, public knowledge, 194–98
   and Cambodian genocide, 196, 206
   U.S. resistance to, 193–94
consecration, law of, 273
continuum theory (of Book of Mormon), 151–53, 172–73
Cowdery, Oliver, 291
Cuba, 192, 194. *See also* Grenada.
Czechoslovakia, 8n4

D

D'Sousa, Dinesh, 41
defense. *See* self–defense
dissenters, Nephite, 55, 76–77, 80n25, 142n20, 283
Doctrine and Covenants 98
   and Hugh Nibley, 95
   and LDS framework, 254–55
   and pacifism, 156–64, 173
   and repentance, 252–53
   and Spencer W. Kimball, 261
Dodd, Chris, 207
double effect, doctrine of, 10–11, 14, 36. *See also* noncombatants
Dworkin, Ronald, 24n16

E

Egyptians, 28, 31n24, 98, 100, 183, 261–62
Einstein, Albert, 214
Elisha, 28n2198–99
England, Eugene
   on abortion and capital punishment, 180–81
   ambiguity regarding pacifism, 45
   on Ammonite pacifism, 172
   anti-violence views of, 159–160, 175–76, 225–26
   and David O. McKay, 191–93, 206, 207, 209
   on Hugh Nibley, 44
   on Nephi, 176–79, 226
   and Old Testament, 182–84
   on Sermon on the Mount, 225–26, 229n18
   and Spencer W. Kimball, 263–67
   and pacifism, 159–160, 175–76, 225–26
Enoch, 99, 101, 248, 265
Eyring, Henry B., 123n31

F

First Presidency statements,, 17, 223–24, 232
flood (Noah's), 183
forfeiture of rights, 22, 28–31, 278
framework, LDS, 2–3, 271–78
French Revolution, 196–97
Fried, Charles, 24n16

G

Gadianton, 241–42
Gadianton robbers,
   divine protection from, 242
   and terrorism, 257
   war with, 51, 79–80, 167
Gandhi, 41, 165, 166n45
Giddianhi, 241–42
Gidgiddoni, 19, 98, 107, 247–48
Girard, René, 142–47
gospel of Jesus Christ
   and LDS framework, 223, 275–78
   preaching of, 105, 242–43, 260, 263, 278
   and self–defense, 229
   Sermon on the Mount and, 224, 240
   and vengeance, 158
Great Britain, 11–12
Grenada, 192–94, 198–99, 205

Grotius, Hugo, 7n1
Gulf war, 41–42

H

heads of state, 38, 42
Hinckley, Gordon B., 161–64
   and David O. McKay, 277
   and Spencer W. Kimball, 268–69
Hitler, Adolf, 11–24, 239. *See also* Nazi Germany
holocaust, 206–9
Hudson, Valerie, 274–75

I

intention
   and doctrine of double effect, 11
   and just war, 8, 14
   and pacifism, 33–34
   and pre–emptive action, 202, 204
   regard for humanity, 36
Israel, 52, 95, 100n15
   at Red Sea, 98, 183, 249, 261–62
Israel, house of, 52

J

Jacob, 113–15
Japan, 39–41, 156–58
Jarom, 55, 79–80, 89–90, 119, 288
Jesus Christ
   clearing of the temple, 160, 183, 227n14, 234–35
   conduct of, 188–89
   Eugene England on, 159–60, 175–76, 225–26
   examples of violence, 159–61, 183
   God of the Old Testament, 182
   and war in heaven, 189–90
Johnson, Paul, 196, 197
Joshua, 95
jus ad bellum, 8–9, 33–34, 39, 271–73
jus in bello, 9–14, 33, 34
just–war theory
   and Aquinas, 7
   and Augustine, 7
   as divine strategy in continuum theory, 151
   general condemnation of war, 19
   and Grotius, 7n1
   in LDS framework, 271, 273
   and pacifism, 17
   presupposes evil of war, 18
   two components of, 7

K

Kamm, F. M., 13n13, 22n12, 24n15, 181n23, 204n40
Kant, Immanuel, 24n16, 27n20, 185, 226n13
   Eugene England on, 180,n21, 180n22, 184, 186n35
Kimball, Spencer W., 223, 258–67

L

Lachoneus, 90n6, 242, 244
Lamanites
   as aggressors, 60–61, 66, 76–77, 147
   agitation by Nephite dissenters, 55, 76–77, 80n25
   conversions of, 140–42
   delight in murdering Nephites, 56, 57, 59, 60–61, 62, 66
   wars against Nephites, 54–55, 60–61, 62, 66, 67, 147
   wickedness of, 55–56, 57, 59–63
Lamoni, father of, 54, 56–57, 61, 105, 147n29, 281
Lehi, 90n6, 119, 165, 287–88
Levinas, Emmanuel, 24n16
Limhi, 154–55, 271n3
Lippman, Walter, 18
Lon Nol, 207
Luther, Martin, 236

M

McKay, David O., 191, 200n31, 191, 193–209, 224, 276–77
   Eugene England on, 191–92
Machiavelli, 2n2
Mao (Chairman), 194

Marat, Jean-Paul, 196–97
Maxwell, Neal A., 123n31
Mill, John Stuart, 36n7
Monroe Doctrine, 193–94, 198
moral innocence, 34–37
moral theory, 36n7
Mormon
    contradicts pacifism, 131–32
    Hugh Nibley on, 87–88
    and LDS framework, 278
    narrative approach to, 131, 133–34, 149n30
    and non-pacifist peace, 19
    presupposes Lord's help in battle, 119
    prophet, 90n6
    warning of Nephite destruction, 138
    views on military conduct, 131–32
    on Captain Moroni, 113–14
Moroni 19, 91, 165, 238, 278
    Hugh Nibley on, 87–88
Moroni (Captain)
    strengthened by God, 96
    compared to Alma and Ammon, 243
    examples of, 19, 91, 98–99, 106–7, 257
    minimizing bloodshed, 249–50
    righteousness of, 243–44
    roles, 242, 244
Mosiah, 121–22
murder, 59–63, 167–68, 218–19

N

Nagel, Thomas, 10, n8, 20
narrative approach, 109–29, 148–49
    biases of prophets, 115–16, 118
    Book of Mormon as anti-war text, 110–12
    burden of proof, 116n25
    Christ as pacifist, 110, 129, 138–42
    Lamanite conversions, 110, 140–42
    and Mormon, 109, 111, 131–32, 148
    and Nephi, 111–12, 126–29, 142, 148–50
    plausibility of, 112, 115, 118, 125, 127–28, 149n30
    problems with, 113–16, 138–42, 146, 148–50, 289–92
    rejection of violence, 110, 111
Nazi Germany, 1, 7, 11–12, 41, 195–
Nephi, 169–70, 172n67, 278
    Eugene England on, 176–79
    example of, 53, 90, 278
    fought against Lamanite assault, 53
    and LDS framework, 278
    as liar and/or murderer, 111–12, 126–27, 142, 169–70, 172n67
    and narrative approach, 111–15, 126–28, 142–49
    slaying of Laban, 78, 111–12, 126–27, 142, 169–70, 172n67
Nephites, 77–93, 102–5, 143
    compared to Lamanites, 76–77
    destruction of, 134
    Hugh Nibley on, 102, 108
    victims of Lamanite aggression, 53–55, 60–63, 66, 147
Newton, Isaac, 214
Nibley, Hugh
    on Alma and Amlici, 75, 103–5
    on Ammon, 105–6
    on Ammonites, 48, 49–50, 60–63, 65–71, 73–75, 81–85, 102, 151–53
    and defensive conflict, 89–94, 102
    on discussion to avoid conflict, 85–87, 102
    on Mormon and Moroni, 87–88, 102
    on Nephites, 45, 73–75, 76–77, 80, 102n17
    and pacifism, 43–45, 49–50, 75
    on Teancum as similar to Amalickiah, 103, 108
Niebuhr, Reinhold, 2n2, 229n18
noncombatants, 9–13, 33–37
Nozick, Robert, 37n8, 214n4

O

offensive tactics, 246–48
offensive war
    condemned by David O. McKay, 276–77

Index   311

prohibited, 46, 147–48, 250
Orend, Brian, 7n2, 8n3, 11n9, 20n7, 22n12
Orwell, George, 41
Orwellianism, 106–7, 220

P

pacifism
   Ammonites claims, 66–71
   anti-violence version, 20–31, 218, 225–30, 238–39
   anti-war version, 33–42, 218
   a priori commitment to, 216
   common-sense view of war, 2
   contingent, 33–34
   defined, 2, 17, 18, 20, 33
   intellectual revisions and, 213, 215–17, 220–22
   misleading characterizations of, 17–20
   and Sermon on the Mount and, 225–30
Packer, Boyd K., 123n31, 233n27
patriotism, 260, 261
peace
   and Captain Moroni, 86–87, 261
   David O. McKay on, 258n5, 276
   and D&C 98, 121, 250, 253
   First Presidency statement, 17
   general preference for, 2
   Gordon B. Hinckley on, 257–58
   "immutable covenant" of, 156, 161–62
   Hugh Nibley on, 232–33
   LDS framework, 271, 273
   and non-pacifism, 17–20
   purpose of war, 106–7
Poland, 8n4
pre–emptive action, 192–205, 246–250
prophets, 90n6, 110, 115–18, 120, 125, 129, 149–50, 161–64, 213
proportionality, 8–10, 23n14, 201–5, 271, 273

R

Reagan, Ronald, 194, 197–98
Red Sea, 98, 183, 249, 261–62
Reign of Terror, 197

repentance, 136–38, 257–58, 264, 271–72, 275
revelation, 121–25, 123n31, 254n13
Richards, George F., 239
rights and obligations, 22–31, 278
Robespierre, Maximilien, 197
Romney, Marion G., 123n31
Ross, W.D., 36n7

S

Samuel (Lamanite), 55–56, 57, 90n6, 138
Sartre, Jean-Paul, 197n28
scapegoating, 142–46
self–defense.
   and all Nephite fighting, 60–63, 66, 76–77, 147
   and Cain, 22–23, 29–30, 31
   and LDS framework, 271–75
   David O. McKay justifies, 191, 200n31, 276–77
   God helps people in, 94–102, 109
   Gordon B. Hinckley justifies, 257–58
   legitimacy of, 93–94, 158–59, 246, 250, 257–58
   Hugh Nibley on 89–94, 102
   pre–emptive action and, 192–205, 246–48
   right of, 22–23, 27–31, 201–3
self–sacrifice, 70–71, 152–53, 188
   overruled by the Lord, 152–53, 188
Sermon on the Mount
   and Alma and Amlici and, 236–38
   ambiguity in D&C 98 and, 229n17
   anti-violence readings of, 225–30
   and Augustine, 230n19
   and Captain Moroni, 243–44, 268
   does not prohibit self-defense, 232–33
   in LDS framework, 272
   love for enemies and, 232–33, 239–40
   and Spencer W. Kimball, 260, 261
   unity of, with other key texts, 268–69, 275
   and war, 231
Shawcross, William, 207n47
shields, human, 12–13, 37n8
Shule, 245–46

Skousen, Royal, 52n17, 76n18, 245n3, 281n2, 283n4
Smith, Joseph, 93–94, 135–36
Soviet Union, Grenada and, 192, 194–95

T

Teancum, 103, 165
terrorism, 21, 198n29, 257
threat
  direct, 10
  immediate, 37, 197–99, 205
  justifiable defense, 37–38, 42
  key concept in just–war theory, 34
  and moral innocence, 34–35, 37–38, 42
  and noncombatant status and, 10
  proximate, 37, 198–200, 205
  unintentional, 202n37
Tolstoy, Leo, 20–21, 42

U

United States, 12, 171, 192–95, 198, 205, 274–75
Utopia, 196–97

V

vengeance, 76n17, , 158–59, 161, 163, 164, 168, 183, 227n14, 248
victims,9 , 31, 92–93
Vietnam, 208–9
violence
  character of, 22–23, 27–30, 31, 201, 204, 236–39, 278
  and Christian discipleship, 277–78
  God's, 93–94, 108, 119, 146, 160–61, 182–84, 227n14
  Lord's abhorrence of, 146, 277–78
  right not to suffer, 26, 29–31
  self–contradiction regarding God's, 265–67

W

Walzer, Michael, 7n2, 8n10, 11n9, 12n10, 13n11, 42n24, 91, 205n15, 248n4
war
  causes of (secular), 275
  complexity of understanding, 277n16
war in heaven, 189–90
Warner, C. Terry, 24n16, 234n38, 235n30, 237n33
weapons
  Ammonites' burying of, 63–64, 65
  heinous, 10, 272
  modern, 35–36, 42
Woodruff, Wilford, 291–92, 292n16
World War I, 1
World War II, 1, 7, 41
  David O. McKay's support for, 191, 276

Z

Zeniff, 55, 57n24, 60n2
Zerahemnah, 246
Zion, 273–74, 273, 275

Also available from
GREG KOFFORD BOOKS

War & Peace in Our Time: Mormon Perspectives

Edited by Patrick Q. Mason, J. David Pulsipher, and Richard L. Bushman

Paperback, ISBN: 978-1-58958-099-2

"This provocative and thoughtful book is sure both to infuriate and to delight. . . . The essays demonstrate that exegesis of distinctly Latter-day Saint scriptures can yield a wealth of disputation, the equal of any rabbinical quarrel or Jesuitical casuistry. This volume provides a fitting springboard for robust and lively debates within the Mormon scholarly and lay community on how to think about the pressing issues of war and peace." - ROBERT S. WOOD, Dean Emeritus, Center for Naval Warfare Studies, Chester W. Nimitz Chair Emeritus, U.S. Naval War College

"This is an extraordinary collection of essays on a topic of extraordinary importance. . . .Whatever your current opinion on the topic, this book will challenge you to reflect more deeply and thoroughly on what it means to be a disciple of Christ, the Prince of Peace, in an era of massive military budgets, lethal technologies, and widespread war." - GRANT HARDY, Professor of History and Religious Studies, University of North Carolina, Asheville, Author, *Understanding the Book of Mormon: A Reader's Guide*

"Mormons take their morality seriously. They are also patriotic. Tragically, the second trait can undermine the first. When calls for war are on the horizon, it is possible for well-intended Saints to be too sure of our selective application of scripture to contemporary matters of life and death, too sure that we can overcome evil by force, that we can control the results of military conflict, that war is the only option for patriots. Yet pacifism has its own critics. This collection of differing views by thoughtful scholars comprises a debate. Reading it may save us in the future from enacting more harm than good in the name of God, country, or presumption." - PHILIP BARLOW, Arrington Chair of Mormon History and Culture, Utah State University, Author, *Mormons and the Bible: The Place of the Latter-day Saints in American Religion*

Common Ground—Different Opinions:
Latter-day Saints and Contemporary Issues

Edited by Justin F. White
and James E. Faulconer

Paperback, ISBN: 978-1-58958-573-7

There are many hotly debated issues about which many people disagree, and where common ground is hard to find. From evolution to environmentalism, war and peace to political partisanship, stem cell research to same-sex marriage, how we think about controversial issues affects how we interact as Latter-day Saints.

In this volume various Latter-day Saint authors address these and other issues from differing points of view. Though they differ on these tough questions, they have all found common ground in the gospel of Jesus Christ and the latter-day restoration. Their insights offer diverse points of view while demonstrating we can still love those with whom we disagree.

Praise for *Common Ground—Different Opinions*:

"[This book] provide models of faithful and diverse Latter-day Saints who remain united in the body of Christ. This collection clearly demonstrates that a variety of perspectives on a number of sensitive issues do in fact exist in the Church. . . . [T]he collection is successful in any case where it manages to give readers pause with regard to an issue they've been fond of debating, or convinces them to approach such conversations with greater charity and much more patience. It served as just such a reminder and encouragement to me, and for that reason above all, I recommend this book." — Blair Hodges, Maxwell Institute

Saints of Valor: Mormon Medal of Honor Recipients

Sherman L. Fleek

Hardcover, ISBN: 978-1-58958-171-5

Since 1861 when the US Congress approved the concept of a Medal of Honor for combat valor, 3,457 individuals have received this highest military decoration that the nation can bestow. Nine of those have been Latter-day Saints. The military and personal stories of these LDS recipients are compelling, inspiring, and tragic. The men who appear in this book are tied by two common threads: the Medal of Honor and their Mormon heritage.

The purpose of this book is to highlight the valor of a special class of LDS servicemen who served and sacrificed "above and beyond the call of duty." Four of these nine Mormons gave their "last full measure" for their country, never seeing the high award they richly deserved. All four branches of the service are represented: five were Army (one was a pilot with the Army Air Forces during WWII), two Navy, and one each of the Marine Corps and Air Force. Four were military professionals who made the service their careers; five were not career-minded; three died at an early age and never married. This book captures these harrowing historical narratives from personal accounts.

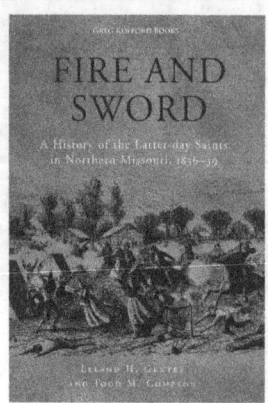

Fire and Sword: A History of the Latter-day Saints in Northern Missouri, 1836-39

Leland Homer Gentry and Todd M. Compton

Hardcover, ISBN: 978-1-58958-103-6

Many Mormon dreams flourished in Missouri. So did many Mormon nightmares.

The Missouri period—especially from the summer of 1838 when Joseph took over vigorous, personal direction of this new Zion until the spring of 1839 when he escaped after five months of imprisonment—represents a moment of intense crisis in Mormon history. Representing the greatest extremes of devotion and violence, commitment and intolerance, physical suffering and terror—mobbings, battles, massacres, and political "knockdowns"—it shadowed the Mormon psyche for a century.

Leland Gentry was the first to step beyond this disturbing period as a one-sided symbol of religious persecution and move toward understanding it with careful documentation and evenhanded analysis. In Fire and Sword, Todd Compton collaborates with Gentry to update this foundational work with four decades of new scholarship, more insightful critical theory, and the wealth of resources that have become electronically available in the last few years.

Compton gives full credit to Leland Gentry's extraordinary achievement, particularly in documenting the existence of Danites and in attempting to tell the Missourians' side of the story; but he also goes far beyond it, gracefully drawing into the dialogue signal interpretations written since Gentry and introducing the raw urgency of personal writings, eyewitness journalists, and bemused politicians seesawing between human compassion and partisan harshness. In the lush Missouri landscape of the Mormon imagination where Adam and Eve had walked out of the garden and where Adam would return to preside over his posterity, the towering religious creativity of Joseph Smith and clash of religious stereotypes created a swift and traumatic frontier drama that changed the Church.

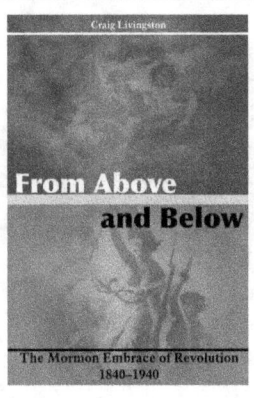

From Above and Below: The Mormon Embrace of Revolution, 1840–1940

Craig Livingston

Paperback, ISBN: 978-1-58958-621-5

Praise for *From Above and Below*:

"In this engaging study, Craig Livingston examines Mormon responses to political revolutions across the globe from the 1840s to the 1930s. Latter-day Saints saw utopian possibilities in revolutions from the European tumults of 1848 to the Mexican Revolution. Highlighting the often radical anti-capitalist and anti-imperialist rhetoric of Mormon leaders, Livingston demonstrates how Latter-day Saints interpreted revolutions through their unique theology and millennialism."
--Matthew J. Grow, author of *Liberty to the Downtrodden: Thomas L. Kane, Romantic Reformer*

"Craig Livingston's landmark book demonstrates how 21st-century Mormonism's arch-conservatism was preceded by its pro-revolutionary worldview that was dominant from the 1830s to the 1930s. Shown by current opinion-polling to be the most politically conservative religious group in the United States, contemporary Mormons are unaware that leaders of the LDS Church once praised radical liberalism and violent revolutionaries. By this pre-1936 Mormon view, 'The people would reduce privilege and exploitation in the crucible of revolution, then reforge society in a spiritual union of peace' before the Coming of Christ and His Millennium. With profound research in Mormon sources and in academic studies about various social revolutions and political upheavals, Livingston provides a nuanced examination of this little-known dimension of LDS thought which tenuously balanced pro-revolutionary enthusiasms with anti-mob sentiments."
--D. Michael Quinn, author of *Elder Statesman: A Biography of J. Reuben Clark*

Hugh Nibley: A Consecrated Life

Boyd Jay Petersen

Hardcover, ISBN: 978-1-58958-019-0

Winner of the Mormon History Association's Best Biography Award

As one of the LDS Church's most widely recognized scholars, Hugh Nibley is both an icon and an enigma. Through complete access to Nibley's correspondence, journals, notes, and papers, Petersen has painted a portrait that reveals the man behind the legend.

Starting with a foreword written by Zina Nibley Petersen and finishing with appendices that include some of the best of Nibley's personal correspondence, the biography reveals aspects of the tapestry of the life of one who has truly consecrated his life to the service of the Lord.

Praise for *A Consecrated Life*:

"Hugh Nibley is generally touted as one of Mormonism's greatest minds and perhaps its most prolific scholarly apologist. Just as hefty as some of Nibley's largest tomes, this authorized biography is delightfully accessible and full of the scholar's delicious wordplay and wit, not to mention some astonishing war stories and insights into Nibley's phenomenal acquisition of languages. Introduced by a personable foreword from the author's wife (who is Nibley's daughter), the book is written with enthusiasm, respect and insight.... On the whole, Petersen is a careful scholar who provides helpful historical context.... This project is far from hagiography. It fills an important gap in LDS history and will appeal to a wide Mormon audience."
—Publishers Weekly

"Well written and thoroughly researched, Petersen's biography is a must-have for anyone struggling to reconcile faith and reason."
—Greg Taggart, Association for Mormon Letters

www.ingramcontent.com/pod-product-compliance
Lightning Source LLC
Chambersburg PA
CBHW052051230426
43671CB00011B/1872